A HISTORY OF GARDENS
AND GARDENING

Dedicated with love to Betty and Max Ealk

Also by EDWARD HYAMS

Soil and Civilization, Vineyards in England, Pleasure from Plants, From the Wasteland, Dionysus, The English Garden, Irish Gardens, The Gardener's Bedside Book, The English Cottage Garden

A HISTORY OF GARDENS
AND GARDENING

by EDWARD HYAMS

*with thirty-two pages of colour plates and
391 black and white illustrations*

LONDON: J. M. DENT & SONS LTD

Made in Italy by Officine Grafiche A.Mondadori, Verona
for J.M.Dent & Sons Ltd, Aldine House, Bedford Street, London

ISBN 0 460 03808 7

CONTENTS

ILLUSTRATIONS

COLOUR PLATES

ACKNOWLEDGMENTS

Permission to reproduce photographs and other illustration material is gratefully acknowledged to the following (italic numbers refer to colour plates):

The Earl of Derby, 226, 228; the Earl of Rosse, *13*, *26*, 338; Mary Bacon, *6*, 6, 151-3, 168-9, 189, 209-11, 292, 306, 308, 312, 313, 322, 326, 360, 361; J. E. Downward, 347, 348; Marcel Gautherot, Rio de Janeiro, *28*, *29*, *30*, 359, 362-7; Leonard and Marjorie Gayton, 280, 349; G. Hampgler, Longwood Gardens, Pennsylvania, *23*, 354-8; Nicholas Horne Ltd, 329-31, 380-1; Claude Johnston, Missouri Botanical Garden, 287-91, 368-70, 372; A. F. Kersting, 279; Kenneth Lemmon, 1-5, from *The Golden Age of Plant Hunters* (1968); Quentin Lloyd, 339-40; William MacQuitty, *6-12*, *18-22*, *27*, *31-3*, 69-71, 73-93, 95, 170-1, 175, 208, 212-13, 224-5, 238, 272, 278, 304-5, 307, 309-11, 314-18, 323-5, 327-8, 371, 375; Manuchehr Sanei, Civil Adjutant to his Imperial Majesty the Shah of Iran, 252-5; Georgina Masson and Thames & Hudson Ltd, 65-6, 165, 167, 172; Nigel Nicolson, 345; Edward Pilkington, Wye College, *24*, *25*, 334; Edwin Smith, 149-50, 154-64, 166, 176, 182-3, 185-6, 192-8, 214, 223, 250-1, 260-2, 264-5, 267-8, 285-6, 293-300, 303, 319-21, 333, 341-4, 350-3; Philip Truex, Brancheville, New Jersey, and Gottscho-Schleisner Inc., 386-91; Douglas Weaver, 332; Paul V. Wheeler, *15*, *16*, *17*, 269-71, 273-7, 281-4.

The British Museum 1, 2, 14, 67, 68, 72, 94, 239-44, 257-9; Colonial Williamsburg, Williamsburg, Virginia, 227; The Commissioners of Public Works in Ireland, 335-7; the *Daily Express*, 373-4, 376-7; the *Daily Mail*, 378-9, 382-5; Deutsche Fotothek, Dresden, 173-4, 200-7, 217-22; the French Government Tourist Office, London, 177-81, 184, 187-8, 190-1, 301-2; the Thomas Jefferson Memorial Foundation, Colonial Studio, Richmond, Virginia, 236-7; the University of Leyden, *4*; the Linnean Society of London, *1*; the Mount Vernon Ladies' Association of the Union, 230-7; the Director, Museum of Far Eastern Antiquities, Stockholm, *3*, 21-58, reproduced from *Gardens of China*, by the late Osvald Sirén, copyright 1949 the Ronald Press Company, New York: plate 24 also by courtesy of the Freer Gallery of Art, Smithsonian Institution, Washington, D.C., plate 25, map from *A History of the Peking Summer Palaces under the Ch'ing Dynasty* by C. B. Malone (1934), also by permission of the University of Illinois Press, plate 26 also by permission of the Bibliothèque Nationale, Paris, plates 21 and 45 after *Chinese Houses and Gardens* by Henry Inn and Shao Chang Lu (1940), Honolulu, plates 27 and 28, originals formerly in the possession of C. T. Loo, New York, plate 38, map, after *Monumenta Serica*, volume v (1940), published by Henry Vetch, Peking; the National Portrait Gallery, London, *7*; the New York Historical Society, 229; Radio Times Hulton Picture Library, 199, 215-16, 245-9, 259; the Spanish National Tourist Office, London, *5*, 96-7; the *Sunday Times*, 59-64.

Plates 9-20, after Sir John Gardner Wilkinson, *Manners and Customs of the Ancient Egyptians*, 1837 and 1841; plates 98-107, after Sir Frank Crisp, *Mediaeval Gardens*, 1924; plates 135-46, after A. Gheerbrant, *The Incas* (1963), by permission of Cassell and Co. Ltd; plate 147, from *The Ancient Past of Mexico* by Alma M. Reed, © 1966 by Alma Reed, is used by permission of Crown Publishers, Inc., New York.

1 *The Wardian Case made transport of live plants safer and easier.*

PLANT MATERIAL

This book is a history of the art of making gardens. Horticulture as the cultivation of plants for food and medicine in some kind of plantation is of Neolithic origin, and is therefore older than civilization and one of its basic elements. But that is not garden making, and it is not profitable, even if it were possible, to separate prehistoric horticulture from prehistoric agriculture, which probably grew out of it since fruit trees, date palms in the East and apple trees in the West, are perhaps earlier than cereals in cultivation and were planted in Neolithic times.

But I think that just a little should be said about one of the elemental materials of any garden. Of the four, three were to hand for the using at any time and almost anywhere in the world: earth, water and stone; but the plant material, or rather a considerable part of it, was made; and as man-made material it has a very ancient history. For the selection, segregation and cross-breeding of plants predated our knowledge of the principles involved by thousands of years, and one could write a specific history of plants as artefacts.

The earliest gardeners — and their successors have been doing as they did ever since — dug up plants in, or took seeds from, the wild, planted them in plantations and cared for them. In so doing they unwittingly ensured the fixation and improvement of the qualities for which they had chosen these particular plants. As Darwin taught us, species originate in natural selection: briefly, what happens is that when a mutant appears either better or as well adapted to the environment as the others in its genus, and if it is segregated by, for example, a geographical or climatic accident so that inbreeding is ensured, then it may give rise to progeny ancestral to a species with the new attribute. Every new species, and every new group of plants produced artificially with a new *genetically ensured* attribute, originate in a mutant individual.

Natural selection usually operates to segregate and fix new mutant attributes which make the species better able to survive, better adapted to its environment. But when man is the selector, he chooses his wild plants for some qualities useful or pleasing to himself, for example size in vegetables; size, flavour and fruitfulness in fruit plants; colour and form in flowers. He excludes from his plantations the less satisfactory individuals of each kind. If the outstanding attribute for which he chose an individual plant was not simply due to very favourable local conditions, but to a genetical mutation, the geographical isolation of the plant in an artificial plantation, enforcing self-pollination, may very well act to segregate and fix the desirable attribute. In short, the earliest gardeners made use of the, as it were, apparatus of natural selection without knowing that such a thing existed, and so created races of artificial plants; plants which not only could not be found so fine in one or several particulars in the wild, but which could survive only under artificial conditions. These were the first garden plants.

Also very early came the practice of vegetative propagation, which is another way of perpetuating desirable plants without change. Any piece of the vegetation of a plant broken off and replanted to strike root, what we call a cutting, is, of course, identical with the original plant of which, philosophically speaking, it remains a part. A few of the plants still in our gardens or orchards are, in this sense, parts of plants which were inadvertently cross-bred or mutated and were selected well over a thousand years ago. The grapevine cultivar 'Pinot Meunier' is a case in point; and until comparatively recently some German-Swiss orchards had trees of an apple which was first cultivated in Neolithic times: the apple called 'Campaner'.

Of course very few of our present-day garden plants remain unchanged like this, but on the other hand many are extremely ancient as artificial plants. The great difference between wild and cultivated cabbages, for example, was initiated when the pre-Celtic peoples of west Europe began to cultivate cabbage. Celery is mentioned in the *Odyssey*. We owe some of our onions to the most ancient Egyptian gardeners, others to the village farmers who foreran the citizens of Sumer and Akkad, and perhaps others to the Indus valley gardeners of over four thousand years ago. Peaches, apricots and grapes were first cultivated in ancient Armenia and Iran, and grapes, at least, were already artificially improved by the time they reached the Egyptians of four or five thousand years ago. Many fruit trees and vegetables can be traced back in this way to a prehistoric origin as 'garden plants'.

But if it is fairly easy to discover the ancient history of many vegetable, fruit and salad plants, it is not so in the case of flowers grown simply as ornaments. Any modern garden of considerable size has in it ornamental plants which were first 'made' by the gardeners of virtually all the ancient civilizations. Perhaps the pleasantest way to make this point without going into tedious detail will be to walk round a good Western garden and note briefly the origins of a few of the plants we find in it.

There will, of course, be roses; they are the most popular of flowering shrubs all over the world where they can be grown. All the ancient civilizations grew them, from those of the Mediterranean basin in the West to China in the Far East. Our garden roses derive principally from Asiatic species; even the old 'Provence' or 'Cabbage' roses were made out of the East Caucasian species *Rosa centifolia*, and this rose was made as a garden plant by the Persians of the Arab period whose gardens it dominated to such an extent that their word for rose, *gul*, is also the general word for flower. The same rose was cultivated on an enormous scale in the Near East and in eastern Europe for the making of attar of roses. Arab gardeners were also responsible for the improvement of the species *R. damascena*, this time in Syria. The Persians were the first to make yellow garden roses, out of the species *R. foetida*. A new scent came from the northern Indian Moghul gardens with *R. moschata*. The two most important components of our own modern garden roses are both Chinese, *R. odorata* and *R. chinensis*, which were anciently cultivated in China.

Perhaps there is a shrubbery of rhododendrons and camellias, underplanted with lilies since they like the same kind of soil. The most beautiful *Rhododendron* species are Chinese, but the genus does not seem to have attracted Chinese gardeners, although they and the Japanese, the latter much later, made good use of, and created, new artificial forms of the *Azalea* series of that genus. Until the second half of the eighteenth century the genus was hardly used in Europe or anywhere else in the West, and in England not at all. Between then and about 1850 half a dozen species were brought into cultivation.

But from 1849 to 1891 J. D. Hooker, son of the then Director of Kew, was in Sikkim plant collecting, and he sent home seeds of thirty species of rhododendron until then unknown to botany. A little later the Indian and Japanese azaleas began to reach England from the Continent, and by 1900 there were probably about one hundred species of the genus in cultivation in Britain, whence they spread to Europe and America. It was as nothing to what was then to come. The plant breeders were already busy using all this new material to create splendid cultivars. During the next decade Neilson, collecting new plants in China for the famous firm of Veitch, sent home at least forty new species of rhododendron. And George Forrest, collecting farther south in China for some rich garden-loving patrons, notably for J. C. Williams of Caerhays in Cornwall, did even better: his rhododendron introductions were not fewer than 120 new species. These

2 *Douglas's winter camping arrangements.*

3 *Plant-collecting in North America: the transport problem was difficult.*

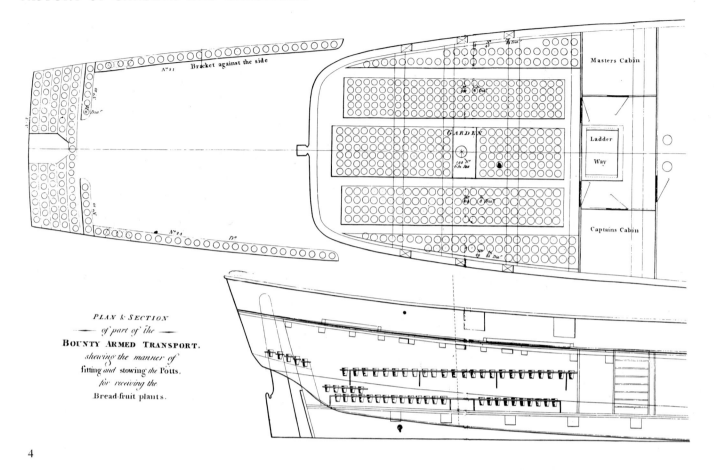

PLAN & SECTION
—— *of part of the* ——
BOUNTY ARMED TRANSPORT.
shewing the manner of
fitting and stowing the Potts.
for receiving the
Bread-fruit plants.

4

varied in habit from prostrate, rock-covering hardy dwarfs to forest trees. He was followed by Kingdon-Ward, Ludlow, Sheriff, and Taylor. Between 1850 and 1950 something like 850 species were brought into specialized gardens in Britain, and were distributed to every part of the world where they could be grown. Several hundred species and hybrids are commonplace in amateur gardening. So the rhododendrons are modern; even the made ones.

Camellias, on the other hand, are very ancient garden plants, although there were none in Europe until the early eighteenth century, when made plants reached us from China. There they had been cultivated in the gardens of Buddhist monasteries and in noblemen's gardens since before the Christian era, and they have been important in Japanese gardens since about AD 700. The first to reach Europe were, as I have said, made plants very different from anything which could be found in the wild. One species, of course, was of great economic importance, first in China, then in Japan, finally all over the tropics — the tea bush.

As for lilies in the shrubbery, only one kind is ancient in gardens, *Lilium candidum*; the Madonna lily. This was first cultivated and improved in Anatolia about 3,500 years ago, for the medicinal salve made from the bulb; the Egyptians, who grew it chiefly for its bulb which they ate, had it from there. The Greeks imported first the salve, then the plant, and it reached our own gardens by two routes: from Greece via Rome; and from Egypt via Moorish North Africa and Spain. It was established in western European gardens before Chaucer's time. But it is doubtful whether any other lilies were in European gardens before the fifteenth century, and most kinds are of much more recent introduction. In Japan some species are relatively ancient in cultivation.

Our imaginary garden will have spring bulbs. Wild daffodils were perhaps used in Roman gardens, and certainly in England as early as the twelfth century. But there were no made daffodils, of the kind we are now familiar with, until very much later: the latter half of the nineteenth century. The Persians began the making of our garden tulips, the Persian and Syrian slave gardeners of the Ottoman Empire

4 *Arrangements for storing breadfruit plants in H.M.S.* Bounty

5 *David Douglas.*

5

continued it, and the Dutch, who had their tulips from Turkey in the sixteenth century, completed the work. Hyacinths were made in Holland, as it were, also in the sixteenth and seventeenth centuries: there were a few varieties reminiscent of our own in existence by about 1600.

Herbaceous and perennial and annual garden plants are partly of European, partly of Asiatic and partly of American origin. The making — largely as inadvertent as in Neolithic times — of garden flowers out of such wild ones as foxgloves and flag iris began in Europe in the thirteenth and fourteenth centuries. Such American plants as the 'French' and 'African' marigolds, *Lobelia cardinalis*, and tradescantias, many Michaelmas daisies, dahlias, rudbekias, etc., reached the Old World gardens from across the Atlantic between 1600 and 1800. Among the garden plants which were created out of wild species by the ancient native American civilizations of the Andes and Mexico, and reached us in due course, were the tomato and the pineapple. Although these were doubtless accompanied by many flowering plants from the ornamental gardens of the Inca nobility and the Aztec lords, who, as we

shall see, made much of great gardens, these early introductions are not well-documented. The Aztec gardeners almost certainly cultivated and improved their native dahlia, for the three forms which reached Madrid from Mexico in 1789, and Kew from Madrid in 1798, do not seem to have been botanical species.

The garden we have imagined will have many flowering shrubs as well as rose, rhododendron and camellia. The mock orange, *Philadelphus*, was probably first cultivated in Byzantine Greek gardens, was taken over by the other civilized peoples of the Near East, and reached western Europe in the fifteenth century. Over four centuries later it was remade as a garden plant when an American species reached Europe, and was crossed with the ancient cultivar to give us the range of superior modern ones. Lilacs were first cultivated in Iranian gardens, the species being *Syringa persica*. Europeans began to cultivate another species, *S. vulgaris*, in the sixteenth century — it did not reach England until about 1600. Once again, when the two were brought together and crossed, they yielded the garden lilacs which we have now, and these

5

6

have been further diversified and improved by bringing still other species into the breeding programme. 'Japonica', *Chaenomeles lagenaria*, was of ancient cultivation in China, later in Japan; it reached Europe by way of England in 1796, to be followed later by *Chaenomeles japonica*.

Being a good one, our garden will include some paeonies. Species of herbaceous paeonies are native across most of Europe and Asia, and consequently the breeding of the made, garden kinds is extremely mixed. A number of different peoples brought paeonies into cultivation in various places at various times, but certainly the Chinese gardeners were the first to bring them into gardens from the wild and to begin the making of garden varieties. The genus has probably been in cultivation for not less than 2,000 years.

As for the woody or 'tree' paeonies, the moutans (*mow tan* = great flower), the earliest written record suggests that they must have been taken into cultivation not later than about AD 400, but perhaps much earlier; probably in the province of Szechuan, or maybe Shensi. This account, written in AD 536, implies that the time of first cultivation was long

ago. The species are, and perhaps already were, rare, even very rare, in the wild. But certainly by AD 700 many garden varieties had emerged, partly as the result of a vogue for them among the rich of the T'ang period (618-906); a fashion which sent prices for new and improved garden kinds to fantastic heights. In his excellent book *The Moutan*, Mr Michael Haworth-Booth cites an account of one hundred ounces of gold being paid for a single plant of a cultivar called 'Pe Leang Kin'. The first published descriptive list of garden moutans, the *Mow Tan Poo*, appeared early in the eighth century, and at about the same time plants first reached Japan, whose gardeners were soon at work improving them by selection and perhaps cross-breeding, producing kinds of greatly superior grace, bearing and colour. In 1789 the first moutan reached Europe — Kew Gardens — on the initiative of Sir Joseph Banks. Thereafter other cultivars, and later the wild species, were introduced. Europe did not receive the exquisite Japanese cultivars until 1844, when Philip von Siebold sent forty of the best to Holland. Today the making of new kinds still continues, chiefly in the United States.

Although, then, much of the plant material which we use

7

8

in our garden making is extremely ancient, and a little of it older than urban civilization itself, almost forming an unbroken link between the late Neolithic and our own gardens, a lot of it is relatively modern and a little of it brand new, since new made plants appear in commerce every year. The raw material for much of the later plant making came from South Africa. It is, for example, likely that our garden will have some gladioli, if only for cutting. The genus is concentrated in South Africa; introduction of wild corms into Holland late in the seventeenth and early in the eighteenth centuries led to the making of garden kinds, which was later carried on in Britain and in the United States. The huge modern florist's varieties, enormously more spectacular and less graceful than the original wildings, are the product of the late nineteenth and the twentieth centuries. Other introductions from the same source were *Watsonia*, *Freesia*, the Cape heaths, chincherinchee (the name comes from the screeching sound of the stalks rubbing together), *Ixia*, *Schizostylis*, *Dierama*, *Nerine* and others; they were mostly nineteenth-century introductions. The *Agapanthus*, also from the Cape, did not reach Europe, later America, until some time after 1700, but it has since naturalized itself in a few parts of

Europe, including Britain, and America. The Cape proteas had a vogue in English greenhouses late in the nineteenth century, and established themselves in Australian and some American gardens; but they are not 'made' plants.

Still more recent were the introductions from Australasia and from the wilds of South America — as distinct from those which came to us as garden plants from the Inca gardens. But once again they were not made plants. In Australia and New Zealand today cultivars of such genera as *Leptospermum* and *Callistemon* are now beginning to embellish the gardens of the world's youngest high civilization. But they do not yet belong to history; they are still news.

In the following chapters I shall revert, from time to time, to this subject of the making of garden plants as material for the making of gardens. It has been used here to establish an important fact: that from the beginning of this art, gardeners shaped not only their inanimate materials, earth, water and stone, but the living material as well.

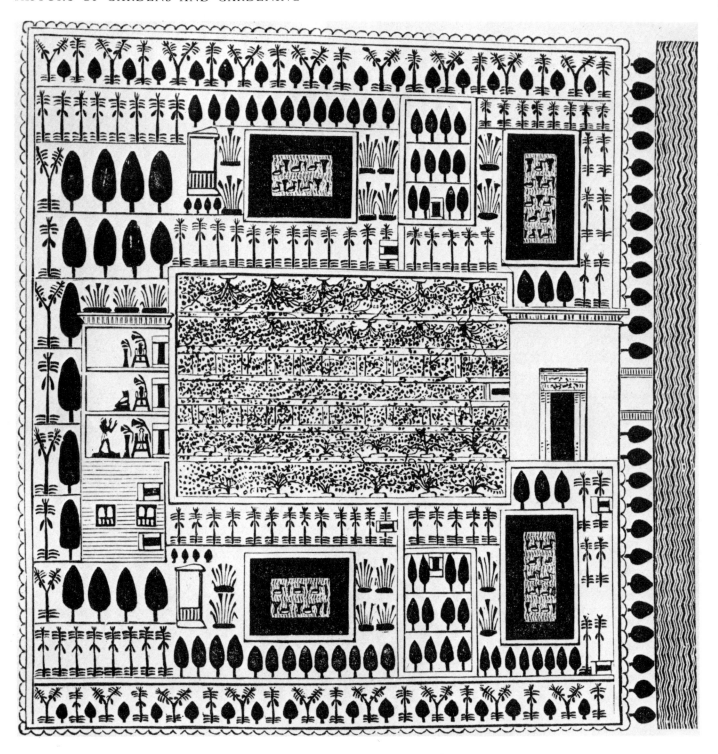

9 *A large garden, with the vineyard and other separate enclo-*
sures, tanks of water and a small house.

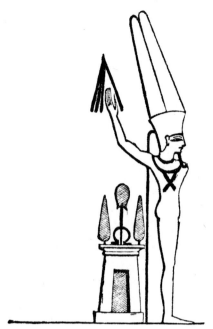

10 *Khem, god of gardens in Ancient Egypt, with his tree emblems.*

NEW STONE AGE TO FIRST CITY GARDENS

The inventors of gardening were people — almost certainly women — of the New Stone Age. To these Neolithic 'peasants' and 'villagers' we owe the fundamental tools and techniques of the craft. The digging-stick, its point hardened by charring, foreruns the spade and the plough. A stick with a truncated crotch makes a hoe; if, after centuries of using it, you suddenly have the bright idea of lashing an oyster-shell or the shoulder-blade of a game animal to the shorter leg of the crotch, your hoe is much improved.

Planting in straight rows makes for ease and economy of labour. These ancient people had as good brains as ourselves and used them as we use ours, to save their muscles. Straight planting was the first act of garden design, and the second was mounding the soil to facilitate irrigation. From the mounding of soil to make little channels for irrigation water derived the irrigation system of canals which made Mesopotamia one vast garden or farm. Crops have to be protected from wild animals; the first fences were probably dead acacia thorn bushes. But stakes cut and trimmed with flint rasps (the so-called choppers of the 'Abbevillian' and 'Clactonian' Lower Palaeolithic) and with their points hardened in fire had been invented thousands of years before the garden, for making animal traps. Regular stake fencing was an obvious development, and we may call it the third act

of garden design. Where irrigation was necessary, it saved labour to dig a pool filled from a spring or diverted stream: this pool has been in gardens ever since. Among the earliest plants brought into cultivation was the grape-vine, *Vitis vinifera*: it was first grown flat on the ground, but its wild habit taught the early gardeners to train it up living trees, or up poles. Two poles forked at the top to carry a cross bar were better. Out of them developed the pergola, one of the earliest elements of garden design.

So my guess is that before the rise of any urban civilization and the use of metals, and contemporary with the development of horticulture into agriculture, of the digging-stick into the two-man plough, the elements of garden design were in being — enclosure, rectilinear order, pools, and pergolas.

The crops were certainly all edible and, a little later, medicinal. The ornamental gardening we are here concerned with is a product of urban civilization. The discovery of healing properties, as of toxicity, in plants was, of course, empirical. According to Arambourg (1967) all prehistoric societies were dominated by the magic which developed into religion. Magic — the imposition of the magician's will by fascination, hypnosis of a kind assisted by ritual — works only on living creatures; but the magicians wished

9

11 *Egyptian tree with earth raised round the roots for watering; the same as we should represent it.*

12 *Egyptian vineyard and orchard.*

and needed to work on the inanimate as well as the animate world; to make things as well as beings do their bidding. So they regarded all things, stones and sticks, as animate; and, of course, plants. A poisonous plant was malevolent, a healing plant benevolent, and the spirit of the plant could be used by the magician for evil or good. Medicinal plants were little gods, and as such they came under the control of the greater deities. It was for this reason, or something very like it, that at least one other element of garden art first came into the Neolithic garden: the statue. It was not there for aesthetic reasons, but to make the garden plants grow and maintain their benevolence. It was almost certainly a representation of the oldest deity, the earth or mother goddess with her grossly steatopygous and big-breasted attributes. For even such highly specialized industrialists as the Grimes Graves (Norfolk, England) flint-miners (*c*. 10,000-500 BC) and manufacturers, who grew no crops but exchanged their manufactured goods for food by trade, had her image in their mines, perhaps to promote the increase of the flints. So this statue, ancestor of Astarte and Aphrodite, was also the ancestor of our garden statues and ornaments. Another element of later gardens, the 'specimen' tree, came very early (as the sacred tree) into garden design, but this was almost certainly later than Neolithic.

The question — where were these earliest gardens to be found — cannot be answered with absolute assurance, but a hypothesis is possible. At Tell Hassuna, across the river and downstream from the site of ancient Nineveh on the river Tigris, has been found the debris of the lives of generation after generation of a settled people who were certainly gardeners, for this debris includes stone hoes fastened to the handles with bitumen (probably from the bitumen

lakes near Hit).* Their soil being fertile Tigris mud constantly renewed by silting, they were able to remain in one place indefinitely, without either exhausting the soil or inventing manuring. One of their crops was a grain grass, for they had stone sickles; of the others we have no knowledge. They flourished about 5000 BC. Similar finds have been made at Tell Halaf, Arpachiya and Tepe Gawra in the same region. Out of such communities as these arose larger village communities subsisting first on horticulture, then on agriculture; and out of them, as surplus food accumulated and organization was imposed by the magician-priests and soldiers, arose the first City States in the world.

Since gardening was the begetter of agriculture, agriculture of surplus wealth, and surplus wealth of urbanization, gardeners may claim that men and women of their trade were the creators of civilization itself.

GARDENING CIVILIZED

Since the first makers of gardens were ancient Mesopotamians, and if the archaeologists and palaeontologists are right in judging urban civilization to have made its first appearance in Mesopotamia in and between the valleys of Nile and Euphrates, then it is likely to have been there that the first gardens designed for pleasure as well as profit — later simply for pleasure — came into being. There are several reasons for thinking so: for example, scientific irrigation was a Sumerian invention. Then, the earliest known works of architecture with aesthetic merit belong to that part of the world, and garden design has always — except for short

* See Hyams (1952).

12

periods in the cultures of China, Japan and England when it was raised to the level of a fine art — been a branch of architecture.

Unfortunately, what we know of this west Asian garden designing and layout is little enough; just sufficient to make it quite clear that it contained every element of formal gardening.

First there were the *ziggurats*. They were artificial, stylized hills created in a flat land by a people who yearned for the hills they had migrated from and whose gods and temples had to be set on high places. They were pyramids built up of decreasing terraces, rectangular in plan. Their internal structure was surprisingly complex and sophisticated, providing for irrigation and drainage. They were planted with trees, shrubs and vineyards. On top were the temple and a sacred grove of trees. Planting was formal and rectilinear. An inscription of Sargon I, creator of the Sumerian empire, found at Akkad, makes it clear that the gardeners of these *ziggurats* and perhaps other gardens were honoured. According to legend Sargon was found as a baby in a wicker basket floating among reeds in a canal (the story is plagiarized much later in that of Moses); he was brought up by an irrigation officer who found him, and he was trained, perhaps by apprenticeship, as a professional gardener. He tells us in his inscription: 'My service as a gardener was pleasing to Istar and I became King.'

In the Gilgamesh Epic, the oldest work of literature in existence, which was engraved on earthenware tablets discovered at Kuyundjuk and now in the British Museum, there is a description of an idealized and sacred vineyard. It

is clearly based on a real one.* In the same poem there is also a description of a sort of landscape garden or park which is clearly also a holy place, for there is 'a cedar-mount, the dwelling of the gods, sanctuary of the Irnini'.† Again this is idealized, but quite clearly based on a reality.

Sennacherib, son of Sargon II of Assyria, was also a garden-maker. He made gardens, moreover, 'in the Upper and the Lower Town', so perhaps they were, in some sense, public parks and not simply palace gardens or temple gardens. He sets it among his many self-proclaimed virtues that he 'brought plants from the land of the Hittites' — i.e. from mountain country. No flowers are mentioned, but trees including fruit trees, shrubs and spice plants such as myrrh. In one place, using prisoner-of-war slave labour, Sennacherib made a five-acre temple garden on naked rock by mining out planting holes and water channels to a depth of five feet.

Even the atrociously militarist Assyrians loved and made gardens. In one of his inscriptions Tiglath-Pileser (c. 1100 BC) records: 'Cedars and Box, Allkanu-wood have I carried off from the lands I conquered, trees that none of my forefathers have possessed, these trees have I taken and planted then in my own country, in the parks of Assyria have I planted them.' Not that this was the first example of plant introduction and acclimatization; it had by then been going on for centuries and in more than one place.

From the general style of the ancient Mesopotamian cultures and from the few fragments of images we have, we may take it that the gardens were formal, architectural and rectilinear. Part of a tablet from Sennacherib's reign depicts

* See Hyams (1965a).   † See Gothein (1928).

11

what looks like a rather less formal landscape garden, but the picture is confused and in any case rectilinear terraces give it a curiously 'Italianate' appearance. Water, in pools often planted with aquatic plants, and in canals, was a feature of all these gardens.

The Hanging Gardens of Babylon attributed to the reign of Semiramis (814-810 BC) and described by several authors, including the great geographer Strabo and the historian Diodorus Siculus, both working from older source books, were apparently based on the *ziggurats*; far from being an invention of that period or confined to Babylon, they were, as I have described them, already very ancient. It is quite possible to get a general idea of what they probably looked like by paying a visit to Lake Maggiore and looking at Prince Borromeo's Isola Bella from a boat in the lake before landing to see it from the inside.

Did the Sumerians, Hittites, Assyrians and Babylonians grow any flowers in their gardens? Very few appear in inscriptions or in reliefs, but some which do are recognizable, notably *Lilium candidum* in the northern palace of Kuyundjuk.

A flower often identified in reproduction as 'lilies' in another relief from the same Assyrian source, depicting a hunting-park, is clearly nothing of the kind but probably some kind of composite, or else simply a stylized flower. In the same palace Assurbanipal and his queen are shown dining in the garden under the shade of palm trees and holding flowers in one hand; the flowers are unidentifiable but the implication of a flower garden is clear.

To sum up this point: horticultural plantations were first made in Neolithic times not less than 7,000 years ago; before the age of metals these plantations had evolved into gardens proper, in that they were enclosed and well ordered. In the earliest City States between Tigris and Euphrates, gardens first became emancipated from purely economic purposes; the rich and mighty developed them into pleasances, formal and architectural parks of trees, and water-works. Finally, this originally Sumerian — with Hittite borrowings — grand and formal style of garden making lasted well into historical times throughout western Asia with only minor changes, and influenced the garden making of subsequent, alien civilizations all over the world.

13 *Orchard or vineyard, with a large tank of water.*

14 *Frightening away the birds with a sling.*

EGYPT*

Because of the wealth of pyramid murals and inscriptions, we know a great deal more about ancient Egyptian gardens than we do about those of the west Asian proto-civilizations. Egypt probably learned her gardening, as she did much else, from the people of the Two Rivers. On the other hand it is a mistake — one upon which whole theories of the evolution of culture have been built — to assume that tools, techniques and styles are invented in one place once and for all and copied elsewhere. As I have said, for tens of thousands of years the brains of men have been of the same calibre, and the taste for creating beauty is as universal as it is our best claim to respect as a species. Like problems evoke like solutions in like conditions. We shall come in due course to a striking demonstration of this in the independent invention by the Chinese and the English of the picturesque or landscape garden. Happily the like solutions are unlike in detail: hence the lovely diversity of cultures. What Egypt inherited, and what she invented, we shall never know.

Egypt, like Mesopotamia, had one very great advantage over the rest of the Old World in the West as a cradle of horti-culture: a soil which was annually renewed by the silt of the Nile flood, so that manuring was hardly necessary.

At the earliest stage for which we have pictures, usually tomb-paintings concerning which I shall have something more

* Most of the facts and figures on which this section is based are taken from Wilkinson (1878); Lepsius (1849-59); one or two more specialized works, e.g. Naville (1898-1908); Petrie (1894); Gothein (1928); and Hyams (1965b).

to say, Egyptian gardens were planted in regular rectangles with trees, vegetables and grape-vines. The trees were for both fruit and timber, the vines for wine, and among the vegetable and culinary herbs were probably medicinal herbs as well (see below). In the early days the most important garden tree was *Ficus sycomorus*, the 'sycamore fig' or 'mul-berry fig' (which has nothing whatever to do with sycamore). And this tree, useful in all its parts as well as providing shade, remained the Egyptian garden tree *par excellence* throughout the thousands of years of Egyptian horticulture. To say that it was held sacred is not to distinguish it; as we shall see, all trees were sacred. From one or two tomb-paintings it

15 *Pomegranate tree. Egyptian tomb painting. Thebes.*

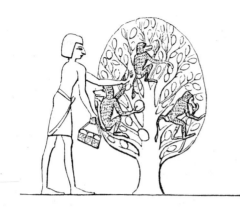

16 *As depicted on this Egyptian tomb-painting from Beni-Hassan, Egyptian gardeners were the first to train monkeys to help gather the fruit harvest.*

seems that this tree had a third use: the leaves were fed to goats and perhaps to other cattle, as were vine leaves (and the leaves of *Arbutus unedo*, later, in Greece), by way of winter fodder. One curious little picture shows monkeys helping the gardener to gather the sycamore-figs. In Malaysia in modern times monkeys are trained to gather coconuts; and at the Singapore Botanic Garden before the Second World War Professor E.J.H. Corner, now of Cambridge, trained eight monkeys to help him in collecting botanical material such as high-growing flowers and epiphytes, from unclimbable trees in the jungle; the tradition is clearly an ancient one.

Egyptian gardens were very early enclosed; first in reed or thorn fences, later in brick walls. The Sumerian pergola was copied, elaborated into an arbour or complex of arbours; later its poles were carved and painted; finally it was made of decorative brickwork, at least in some of the greater gardens. Such complexes of pergolas, supporting grape-vines, were in every Egyptian garden of any importance. There is no evidence that the pergolas were ever used to carry any climbing plant but the grape-vine. The earliest of their vines must have come from western Asia, and the grapes were presumably black. By the seventeenth Dynasty there were a number of varieties, with purple, white, pale green and even red grapes, which means that Egyptians were apt to spot and propagate mutant forms. The vines were not only irrigated; they were also mulched.

The early Egyptian gardens seem to have had no flowers, being confined to the cultivation of fruits, including melons and perhaps water-melons; salads, including chicory; and pot herbs, although we do not know what these were. How-

ever, they certainly included onions. Some writers credit the Egyptian garden with citrus fruits and bananas. Citrus fruits were domesticated in Indian and Chinese gardens at a later date, and cannot have been in the ancient gardens of Egypt; still less bananas, which are from the Indo-Malayan source of cultivated fruits.[*]

Like the monasteries later in Europe, in ancient Egypt the temples were centres of horticulture, garden design improvement, and experiment with new plants. First in temple gardens, later also in royal and noble gardens, exotic trees, shrubs and herbs brought home by the princes commanding Egyptian imperial armies, and by travelling merchants in the export and import trade, were acclimatized. Exotic trees were particularly valued, for Egypt had few of her own; and like the native ones, they were held sacred. Every temple park had its groves of trees, and if their first purpose was religious, they were also a source of revenue and the subject of scientific study — the first botanical arboreta were in Upper Egypt. Trees were also planted to shade the temple portico and about the garden pools.

Again as in Europe some thousands of years later, temple gardens were medicinal; that is, they were physic gardens to which medical schools were attached. In short, the clergy were the cultural descendants of the Neolithic plant-magicians and, as such, for long had a monopoly of the medical profession. The Egyptian pharmacopoeia from the time of the great physician Imhotep (c. 2700 BC) contained about 500 herbs or herbal remedies, rising to 700 a thousand years later; evidence of a steady programme of research and plant introduction. It was probably as a mere by-product of medicinal gardening that flowers first came into Egyptian gardens, since it is fact that such plants as Madonna lily, autumn crocus, poppy, the great yellow-flowered gentian, water lily, bluebell and others were cultivated primarily for their medicinal properties.

But it was less in the temple gardens themselves than in new gardens made for temples by royal or rich benefactors that garden design as such, emancipated from religious rules, economic needs and scientific purposes, came into its own as a branch of architecture. It was formal and rectilinear, as we should expect of the people who built the pyramids. A gentleman's garden of, say, the eighteenth to the fourteenth

* See Vavilov (1951). An earlier authority, A. de Candolle (1884), is equally sure of this and has interesting articles on both plants.

14

1. *Tomb painting, Egypt, 1900 B.C., entitled 'Gathering Figs'.*

2. *A painting from the tomb of Nembamun; private garden with ornamental water.*

3. *Painting of a Chinese garden. From* Gardens of China *by O. Sirèn, 1949.*

ACANTHUS
POLYSTACHYUS
B.B. DEC. '43.

4. Acanthus polystachyus. *Painting by Berthe Bake*. Hortus Academicus.

century BC was enclosed in a high brick wall which was later coped with tiles and broken by decorated gateways and gates. The walls were shaded by rows of trees planted on the outside; perhaps also on the inside. The house might be at the centre of the garden, or near the wall. The path to the door of the house was shaded by trees or by a vine pergola. One large rectangular section of the garden was a vineyard with the vines trained high on a complex of pergolas to form a vast arbour. This provided not only a pleasant place for walking as well as grapes for the wine-press, but the manner of training shaded the soil and so reduced loss of water by evaporation. The rest of the garden was divided into rectangular areas by low brick walls and walks. The ponds and canals, with their water lilies, rushes, fish and waterfowl, were also rectangular, as were the garden pavilions. Some of the divisions were planted with trees in straight lines, others with vegetables, and some with flowers in pure stands, for the Egyptians seem never to have mixed species.

In fact, as far as one can judge from plans so stylized and diagrammatic that interpretation is not easy, flowers and foliage plants were planted to give solid blocks of colour less in the manner of Victorian carpet-bedding than in that of Senhor Burle Marx in his abstract tropical gardens in Brazil and Venezuela today. Fruit trees were important; there may have been some flowering shrubs grown for their beauty alone, but if so, I do not know what they were. Small trees and bushes were, in the later periods, planted in big earthenware vases set at regular intervals about the garden.

The Egyptian gardens of which we have any knowledge were large. The formal lake which the Pharaoh Amenhotep III made in one of his parks for his queen was about a mile long and quarter of a mile wide, and was used for ceremonial boating and water festivals. Of course that was exceptional, but the gardens of the rich and mighty were certainly as large as a gentleman's park in England in the eighteenth century.

The introduction of exotic trees from abroad had one curious effect in temple gardens, in that each temple could and did have its own particular sacred species. We have very incomplete records of the trees introduced and most of them cannot even be identified, but at least twenty species of exotics were being widely grown by the fifteenth century BC, always in pure stands as sacred groves.

From the ground plan of a high official's villa at Thebes in the reign of Amenhotep III (1405-1378 BC) we get a fairly

17 *Egyptian shadouf for watering gardens.*

good idea of what a great garden was like by then. The most obvious conclusions to be drawn from it are that the vineyard with its several straight walks was of the first importance; that trees were numerous, planted with strict regularity, and second only to vines in importance; that garden pools were large and rectangular; that there were several pretty little garden pavilions or summer houses; and that absolute rectilinearity of layout and planting was the rule.

In short these gardens were outdoor living-rooms designed for human intercourse; a style which was to endure throughout the Old World in the West for another three thousand years or more. The Egyptians' gardens were not for looking at; they were for living in.

A tomb painting from Thebes known as the Apoui Garden shows the porch of a very handsome villa, its steps flanked by plants, garden on both sides, fruit-laden trees, two pools or canals, and gardeners at work irrigating with the ancient water-lifting device called the *shadouf* which is still in use as far afield as south India. There are two flowerbeds whose plants have been rather questionably identified as cornflower, poppy and papyrus.

In all the Egyptian tomb paintings date palms appear, and were clearly as important as any other fruit tree. *Ficus carica*, the fig of history, was also grown. In a plan of house and garden of the High Priest of Mērirē, Tell El-Amarna, one division of the garden shows a rectangular sunken pool in the midst of a grove of trees and bushes, including obvious date palms and a small palm-like plant (which could have led

15

to that banana solecism) that could conceivably be a cycad. The esculent 'Rain Queen' cycad of South Africa is apparently confined to that country, but do we know for sure how far south Egyptian sailors penetrated, and what plants they may have brought home? This pool and grove must have been a pleasantly shaded and cool place in the height of summer.

The architectural garden of tiered terraces rising one above the other on a steep hillside by means of grand stairways or ramps of dressed stone, with cloisters, or arcades, the whole laid out formally and geometrically with flower-beds, ponds and groups of trees — the style to be copied by the Renaissance Italians — was invented and first carried out in Egypt (*Deir-el-Bahari*) for Queen Hatshepsut (1505-1483 BC). It was a temple garden with the shrine on the uppermost terrace. The trees were accommodated by excavating large

planting holes in the naked rock and filling them with Nile mud. The Queen became a plant-introducer in furnishing this grand formal garden, in which she planted thirty-two incense-bearing trees as well as many other plants fetched from Punt (Somaliland). The Egyptian gardeners were skilled in the transplanting of grown trees; they dug them up with the soil-ball of the roots intact, transferred them to huge pots which were then slung by straps to carrying-poles and carried on board ship by half a dozen labourers. They understood that this was best done when the trees were dormant.

Another great plant-introducer and gardener among the Pharaohs was Rameses III (1198-1166 BC). During his reign the practice of planting small trees and shrubs in large, decorated earthenware vases seems to have developed — another of the garden art elements to be copied later by the

18

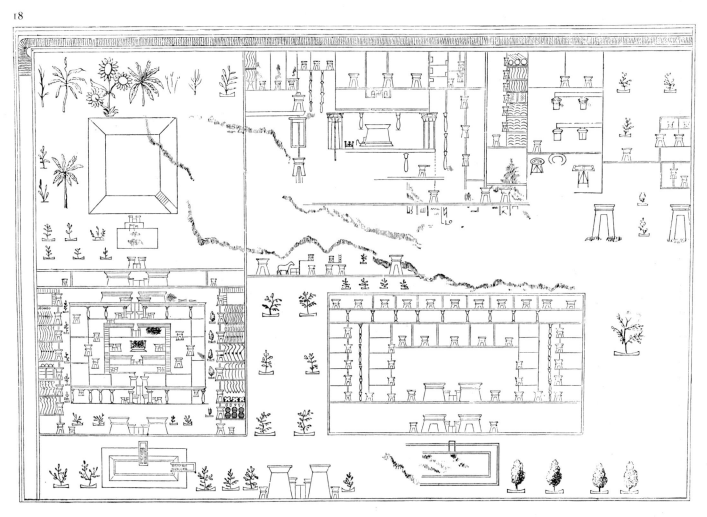

19

18 *Layout of an Egyptian villa.*

19 *Egyptian gentleman's villa, Thebes.*

Roman and Renaissance Italian gardeners. A list of this Pharaoh's donations to the city of Heliopolis includes the following passage:

'I give to thee great gardens with trees and vines in the temple of Atuma, I give to thee lands with olive trees in the city of On. I have furnished them with gardeners... I give to thee trees and wood, date-palms, incense and lotus, rushes, grasses and flowers of every land to set before thy fair face.'*

In the course of his reign Rameses III gave 514 gardens or garden sites to temples. In many cases, of course, they were intended to provide the temple with revenue in the form of oil, wine, timber and incense as well as with pleasure-grounds.

There were small as well as great gardens in Egypt, not only around private houses but also around graves. These grave-gardens were highly stylized, which suggests that they were ritual. Evidently the soul was to continue to enjoy the garden after death. (Hence, also, the numerous tomb paintings of gardens.) One of these gardens of the dead

'...is at the tomb of the writer Inny, close to his own beautiful garden. Surely by this was intended some sort of ceremonial or symbolic garden of the dead, and maybe Sinuhe's Necropolis-garden should be regarded in a similar way...† It seems just as likely that it is a very ancient garden style, handed

* Wilkinson (1878).
† The reference is to another and larger garden.

17

20 *Water-tank between date palms in an Egyptian garden.*

down deliberately in the books that record sepulchral monuments. In the Middle Period we certainly found gardens of the living not very different from these, at any rate in the case of vegetable gardens. But it is quite possible that our pictures go back to a still earlier time of which as yet no records have been discovered.'†

The pictures referred to in this passage show a group of five or seven palms, a water-tank drawn diagrammatically to imply that there is water on both sides of the palms; and a chessboard-like diagram of a vegetable garden. They could have derived from a west Asian source, and be representations of the earliest Egyptian gardens.

What did Egyptian gardening add to the art of garden making which had not been invented by the peoples of the Two Rivers before them? Although nothing is more difficult than identification of their flowers from their stylized pictures, there is no doubt that a number of new species were either brought into cultivation or introduced as exotics from countries where they had been grown but where gardening was much less sophisticated than in Egypt. In the matter of design they laid down, not only for the thousands of years of their own history but for two alien civilizations to come, the lines of two highly formal and architectural styles. These were the flat, strictly rectangular style given a third dimension by rectangular blocks of trees; and the grand tiered or formal terraces for a hillside site. There can be no doubt whatever that Hatshepsut's great temple garden of rising terraces, arcades and trees is ancestral to the Roman style, which was resumed and perhaps improved on by the Italian garden architects of the Renaissance.

† Gothein (1928).

18

21 *Fan grating design for garden pavilion window.*

CHINESE GARDEN ART

If, respecting the chronological plan of this book, I turn now to the subject of Chinese garden art before continuing with the development of the art in the West, it is as much on general principles as for specific reasons. We know that China was one of the three places in which civilization first developed, and one of the first three countries in which men learned to live by cultivating plants. And Chinese writers assure us that garden making is, indeed, a very ancient art in their country.* But although no records or pre-Christian era gardens survive, we have rather more evidence (although it is circumstantial) than simple assertions for the antiquity of Chinese garden art. For although the earliest description of an actual garden — clearly idealized and rhapsodical at that — dates from the second century BC only, the garden described — or rather gardens, for there are several such rhapsodies — were clearly the late and sophisticated products of a long tradition, and by no means primitive works of art.

The Egyptians, as I have tried to show, created and stylized formal, geometric, highly 'unnatural' gardens which were essentially works of architecture. Living in a land which is virtually featureless and in which most beauty was man-made, they could not have done otherwise. The Chinese garden,

* See e.g. Kan To, *Yüan Yeh* (1933); Boynton, G.M., in *The China Journal*, July 1935; and Sirén (1949).

from the earliest of which we have any kind of record, is the antithesis of the Egyptian garden, chiefly because the Chinese became lovers of that kind of natural scenery of which the Egyptians had none to love.

The gardens we first hear of in China in any kind of detail were made during the Ch'in and the Han dynasties. They were royal palace gardens, landscaped hunting parks as much as gardens, and had religious as well as aesthetic and recreational purposes, for they were laid out under the influence of Taoist nature worship. Such were, for example, 'Ah Fang Kung', the Ch'in Emperor Shih Huang Ti's great park; and the Han Emperor Wu-ti's 'Wei Yang Kung'. Both these, and other garden-making emperors

'... desired to transform their residences into earthly paradises or fairylands where with the aid of secret elixirs of life, and of yoga exercises, they hoped to attain immortality...'

We do not really know what these ancient gardens were like, for although the history of the five centuries before Christ in China is fairly well known there is no contemporary description of a royal garden. What we have are imaginative pictures in paint and in words, created long afterwards from mere traditions, by Sung landscape artists and by one or two Ming painters. Their paintings were, of course, no more than romantic inventions and quite worthless as documents.

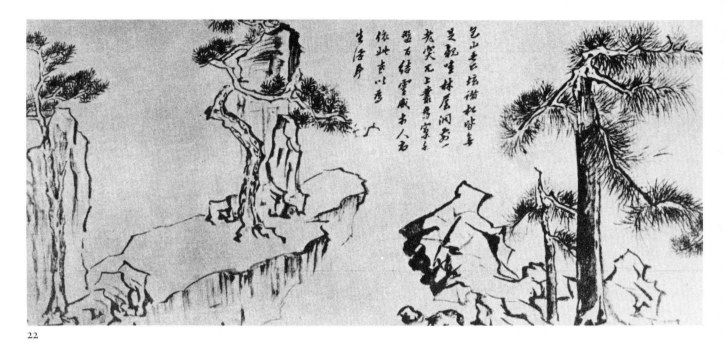

22

22 *The spirit of Chinese landscape gardening is implicit in this painting by Huang Tao-chu.*

23 *Poet's small garden. After Hsiang Mo-lin c. 1560.*

24 *Paintings such as this thirteenth-century landscape by Hsu Shih-chang influenced Chinese and later Japanese garden design.*

Verbal descriptions more nearly contemporary tell of artificial mountains built as dwellings for immortal Beings (see chapter 5 on the subject of *Horai* in Japan), grottos, fishponds, rare trees and flowering shrubs, streams and winding paths. Most important were the 'mountains', made of enormous old water-eroded limestone rocks; and the various uses of water. What these descriptions do reveal is that these were highly selfconscious, romantic landscape gardens, and therefore at the end rather than at the beginning of a creative tradition; that these gardens of the third and second centuries BC had their origin in much earlier ones; and that, since the Chinese gardens made in the twentieth century were much the same, Chinese garden art was massively stable and almost incredibly conservative for more than twenty-five centuries.

Garden art did not develop, in so far as it developed at all, of its own accord in Chinese culture; as in Japan later, and in England still later, it was a branch of landscape painting. Some artists worked with paint on paper, some with ink on silk, and some with rocks and water and trees on a piece of land. Very often the painter, poet and garden designer were the same man, and a remarkably large number of great Chinese landscape painters were equally famous for their gardens. Painters and garden-artists alike were, from at latest the fourth century BC, under the influence of the Taoist back-to-nature movement, in itself typical of the kind of anti-urban reaction which occurs only at the height of an old urban culture. Only an old, very sophisticated and complex civilization produces and supports men like the Taoist philosopher-artists who selfconsciously retired to country cottages to plant little gardens of rocks, willows, plum trees and a few chrysanthemums, and to live the simple life. These artists created the elements of which greater gardens were composed, and wrote pieces such as the poet-gardener Tao Yüan-ming's:

'Homeward bound! Fields and garden at home are growing

23

24

wild; how could I not return? Of my own accord I have forced my soul to serve as the slave of my body; to what end further torment and care? The boat rocks in the light breeze. The wind plays in my fluttering robe... Now my eyes light upon my door and the ridge of the roof, exultingly I hasten forward... The paths are overgrown, but the pine-tree and my chrysanthemums are as of yore... To ramble in my garden is my daily joy; its stillness is guarded by a constantly closed gate. The evening mist rises lingeringly out of the valleys; tired birds find their way home. The shadows float out and soon they have disappeared; leaning with my hand against my solitary pine, I linger.'*

For many centuries garden art continued in this vein and feeling. The great gardens of the rich were as selfconsciously simple and natural — but it was a very subtle simplicity and a very conventionalized nature — as the cottage gardens of the Taoist poets and painters. But in the fourth century AD Buddhist ideas, which had been gaining ground against

Taoism for a long time, began to affect garden art. Buddhist monastic orders always chose beauty spots for the building of their monasteries, and the monks gardened the surrounding lands. Typical of such foundations was that of the Society of the White Lotus founded by the Buddhist convert Hui Yüan in AD 370. The parklike garden in which disciples received instruction became a model for similar parks made by graduates of this school in many parts of China; they were called, after the mother house, Lu Shan parks. There was no real conflict between the old and new religion, for Buddhism as introduced from India was readily Taoized. As a result the Buddhist influence on garden art, as on painting, was quite as 'natural' and, as it were, un-architectural as the Taoist. Here, from a Chronicle published in 547, † is a description of a garden which the rich Chang Lun bequeathed to a monastery in return for a good place in heaven:

'With its hills and ponds this garden excelled in beauty

* Quoted by Sirén (1949).

† Lo-yang Chia Lang Chi, quoted by Sirén (1949).

many princely pleasure grounds. Here had been built up a number of hills that were called the Chin Yang Mountains; they looked as if they had been formed by nature. Within these heights there were double peaks and curving ridges by the side of deep streams and valleys. There were plenty of tall, leafy trees which afforded protection against the rays of sun and moon, and hanging creepers which did not prevent the mist from stealing in. The paths ran zigzag up the hills and down in the valleys; it looked as if they had suddenly been broken off at certain points, although actually they continued in another direction. The stony and curious water-courses flowed in some places in winding bends and in other places straight on. Nature lovers were so captivated by this spot that they forgot to go home.'

But in China the affinity between great and little gardens was always maintained. There was not one style for cottages and quite another for palaces. The rich and mighty had the means; but the learned and gifted poor had the genius, and it was still to poets like Hsieh Ling-yin (c. AD 410) that the

25 *Sketch map of the Yüan Ming Yüan, the Garden of Long Spring.*

26 *Yüan Ming Yüan, Tz'ü Yün P'u Hu, landscape garden on an island. From a painting by T'ang Tai and Shên Yüan.*

25

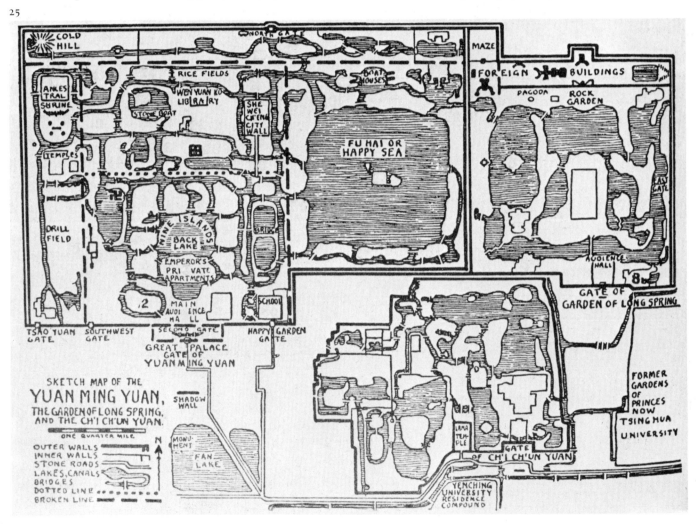

26

rich men looked for the elements of their gardens, for that 'atmosphere' implicit in Hsieh's:

'I have banished all worldly care from my garden; it is a clean and open spot. I chose the place in the lee of the mountains to the north; the windows open towards the hills in the south. I have dammed up the stream and built a pond. I have planted roses in front of the windows, but beyond them appear the hills...'*

But the poets were not the only creators of garden elements. Among the many painter-gardeners of the sixth century, the great Chang Seng-yu was outstanding. He designed many gardens, but in a sense they were all the same garden, for he established and himself held to a convention. A thatched cottage for the resident philosopher-hermit was set among trees at the foot of a mountain; there was a stream, a lily pond, some chrysanthemums, a few fruit trees grown for their blossom, an old and preferably gnarled pine, perhaps a

* *The China Journal*, London, 1935.

clump of bamboo, and some fantastic rocks. And this convention endured for centuries, for we have it still living in Po Chü-i's early ninth-century poem *T'ao t'ang Chi*, in which the author describes his own cottage on the lower slopes of the Kuang-lu mountains in Kiangsi:

'...Before the hut extended an open court covering about 100 square feet, and in the middle of the court rose a terrace. On the south side lay a square pond, twice the size of the terrace. Around the pond were planted bamboos from the hillside and wild flowers. White lotus flowers and white fish were placed in the water. Further south wound a stony stream, and along this grew pines and other conifers; bushes throve at their feet. The paths, which led in and out, were paved with white stones. To the north the hall steps had been hewn in the mountainside, so that one could ascend to the top, and on cleared places where stones were piled up.* There were also a spring and a tea plantation, inviting to the pleasure of tea drinking. On the eastern side of the hill the water fell from a height of three feet, and on the

* i.e. as 'mountains'.

23

27

28

opposite side it was led from the height by an open bamboo pipe to above the house whence it flowed down by a terrace...'†

In half a dozen such passages 'mountains and water' are used in such a way that the phrase can be freely translated as 'garden'. In this same period the poet-statesman Li Te-yu laid out a much larger garden on the same principles: it was called P'ing ch'uan and included many rare trees, shrubs and herbs, 'mountains', water in both streams and ponds, and several pavilions. Li's garden, like his vices, if vice be the right word for the practice of taking hallucinatory drugs, was designed to help him attain the Taoist ideal of making contact with 'invisible worlds'.

In short, Chinese Taoist gardening was, like the English gardening of the nineteenth century, 'paradise' gardening, romantic, escapist, and in absolute opposition to the spirit of classical, Italianate garden design. And it is in just this fact that one can find evidence for the very great antiquity of Chinese garden art; it is barely conceivable that there was

† Quoted by Sirén (1949).

24

not, at a time before this kind of romanticism became fashionable, some kind of formal and architectural gardening; the kind of garden design proper to a culture before its people have shed their fear of nature and, from looking upon natural forces as their enemy, make a sort of pet of them.

In landscape gardening flowers are not important until, at a certain point in time, it is transformed into 'paradise' gardening. Flowers became important in Chinese painting (see below) and in Chinese gardening late in the T'ang period and in the succeeding disruption of the empire under the Five Dynasties (AD 907-960). For rather less than a century flowers became as important as design in garden art. I shall have more to say about this. With the restoration of central imperial power by the Sung came a restoration of the simplest kind of Taoist gardens. Under the influence of painters rather than poets, those monochrome landscape painters who were also to have such a revolutionary effect on Japanese garden art, stone and rocks ('mountains'), always important in Chinese gardens, became predominant.

27, 28 *Garden scenes, Han period; scroll illustrations ascribed to Ch'in-Ying.*

29 *A garden kiosk with 'mountain' stones, Peking.*

30 *Stones and water, Suchow.*

29

30

The man whose influence on garden art at this time was overwhelmingly great, through whom the landscape painters' ideas were popularized among the rich and educated classes, was the emperor Hui Tsung (1100-25). Far from being merely an emperor, he was a great artist, a painter of exquisite talent, an expert on floriculture, and above all a lover of stones. As Osvald Sirén (1949) puts it, the emperor 'collected water-modelled garden stones with the same zeal as he collected paintings and old bronzes, and he had them fetched not only from the beds of lakes, but from older private gardens'. These garden stones seem never, in China, to have been religious symbols, which is what they were in Japan where in any case they were of a different kind. For the Chinese they were simply beautiful objects, although occasionally invested with an almost human, or even divine, spirit by the anthropomorphism of Taoist feeling.

Hui Tsung not only collected remarkable stones for his Ken Yu garden with such enthusiasm that for a time 'they blocked all other traffic on the canals round the capital',

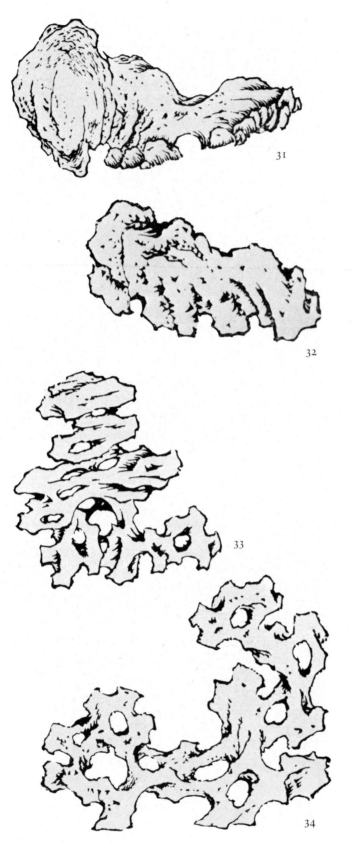

but he sent a special officer with extraordinary powers, one Chu Mien, to collect plants and trees in the southern provinces. Chu Mien, who also collected still more garden stones, was a very efficient and absolutely merciless official who used his powers to take stones and old trees from private citizens as well as from the wild, and to force the local population to provide the necessary labour. China, like Egypt a couple of thousand years earlier, and Europe eight hundred years later, provides too many examples of public resources being overtaxed in order to create great works of architecture and garden art.

The stones which were so important in Chinese gardens were of a peculiar kind and used in a special way, and there is nothing quite like them in the garden art of any other country. Chinese writers and painters were always much preoccupied with rough, towering and picturesque mountains, and it is from this same feeling that the gardeners' preoccupation with rocks derives. The *Yüan Yeh* tells its readers that the 'mountains' in their gardens should look wild, should resemble real mountains, should be after Nature, and yet that the garden designer should constantly bear in mind that the work is being executed by human hands: in short, that what is being made is a work of art. The instruction applies as much to painting as to gardening. For rocks were

31, 32 *From the poet Li Tê-yü's garden in P'ing Ch'uan (8th-9th century).*

33, 34 *T'ai Hu garden stones. After Lin Yu-lin, Su Yüan Shih P'u (Ming period).*

35 *From a derelict garden in Suchow. A T'ai Hu stone.*

36, 37 *Garden stones: from the* Shih Chu Chai Shu Hua P'u.

as important in the Northern Sung monochrome landscape painting as in the gardens of the time.

The rocks favoured above all were ancient, water-eroded masses of limestone of weird and fantastic shapes; rocks looking 'like goblins or savage beasts, lying crossways or in the horizontal or in the upright position, on the surface of which grew moss and lichen with mottled hues, or parasitic plants...' ★ The stones were grouped with special regard to the picturesque play of light and shadow in their hollows and rough surfaces. A single stone of especially remarkable shape might be set up as we set up statues; or many such stones might be assembled to form grottoes.

Many of the best rocks were large pieces of eroded limestone fished up from the bottom of Lake Tai Hu. Other sources were used, but Tai Hu stones were most highly valued. They were of very strange shapes, honeycombed with holes, from white to slate blue or even black in colour. The largest used were above six feet tall. But very small examples, used with seashells and coloured gravels to make tray gardens for interior decoration — the art later perfected

★ T'sao Hsüeh-c'hin (1792).

36

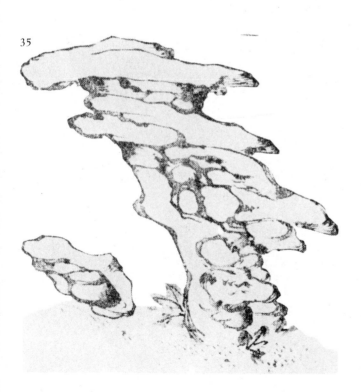

35

37

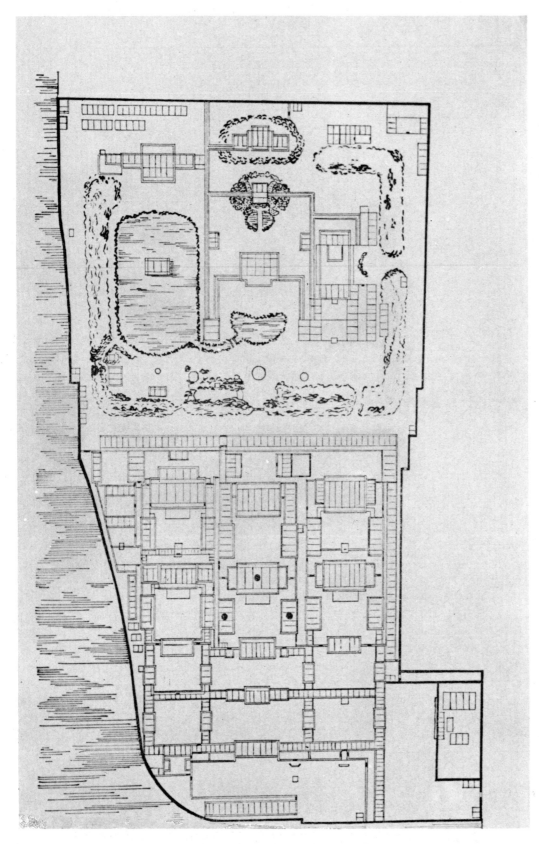

39 *A small garden with chrysanthemum beds. Woodcut from Lin Ch'ing,* Hung Hsüeh Yin Yüan T'u Chi.

in Japan as *bonseki* — were also valued. Such stones continued in use for many centuries. A seventeenth-century writer, discussing Tai Hu stones, says: 'They have been collected since time immemorial and are now very rare.' Being very rare, they were also very dear, and a really ancient and beautiful stone, regarded exactly as a work of fine art, might sell for as much as '200 measures of rice'. So expensive did such Tai Hu stones become, in fact, that they were well worth faking, and clever craftsmen created faked Tai Hu stones well enough to deceive all but the most experienced judges. A curious fact is that the man who sought, found and brought back from some remote and difficult place a really fine stone with all the desired attributes was regarded and honoured as an artist, as if he had made it: this was, in short, the first art of *objets trouvés.*

I have referred more than once to the affinity, amounting almost to identity, between landscape painting under the Sung and garden making. The *Yüan Yeh* goes to the length of suggesting that Tai Hu, or some lesser but good stones, be set up by the landscape gardener against a white garden wall:

'The white wall serves as paper and upon this one paints with stones. Those who perform such works should in the first place pay attention to the furrows and lines of the stones, and then dispose them in the light of the old masters' ideas. One may then plant Huang-shan pines and firs, or old plum trees or beautiful bamboos. If one contemplates such a painting through a round window, it is like wandering in a mirror.'*

* Quoted by Sirén (1949).

29

40

To such lengths did the stone-loving artists go that the great painter and art critic Mi Fei (early twelfth century) used always to bow reverently to a certain wonderful old Tai Hu rock in his garden when he passed it, and he never failed to greet it respectfully as his elder brother. The cult developed all through the Sung and subsequent periods until many different kinds of stones, all named and from many different sources, were valued, traded in, used and re-used according to a growing body of traditional practice.

The basis of any Chinese garden, then, from the earliest time of which we have any record until the collapse of traditional Chinese culture under Western pressures, was 'mountains and water'. But trees, shrubs and herbaceous plants were also important, and were never, as they were in Japan (see chapter 5) entirely banished from the garden. Osvald Sirén says that there was never, in Chinese garden art, anything like the European parterre of flowers, and lawns were entirely unknown. There seems no doubt about the absence of lawns, but I think it probable that flowers may have been used in formal patterns at a very early date, before the triumph of landscape over architecture; though that is mere conjecture.

The difficulty in discovering how the early Chinese gardeners used flowers and felt about them lies in the fact that what we know about this was all written by authors of the Ming

40 *The Lan-t'ing garden near Shan-yin in Chekiang. Woodcut from Lin Ch'ing,* Hung Hsüeh Yin Yüan T'u Chi *(early nineteenth century).*

41 *The Silver Pavilion, Garden of Ginkakuji.*

41

(1412-1712) and later periods, whose refined romantic aestheticism was such that one suspects them of remaking the past to suit a literary convention, like our own pre-Raphaelites who invented an entirely imaginary Middle Ages. Seventeenth-century poet-painters of the *hsieh-i* ('idea writing') school write about flowers as if they were people, with no more objectivity than the most sentimentally whimsical of English garden writers. For example, this kind of thing from the pen of Yuan Chung-lang:

'When they stand in the sun and their sensitive bodies are protected against the wind, they are happy. When they look intoxicated or silent and weary, and the day is foggy, then the flowers feel sad. When the bloom-laden branches droop and are not able to draw themselves up, it is as if the flowers were dreaming in their sleep. When they seem to smile and look around with a gleam in their eyes, the flowers have awakened from their slumbers.'*

Records of flowering plants familiar in gardens, all of them celebrated paintings, do not go back beyond the first half of the tenth century. But this is a mere accident of lost records, and by that time, no doubt, the plants commonly depicted had been in cultivation for more than a thousand years, and perhaps for very much longer than that. Favourite subjects were roses, including monthly roses, lilies, paeonies, chrysanthemums, hollyhocks, water lilies, narcissus, and some

* Quoted by Sirén (1949).

31

42

orchids; poppies, too, of course, and for their beauty, not their opium, for opium was a Western introduction. Of flowering trees, the plum was by far the most important; plum trees were planted in thousands, written about in innumerable poems and treatises, painted by all the great painters, and were almost objects of worship.

In the seventeenth century two books for art students — *Shih Chu Chai Shu Hua P'u* and *Chieh Tzu Yuan Hua Chuan*, the latter appearing in parts from 1679 to 1701 — were first published. Owing to the importance of flower-painting in China, these books tell us something about Chinese garden flowers. The principal ones seem to have been bamboo, hardy

orchids, plum trees of course, tree paeonies (*Paeonia suffruticosa* only), hibiscus, chrysanthemum, roses, water lilies, pomegranates, persimmons, cherries, lemons and oranges. Bamboo was very highly valued, and by Middle Sung times (eleventh century) about a hundred cultivars were distinguished by nurserymen. Rather later than the others, peach trees were valued for their flowers and fruits, and later still apricots.★ The orchids cultivated seem to have been cym-

★ Both were introduced from Persia, as were many other plants, the most important being the grape-vine and alfalfa. A number of important introductions were made in the second century BC under the Han emperors. General Chan K'ien, an officer of the Emperor Wu, was responsible for some of these. See, for others, Laufer (1890).

43

42 *Garden entrance with stones and climbing plants. From a woodcut from a seventeenth-century drawing illustrating a scene in the play* The Story of the Western Pavilion.

43 *Garden pavilions: after a woodcut illustrating* The Story of the Western Pavilion.

bidiums. On the whole the Chinese valued flowering and other plants less for their colour than for distinction of habit, grace; white was the favourite colour for flowers, and scent and form were more important in a plant than any more spectacular attribute. This, again, was probably due to the influence of monochrome landscape painting.

By far the most important herbaceous genus was the chrysanthemum, and yellow-flowered kinds were considered superior to all others. This had been so at least since the fourth century, when the chrysanthemum garden of the author T'ao Yüan-ming became famous. Second in importance were paeonies and notably the moutan, *Paeonia suf-*

33

fruticosa. White varieties were valued above all others and they were cultivated in special nurseries. They were used rather more sparingly in gardens. Water lilies were grown not only in ponds and lakes but in urns, vases and other large vessels. The importance of these lotuses in gardens was much enhanced by the advent of Buddhism. The eleventh-century poet Chou Tun-i gives us an idea of the garden taste of the times in the following passage:

'Since the beginning of the T'ang dynasty it has been the leading fashion to admire the paeony, but my favourite is the water lily. How stainless it arises from its bed of mud. How modestly it reposes on the clear pool — a symbol of purity and truth. It emerges symmetrical and perfect in its spotless purity; its subtle perfume is wafted far and wide... something to be reverently admired from a distance, and not profaned by familiar approach.

'In my view the chrysanthemum is the flower of retirement and culture; the paeony a symbol for high rank and wealth; the water lily is the matchless lady of virtue. But few have loved the chrysanthemum since T'ao Yüan-ming, and none now loves the water lily like myself, whereas the paeony is a great favourite with all mankind.'*

Among other identifiable garden flowers in popular use, the following are probably the most important. *Lilium regale*, or a similar trumpet-lily, seems to have been the only true lily; but there were two kinds of hemerocallis. Monkshood, several mallows, several poppy kinds, a luteola, a gentian and one begonia were among the herbaceous plants. Among shrubs the most commonly planted were camellia, roses, gardenia, hibiscus, hypericum and hydrangea, but above all the moutans. The climbing plants depicted in Chinese painting and on pots and vases are not easy to identify, but some tecomas and ipomaeas are obvious. As for trees, as well as the half dozen conifers so highly regarded, the typical deciduous trees of a big Chinese garden were *Sophora japonica*, *Gleditschia sinensis*, *Robinia pseudo-acacia*, *Albizzia julibrissin*, *Catalpa ovata*, *Ailanthus altimissima* and *Ginkgo biloba*. Of course some other genera, including the Acers, were grown, and

* The translation is from Giles (1901).

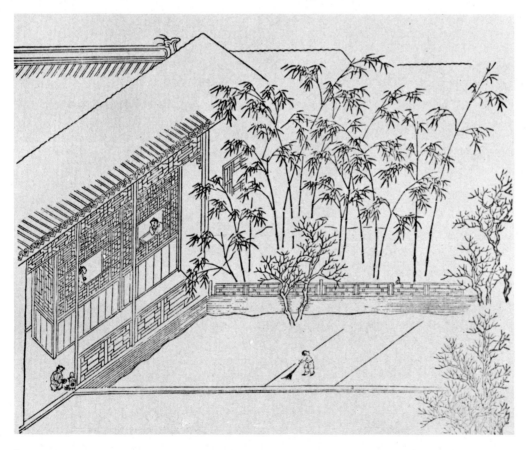

44. *The little Chu Fang garden at the house in Ch'ing-chiang-p'u, where Lin Ch'ing lived in retirement.*

especially the fruit trees for their flower, including pomegranate, loquat, lichi and apple. In the south of China the
citrus trees and the banana were important garden subjects.

Both great and small Chinese gardens had, from as early as
we have records, some architectural elements. As a rule they
were used strictly to enhance the landscape picture and not
in any formal style, yet it is possible that they were a vestige
of some much earlier and formal or architectural style of
gardening; one in which house and garden were created as
an entity in the early Japanese manner, and in the manner
we have been familiar with in Europe since Roman republican times. But in the Chinese gardens which we know, the
hermit's hut or cottage was used as a romantic ornament in
great gardens, or as a weekend cottage in a small one. In the
greatest gardens the principal architectural features were
walls, pavilions and bridges. The pavilions were of all sizes
and two types: closed, or open like verandas. They had
beautifully tiled roofs, and ornamental balustrades in a whole
series of stylized patterns were important; so were the fanci-

45 *An ornamental garden pavilion window.*

*46. Yü Ch'un-ting garden
in Hui-chou, showing paved path
leading to the rampart of the
city wall: from Lin Ch'ing.*

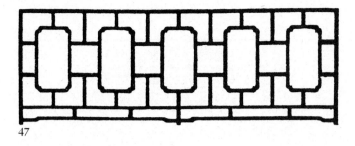

47

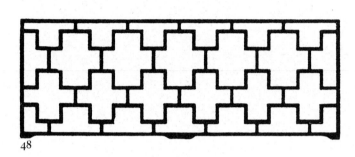

48

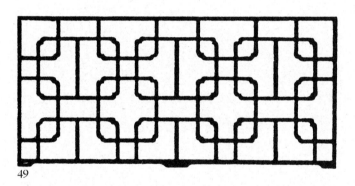

49

50

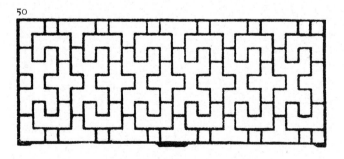

47-53 *Ornamental balustrade patterns, some of them based on sun-flower and plum blossom petals; these were for garden pavilions. From the* Yüan Yeh, *c. 1634.*

ful doorways, shaped like shells, lotus-petals, gourds, vases or according to some geometrical convention. Equally, the ornamental windows were often stylized leaf or flower shapes, but as often elaborate geometrical shapes were used. Paths and floors, both in the pavilions and in the open, were often mosaics laid either in conventional or *trompe l'oeil* geometrical patterns, or to form pictures of animals.

In the garden art of Europe there has been much change from time to time; one style has replaced another as first Italy, then France, and finally England led the fashion in art. Nor were the changes simply a matter of fashion, for other influences were often at work to change the manner of gardening. For example, that of scientific horticulture, the making of new garden plants by breeding and selection; and that of botanical gardening and of plant collecting, which resulted in such an enrichment of plant material that the garden picture was transformed. We shall come to that in its place. The point here is that, on the whole, both these influences were wanting in China; moreover, the culture was so massively conservative that change was extremely difficult to bring about. Conservatism of style and taste is inevitable in a land of ancestor-worship, and in a culture with so clumsy and inflexible a system of writing as the ideographic.

Consequently, once the general style of garden art in China had been fixed — romantic landscape based on rocks and water as the principal elements — it is almost true to say that it ceases to have a history; it simply repeats itself, and there is little left for the historian but to describe the finest works of this long-sustained but now extinct art.

The Yangtze valley was the centre of garden art in China, notably the ancient provinces of Anhui, Kiangsu and Chekiang. Of all the ancient cities of China perhaps Suchou, home of artists, poets and philosophers, had the most and best of the famous private gardens, although Hangchou must once have been as great a centre. Marco Polo was there shortly after the end of the Sung period. He describes the palace grounds, which were ten miles round, and the extraordinary garden planted about a lake, with its flowering and fruit trees, its preserved game for polite hunting, its groves of lofty trees. By his time it was a partial ruin as a result of the conquest of the Middle Kingdom by the Mongol Khans, but the city's many fine public gardens were still maintained, although from what he says one gathers they were for the recreation only of the richer citizens.

Suchou was at its zenith as an art centre in Ming times. The artists who settled there gave expression to their talent not only in painting and poetry but in garden designing. The most celebrated of these was Wen Cheng-ming: Sirén saw and photographed this artist's wistaria still flourishing among weirdly shaped rocks in its fourth century, about thirty years ago. For at least two centuries Suchou continued predominant as a city of painters, poets and garden artists, although the greatest painter-gardener at the end of the Ming period was a Yangchou man, Shih-t'ao, whose fame as a maker of picture gardens became nation-wide.

Shih Tzu Lin, the 'Lion Grove', was probably typical of the Suchou gardens. Originally a temple garden, it was laid out in 1342. Large water-sculpted rocks, a little resembling lions, were set up on a hillock among old, gnarled pines; other equally remarkable rocks were set up in the lake so that their effectiveness was doubled by reflection in the water. The hillock is tunnelled, and the paths wind through its grottos as well as over the top. There are several pavilions in the shade of tall bamboo groves and coppices of trees.

That there was little change in garden art styles during more than twenty centuries is clear from the nature of one of the last gardens made late in the nineteenth century, by Prince Kung, at the palace called Kung Wang-fu. A measure of architectural design, necessary to marry the garden to the palace, is apparent; it may have been borrowed from Western garden architectural ideas. But the elements, as will be clear from the following description, are all in the very ancient landscape picturesque tradition:

'On entering the visitor is confronted with stately rock formations, including one in the shape of a tall portal, the top of which is formed by a recumbent block, a stone structure executed with great boldness combined with skilful distribution of the masses of light and shade playing on the soft background of greenery.

'At the entrance to the first big court there lies a pond with a feeding canal, in a setting of unhewn rustic stone blocks, some of which also serve as stepping stones. The pond is shaded by willows and *Gleditschia sinensis*; but as there is no water the trees do not appear to best advantage.* On a stone platform behind the pond lies a long pavilion with a jutting veranda... It stretches out its arms in the form of sloping galleries to east and west, being thus connected to the long side galleries running north and south. The decorative effect must have been extremely fascinating when the water mirrored the trees and with its reflections enriched the play

* Originally, of course, there was water.

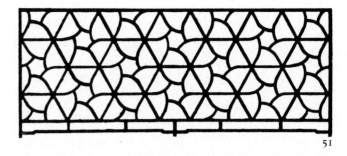

51

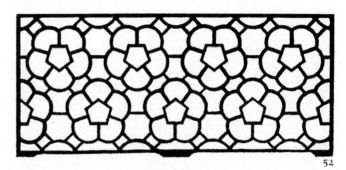

52

53

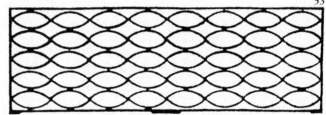

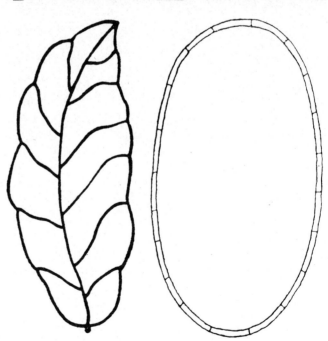

54 *Garden pavilion windows; from the* Yüan Yeh.

55

of light and shade between the pillars of the buildings.

'The court behind this is somewhat broader... In the middle of the background, dominating the whole court, is a huge mountain built up of hollowed and jagged stones, in front of which a narrow stream formerly wound. In the middle of the mountain yawns a grotto, and on either side of this run winding tunnels which lead to the yonder side where sloping galleries take one to an open hall behind the crest of the mountain. The mountain is called Ti T'sui Yen (The Gorge of Dripping Verdure), a name originating in the fact that from a receptacle placed on the mountain water seeped down into the grotto and thence into a little pond before the mountain. The grotto itself, named Pi Yung Tung (Grotto of the Secret Clouds), was regarded as one of the most fascinating and wonderful parts of this extensive pleasure ground.'†

The description continues with an account of the way in which the mountain formed a summit to the whole garden; and with an account of the open-air theatre also included in the garden. For the rest there is a repetition, with variations, of rock and water themes throughout the whole garden.

† Quoted by Sirén (1949).

38

55. *A garden in Nanking laid out c. 1757 by the poet Yüan Mei.*

56. *Small landscape garden, Kiangsi. Woodcut from Lin Ch'ing, Hung Hsüeh Yin Yüan T'u Chi.*

57. *Pond of the Black Dragon, near Peking.*

Some of the pieces of water were very large, but were kept filled by a water-wheel pump driven by asses. They had to walk round and round ceaselessly, for the ponds were not paved; the bottoms were of earth so that aquatic plants could grow in them, and this endless refilling was essential.

Here, to sum up what Chinese garden artists were trying to accomplish from about 500 BC if not earlier, to the first decades of the twentieth century, is what a Chinese art critic told Father Cibot, s. j., who included it in his *Essai sur les jardins de plaisir des Chinois* (Paris 1782).

'What is it one seeks in a pleasure garden? What has one always enjoyed therein? All the centuries have given the same answer to this question: it is the substitute for the perpetually new, fresh and delightful charms of the country, man's natural home. A garden ought thus to be a living picture of all that is proper to a natural landscape, so that it may arouse the same feelings and offer to the eye the same charms as this. The art of laying out a garden lies in bringing together in a natural way the beauty, the verdure, the shade, the views and the wealth of variety proper to the country-side, so that the eye believes it beholds these things, the ear listens for their silence and peace, and all the senses are filled with the serenity which makes it so delightful to live there. Thus, the wealth of variety, this constantly recurring fundamental feature of the natural landscape, should be the first thing to aim at in arranging the ground. Even if it is not sufficiently extensive to contain all the many kinds of hills and mountains that nature models and separates from one another with valleys, glades and groves, and all the water-falls and winding streams among the heights, or the natural pools that are shaded by water plants, and the rocks that stand straight and erect or lie flat on the ground, or the dark grottos and the leafy bowers, one should nevertheless give to the plan a natural variety, and not let oneself be tempted by a misleading first glance to produce a stiff and hard symmetry, which is as tiresome and cold as it is monotonous... The ingenious art that can vie with and even excel nature, may be recognized above all in the ability to arrange the 'mountains', the clumps of trees, and the streams in such a way as to reveal the beauty of Nature, enhance its effect, and offer an infinite variety of shifting views.'

How this Chinese critic would have detested the great French gardens of the seventeenth century; and how he would have admired the ones which the English were soon to be making.

58 *Like the Romans and Renaissance Italians, Chinese architects erected house and garden as a unit. A courtyard of Lin Ch'ing's garden in Peking.*

59

HELLENIC
AND HELLENISTIC

HELLAS

There is not a trace of any kind of evidence for a garden art in ancient Greece until well past its cultural zenith. In the Hellenic world garden art was a product of the decadence of the culture, of the period of transition from national culture to world civilization. Marie Luise Gothein, in her great *History of Garden Art* (1928), has a possible, and in any case interesting, explanation of this:

'The reason for this remarkable gap in Greek art of the best period is the constitution of the cities: a sort of frame enclosing the whole life, intellectual and political, of the Greek, allowing no space, even at the time of its greatest expansion, for the cultivation of private gardens. In all ages any important development of the art has been due to the educated class, politically powerful and artistically refined. But the growing democracy watched with a jealous eye lest any mental superiority should raise a man's family to high station. If in spite of this the Greek spirit has proved important in its results [for garden art], we must seek for garden development in quite a different place.'

In earlier periods of Hellenic culture, using the word Hellenic in its very broadest sense, the case was perhaps different. The great Cretan palaces must surely have included pleasure-grounds; and we may choose to regard as evidence for this the trees and flowers which the Cretan artists painted on their vases and their walls. But without going back to a time so remote, we do hear of gardeners in Homer and, by implication I suppose, in Hesiod.

Even so, as Homer no doubt lived and wrote long after the period in which his poems are set, it is at least possible that the poems reflect the customs and manners, to some extent, of his own times rather than those of the times he was recalling. It is notorious that historical novelists, even the best of them, are full of anachronisms, especially in fields as technical as horticulture. Shakespeare's Italian gentlemen, and still more his Italian clowns, are, in fact, very English of his own time. But for what it may be worth, we note that Laertes, Odysseus's father, had a garden in which fruit trees were the most important plants; that his fruit and vegetables were planted with regularity; that the garden was enclosed; and that as a boy Odysseus was made to work in it. There is no question of an ornamental garden.

Two other gardens in the poems, both the property of Alcinous, are of the same utilitarian kind; virtually kitchen-gardens. These gardens were walled and closely integrated with the house or palace. They were, in fact, simply planted courtyards, and if the Cretans did have gardens, they would have been of the same kind. The species planted in the Homeric gardens are apple, pear, fig, olive, pomegranate and grapes; the grapes were grown separately in a vineyard. There was a separate vegetable garden.

It was probably in the vegetable garden, or in a part of it devoted to culinary and medicinal herbs, that flowers were first cultivated, simply as a by-product. For example, *Lilium candidum* was first known to the Greeks as the origin of a salve imported from Asia, where their Ionian cousins, in touch with west Asian gardening, were far more advanced than they were themselves. Next the bulbs were imported so that the salve could be made at home. Finally, the plants were grown, still as a source of the salve. Now many culinary and medicinal herbs have pretty flowers. In one early poem parsley is equated for beauty with the violet. Roses were important for the extracted scent long before they were grown as ornamentals.

At all events, we may take it that rich Greeks of the seventh century BC had kitchen gardens, orchards and vineyards attached to their country houses; and that they had no ornamental gardens.

The kitchen-garden and orchard comprised one of the two origins of the art of gardens in Europe; the other was the sacred grove and the Nymphaeum. Sacred groves of trees might be in open country; or they might be planted in temple precincts, in which case they were in the cities. The Nymphaeum seems at first to have been a wayside shrine, such as one still sees in Catholic southern Europe. But it was more elaborate: a suitable site along the course of a stream would be chosen, a stone basin constructed to hold and spill the water. Poplar trees were then planted to shade the place, and an altar placed on a hillock where offerings could be made to the Nymphs. Such Nymphaea, too, were made inside the cities in due course, and much embellished with statuary.

The sacred grove and the Nymphaeum became a feature of Mediterranean gardens all over the Hellenic world. They still are, though we may not readily recognize them as such.

Only fortuitously ornamental, kitchen-gardening continued the rule well into historical times. It is true that by the sixth century BC both sectaries and victims at religious rites of many kinds were being crowned with wreaths of flowers, and that this has been taken as evidence for floriculture. It is nothing of the kind. No Greek city was large by our standards until very late in the imperial epoch, and wild flowers were doubtless plentiful in their seasons. However, it is possible that by way of the culinary and medicinal herb garden, a few flowers were cultivated, probably hyacinth of some kind, violets, lilies, poppies, crocuses. Roses were early in cultivation, and must have been commonplace by the fifth century BC. They first occur in the literature only by implication; and probably, like lily bulbs, they were introduced for medicinal or cosmetic use, from Persia by way of Macedonia — notably for the making of the kind of rose-scented oil with which Aphrodite anointed the body of the dead Hector. True, in the very ancient Hymn to Demeter, Persephone gathers roses, so-called: but she gathers them from the grass of a meadow, as if they were primroses. She also gathers crocuses, violets, irises and narcissi.

The first reference to an identifiably authentic rose-bush occurs in a fragment of Archilochus; rather over a century later, Sappho made the rose her favourite flower. By the time of Herodotus, moreover, the rose had acquired sixty petals — i.e., it was a *Rosa gallica* of Persian origin.

Translations of the Bible are quite unreliable as a source of information about what flowers were grown in the Mediterranean world between, say, 1000 and 700 BC. What, for example, was meant by the Hebrew word *Susan*? English translators have 'lily'; but Luther used 'rose'. It may have been some kind of fritillary or one of the wild, red lilies; Victor Heyn (1885) thought this likely. And the same scholar, as philologist, gives us good evidence for the introduction of both the cultivated rose and the cultivated lily from Persia when he points out that *rhodon* (Gr. *rose*) and *leirion* (Gr. *lily*) are originally Iranic words. And this is what we should expect, for Iran was, horticulturally, a province of the earliest, west Asian, civilizations.

'Adonis gardens' may, as Gothein (1928) suggests, be another source of garden art. At midsummer Athenian women celebrated an unofficial but tolerated Festival of Adonis, clearly of enormous antiquity, by setting up a figure to represent Adonis on the roofs of their houses, surrounded by pots of soil in which they grew lettuce, fennel and other herbs. The withering of these plants symbolized the death of the god, Aphrodite's lover, whom the women then lamented in dirges. Something like the Adonis garden, but much elaborated, got into the design of gardens much later. The cult, like their knowledge of horticultural practice, reached the Greeks by way of Syria.

*60 Reconstruction model
of the Roman garden at Fishbourne,
Sussex. See plan below.*

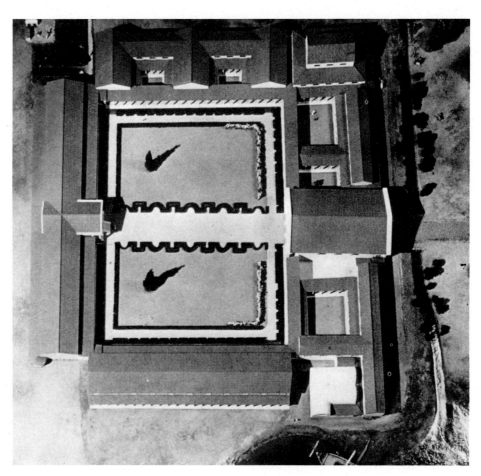

*61 Plan of the Roman garden
at Fishbourne.*

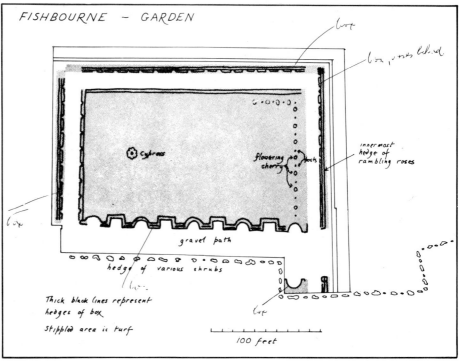

FISHBOURNE ~ GARDEN

box

box, roses behind

innermost
hedge of
rambling roses

Cypress

flowering
cherry

posts

box

gravel path

hedge of various shrubs

box

box

Thick black lines represent
hedges of box

Stippled area is turf

100 feet

43

62 *Excavation of the Roman garden at Fishbourne.*

Such gardening as there was could develop only on the country estates of the Attic gentry and the gentry of other Hellenic cities. As the growth of Periclean democracy tended to deprive them of their lands, wealth and privileges, and as the devastation wrought by Spartan raids into Attica in the first years of the Peloponnesian War forced country gentlemen to take refuge in the city, garden art in Attica suffered a severe setback, while in Sparta itself, and in Boeotia and other Hellenic city states, it remained strictly utilitarian. Probably at this time only the Asiatic Greeks were making ornamental gardens on the Syrian model, derived from Persia and thence from Babylonia.

But, to return to Athens, even in a society where war and taxation deprive the gentry of the means to make gardens, the community itself may still make them, for example in the form of public parks and temple gardens, as in Egypt and China. Sacred groves planted in temple precincts became gardens; so did the small orchards planted for the benefit of

the temple servants. And the movement was helped forward by the fact that trees were venerated and consequently carefully tended.

But not until late in the fifth century BC, under Cimon, did the Athenians really take to making public gardens in their city. Cimon had the Agora planted with trees, and he was probably the first planter of street trees, at least in Europe. This Athenian example was followed in Thebes; and in Sparta the central place, the *Platanistas*, took its name from its fine plane trees. The species was *Platanus orientalis*, one parent of the London Plane which is now planted all over the world. Corinth, too, had public gardens. Moreover, in each of the major Hellenic cities the old Hero sanctuaries associated with the gymnasia developed into parklike gardens.

However, we cannot find a trace of evidence for gardens planted, in the Chinese or English spirit, for their own sake, as works of art. All Greek gardens were planted courts

44

63 *Excavation showing drainage channels for the Roman garden, Fishbourne.*

associated closely with buildings and serving the same purpose as public rooms — temple courts, gymnasium courts, courts for political debate. In short, Greek gardens were outdoor public assembly rooms in which to carry on the business of living, decorated with living plants as well as with works of art and architecture. This is of the first importance to our subject because it established a pattern for garden design throughout the whole Hellenic world, a pattern which has lasted around the Mediterranean until the present day. The garden in Greece was as much a work of architecture as, in China, it was a work of anti-architecture.

From the idea of holding schools in gardens of trees and grass — the public gymnasia — grew the idea of the private academies held in such gardens as Plato's; and, horticulturally more notable if philosophically less distinguished, the garden-school of Epicurus near the Dipylon Gate in Athens, a generation later. We have little information about the physical attributes of this Epicurean garden-school, except that it was large and famous for its beauty. Pliny wrote, in a rather snide spirit, that it 'brought the country into the town', and seemed not to admire the idea. Pliny notwithstanding, the *magister otii* had set an example which many rich Romans were one day to follow.

So integral were the garden and house courts of these academies — Theophrastus was making one at the same time as Epicurus — that it is of their halls, porticoes and pavilions that we read. All we know of them is that they consisted of meadow or lawn with some flowers and many trees. It cannot be over-emphasized that all Greek parks and gardens were for some definite use. The *palestra*, even, was not what we should call a park; it was a playing-field.

No influence from outside made any difference to this rule; but some influences did enrich the plantings of Greek court-gardens. For example, the influence of the Asiatic Greeks led to some plant introductions. But not until after the vast expansion of the Hellenic world following Alexander's conquests, and the creation of a Hellenic Empire, was there

45

much change. The Greeks were staggered at the extent and beauty of the oriental gardens. And although that did not make them change their own style, it did make them enrich it — fatally, in the long run, because it became vulgar. The oriental influence can, as a matter of fact, be traced much earlier. Xenophon, in the course of that great March to the Sea immortalized in literature as the *Anabasis*, saw and was much impressed by some of the great parklike gardens of Iran; and as a country gentleman who wrote an excellent book on running an estate and its farms (the *Oekonomikos*) he had some influence on the horticulture of his time.

The orientalization, the great broadening of the Greek notion of a garden following Alexander's conquests, had at first more effect on the successor states of the empire than on metropolitan Greece. Alexander himself took some interest in new plant introductions, bringing European plants to Babylon. The orientalization of his manners led him to prefer to hold court in one of his gardens than under a roof. Another consequence of contact with the East was the planting of botanical gardens such as that of Theophrastus, where exotics, difficult or impossible to identify now, were acclimatized. Theophrastus grew gladioli, paeonies and anemones as well as the flowers already mentioned.

Among Alexander's successors, the Seleucids were responsible for introducing a number of new plants to their domains, among them spikenard, cinnamon and, according to report, some new anemones. The Ptolemies, inheriting the whole wealth of Egyptian garden traditions and plants, were more in a position to give than to receive; under their aegis, the Hellenized Egyptians and Egyptianized Hellenes became crazy about gardens, and particularly about floriculture. The Greeks, fascinated by the floricultural wonders which could be wrought in the climate of Egypt, became profligate in their use of flowers. Ptolemy Philadelphus even had his floors strewn with them. In the new Hellenic cities of Asia and Africa, space was at last allowed for private urban gardens. Royal and public gardens occupied a quarter of the whole area of Alexandria — the Museum garden, the garden of the Great Gymnasium and the Paseion, an artificial mountain garden. Alexandria's suburbs were garden-suburbs; and even the cemeteries, public and private, were gardens. In Antioch, the main street is described as a continuous portico with houses on one side, and, on the other, gardens occupying the entire length. The gardens were full of pavilions, fountains and statues, and probably the only plants used were trees. But Antioch was famous for its rose gardens;

the rose park of Daphne to the south was enormous, and as famous for its great cypresses as for its roses. But again, all those gardens were pleasure grounds in which buildings were more important than plants, and which had far more affinity with architecture than with horticulture.

The fashion for gardens spread back from the Hellenic world overseas to Greece itself in the third century. Thebes became famous for her gardens. The Greek house was built round a court, and this court was the more important in that the rooms in the house were tiny; hardly more than sleeping-niches. The court was the most important living-space in the dwelling. It was planted with some trees, and with ornamental plants in big terracotta pots, perhaps on the model of the 'Adonis gardens'. Thus Greek gardeners set a pleasant fashion which has endured for more than 2,000 years. Gothein

64 *Roman garden drainage, Fishbourne.*

(1928) suggests that the peristyle itself (extensible since, unlike the Roman atrium, it was unroofed) was used for growing flowers.

Curiously enough, despite the formal and architectural quality of Greek gardens, there was a fashion for building artificial grottoes not unlike the Chinese in spirit. It probably derived from the Nymphaeum. It was selfconsciously rustic and moss-grown. Pliny has an account of a gigantic hollow plane-tree inside which a grotto was constructed with pumice-stone and mosses, so large that eighteen people could dine in company inside it. He was a credulous reporter, but perhaps it was true. One is reminded of the great Dragon Tree of Icod in the Canary Islands within whose hollow trunk first the Guanches and later the Spaniards made a chapel; a dozen or more people could hear Mass inside that tree.

'Even in a modest park (described by Alciphron) in the neighbourhood of a Greek town, possibly Corinth, there stood an ivy-clad rock grown over with laurel and plane, and set about with myrtle. At intervals nymphs were stationed and behind them stood Pan gazing at them. With all this ornament one may safely guess at grottoes inside the rock. The rest of the garden arrangements at the villa are quite modest — only groups of cypress and myrtle and a small flower garden.'*

Vulgarity set in in the third century BC. Hiero II of Syracuse, for example, had an immensely costly garden made for him on the deck of an enormous ship built by Archias of Corinth with the help of the famous Sicilian engineer Archimedes. The flowerbeds were made in lead trays; ivy and grape-vines rooted in pots were trained over the pergolas which

* Gothein (1928).

shaded the walks. There were two garden pavilions: one a small library of books; in the other, which was floored with agate and precious stones, three people could recline. Not even the Cunard Line has come up to that standard of ostentatious ocean-going luxury.

Despite that kind of thing — a typical product of an affluent tyranny — the older and simpler garden persisted; what we might call the cottage garden, the garden of Laertes or of Alcinous. We know this because such little gardens of fruit trees, vegetable and salad plots, and a few flowers, were typical settings for the romances written by novelists from the second to the sixth century AD. Partly, no doubt, we have here a cliché in popular literature; but such gardens were probably common. Descriptions of large gardens made in the same simple traditions show that one did not have to be as vulgar as the Sicilian tyrants and rich men. All make a point of a site set high and with a good view of the sea and passing ships. The garden was enclosed on at least two sides by screens of plane trees, cypresses, laurels and pines or firs, 'entangling their branches' (possibly the origin of pleaching unless, as we have suggested, that was invented by the Egyptians much earlier). Trees were deliberately over-grown with ivy, a practice which, contrary to common prejudice, does them no harm. These screens protected fruit trees, olives and vines. There was a small flower garden with violets, hyacinths, lilies and roses.

To the last the Greeks remained strictly utilitarian garden-ers, sweetly rationalist and, as it were, anti-Taoist. The *Geo-ponica* may recommend the planting of violets, roses and crocuses between the rows of trees, each according to its kind in pure stands; but that was as much or rather more because the flowers were 'food for bees' and would thus increase the revenues of the property, as because they were pretty. There is, in the Greek gardener's mingling of sense and sensibility, a pleasant lingering, long into the decadence of Hellenic culture, of that μηδὲν ἄγαν which is so much more pleasing than the whimsicality of the Chinese aesthetes.

ROMAN AND BYZANTINE HELLENISTIC

There is no need to concern ourselves with early Roman gardens: the Romans, great soldiers, lawyers, politicians and organizers, had no genius in the arts and sciences. The strength of the Latin language in both elements and structure made poets of some of them, often provincials rather than born Romans. But in the arts generally they relied on a brain-drain from their cultural sources, Greece and Syria; and even from the Celtic west. Their gardens, like their architecture and sculpture and engineering, they owed to the Greeks. It is, for example, significant that whereas the Greek country gentry really liked living outside the city and cultivating a garden, the Romans were self-conscious about it; country life, withdrawal from the crowd's ignoble strife, was some-thing of a fashionable, sophisticated attitude rather than a genuine taste.

The fact remains that they were quick learners, and that they had the money and labour to make great gardens. It was thus that they transcended the achievements in garden making of their Greek masters, and made the most remark-able gardens in all the lands of the Hellenistic culture.

It is just to admit that they had some predisposition for the art, or at least for the technique and economy of gardens. The original citizen's small-holding in early and middle Republican times was called neither a farm nor a villa, but a *hortus*; it was, in fact, a fruit and vegetable garden for both subsistence and cash crops. It was out of such market-gardens, or kitchen-gardens, that the *villa rustica* of the richer families developed; a country house-cum-garden (they are inseparable and designed as a unit) which provided the household with vegetables, fruit and wine and perhaps some dairy produce. And it was out of the *villa rustica* that the *villa urbana*, in which ornamental gardening could be prac-tised, developed in its turn.

It must also be admitted that the special Roman sense of order itself imposed a shape on their gardens which was native — for example the *quincunx* formation which is typical and which, incidentally, makes better use of soil than the Greek straight lines.

Real garden art in Italy began with Cicero's introduction of the Gymnasium park, an introduction which can be taken as implied in some of his Dialogues. He and his friends, by marrying the gymnasium to the *villa urbana* style, produced what may fairly be called the Roman garden. It had nothing much of the *villa rustica* left, there was nothing cottagey or kitcheny about it. Such parks were called Academies, after the Greek example. They were often large, and they con-sisted of a grass enclosure, with a portico and statues and groves of trees, for the most part plane and cypress. There might also be grottoes and pergolaed walks, likewise in the Greek style. The well or pond for irrigation of the earlier

65 *Hadrian's Villa. Detail of the Canopus Canal.*

gardens developed into water works which finally, in Byzantium, became very elaborate and vulgar displays of wealth and ingenuity. The Amaltheum, a Greek garden either real or legendary, provided the model for grottoes with streams running through them, such as Henry Hoare was to make at Stourhead in England seventeen centuries later. The interior of the grottoes was lined with rough pumice stone or with tufa rock-work, and mosses were planted by this water. They were, in short, a sort of Nymphaeum in origin.

As I have said, ornamental waters in gardens developed out of the need for irrigation. This was often laid on in large gardens by means of canals, which consequently came to be described in such hyperbole as 'like the Nile' or 'like the Europus'. The Canopus in the Villa Adriana, which we shall come to presently, was a lineal descendant of such canals. Another development of this period was the terraced villa, an advance on the great garden of Queen Hatshepsut and of the ziggurat gardens of the Mesopotamian cities. The house was built on a hillside; the villa, a complex of gardens and buildings and statuary, lay below it in a series of terraces down to the Academy at the bottom. The Academy was a

grove of trees with statues, probably a fountain, and seats shaded by trees or shrubs which were later trimmed or clipped. The development of more elaborate water-works, with more fountains, water-staircases, water curtains and so forth, was assisted by terracing, with its steep fall in level. The agronomist Columella grumbled against such elaborate devices as pernicious luxuries.

Towards the end of the Republican period Italy had so many vast villas that there was a dangerous encroachment of ornamental parks on agricultural land. Such villas had long avenues of trees, flower gardens with formal parterres arranged in geometrical patterns, lakes, pools, streams, canals and all the paraphernalia of ornamental waters, high towers, and of course statuary. The high towers were for the enjoyment of distant views. Such gardens were not only all round Rome, and all round Naples, and between Rome and Naples, but even inside the cities. Lucullus (p. 52 below) had several, as did Metellus and other millionaires who had enriched themselves fabulously by looting the provinces entrusted to them by the Senate and People of Rome. Still other, more natural parks were stocked with game animals

49

and were, in fact, vast 'shooting boxes' in the Persian style. Varro, in *De re rustica*, describes one such belonging to Quintus Hortensius where the animals seem to have been tame. That did not save them from being slaughtered by the *nouveaux riches* sportsmen. There is a curious and distasteful flavour of Edwardian England about all this.

But the Hellenic spirit, with its glorification of architecture, still ruled and there was not much that was natural about most Roman gardens. Trees were planted in geometrical, symmetrical blocks in the manner which Le Nôtre was to revive in France in the seventeenth century, and the whole layout was likewise formal and geometrical. Strabo described many Roman urban and suburban and rural villas, and they are all alike; there is no more originality in them than in the Roman arenas which were built for the games all over the empire. The only variation is in the richness of sculpture and ornament. A few Roman garden makers are credited with the introduction of new plants; Lucullus, for example, may have brought new cherry trees to Rome.

Probably typical of the smaller, simpler gardens, more in what we think of as the Roman spirit and less orientalized, was the Portico of Livia. This was a public garden which Augustus caused to be made on the site of a millionaire's great flashy palace which had been bequeathed to him and which he immediately had razed to the ground. The emperor liked to make such gestures from time to time; they made an excellent impression on the plebs who were his allies against the plutocracy. It was a sunken garden about 125 yards long and 80 yards wide, probably paved but possibly grassed, perfectly rectangular and with a very grand stairway leading down into it. There were niches for statues all round the walled sides, a rectangular pool in the middle, and, for the rest, geometrically planted groups of trees, and flowerbeds.

The nature of the small town gardens of citizens who were not immensely rich can be deduced from such remains as Pompeii, at least for Republican times. They were like the Greek courtyard gardens in the colonnaded atrium (in Naples it might be, rather, a peristyle), with a small pool or a narrow canal right down the centre, crossed by little bridges. The plants were in big terracotta or even stone pots, with herbs and small flowering plants in rectangular flower beds or parterres. House and garden were integral, as they were later to be at one great period of Japanese garden art (see chapter 5).

That the very early Roman gardens were only kitchen-gardens is evident in the fact that for centuries Latin had no word for gardener. *Oliter* was specifically a grower of vegetables, which might not, of course, deter him from cultivating a few flowers; *arborator* tended the trees, including fruit trees. Growing trees for firewood was a profitable business in the neighbourhood of big cities, and coppice wood was a crop, as it still is (though for a different reason) in Kent and Sussex today. Then there was the *vinitor* who tended the vineyard. Not until Cicero's time did the word *topiarius* appear; it became, in time, the word for a gardener in general. Topiary did not mean, in Roman Italy, what it means in the modern world. The derivation of the English meaning is, however, obvious, because the principal task of the *topiarius* in the great Roman gardens was the training of ivy over statues and architectural ornaments. He also had other shrubby plants to care for: oleander, bay laurel, *Daphne laureola*, box, cypress and myrtle; these were the ones in common use. Cypress and box were the first subjects of topiary in our sense — the clipping of evergreens into both formal and fantastic shapes. The Romans called the products of this craft *nemora tonsilia*. Then, as for flowers, the *topiarius* cultivated all the same ones as the Greeks; but he had more species of *iris*, and of narcissi including daffodils; colchicums, lavender, cyclamens and periwinkles were popular garden flowers.

The *topiarius* was presumably at first a man who made *topiae*. These were miniature landscape gardens, almost a sort of *bonseki*, planted in the peristyle. According to the Elder Pliny dwarf planes, artificially dwarfed, and dwarf conifers were used for these, and also some small ferns including maidenhair. Georgina Masson, in *Italian Gardens*, points out that

...some idea of what these toy landscapes were like may be imagined from the enchanting miniature garden in the courtyard of the Casa di Mario Mucrezio, with its tiny water-staircase and pool adorned with Lilliputian herms and statues and representations of water-birds.'

If Pompeii, again, is anything to go by, the Roman garden would probably have been not much to our taste. The use of painted landscapes and scenes of domestic action on the garden walls, to increase the perspective; and the practice, borrowed from Greece, of painting statues in a lifelike way must surely have been as grotesque, in our eyes, as some of the contrivance-filled Jacobean gardens.

I have referred to the fact that Lucullus had a number of

66 *Hadrian's Villa.*

gardens; they were so placed about Italy that he could choose his weather to suit himself, and each of them was magnificent. His Roman garden was at the top of the (now) Spanish Steps, or rather the house was there. It was approached by rising tiers of terraces and stairways, the garden proper. As reconstructed in a drawing by the Renaissance architect Pirro Ligorio — Roman architectural gardens were less ruined then than now — this garden became the model for the great terraced gardens of the Italian Renaissance. This is to say that a rich Roman's garden was far more a work of architecture than of horticulture; a work of walls, paved terraces with balustrades, colonnades and statuary. Some flowers were grown, but the plants were chiefly evergreen trees, planes and poplars, and clipped evergreen shrubs. Part of the villa as a whole, but not of this formal garden, would be orchard, vineyard and vegetable garden. There would be an enclosure for raising some game animals and birds, and aviaries. There might be a shrubbery especially attractive to songbirds, but much less for their song than for their flesh, for the Romans netted them for the pot. But the ornamental quality of some birds, such as peacocks, was appreciated. Many great gardens included fishponds.

In the letters of the Younger Pliny, nephew and heir to the great natural historian, *consul suffectus* in AD 100, and a professional man of letters who happened to be immensely rich, we have accounts not only of his own numerous villas, but also of others belonging to his friends. These descriptions make it very clear again that house and garden were integral, married by long porticoes so that the garden was virtually a series of courts so contrived that every major room in the house opened into some part of the garden, commanding a view over it and over some part of the country beyond. Some of the court gardens were open to the winds; others were completely sheltered. They were rectangular, with straight paths defined by clipped box or rosemary and provided with groves of trees. The paths were often shaded by pergolas and the flowers, violets for example, planted in dense masses, partly in order to concentrate the scent. Garden pavilions might include one especially for sun-bathing — the *heliocaminus* — open to the sky but sheltered from the winds and in some cases centrally heated for use on sunny days in winter. Some villas had heated swimming pools in the gardens, and courts for ball-games, usually associated with the typical Roman baths.

Two other features were common to many Roman villas. These were terraces laid out with geometrical and highly formal parterres edged with clipped box, and gardens of topiary animals enclosed in clipped evergreen hedges. Parterres were probably not planted with flowers. They were themselves ornamental by reason of their shape. The other feature was a drive — or perhaps a ride is the correct word — laid out in the form of an oval round an area planted with box or sometimes another evergreen, clipped into fanciful shapes.

Pliny's Tuscan villa included a court garden private to, and opening out of, his own personal suite of rooms. Central to it was a fountain, and at the four corners were plane trees — the Italians introduced *Platanus orientalis* from Asia Minor for its great value as a shade tree which would stand pollarding or could be grown naturally. The enclosing walls of this private garden were painted with landscapes. Another part of the villa was a feature called the Hippodrome, which Georgina Masson says '...probably looked like its lineal descendant, the Boboli amphitheatre, and the Piazza di Siena of the Borghese gardens.'

Enough remains of one very great Roman villa for us to be able to visit it and form some idea of its appearance. This is the Villa Adriana, the great complex of palace and garden built by the Emperor Hadrian between AD 118 and 138. He was a man of very wide culture, and it seems likely that he was his own architect. It is at Tivoli in the foothills outside Rome, and originally covered 600 acres. It was, and can still be seen as, a complex of buildings and gardens so interpenetrating that the whole is a unity. Set in gardens, and with garden set in them, were living quarters, picture galleries, art collections and grottos. In the sixteenth century it was much less badly ruined than it is now; its present state is due to the Renaissance villa builders who looted and cannibalized it for their own gardens, just as the Chinese raided old gardens for materials to make new ones. The central block of buildings and gardens is planned and regular, but for the rest there is no plan, no regularity, and the principal features are scattered about all over the vast area of the villa; that is all over the huge pleasure park. The element which unifies the whole is water used in streams, canals, lakes, pools and fountains.

The most spectacularly beautiful feature still intact is the Canopus. It is set in a small valley, part natural, part artificial, on a flat open space between wooded hillsides which originally had walks, booths and even, at one time, a sort of market. The valley floor is about 400 yards long and 60 yards wide. Half this space is filled by a long, narrow rectangular sheet of water in a beautiful stone basin, the so-called Canopus Canal. It was, and in part still is, flanked and partly surrounded by a most graceful colonnade of light arches, used as a pergola for climbing plants, probably grape-vines. This is enriched by statues and, on one side, there was formerly a loggia supported by caryatides, some of which were copies of the Athenian Erechtheion caryatides. At the far end of this perfectly proportioned perspective of water and statuary is the triclinium, the semicircular dining-hall. This is roofless, in the form of an apse. In it stands an enormous stone dining-table with a channel down its long axis. This was either used for cooling wine, since water flowed through it, or even, perhaps, for floating dishes down the length of the table. The dining-hall could be screened from the heat of the day by an extraordinary curtain of water falling from above, and thereafter flowing over marble steps and joining the streams which also flowed round the reclining benches of the diners, to cool the air in the height of summer. From the dining-hall, and along the lovely perspective of the Canopus, the view was of rising ground beautifully set with magnificent cypresses.

Another enchanting feature of this great garden, final expression of the Roman style in garden art, is the Marine Theatre. A circle of water in a stone channel surrounds an island reached by decorative bridges. On the island stands a little pavilion central to a garden of parterres, and a fountain. The whole is surrounded by a circular colonnade. One of the most perfect jewels of garden architecture anywhere, Hadrian's Marine Theatre was copied in two superb Renaissance gardens which we shall come to in their place.

Another and very different Roman garden which is still visible is the Temple of the Sybil above the waterfalls at Tivoli, a noble and impressive sight. It represents a type of small Roman landscape garden, usually part of a villa, in which the natural beauty of the site, enhanced and focussed by a work of formal architecture, was of more importance than the formal design. A small and beautifully proportioned circular temple stands on rocks grown through and over by evergreen trees and shrubs. There were apparently other such small, sacred landscape gardens, but this seems to be the only survivor. They all had a specific dedication, for example to the Nymph Amalthea or, in the Tivoli case, to the Tiburtine Sybil. Georgina Masson suggests that if the best-loved landscapes of Italy inspired her poets, her poets, with their idealizations, inspired the landscape gardeners.

It should be remembered that these were not landscape gardens in our sense; they were very small and, as it were, fragments of a picture. There were some much larger landscape gardens, the most remarkable being that of Nero's 'Golden House' of which we have two brief descriptions, both from illustrious pens. Suetonius says:

'His wastefulness showed most of all in his architectural projects. He built a palace stretching from the Palatine to the Esquiline, which he called the Passageway; and when it burnt down soon afterwards, rebuilt it under the new name of the 'Golden House'. The following details will give some idea of its size and magnificence. A huge statue of himself, 120 feet high, stood in the entrance hall and the pillared arcade ran for a whole mile. An enormous pool, more like a sea than a pool, was surrounded by buildings made to resemble cities, and by a landscape garden consisting of ploughed fields, vineyards, pastures and woodlands, where every variety of wild animal roamed about...'[*]

And Tacitus:

'...its wonders were not so much customary and commonplace luxuries like gold and jewels, but lawns and lakes and faked rusticity — woods here, open spaces and views there. With their cunning and impudent artificiality Nero's architects and contractors outbid nature...'[†]

Tacitus's description makes the garden sound like an English garden of the late eighteenth century and perfectly inoffensive. But the fact is that this kind of garden art was not in the Roman taste. The Roman contribution to the art was that of perfecting, and perhaps improving on, the Greek architectural garden.

And in a sense this style was being returned home when the Emperor Constantine moved the capital of the Empire to Byzantium, a typical small Hellenic city with gymnasia and other gardens in the Hellenic tradition. In AD 330 the first Christian Emperor began to build his palace and lay out his gardens. We know nothing about these, but it is safe to say that the complex would have been on the same lines as the Villa Adriana, perhaps showing a measure of orientalization.

Orientalization sums up the changes which occurred in gardens during the following centuries. Marie-Luise Gothein (1928) writing of the Trichonos palace built by the Emperor Theophilus early in the ninth century, describes it as follows:

[*] Suetonius, *Nero*, translated by Robert Graves, Penguin.
[†] Tacitus, *Annales*.

53

'...in some parts reminiscent of Hadrian's Villa, though it of course betrays Asiatic influence as well. This Trichonos is like a triple shell, as its name implies... On the middle of the steps was a kind of arbour on pillars... The staircase leads down to a court, which is really a peristyle, having a shell fountain in the middle made of brass, with a border of silver and at the top a golden pineapple.★ The basin was filled at specially festive occasions with all procurable kinds of fruit, including pistachios and almonds...'

More in the same tenor makes it clear that by the ninth century Byzantine gardens were Roman villas plus a lot of ingenious Asiatic metalwork and ornamentation, and perhaps some new plants.

In the romantic novels of the Byzantine culture gardens are often described as backgrounds for amorous assignations. They differ little from gardens described in much earlier, Greek novels, but such differences as there are, are again in the way of orientalization. Every considerable garden had baths, fountains, porticoes and statues. There was much use of coloured marble, and of statues of birds and animals, often made of precious materials, or at least plated with gold. They were often used as parts of a complex fountain, and had water pouring from their beaks or mouths in a very unnatural fashion. Fountains were made to reproduce bird calls by directing the water through ingenious whistles.

Seats and couches were shaded by arbours of clipped evergreens; myrtle was in common use for that purpose. But often even trees, as well as such animals as the Emperor Basil's golden lions which beat the ground with their tails and roared realistically, were made of brass covered with gold or painted gold. They derived from a very ancient Persian model, and the golden plane trees appear in innumerable stories. But the Byzantines had a perfect mania for putting models of plants and animals, made of silver, gold or bronze, in their gardens; one equalled or surpassed only by the similar mania of the Incas.

The rich Byzantines all had country houses and round them great hunting parks which might contain gardens.

But by the eighth or ninth century Byzantine gardens had reverted so much to the Persian model — the new Persian model, however, as created by the Arab gardeners — that thereafter the story of the garden in Asia Minor generally belongs to the story of Islamic garden art.

★ Not really. Pineapples were unknown in the Old World before c. 1550. The source of this design was probably the pinecone.

67 *Japanese ladies' clothes for garden visiting
had to match the season.*

5

JAPAN: GARDENS
IN THE ABSTRACT

Still keeping to the rule of chronological order, we now return to the Far East; and this time to the gardens of a people among whom, almost from the beginning, garden making was one of the fine arts. Moreover, the Japanese carried the art much further into the realm of the abstract than any other people in the world either before or since. Among the greatest, as they were among the earliest, of plant makers, improvers on nature's flowers, they excluded first flowers and later, in one most important school of garden art, all plants whatsoever from their gardens.

The art of garden making was not original to the Japanese; it reached them, by way of that colonial outpost of Chinese culture, Korea, in the sixth century. But they completely transformed it to their own taste and to give expression to their own philosophy and their own religion. So much so, indeed, that before we attempt to follow the history of Japanese garden making chronologically, it will be necessary to do something which will not be necessary in the case of any other culture: to define a few of the terms and symbols which became the elements of Japanese garden design during a period of about thirteen centuries.

The oldest symbolic element in the Japanese garden is probably *Horai*, although it is possible that *Shumitsen* (or *Sumisen*) is even more ancient. In Chinese Taoist legend

Horai was the name of, or designated the idea of, an island somewhere in the ocean, shaped like a tortoise and inhabited by tortoises, cranes and immortal beings. For this reason *Horai* was 'auspicious', for it was believed that tortoises lived 10,000 years and cranes 1,000 years. The influence of *Horai* was thus favourable to longevity. It is by no means clear when representations of *Horai*, for example in the shape of crane-shaped pools with tortoise-shaped islands, first appeared in Japanese gardens. The issue is confused by the fact that *Horai* as a garden element became established and fashionable only when the example of the Shogun Yoshimasa (1435-90), a great gardener and exponent of *ikebana*, made it so by his insistence that 'auspicious' elements must be included in the composition of any flower arrangement or any garden. But *Horai* was in gardens centuries before the time of Yoshimasa; it has been traced back by some historians, perhaps rather dubiously, to the first century AD; dubiously because at that time it is very doubtful if Japan had anything which could properly be called gardening. On the other hand those who place its appearance as late as AD 900 are ignoring much evidence for its earlier use.

So, then, one element in a Japanese garden had to be *Horai*, usually in the shape of tortoise-and-crane symbols in some form, however highly stylized.

68

Buddhism, like the art of garden making, reached Japan from China by way of Korea in the sixth century. With it came the idea of *Shumitsen*. It was very soon so confused with *Horai* that garden compositions of rocks and water in which both the Taoist and Buddhist elements were mingled became usual, and it is very difficult to analyze them; in fact, for a foreigner it is impossible. *Shumitsen* was of Hindu origin, but it was borrowed from Brahminism by Buddhism and then exported to the lands which the Buddhists evangelized. *Shumitsen* was Indra's heaven and in its material form was the central mountain or hub of the universe: it was of majestic height, it shone brilliantly, and around it were eight circles of mountains separated by eight oceans. *Shumitsen* appeared in Japanese gardens as a group of rocks, one being dominant; but the rocks might also be *Horai* at the same time.

The play on the use of rocks in Japanese gardens, entirely

different in kind and spirit from the rocks in Chinese gardens, is infinitely diverse and subtle and quite beyond most westerners. I shall have to say a little more about this when I come to the element *Ryoan-ji*, named for the monastery where it was first stylized but probably did not originate.

One of the reasons why there were so few kinds of plants in Japanese gardens was that only 'auspicious' plants could properly be used, until the decline of the religious significance of the art. *Sho chiku-bai* gardens were gardens in which *sho* (pine), *chiku* (bamboo) and *bai* (plum), all 'auspicious', were used. *Sho chiku-bai* gardens as such were rather late-comers to the art. They became common only after about 1603; later they were syncretized with other 'auspicious' gardens. But certainly the three auspicious plants were an element in earlier Japanese gardens, and perhaps even the earliest.

56

68 *The elements in this painting were also the elements of any good Japanese landscape garden.*

69 *Garden beside the entrance to the Moss Temple, Kyoto.*

69

Ryoan-ji gardens are gardens in which the focus, and in the purest form the only element, is a group or groups of rocks arranged in a certain manner. In the original *Ryoan-ji* garden (which, as it happens, is also one of the prototypes of the abstract or Dry Landscape garden, of which more below), the rocks were laid in sand. But a similar arrangement of rocks might be used in a sheet of water, a lake or a pool. The origin of this element appears to have been a legend concerning a fleet sent from China to seek the treasure — Eternal Life — of *Horai*. The rocks may represent fifteen ships roughly in line ahead, but in three groups so that they could be arranged in 'auspicious' numbers: seven, five and three. In the *Ryoan-ji* monastery garden there are, however, five groups; but that is good also, because three and five are auspicious. It was easy to combine the elements of *Ryoan-ji*, *Horai* and *Shumitsen* into a single composition of rocks and water, or rocks and sand, since the *Ryoan-ji* 'ship' rocks could

be seen approaching *Horai*; and the central rock of *Horai* could also be *Shumitsen*.

Why are the numbers seven, five and three auspicious, which for so long controlled the placing of rocks and even the planting of trees in Japanese gardens, and which sometimes dominate the composition of *bonzai* even now?

'With Taoism came the theory of *in* and *yo* which maintained that the universe was produced by the interaction of male or positive (*yo*) and female or negative (*in*) principles. The association with the theory of numbers is that seven is unchangeable and appropriate to *yo*, five is a combination of *in* and *yo*, and three signifies heaven, earth and man. This theory is still applied in various forms of Japanese art including the garden. For instance in planning artificial hills, if one is made rugged and precipitous and dynamic in mood, another will be smooth and serene and static. If one waterfall

57

70

71

70 *Ryoan-Ji, Kyoto. Outside the dry landscape garden.*

71 *Tree and water garden surrounding the dry landscape garden, Ryoan-Ji, Kyoto.*

72 *Landscape painting and landscape gardening shared the same inspiration.*

gives the impression of masculine power, another should suggest feminine grace. If there is a peninsula projecting into the lake, there should be a bay to balance it. In laying out stepping stones, if a concave-shaped stone is used, it should be followed by one with a projection. Beside a large rock standing erect there should usually be a low reclining one, The principle of positive and negative is applied to the layout, to the selection of materials, and also to the details of construction.'*

These are probably the principal symbolist styles in Japanese garden design, or rather elements of those styles. I am all too aware that a Japanese reader would find my exposition of the subject very crude and incomplete, but one would have to be brought up in the Japanese culture to understand the inwardness of these elements. There are also many other, lesser, religious elements. The stone lantern we regard as characteristic of the Japanese garden is a sixteenth-century addition. In 1549 Saint Francis Xavier brought Christianity to Japan; it was prohibited on pain of death forty years later. But it made some converts, and one of them was

* Harada (1956). Most English readers will be more familiar with the Chinese terms *Yin* and *Yang*.

72

Oribe, a disciple of Rikuyu, the great sixteenth-century master of the tea ceremony in the garden. Oribe, like his master, was an exquisite designer of gardens, and to honour his religion he designed the stone lantern in which the pillar is the upright of the cross and was often carved with a representation of the Virgin Mary.

A waterfall in a Japanese garden may be, but is not necessarily, a symbol for Fudoo Myoo, chief of the five rajahs (*myoo* is Japanese for *rajah*) who were Buddha's messengers.

It is by no means easy to know what is signified by any particular grouping of rocks or trees; but it is certain that not until the end of the Shogunate in the nineteenth century were any elements in a well designed garden placed with regard to aesthetics alone. On the other hand, and to quote Jiro Harada once again:

'... the ideal of the great garden-masters such as Soami, when they designed Japanese gardens, seems to have been to recreate a landscape and infuse it with spiritual values so that the garden might represent the Mandara (expressing the doctrine of the two realms, one the principle and the cause, the other the intelligence and effect) in Amida's paradise in the West.'

It was in trying to accomplish this that the garden masters learned to syncretize styles in the manner described above. But it would be a great mistake to think of the Japanese garden as simply a kind of outdoor temple. The landscape gardens of Japan are also picture gardens; they are also open-air living-rooms and play places. They are, in fact, everything any garden anywhere has ever tried to be, except flower-gardens.

Yet even this was not always true:

'The classical Japanese garden, however, which expresses the people's great love of nature, does not appear until the tenth to twelfth centuries. This was the period of palace building in the Shinden-Zukuri style which was clearly based on the principle that the individual parts of the building should be merged as much as possible into the garden.'[*]

A comparison with one spirit that governed the design of the great Roman garden villas, such as Hadrian's, immediately comes to mind. Tetsuro Yoshida continues:

[*] Yoshida (1957).

59

73

'The main wing, Shinden, comprising the master's living and reception rooms, opens on its south side into the garden. Corridors running east, west and north connect it to symmetrically arranged subsidiary buildings. Two further corridors run from the east and west wings in a southerly direction and enclose the large garden which lies between them. Both finish in an open garden house beside the lake.'

Here again is that likeness to the spirit of Roman villa design, and even some suggestion of a likeness to the sort of Egyptian garden which was made after Queen Hatshepsut's innovations. There is absolutely no suggestion of culture-diffusion here: it is simply the case that human beings, wherever they are, find like solutions to like problems; the problems, in the aesthetics of daily living, being set by taste.

'In the lake which is at some distance from the main house and in the middle of the garden, there is a small island and

73 *Heian Shrine, Kyoto.*

74 *Buddhist Temple garden, Eikando, Kyoto.*

74

behind the lake a hill with an artificial waterfall. An arched bridge and an ordinary bridge lead from the bank to the island and from the island to the hill on the opposite side. A little brook winds its way from the north underneath the corridors of the buildings, flows into the eastern end of the lake and flows out again at the western end. It was also possible to boat on the lake: festivals saw the art-loving aristocracy being rowed out in splendid Chinese boats and listening to music and poetry across the water. On these occasions the ladies wore their festival kimonos whose colours reflected various plants or blossoms according to season and were also named after them; in the spring they wore the colours of the plum blossom, the cherry blossom, or the willow, in summer of the Unohana blossom (*Deutzia scabra*) or the blossom of the Kakitsubata (*Iris laevigata*), in the autumn of the Hagi or 'sweet clover' (*Lespedeza bicolor*) or Onimaeshi (*Patrinia scabiosaefolia*), and in the winter of withered leaves or of fields bare after harvest. The plum-blossom kimono was white with a crimson lining, and in the winter the colour was yellow and the lining bright blue...'

In the kind of garden here described the Japanese were still using not only the plants mentioned, but such flowering shrubs as azalea, paeony and camellia; their gardens were still bright with flowers. But, as we shall see, this was not to last.

Japanese historians divide their history into periods which I shall more or less follow, because with each major political or economic change came some change or evolution in garden style. The earliest clearly recognized period is called Asuka and lasted from AD 552 to 644*. Society was feudal and simple, but many of the arts of civilization were advanced. It is the period of Buddhist missions from Korea, bringing with them more of those arts. A curious legend of the time tells how a man from Korea called Shikimaro

* Some authorities give very slightly different dates for the periods of Japanese history named in this chapter.

had his skin mottled white all over his body and that for this inauspicious blemish he was condemned to be thrown into the sea to drown. By claiming to be able to build a mountain with rocks, he won a respite. He built a mountain in the grounds of the royal palace on an island in the lake; this was *Shumitsen*.

From what little evidence has survived from the later part of this period, gardens may already have been syncretisms of *Horai* and *Shumitsen*, that is of Taoist and Buddhist elements, with the lake or pool as the most important feature; in it probably a tortoise island connected to the mainland by an arched bridge. As for plants, as we have seen already flowers were allowed in the garden at this time and for another five centuries. Probably plum, cherry and kerria were the most important flowering shrubs.

The same, with lespedeza, were also the predominant garden plants of the Nara Period, AD 645 to 782, plus perhaps some deutzias. The principal garden feature was still the lake or pool, often crane-shaped and with a tortoise island. The *Horai* and *Shumitsen* rules were sufficiently relaxed to enable garden designers to use them less as principal features, and more as decorative elements of large landscape gardens designed as pictures. The same tendency continued during the subsequent Heian Period 784 to 1183, when so literally 'picturesque' did gardens become that some seem to have been portraits of actual places notable for scenic beauty. According to Jiro Harada (1956), for instance, the palace garden of Shosei-en, part of which still survives in its original form, was laid out by Minamoto-no-Toarn to portray the Shiogama district. But this kind of picture-gardening must not be confused with the infinitely more subtle and sophisti-

75 *Shogakuin, Imperial Palace, Kyoto. Part of the gardens.*

5. *A courtyard fountain: the Alhambra.*

6. *Predominantly French, Schönbrunn's great palace garden shows Italian influence.*

7. *The Renaissance style persists in the Nikitsky Sad, Yalta, U.S.S.R.*

8. *Cairo Botanic Garden. The layout is French.*

cated landscape gardening of a later epoch, to which we shall come below.

It was in the tenth century that Japanese gardeners seem first to have taken to earth-moving on a large scale in the creation of landscape gardens. *In-and-Yo* gardens could be made by creating an artificial mountain with the spoil dug out in making an artificial lake. This, too, is the first period of garden-cum-house designing. Towards the end of it, however, there was less realism in the imitation of natural scenes, and more of a tendency towards stylization.

We come now to the first great, and incidentally well-documented, period, Kamakura (1183-1333). Kamakura was a small town on the coast which became the headquarters of the warrior-caste which, inspired and initially led by Minamoto-no-Yorimoto, dominated Japan during this period, in opposition to the aristocracy of Kyoto. As it happened, Yorimoto was a garden enthusiast. The great garden for which he was personally responsible was laid out, with an enormous number of rocks gathered from all over the country, for the Eifuku-ji monastery in Kamakura. This was not wanton extravagance in indulgence of Yorimoto's personal taste: it was, exactly like church building in the West, a religious act. We know nothing about this garden except that it stimulated rhapsodies of praise for its extraordinary beauty.

But the real interest of this epoch is in what happened after Yorimoto's death; for Japanese garden art then came under the influence of a school of Chinese landscape painting, just as, from about 1720 onwards, English garden art was to fall under the influence of a school of European landscape painting.

76 *Shogakuin, Imperial Palace, Kyoto. Part of the gardens.*

Three major influences were at work in the shaping of garden styles in this epoch. One was the monochrome landscape painting of the Chinese Northern Sung school, the impact of which in Japan was as great as that of the 'Romagna' landscape painters in Italy and France in England six centuries later. Another was the reforming Zen Buddhist missions which began to reach Japan at this time and which were relatively puritanical. The third was the equally puritanical austerity of taste of the ruling warrior caste, reacting against aristocratic luxury and self-indulgence.

The influence on garden art was particularly strong because many of the Zen monks were professional and practising garden architects. If this seems odd to most Western readers, they should bear in mind that garden making was religiously equivalent to church building in the West, so that by practising it one could acquire merit.

Seigen, the designer of Yorimoto's great garden, was a Zen priest, and virtually all the Kamakura garden artists were also priests. On the other hand the Kyoto aristocrats were still designing and laying out gardens, so that there was a

rival, and lay, school of garden artists at work. Among the Kyoto laymen designing gardens at this time were the great poet and calligrapher Sadaie, and the artist Gokogoku Yoshitsume who happened also to be an aristocrat and a rich man, but who was the author of *Sakuteiki* — 'Book on Making Gardens'. These and other garden artists, if they were not all rich themselves, were patronized by the rich. Despite the reigning official austerity, they commanded such resources that they could, for instance, move huge rocks over great distances, dig lakes, make artificial hills, build bridges, and have mature pine, cherry and plum trees transplanted. Thus a garden designed by Gokogoku Yoshitsume in 1205, and made and planted with Sadaie's help, had a number of ancient pine and cherry trees moved into it. Here is a brief description:

'The garden was laid out with the pond as the main feature. A bridge was built to the middle island under the direction of Sadaie. There was a hill built in front, and a waterfall at the foot of it. The rock composition in this garden was especially beautiful. When one was in the garden one had the impression of being in the heart of a deep mountain thickly covered with moss. Especially conspicuous among the an-

77, 78 *Shogakuin.*
Imperial Palace.

79

79 *Shogakuin, Kyoto.*

80 *Heian Shrine, Kyoto.*

cient trees was a pine stretching out its branches covered in dark green foliage.'*

The stay-at-home tastes of the Kamakura *samurai*, and the influence of the Northern Sung monochrome landscape painting already mentioned, led to the creation of the first true picture gardens; gardens deliberately designed to be viewed from a single point — the war-lord's study in the house — or from any of several fixed points. But since the Kyoto aristocrats were still making gardens as play-places, settings for such leisure occupations as boating, poetry-reading and picnics, the older traditions were not lost. Still, the influence of Zen austerity and Chinese painting did slowly gain the upper hand until, in the subsequent Muromachi Period, 1394 to 1572, they produced the first pure abstract gardens in the history of the art.

Even now this development was not immediate. Aristocrats continued to maintain and plant gardens in which flowering

trees, pines, bamboos and water were as important as rocks, and the *Horai* and *Shumitsen* elements still kept their place. These gardens of Kyoto and a few other centres were admired far beyond Japan: admiration for the art of Japanese gardens became fashionable in Ming China, and the first party of wealthy visiting tourists arrived from there to visit them in 1402, other parties following them thereafter. This must, I think, be the first case of organized international garden-visiting tours in history. So much garden making was going on in this period that every new garden laid out and planted meant an old one destroyed, because good rocks and suitably ancient trees were becoming very scarce in the wild and had to be moved from old gardens. Rocks for the garden, and old trees, became fashionable as suitable presents among the rich, and so did the custom of swapping rocks and trees.*

An element which was much honoured and discussed in the

---

* Harada (1956). This description is from the *Masu Kagami*. An account of a method of moving mature trees is to be found, by those who can read Japanese, in the *Meigetsuki*.

* There is at the present time a rock called 'Fujito-seki' still to be seen at the Sambo-in garden. It was first used in making the Hosokawa villa garden, was moved to the Nijo Castle garden when that was being made, was moved again to help in the making of Hideyoshi's villa at Juraku, and was taken from there to the Sambo-in garden. See Harada (1956).

80

garden art of the time is one which is difficult to convey in words and which is rather difficult for the western mind to grasp. It is called *yugen* and roughly speaking its manifest meaning is simply 'mystery'. But it refers to the unseen element, that which is never stated by the artist but which he succeeds in conveying by the implications of what he does state; this he must do so successfully that although it is 'the word unspoken, the view unseen', the *yugen* can reduce the observer to tears of sensibility.

However, to come now to the 'abstract', Dry Landscape (or Symbolic Level) gardens. The element of *yugen* led garden artists to leave out more and more, relying on the sparsest materials to create the mood and feeling, the repose of spirit which was the artist's aim. In the otherwise conventional Silver Pavilion garden created early in this period, a cone and platform of white sand, two pure geometrical shapes, were used. They were perhaps an abstraction drawn from the layout or plan of the garden as a whole, for half of it was a lake (*in*) and the other half a hill (*yo*). Later in the period Zen artists, taking Sung painting as their ideal and using white sand instead of silk by way of 'canvas', and rocks instead of

ink or paint, began to compose abstract gardens from which all plants were excluded. Important though Sung painting was to this art, it should be made clear that the garden artists did not copy Chinese paintings; the Zen and other abstract gardens were original compositions, their makers original artists in their own right. Moreover although their style was new and revolutionary, they kept many of the ancient traditions, and *Horai*, for example, had a revival.

The development of the abstract style of garden art was swift and there was more than one school. In one of these the inspiration came from the Chinese Northern Sung painters Ma Yuan and Hsia-Kuei; in another it came from a southern and later manifestation of Sung graphic art, and notably from the work of Mu-Ch'i. An outstanding example of this Japanese abstract garden is that of the Ryoan-ji temple which, as we have seen, gave its name to a type of garden. This temple garden is — for it is still intact — a rectangle 24 metres by 10 metres enclosed in an earth wall. The level surface is raked white sand; there are, of course, no plants, and the only elements used apart from sand are fifteen rocks of various shapes and sizes used in five groups. The whole

81

82

81 *Rocks and dwarf pines, Daitoku-Ji, Kyoto.*

82 *The Zen-Buddhist Garden of Daitoku-Ji.*

83 *Detail of the Zen-Buddhist Garden of Nanzen-Ji, Kyoto.*

was so placed as to use the surrounding natural landscape as a setting; an intention which has been set at nought by later and careless tree planting.

Rocks and sand had to accomplish more than one purpose, just as an abstract painting 'works' on more than one level. By number and arrangement and shape they might signify *Horai* or *Shumitsen*; but at the same time they might be pure abstraction of a landscape, as, for example, the Daisen-in Dry Landscape garden is an abstraction, in the school of Ma Yuan, of a mountain range composed of a rock $7\frac{1}{2}$ feet high and two rocks 5 feet high, so placed in relation to each other and to the 'canvas' — a flat expanse of white sand — as to 'be' a vast and impressive landscape.

Faithfulness to the chosen landscape school was carried to great lengths. For example, at Daisen-in the rocks were set vertically and taper away at the top in a manner which suggests the brushwork of some Northern Sung masters; whereas in the Taizo-in (Myoshi-ji) garden the manner of slanting the stones is reminiscent of the Southern Sung master, Mu Ch'i.

The move towards abstraction was apparent also in other kinds of garden. Symbolic elements moved away from representationalism. *Horai* was expressed in a single rock; the real waterfall becomes a series of tiered rock surfaces without water. Moreover, by a curious inversion the sheet of real water came to be treated as if it were the raked sand surface which originally signified it, that is to say as a canvas on which to compose a picture with rocks.

This glimmering of what Japanese abstract garden art became by the sixteenth century will have to suffice. It is an endlessly variable and subtle form and nothing at all comparable has ever been attempted elsewhere in the world until very recently in Brazil. We shall come to that in its place. I should just like to emphasize once again that although this kind of monochrome, plantless, abstract garden making came into existence and developed for three centuries under the influence of Chinese monochrome landscape painting, its masterpieces are not attempts to render particular landscapes in three dimensions, but are original works of art.

A curious by-product of fifteenth-century Dry Landscape gardening was *bonseki*, which became very fashionable in the Muromachi period. *Bonseki* is the art of making miniature landscape pictures with small stones and sand in flat lacquer trays. It is an element of interior decorating, and has affinities with the earlier *ikebana* and the later *bonzai*.

The next period distinguished by Japanese historians is the Momoyama, and it extends from 1573 to 1602. This is the first period during which books on garden design became rather common and played an important part in the development of the art. Their tendency, as is always the case with garden design books, was to fix and popularize a number of successful designs and so to discourage original work. By the end of this short period Dry Landscape garden art had passed its zenith, but some new elements were introduced into the older kinds of garden. Of these the most important was the clipped evergreen. It was not, of course, literally new, but became much more popular than ever before under the influence of topiarists who became famous, and

83

84

notably of a gardener named Yasokuro. Several different species were used in this work, but probably the evergreen azalea was the most common. It was never, of course, allowed to flower in a Japanese green garden but was used as we use box or yew. There seem also to have been some plant introductions into gardens. The garden of Nobunaga's castle at Azuchi on lake Biwa was remarkable for its rare trees, palms, and the use of a cycad, *Cycas revoluta*. Grand gardens were made by Hideyoshi: there is a tradition that the castle-palace and garden which he made at Fushimi absorbed the labour of 300,000 men.

The art of using rocks degenerated, but on the other hand an entirely new kind of garden came into being. This was a garden based on the *roji* and called after it, the *roji* being the planted path which led from the house to the *chaseki*, the garden pavilion which became the heart of every gentleman's garden as the social importance of the tea ceremony evolved. *Roji* gardens were for strolling in, and the emphasis was on the style of paving and on the path-side planting. Largely under the liberating influence of this period, which began a kind of renaissance, there was a move away from the garden-as-picture and back to the garden as a realistic landscape and a place for polite intercourse. But there was much sloppy work done at the time, notably in rock work, which has a weak look probably due to the fact that the rocks were no longer deeply embedded in the earth. As any modern rock garden designer knows, and despite the fact that in theory there can be no visual difference, rock work only looks strong and impressive if more rock is underground than showing; shallow-set rocks never look impressive.

The long Edo period from 1605 to 1867 is that of the Tokugawa *Shoguns* and only ends with the imperial restoration. It is divided by historians into three periods. Early Edo almost covers the seventeenth century. Harada lists four principal and several lesser garden styles of this period as popular among the nobility and gentry of the Tokugawa party. The four principal styles are: *Kaiyu-shiki*, based on a lake with paths all round it and vantage points or belvederes from which to view it as a series of pictures. As we shall see, a similar type was to be created by English garden artists a century later and quite independently. *Chisen kansho-shiki* were lake gardens designed to be viewed from a fixed

85

84 *Raking the sand of a dry landscape garden is a special art.*

85 *Detail of the Ryoan-Ji, Kyoto.*

point in the house, and therefore pure picture gardens. *Kare Sansui* were Dry Landscape gardens highly stylized in one of the traditional designs and no longer original works. Then there were *roji* gardens. The first two of these four were very traditional, in that they had to contain the *Horai* elements and be 'auspicious'.

Lesser styles were numerous. In, for example, *shakkei* the Japanese gardeners borrowed an ancient Chinese style, and planted their trees to create false perspectives and draw the surrounding natural landscape into the garden. In the style called *shukkei* natural landscapes were reproduced realistically in miniature.

The tendency of this period was scientifically progressive in the sense that horticultural techniques became more sophisticated and plantmanship developed; but in terms of pure art it was degenerate and reactionary, with reversion to naturalistic realism. Typically, for example, waterfalls now had to be seen to be fed by streams; and that entailed treating rocks simply as rocks and not as elements of an abstract picture.

71

This tendency was continued during the Middle Edo period. For although the Shogun Tsunayoshi, with whose tenure of power the period began, was both a devout Buddhist and a maker and lover of gardens, the religious element in Japanese gardening continued to decline. The symbols might be retained, but chiefly for antiquarian or aesthetic reasons. What counted was the beauty, and not the significance, of a garden.

Another major change affecting garden art came with the eighth Tokugawa Shogun, Yoshimune, and with the end of the civil wars following his decisive victory at Seki-gahara. The Shogun applied a sort of credit squeeze and imposed economic austerity on the whole nation. As one consequence the making of great gardens became impossible. Much smaller

gardens, in which meticulous attention was paid to detail, became fashionable. Water-works were simplified; *Horai* was retained but likewise simplified; crane-and-tortoise islands disappeared; and as the use of very large stones became economically impossible, topiary, to provide solid masses, gained in importance.

As not uncommonly happens when a government tries to check economic expansion by decree, the Shogun's austerity drive, continued by his successor, made matters worse. By 1779, when the period called Late Edo began, Japan was in serious economic difficulties. As a consequence the near-century which ended with the restoration of imperial power in 1868 was a poor one for gardens, and very few new ones of any kind were made. But as it happens one of the few which were made, the Kenroku Park at Kanazawa, was and remains

86

87

86 *Pavilion of the dry landscape garden, Heian Shrine.*

87 *Roof detail, garden pavilion Mara Horyu-Ji.*

88 *Tenryu-Ki (Zen) Garden, Kyoto.*

88

89

90

74

one of the greatest in Japan. It was planted by the Maeda family between 1820 and 1840, but did not receive its present name, which means 'Garden of the Sextuple Combination', until it was made a public park in 1874. The six attributes referred to in its name are vastness, solemnity, endeavour, venerability, water and views. The use of water is remarkable, not least technologically, for the water was brought five miles up-hill on the siphon principle, without the use of pumps. The system still works perfectly. The garden is pure landscape, twenty-four acres in extent, and it incorporates most of the styles we have discussed.

The imperial restoration in 1868 and the decision to westernize Japan had consequences for garden art as for every other Japanese institution. For some decades the Japanese people seemed bent on despising and destroying all their own ancient culture in favour of the European one. As a result gardens made by the rich and by the middle classes were in imitation of European and American gardens. It was as if,

until they were sure of succeeding in their nation-wide and very swift programme of westernization, they could not afford to allow themselves the luxury of confidence in their own ancient institutions. But when their confidence was fully restored by their decisive victory over Russia in 1905, the Japanese could afford to react in favour of their own artistic traditions. But still they remained under the spell of the ideas which had so quickly made them into a great world power, and consequently, in the Japanese gardens made since about 1870, it is difficult to find Japanese traditions unmixed with western styles.

Three kinds of large gardens, not to mention the lesser ones which are innumerable, have been made since that date: *Shakkei-shiki*, landscape gardens designed in the ancient Chinese tradition to draw the surrounding landscape into the picture, and made principally in such mountainous regions as Kyoto; copies of old Japanese gardens or of famous western gardens; and gardens which are a mixture of Japanese and

89 *Katsura, Kyoto.*

90 *Daigo-Ji Garden (Shinto), near Kyoto.*

91 *Heian Shrine.*

91

75

92

93

92 *Imperial Palace, Katsura, Kyoto.*

93 *In the Tenryu-Ji Zen Garden, Kyoto. Typical of Japanese gardening. Dead pine needles were removed by hand.*

94 *Pines, sand and water — basic elements of a Japanese landscape.*

western styles. The almost total abandonment of the religious element in garden art led to a decline in quality which was not quite compensated for by a more careful attention to pure aesthetics and to plantmanship. Japanese gardeners seemed to lose their special touch with rocks and stones. And some critics still maintain that the Japanese have yet to solve the difficult problem of reconciling the great traditional styles in garden art with the modern western architecture of Japanese houses.

Where, in all this, are the flowers? In Japan, unlike Europe, the art of designing and making gardens was one thing, the art and science of growing flowers was another. The reasons are obvious: from the beginning Japanese gardens were landscape gardens. In our own English landscape-garden period, say 1720 to about a century later, flowers were at a discount in great gardens.

94

As we have seen, Japanese gardens were, nevertheless, not always flowerless or nearly so. The monochrome garden was a product of social and religious austerity and of Chinese monochrome landscape painting. From the tenth to the twelfth century the gardens were colourful, although the number of garden plants in common use was remarkably small, and when the strict ideas which had banished flowers from the garden to the florist's nursery were abandoned, and some flowering plants were restored to gardens, their number was very limited.

In the tenth and eleventh centuries plum and cherry were the only important flowering trees. Shrubs included camellia, the shrubby paeonies introduced from China, *Kerria japonica*, and wistaria. Bulb flowers, with the exception of a few irises, were not used at all, or very rarely, and the same is true of herbaceous perennials and annuals. This period is too early

for flower-decoration in pottery to give us any sure hints. Japanese pottery of the sixteenth century in the Musée Guimet in Paris is decorated with admirably painted pictures of flowers. I have listed from such pots double red roses, a narcissus with several heads to each stalk, pink and white moutan paeonies (the moutan identification was made from the beautifully drawn foliage), *Nymphaea* water lilies, *Lilium auratum*, and a flower with heads of dianthus-like flowers, very like 'Sweet Williams', but with feathery foliage, which I have not identified. Flower paintings of the same period in the same museum show chrysanthemum, one of the most important genera grown in Japanese nurseries but, of course, for cutting and use in *ikebana*; an iris which looks like *Iris laevigata*; and diverse paeonies. A screen, again at the Guimet, painted with a decoration of aquatics, shows, surprisingly an unquestionable leaf of *Nelumbo*. Slightly later pots, both Japanese and Chinese, in the same museum show wistaria, paeonies, chrysanthemums, bamboos, ipomaea, cornflower, poppy, a magnolia which looks like *M. denudata*, various *Prunus* flowers, and pomegranate.

The English and American gardener is familiar with the idea of azalea as a Japanese shrub, and it is true that Japanese nurserymen produced, in Kurume, a range of cultivars which startled Western gardeners when they were first introduced. In Japan they were principally for pot use, and the only use which the garden designer had for these evergreen azaleas was as subjects for clipping. The azalea colours would have been very out of place in a classic Japanese garden; the sort of shrub which garden designers preferred was the unspectacular *Lespedeza bicolor*.

Trees used were for the most part pines and a few maples. The Japanese saw little point in chasing after exotic species;

they had perfectly adequate material for their purposes in their own. A work of fine art is not made better, and may be made much worse, by the use of outlandish materials. Such was the feeling behind Japanese indifference to our kind of plantmanship.

Finally, lawns were a part of traditional Japanese garden art, but on the whole they came late to the Japanese garden, and most designers preferred moss crossed by stepping-stones for the making of green surfaces.

95 *Shogakuin. Imperial Palace.*

96

6

GARDENING
IN THE DAR-AL-ISLAM

Although the making of great gardens by the Arabs and their conquered converts in the whole Abode of Islam began at about the same time as the revival of garden making in Europe, Arab culture progressed so much faster and further in the next few centuries, their gardening was so much more sophisticated and had so much influence on the development of gardening in Europe, that we should look at it before coming to the subject of gardening in medieval Europe. The Arabs, like the Europeans, had two great examples before them: the ancient West Asian as they found it evolved and modified in Iran; and the Roman as they found it in North Africa and in southen Europe when they invaded that continent. But the Arabs used these examples first, as it were, and quickly developed a style of their own.

Having regard to the rule of chronology to which I am trying to keep, I should have to carry this short account of gardening in the Dar-al-Islam up to about the year 1200; then take up the story of the garden as it was beginning to revive in Europe; and then return to the later phase of Islamic garden art. It will, however, be convenient to break the rule in this case, and to continue the subject of Islamic gardening to one of its great moments, under Babur in northern India; then to go back a few centuries and start again in Europe; and later to return to the gardens of Islam.

We are apt to imagine that until about the year 650 the Arabs were a people of desert savages. It is true that the armies which so swiftly and irresistibly conquered the whole southern Mediterranean basin were raised among the Bedouin of the deserts; but, of course, many thousands of Arabs were civilized, Hellenized, urban people long before their great period of dominion that followed the series of *jihads* stimulated by the teachings of their prophet Mahomet. There were not only Hellenized Arabs, but Persianized Arabs who had come under the influence of Zoroastrianism. Philip, Emperor of Rome between AD 244 and 249, was an Arab. In short, following their conquests in the seventh century the Arabs did not have to create a new culture out of whole cloth but, like other great 'new' peoples, used and modified the achievements of earlier cultures.

Whatever it may have been in theory, the Dar-al-Islam never became a centralized empire. The governors and emirs of the many provinces were not only independent potentates, owing only nominal allegiance to the Caliph, as European monarchs owed nominal allegiance to the Pope, they were rivals in the arts and sciences as well as (often enough) in politics and war. In their eastern dominions, in the city-states (as they virtually were) of Shiraz, Isfahan, Baghdad and Damascus, for example, Arabian gardens were naturally based on the ancient Persian ones, which had been modelled on the much earlier Mesopotamian gardens. There are echoes of very ancient Babylonian elements, and therefore of elements first used, no doubt, in Ur and Kish and Lagash and Uruk, in the Arabian gardens of the seventh and eighth centuries and into the sixteenth century. Thus the gardens of Islamic Iran were rectangular, enclosed, architectural and formal, with fountains, pavilions and many large shade-trees. Flowers, in urns and vases rather than in parterres, were chosen as much for their scent as for their colour, and were few in any case. In many gardens no flowers at all were grown.

Iran is not a land in which garden making is easy. The Zagros range, against which clouds build up and condense, takes all the rain and leaves very little for the Iranian plain. The winters are bitterly cold, the summers blisteringly hot. There is a beautiful spring in March and April, with myriads of wild flowers, but it is very short. No garden can survive without irrigation, and consequently the nucleus of every garden is water. Water was supplied to the Persian gardens of the Islamic period by the same engineering device as had fed the Achaemenid gardens over a thousand years earlier, the *qanat*. This is an underground conduit or tunnel which may be several miles long and which is sloped so as to raise the water-table at the delivery end to the level of the water-table at the intake end, which will be in foothill country where rainfall is higher. I believe that it must have been on the hydro-engineering skill in 'balancing' remote bodies of underground water, learned by the *qanat* engineers during well over a thousand years of experience, that the Arabs based the extraordinarily elaborate and ingenious waterworks of their later gardens.

The water supplied by the *qanat* was used both for the practical job of irrigation and ornamentally to fill pools, canals and even small lakes, and to work fountains and cascades. As is clear from Persian carpet designs, which are often stylized plan-pictures of gardens (until the process was reversed and gardens began to imitate carpets, notably in parterres of coloured pebbles), the water was often used to fill canals. These, in place of mere drives or walks, divided the gardens into four or more geometrical sections: division into four equal quarters was fundamental to Islamic garden design; subdivision was a matter of taste.

By far the most important flower in Islamic Persian gardens was the rose: so much so that the specific name for rose,

gul, is the generic word for *flower*, and occurs as part of the compounds which were the names of specific flowers, e.g. *gul-i-marges*, narcissus; *gul-i-laleh*, lily or tulip; *gul-i-kakab*, dahlia (a much later introduction, of course). It is true that there is something of the kind in English. In Britain, for example, the rose is paramount in gardens: thus, guelder-rose, rock-rose, sun-rose, Christmas-rose, rose-of-Sharon, etc. But the identification of the rose with flowers in general is complete in Persian.

Fruit trees were of the first importance in all Arab gardens. In parts of Persia they included citrus, principally the orange. Contrary to some accounts these were not introduced by the Arabs, but by much earlier Iranian people, from China. As early as 126 BC the Chinese had emissaries in Fars, from which country they sent horses, grape-vines, alfalfa and other useful animals and plants to China, and in return they introduced Chinese plants to Iran.*

As we shall see later in this chapter, there is in the literature of the subject very little to be found about groundling flowers. The Arabs of the seventh and subsequent centuries loved the native flowers of Iran, and cultivated some of them in their gardens, but there were remarkably few species, if the records are anything to go by (they are chiefly poetical and probably unreliable). Isfahan became famous for tulips, other parts of the country for Crown Imperials, ranunculus, narcissus, stocks, dianthus, jasmines, violets and violas. Roses with petals orange on one side and yellow on the other are described quite early, and were obviously derived from the native Iranian *Rosa foetida* which in our own century has given us so many brilliantly colourful cultivars. Hollyhocks, marigolds and lilacs are among the very early garden flowers of Islamic Iran. Iran is the source of all our yellow roses, and these first reached Europe when they were sent from a Persian emirate, or possibly the Caliphate, to a Moorish Spanish kingdom, Granada. The species in question was *Rosa hemispherica*. The Persian Arab gardeners seem to have done very little, if any, hybridizing — there is a respectable theory that no gardeners of the antique world knew that this was even possible. But they did improve garden plants by selection, and their predecessors had been doing so for many centuries, especially the *gabris* — gardeners, often priests, of the early Zoroastrian period.

Artificial decorative elements were early used in the Islamic

* The interchange of plants between China and Iran can best be studied in Laufer (1890).

gardens. The making of carpet-like parterres with the patterns carried out in coloured pebbles has been mentioned, although it was probably a later development; the other element was artificial flowers and even trees, often made of precious metals and gem stones. The poet Firdawsi describes a tree made of gold, silver and rubies for King Kay Khusraw; its hollow fruits were filled with wine and musk. The Arabs took over this kind of thing with enthusiasm, and used also cheaper materials; even, in due course, paper. Centuries later, after the Mongol conquest, the Khans caught the fashion for artificial plants in gardens, from the Arabized Persians. Tamerlane, of whose gardens I shall have something to say later, had a six-foot tree with leaves made of gold and silver, fashioned like oak leaves, fruits of pearls and emeralds, sapphires, rubies, diamonds and so forth.

The Islamic gardeners early realized that few trees are more ornamental than fruit trees, and made their apples, pears, plums, apricots and peaches serve a dual purpose. Peach, cherry and the fig were not native Iranians, but had early been introduced into that country. The magnificent *Platanus orientalis* is native as far as the Crimea, but it first came into garden use in Iran, whence its use spread all over the world. Other garden trees used in Islamic Persia were sycamore, poplar, ash, elm — above all except the plane — the cypress. Aviaries were often backed by dense but orderly and rectangular plantings of such trees; and in the larger tree gardens gazelles and peacocks were at large.

Iran, like China and Japan, had as a sort of by-product of the love of gardens, a great school of flower painting, chiefly in miniature. In the pre-Islamic period such paintings were usually highly stylized, as they were in carpet design, but by the late seventh century the need for correct representation of plants to illustrate the Arabic medical treatises, which were first based on Dioscorides and only later reflected the advance of original Arab thinking in medical science, encouraged a more naturalistic style among painters. However, this art did not reach its zenith until about a thousand years later, and there does not seem to have been anything comparable, in the way of painting influencing garden design, to the Japanese or English cases. Carpet design did influence the manner of planting, but not, according to such accounts as survive, until the late eighteenth century.

Central to Persian garden design, as I have already implied, was a tank or small lake of water. This was true in all the Islamic provinces of Iran except only Khorasan, where a

more or less endemic water famine led to the development of a kind of dry gardening slightly reminiscent of Japanese Zen gardens, with blue and grey pebbles being used to substitute for water. The garden tanks were slightly sloped along the long axis, so that water very slowly overflowed from the lower end, whence it was carried away, more or less ornamentally, to do other work. Pools and tanks were never 'freely' shaped, like those of a Chinese or English garden; they were invariably regular figures, but very diverse, usually formed of elements of a circle or ellipse or oval, their 'lobes' variously arranged. Some, however, were rectilinear. In a large garden there might be a series of tiered terraces, and in that case each would have its ornamental tank, and each tank would be of a different pattern.

The highest development of the Persian garden belongs to a later date, and we shall return to it after glancing at some other parts of the Dar-al-Islam.

Just as, in Persia, the Arab conquerors adopted, modified and finally improved on the native garden style which they found there, so too in India and elsewhere they found and changed the local styles to suit themselves, for quite often they did not really like what they found, although they were usually ready to learn from it. For example, from about 300 BC onwards the great gardeners in India were Buddhist monks. The gardens which they preferred, as we have already seen in the case of China, were naturalistic parks, whereas the Arabs, their taste shaped by the aridity of their countries, preferred architectural, geometrical gardens based on the exigencies of irrigation. It may be that the native Indian style had some influence in softening the firm lines of the Arab garden — but much later, in the case of the Moghul gardens. The early Islamic gardens in India were designed by Persians and very much resembled the gardens of Iran. In many cases those gardens were superimposed on the old, 'wild' Buddhist gardens, which more or less disappeared.

The earliest and perhaps the best gardeners of what subsequently became Islamic North Africa were the Carthaginians. It is not possible to describe their gardens, because the Romans ruthlessly destroyed every trace of the Carthaginian civilization at the end of the Third Punic War; my statement is based on the importance of Carthaginian horticultural and agricultural writings to the Romans, and even the Greeks, which is manifest in the praises of, for example, the Roman-Spanish agronomist Columella. Carthage and the other Punic cities of North Africa were, despite their long history and tremendous effect on Mediterranean history, never more than colonial settlements of Tyrian or Sidonian origin, and they even paid rent for such land as they had to the Berber princes. Consequently land and water were very scarce and precious, and as a result the Punic cities, notably Carthage, developed intensive cultivation to a very high level of skill. Among the very few books which were deliberately spared when, at the final sack of Carthage, the Romans barbarously destroyed the city's many libraries, was a work of agricultural and horticultural science by Mago, known as 'the Carthaginian'. So greatly did it impress the Roman agronomists that it was at once translated into Latin and Greek, and was later heavily plagiarized by such Roman writers of textbooks as Columella himself, though he did have the grace to acknowledge his source.

But if Carthaginian horticulture was carried on by the Romans more or less competently as they colonized their new conquest after the Third Punic War, the Vandal conquerors of North Africa in the fifth century destroyed all traces of the Romanized-Carthaginian villa gardens. It was then left to the Moors, the 'Arabs' of the African provinces of the Dar-al-Islam, to restore civilized ornamental gardening to North Africa.

As it happens, North African Islamic gardening reached its zenith and can best be studied not in Africa itself, but Spain. The Arab force which conquered Andalusia was nominally Syrian, but was composed of a mixture of peoples — Berbers, Arabs, Persians, many Jews and quite a considerable contingent of Arabized Byzantine Greeks. Whatever they were, they were an improvement on the Visigoths and Vandals; so much so that Andalusia has never, since it was finally reconquered by the Christians of Spain in the fifteenth century, been as productive of able men and valuable ideas as it was during the centuries of Islamic rule. True, these Spanish Moors were not precisely 'Arabs', and just as their medicine, their mathematics and their chemistry were advanced by Jews, their house and garden architecture was developed by Byzantine Greeks. Even their military successes were due in part to a strong contingent of Italian Goths. Did they owe their remarkable success in improving south Spanish agriculture to a Punic element still lingering? Peoples who are said to have been 'exterminated' have curious ways of making a come-back. Still, the great virtue of the Arabs was that they gave the diverse peoples under their aegis a chance to do their best.

The conquerors of Andalusia soon turned to the making of gardens. The Ummayad Abd-ar-Rahman I, who was proclaimed Emir of Andalusia at Córdova in 756, immediately set about making a garden, the plan of it based on his grandfather's garden in Damascus. According to the historian of the period, Al-Makkari, he sent experts to bring him exotic plants from India, Turkestan and his native Syria; and it was he who was responsible for introducing the yellow rose from Iran (see above), the pomegranate and the jasmine to Spain. In shape his garden was a Persian one.

This initiative set many rich men of the province to making gardens, and by the tenth century, in the time of this prince's descendant and namesake, Abd-ar-Rahman III, all the country about Córdova was one great garden. There were, again according to Al-Makkari, 50,000 villas set like stars in the firmament in the countryside all round the city. This figure is presumably a gross exaggeration; but we may safely take it that there were an enormous number of such villas and that, as the historian says, much of the material for building them was taken from demolished Roman villas. This probably means that the old Roman villa gardens had their influence in shaping the Spanish Islamic gardens, but most of the garden architects were Byzantine Greeks who had become sufficiently imbued with Moslem notions to satisfy the tastes of their clients. The contractors and foremen of works were often specialists fetched from Egypt or Byzantium.

The most famous of the earlier Spanish Islamic gardens was that of Medina Az-Zahra near Seville. It was terraced on a hillside, the terraces being built of marble. The garden rides and walks were paved with mosaics. Miles of clipped box, bay and myrtle hedges divided the garden into many smaller gardens, all rectilinear as was the rule. Irrigation canals fed all parts of the garden and worked hundreds of fountains. A garden pavilion where Abd-ar-Rahman held his court contained a fountain made of green marble embellished with ornamentation in gold and precious stones.

In Spain as in Iran, the gardens were dependent on an irrigation system. Out of the ingenious water engineering which they learned in western Asia, Arab and Byzantine engineers developed much more complex systems. In these the water was so balanced in the underground complex of lead pipes that the play of every jet was dependent on the play of every other jet, and manipulation of a single valve could alter the water-pattern of the whole system. Very few of

97 *The Alhambra (Granada).*

these systems are still working, for the waterworks were neglected after the reconquest of Andalusia by the Christians. However, at least one still operates. Neglect of irrigation systems by the Spanish Christians led to worse things than the breakdown of ornamental waterworks; as the irrigation system failed the gardens died, and as the gardens died the villas decayed. And just as they were to destroy the great civilizations of Central and South America, the Spaniards destroyed the Moorish civilization of Andalusia.

It may have been from the Roman example that the Arabs learned to build their villas high on a hillside with the garden in terraces below it. But it was their own taste which made them surround their gardens with very high walls and then to double the measure of privacy and degree of shade by planting trees — sometimes fruit trees, but chiefly cypresses — inside the walls. This tall, dense and evergreen enclosure was, as always, on a rectilinear plan. Central to it was at least one canal, probably two or three parallel, and possibly a whole grid of canals so that the division of the gardens was made by water. Jets of water sprang from the canals and fell into them, but there would be other, more elaborate, fountains as well, often in enclosed or cloistered courts.

Paths in Islamic gardens were never random or winding, always leading straight to some goal, perhaps a pavilion; sometimes to a view through an ornamental unglazed window in the outer wall; often to an arbour or kiosk made of wood or stone or bricks, brightly tiled, with vines trained over it. The last feature was to become known in later Spanish gardens as a *glorietta*. The beds for trees and evergreen or flowering shrubs were sunk below the level of the paths, which were always paved, pebbled or covered with mosaic. Where any flowers at all were grown, they were planted in large earthenware pots or vases. Lawns were unknown; some gardens were paved all over except for rectangular beds left uncovered for planting. Walls, balustrades, seats, the sides of fountains and all such vertical surfaces were apt to be covered with brightly coloured tiles, a practice which can best be seen today in some old Portuguese gardens such as that of the Peña Palace. There were, of course, no statues in Islamic gardens, since the Koran, following the Old Testament, forbids the making of graven images.

What the Arab gardeners of the Dar-al-Islam regarded as correct rules for planting, and some of the garden plants which they favoured, can be gathered from an authoritative twelfth-

century work on agriculture and horticulture written by the agronomist Yahyā ibn Muhammad (Abū Zakarīyā). This book, if it owes something to the late Greek editions of Mago the Carthaginian and to the works of Columella, is nevertheless an original work and closely based on practical knowledge and experience. Abū Zakarīyā says that all garden doorways should be framed by clipped evergreens, that cypresses should be used to line paths and grouped to mark the junctions of paths. He objects to the mixing of evergreen with deciduous trees. He liked to see canals and pools shaded by trees or bowers, to prevent excessive loss of water by evaporation. Plants named in his text include lemon and orange trees, pines and most of our common deciduous trees, cypresses, oleander, myrtle and rose as the only flowering shrubs, violets, lavender, balm, mint, thyme, marjoram, iris, mallow, box and bay laurel. He lays much stress on aromatics, as, indeed, did all the Islamic gardeners. His climbing plants are vines, jasmines and ivy.

Turning from Spain to India once again, there was a first great period of Islamic gardening in that country under the ruler Feroz Shah, in the mid fourteenth century, at Ferozabad (a few miles from modern Delhi). Unfortunately we know very little about these gardens except that they were typically Islamic in imposing straight lines on the old Buddhist gardens which they replaced, and that their planting was accompanied by street and roadside tree-planting on a very impressive scale. But the greatest Islamic gardens of India were those planted by the Moghul emperors, beginning with Babur and his Ram Bagh at Agra. The zenith of this school of garden art came in the reign of Jahangir and his garden-loving wife, who was Persian.

The Moghul gardens all had a great central pavilion, virtually a palace, which served as a tomb after the royal builder's death. The gardens were very large, rarely less than fifty acres, often more, and in any case quite enclosed by a high wall as in Spain. Near the central pavilion was a great tank — that is, a rectangular lake — from which flowed four canals to divide the garden into four quarters which were, in their turn, divided into smaller parts by lesser canals. Canals were often lined with blue tiles. All trees were planted in straight lines or rectangular blocks. Canals were shaded by such lines of trees, and the principal walks were avenues.

Some of the square plots defined by the lesser canals were raised platforms of turf or, more often, stone, sheltered by a tree at each corner to give shade and, covered with carpets, used for picnics. The main canals might have a border for flowers running the whole length, and as such borders were apparently planted with herbaceous perennials, bulbs and aromatics, as well as with shrubs, one cannot help wondering whether, in them, we have one origin of the herbaceous border. But, on the whole, these Indian gardens made by the Moghuls were really Persian gardens; even many of the technical terms used by Indian gardeners were Persian loanwords.

Still, there were considerable local differences. Wherever the fall of land made them possible the Moghul gardeners liked to have waterfalls, which might be simple, or elaborate in the manner of the Roman (and later, Renaissance) water-staircase. They were never, as in Chinese or late English gardens, made 'after Nature'; they were works of formal architecture. The long pergolas in these northern Indian gardens seem to have been of Egyptian rather than Persian inspiration, but the placing of octagonal pavilions at the inner angles of the outer walls was typically Persian.

Refinements in Indian gardening began very early in this period, in the reign of that great gardener Babur, who got his inspiration, as we shall see, in Samarkand. There were, for instance, gardens to be seen only by moonlight; and gardens dedicated to a single flower, like the Emperor's own garden of violets near Kabul, or the famous Rose Garden, the Gulabi Bagh, at Lahore.

Back in Spain, the art of gardens was reaching a zenith even before the Indian peak with the creation of vast, formal, architectural gardens in all the Islamic emirates of Andalusia. Vestiges of a few of these gardens still remain. They were always broken up into numerous small interconnecting enclosures. When, as in two of the surviving cases, they were built on hillsides, a small element of irregularity gave them a charm which was alien to most of these great Islamic gardens. The three principal survivors are the Alhambra and the Generalife in Granada, and the Alcazar in Seville. The surviving and smaller Patio de los Naranjos at Córdova mosque is older than any of these but, except for its antiquity, rather less interesting.

The oldest of the first three is the Alhambra, started in the eleventh century but the finer parts of which were built from 1248 by Al Ahmar. Of the numerous original patios or courts only four remain, but from them we can get some idea of what the whole garden was like in, say, 1400 and

until the reconquest. First, the Court of the Myrtles consists chiefly of a long, broad pool enclosed by galleries and a colonnade on the north and south sides and by clipped myrtle which, despite the clipping, flowers deliciously. The much more famous Court of Lions into which it opens through a decorated doorway dates from about 1350, and is surrounded by a peristyle of alabaster columns supporting Moorish arches, with a pavilion at each end of the long axis. The Lion Fountain from which the name derives is central and feeds four small channels, in the manner of the channels at the Villa Adriana, which divide the area into parts now gravelled but originally occupied by shaped citrus trees and possibly by some flowers.

The third Court, the Court of Doraxa, originally for the use of the harem ladies, is contained by walls lined with fine old cypresses and orange trees. Originally they must have been planted regularly, but time has given them a pleasingly scattered or random look. The fountain in the centre looks as if it had been restored in the Renaissance manner and can hardly be called 'Moorish'. Finally there is a very late (seventeenth century) Court of Cypresses, four immense old trees, with pebbled paving in a design of interlaced bands, and another fountain.

The making of the Generalife began later than the Alhambra but before 1300, and it was built as a summer palace for the kings of Granada. It is on seven levels, the site being a hillside. The highest terrace is the Court of the Canal, which is enclosed on three sides by buildings and on the fourth by an arcade, its name being derived from the narrow canal down the centre of the long axis. Other features of this Court are a miniature mosque, a fountain, and clipped box parterres. At a lower level on one side is a square walled garden, the walls pierced by decorated windows commanding fine views. On the other side is the Harem Court with a horseshoe-shaped canal, ancient cypresses, and oleanders, leading to the next terrace through an arched gateway by way of steps and landings ornamented with pebble mosaics. A belvedere reached by more decorated steps is above this terrace, and from it there is a novel water-staircase, the water being carried down the hollow-tiled balustrade. Stairs lead to the Mirador from which you have a view of the Alhambra, with the *sierra* in the distance.

The Alcazar garden at Seville is on a flat site; and although Moorish in design and workmanship, was in fact created by a Christian king, Pedro the Cruel, as an abode for his adored and abused mistress. The Alcazar we now see was started in 1350, a century after the reconquest of Seville, and what we have left now is only a vestige of its former vast splendour. Its paved paths are raised well above the beds, in which trees and palms are the only plants. Every enclosure is walled or hedged by dense, tall, clipped evergreens. Trained cypresses form the *gloriettas* at the junctions of the paths. The sixteen acres which are all that remain of the once much larger garden include avenues of cypresses and flowering shrubs, elaborate box parterres, a very large bath or tank, and much display of coloured tiling. One suspects, especially in the box parterres, a later, Italian influence.

To return again, now, to Persia. As in the Spanish, so in the Persian Islamic gardens, waterworks and fountains were supremely important. In Spain, fountains of the same interconnected and elaborate kind were used lavishly. The great Hazar Jarib (Safavid) garden at Isfahan had 500 fountains or jets of water of one kind or another. Water was used in simple fountains and in these very complex systems of pattern-forming jets; more simply in open channels lined with tiles, forming stylized streams and cascades; and in still surfaces — either in tiled shallow basins, or in deep tanks without tiles so as to give the water a deep, dark and mysterious look.

If the flowers actually named in accounts of old gardens were really the only ones used by the Arab gardeners, then they were, as I have said, surprisingly few. However, it is impossible to be sure that all were named. The two kinds of documents we can look to for information are poetry, and the carpet designs which (see above) were frequently stylized pictures of gardens. One source is Firdawsi's *Shah Namah* (c. AD 1000), in which there is a good deal of this kind of thing:

> 'Mazanderan is the bower of spring
> Tulips and hyacinths abound
> On every lawn...'

Roses, lilacs and lilies are often mentioned and were clearly widely grown. The lilies would have been *Lilium candidum*. Violets, daffodils and irises were also grown. Trees are hardly ever given identifiable names by the poets, but we have a list of them (see above) from a more reliable kind of writer. Some of the poets' trees which occur often are mythological ones which grow only in one of the Moslem heavens.

Finally, something needs to be said concerning the last great phase of garden making in the Dar-al-Islam before

European influences began to be felt, in and about Samarkand during and immediately following the reign of the great Mongol Khan Tamerlane.

At least fourteen of these Mongol-Persian gardens are named in the literature. The Spaniard Ruy Gonzalez de Clavijo, who was sent by the court of Castille and Leon as ambassador to Tamerlane's court in Samarkand (1403-6), wrote, in an account of his arrival:

'...so numerous are the gardens and vineyards surrounding Samarkand that a traveller approaching the city sees only a hilly mount of trees, and the houses embowered among them remain invisible.'

From Clavijo and two Arab writers, Sharaf ad-din 'ali Yazdi and Ibn Arabshas, and from the Emperor Babur's account of his visit to Samarkand, we can gather that Tamerlane's gardens and those of his descendants and principal officers into the sixteenth century were usually made on hillsides or had artificial hills. They were terraced, geometrical, architectural and formal, and were composed of many enclosures. Trees were of paramount importance. Elm, white poplar and cypresses are named; they were planted in blocks which were all of one kind. There were many pavilions, and there were streams and also 'meadows', which may have been rough lawns. Even the orchards were regularly planted in enclosed courtyards whose walls were pierced by gateways '...most beautifully ornamented with tile work in gold and blue'.

Thus Clavijo, who was received by Tamerlane in the 'Dil-gusha Garden' where the Khan sat beside a fountain whose water fell into a basin in which red apples floated. The flower gardens were laid out with straight walks and square beds, but sycamore trees made the greater walks into avenues. The beds seem to have been planted for the most part with flowering shrubs, roses, of course, and perhaps oleander, lilac and myrtle. But some of the beds are described as 'little wildernesses'. They may have contained spring bulbs, chiefly tulips and hyacinths, perhaps some herbaceous perennials, all growing in grass. The walls of some Mongol-Persian gardens had cloisters or columns throughout their length, and porticoes were also used, doubtless on the Byzantine plan. Other walls were painted with murals, which again may have been copied from Byzantine garden art. Some of the beds were used for fruit trees. Here, again from Clavijo, is a description of the house and palace where he was lodged:

'We found it to be enclosed by a high wall which in its circuit may measure a full league around, and within it is full of fruit trees of all kinds save only limes and citron-trees which we noted to be lacking. Further, there are here six great tanks, for thoroughout the orchard is conducted a great system of water, passing from end to end: while leading from one tank to the next they have planted five avenues of trees, very lofty and shady, which appear as streets for they are paved to be like platforms. These quarter the orchard in every direction, and off the five main avenues other smaller roads are led to variegate the plan... In the exact centre there is a hill, built up artificially of clay brought hither by hand: it is very high and its summit is a small level space that is enclosed by a palisade of wooden stakes. Within this enclosure are built several very beautiful palaces, each with its complement of chambers magnificently ornamented in gold and blue, the walls being panelled with tiles of these and other colours. This mound on which the palaces have been built is encircled below by deep ditches that are filled with water, for a runlet from the main stream brings this water which flows into these ditches with a continuous and copious supply. To pass up unto this hillock to the level of the palaces they have made two bridges, one on the other part, the other opposite... There are to be seen many deer which Timur has caused to be caught and brought hither, and there are pheasants here in great abundance.'*

In some of these enormous gardens whole cities of huge tents were raised for holiday festivals, and the entertainment, apart from gross eating and drinking, included displays of animals such as elephants and even a giraffe, music, singing, dancing, shows of skilled craftsmen's work, and even public hangings. Of one such party which he attended Clavijo wrote:

'At several points of vantage tall gallows had been erected and the populace was entertained by numerous hangings including those of the mayor of Samarkand and of certain butchers caught charging too much for their wares.'

As we have seen, one of the sources for information about the later gardens of the Dar-al-Islam is the Emperor Babur, who gives an account of some of the gardens which he saw in Samarkand in his autobiography. We also have, for this period, a number of miniature paintings of gardens, made by some of the greatest Persian miniaturists, notably by Bihzad and Shah Muzaffar, both of whom worked at Abu'l Ghazi Husayn Bayqara's court at Herat. Perhaps the best way to make use of the source we have in Babur will be to quote

his own account of the garden called Bagh-i-Vafa, Garden of Fidelity, which he made in his own kingdom in 1508, on a height overlooking the Kabul River.

'In the garden is a small hillock, from which a stream of water, sufficient to drive a mill, incessantly flows into the garden below. The four-fold field-plot (the Chahar bagh) of the garden is situated on this entrance. On the southwest part of this garden is a reservoir of water twenty feet square, which is wholly planted round with orange trees; there are likewise pomegranates. All around the piece of water the ground is quite covered with clover. This spot is the very eye of the beauty of the garden. At the time the orange becomes yellow the prospect is delightful.'

As well as this garden Babur owned others which he had not made but bought. One of them was the Bagh-i-Kalan, which means 'Immense Garden', about ten miles from Kabul. It was on a hillside rich in streams, some of which flowed through the garden and naturally had winding courses. It is of interest in the context of taste in garden design that Babur's first care was to have the principal stream straightened, channelled and supplied with fountains; the same was then done for the other streams. In fact, he went to work to impose on this garden the regular and rectilinear plan which was de rigueur in the Dar-al-Islam.

This great imperial gardener was as interested in plants, the material of gardening, as in design. He found time on his interminable travels on official business to note and admire the wild flowers; he counts thirty-one species of tulips in the countryside about Kabul and notes that one is scented like a rose; he named two which were new to him. He ordered flowering shrubs and trees, by name, to be planted in the city squares and to line the streets, and sweet-scented flowers to be planted under them. He also experimented with new plants both ornamental and useful, for example sugar-cane grown in his own gardens, and new kinds of melons and grapes raised from seed and cuttings for which he sent to remote provinces or foreign lands.

Babur, in short, set the pace and style in gardening for his country, and in due course we shall return to take a look at the consequences of this in the seventeenth and eighteenth centuries.

* Quoted by Wilber (1962).

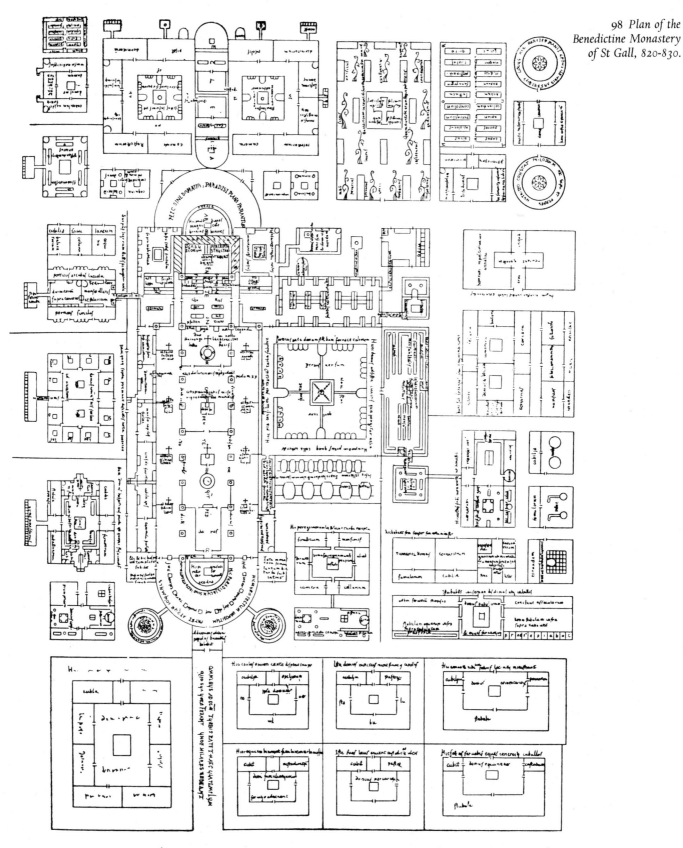

99 *Garden with wattle fence and trees (1435).*

7

THE GROWTH
OF GARDENING IN
EUROPE'S MIDDLE AGES

It is a cliché that the monasteries were the pioneers of garden making in Europe's Middle Ages. What really seems to have happened is that the founders of monasteries took over from the Italians of Roman Italy the idea of schools-in-gardens, the Academies, and the idea of the *villa rustica* supporting the community with its produce. Thus Saint Augustine, telling of the founding of his school at Hippo, says: 'I assembled in a garden that Valerius had given me certain brethren of like intentions with my own, who possessed nothing even as I possessed nothing, and who followed after me.' He was, in fact, founding a Christian version of the classical *academe*. The cloister which was thus early attached to churches, built in the manner of Augustine's, corresponded to museum, exedra and portico in the pagan philosopher's garden; and the court around which the monastery buildings were set was simply the Roman peristyle. But even Augustine was not altogether an innovator in modelling a Christian establishment on the pagan house-and-garden complex, for the oldest Byzantine basilicas had adjoining porticoes planted as gardens. These were called Paradises, a name which was taken over by Western churchmen, although there 'Paradise' did not always mean a garden. It was, at least at first, a sort of courtyard where sinners had to wait before being received back, literally, into the church. Logically, such courts should have been called Purgatories; but they became gardens.

These cloister gardens were the first real gardens of the European Middle Ages. They were being made very early, in Rome certainly as early as the eighth century, when Pope Hadrian I had the cloister of San Paolo Fuori planted as a garden of trees and flowers. This, by the way, puts paid to the notion that these very early ecclesiastical gardens were devoted solely to vegetables and salad and medicinal herbs, for all cloister gardens were tree and flower gardens. When in 1070 Monte Cassino was rebuilt, its Paradise was, according to record, 'in the Roman fashion'. At that time there were still great Roman villas not so ruined as to be useless as models — the Villa Adriana, for one. And when William Rufus, who succeeded his father as King of England in 1087, visited Romsey Abbey he 'went into the cloisters to admire the roses and other flowering plants' — so such gardens were not confined to Italy.

Still, it is true that the vegetable gardens associated with monastic foundations are even earlier than these ecclesiastical Paradises. This was at least partly due to Saint Benedict, whose sixth-century Rule enjoined self-sufficiency in vegetables and herbs on his disciples, and work in the garden for everyone. So that we owe the link between the horticultural science developed by the Romans and our own which derives from it to the Benedictines who, furthermore,

100 *'Mary' garden, from the* Speculum Humanae Salvationis, *with central fountain and plants growing in the ground.*

101 *The wattle garden with the Virgin and six Saints (1450-65) is described as having 'several flowers and lily-like stalked plants to symbolize a garden'.*

were improving gardening techniques throughout the Middle Ages. The garden crops included choice fruits, whose cultivation was another revival of Roman practice, and a very few species of flowers.

A plan for a great monastery drawn in the year 900 and preserved at St Gall in Switzerland includes the following gardens: first, the Paradise, an open court with a portico. It has a 'flowery mead', flowers growing in grass, and these would have been common wild flowers. It has also four rectangular flowerbeds. Probably close to the Hospital and the house of the Infirmarian there is a Physic Garden, in which there are sixteen raised and parallel rectangular beds for herbs. Specifically medicinal herbs grown (marked on the plan as such) include roses and lilies (*L. candidum*) as well as herbs we should call culinary, such as sage and rosemary.

Here is further proof, if any were needed, that the flower garden has, as one origin, the herb garden in which the beauty of the flowers was at first simply a by-product. The School as well as the Hospital on this plan also has its peristyle and therefore its own garden. The Cemetery is also a garden, planted not only with shade-trees, but with fruit trees, set in straight rows with the graves between them, each row of trees being of one kind.*

North of the churchyard, itself a garden, is the large vegetable garden. There, eighteen raised beds are arranged in a square. There is a house for the gardener, for although the monks had, by the Rule, to work in the garden, there was usually a full-time professional.

* Gothein (1928) suggests that here the architect has copied Charlemagne's *Capitulare de Villis*.

102 *Enclosed garden with very low palings and a very curious miniature gate, on which is* MCCCCXVIII — *a doubtful date, which, if correct, would make it the oldest known engraving with a date. There are two trees, but no flowers.*

Flowers began to be important for their own sake when, beginning perhaps in the sixth or seventh century, the Church gave up the policy of condemning them as heathenish, and took over their use in ritual and symbolism. The Madonna lily, having been Aphrodite's flower, became Mary's, and symbolic meanings became attached to violets and to roses. In some monasteries flowers were grown and used lavishly, although few in kind.

The science of garden irrigation was not lost. Part of a contemporary description of Clairvaux Abbey gardens in the early twelfth century runs thus:

'Where the orchard leaves off, the garden begins, divided into several beds, or cut up by little canals which, although standing water, do flow more or less... this water fulfils the double purpose of nourishing the fish and watering the vegetables.'

Again, a plan* of Canterbury Cathedral gardens, vineyards and orchards, dated 1165, shows an elaborate irrigation system.

The advancement of gardening in the eleventh and twelfth centuries in Europe was not solely in ecclesiastical hands. Secular lords were soon learning the worth of a garden from the Church. But there was also another influence at work, that of Norman Sicily. The 'baptised sultans', as they were called, of the Hauteville family took over the gardens of the Moslem emirs whom they had conquered. Those gardens of Islamic Sicily did not differ in any important particular from those of Iran, northern India or southern Spain. Although gardens like this did not survive, travelling soldier-noblemen and priests brought ideas from what they had seen in Sicily

* Now in the Chapter Library.

103

and Calabria into northern Italy, France and even Germany. The Emperor Frederick II Hohenstaufen, known as *Stupor Mundi*, a man of brilliant mind and a culture far in advance of his time, was master not only of Sicily and the south of mainland Italy, but of all Germany. He was, among other things, a considerable archaeologist, and despite the influence of Arab arts including garden art in Sicily, which was the most beloved of his enormous dominions, he made his gardens on the Roman model. At Palermo there was a rectangular pool or bath in the central courtyard, pergolas and trellises of vines, groves of trees and such flowering shrubs as myrtles and oleanders, fishponds and aviaries (Frederick was the first great post-Hellenic ornithologist). Some flowers were grown, chiefly roses, lilies and violets. Gardens of the kind laid out and planted by Frederick and his imitators were the basis of Pietro de' Crescenzi's chapters on the making and care of gardens in his *Liber ruralium commodorum* published in 1305. Pietro deals with three kinds of gardens: little ones — a fountain, a lawn, beds of flowers and herbs; gardens of up to two acres for comfortable burgesses; and gardens of twenty acres or more for the nobility. The last were of the kind which the Sicilians had made.

Pietro's book not only deals with design and layout, the making of turf seats and shady arbours and of walks and waterways, but also touches on the arts of grafting, budding, topiary and pleaching.

The nobles of northern Europe caught the taste for gardens from the churchmen. The ladies rather than the men were the castle gardeners; and like the monks they planted vegetables, salads, medicinal herbs and some flowers, all together in small, neat parterres. They also had little 'flowery mead' gardens of the kind described by Pietro de' Crescenzi, often in enclosed courtyards, consisting of a plot of mixed grass and flowers, a seat shaded by climbing plants or a pleached or clipped evergreen, and perhaps one or two fruit trees. Such bowers were so placed that the lady's quarters opened into them. The principal flowers were roses, violets and marigolds. Some castles, palaces or houses also had what are called tree gardens, or pleasances: fruit trees were the most important element of these, but some other broad-leaved trees were planted for their shade, and the lime or linden was a favourite, particularly in Germany. Lindens were

'...not confined to the tree garden but were also the glory of the castle court, with a lawn and a fountain. It is the proper tree for social life and parties, and it also stands out in the pasture lands. Its branches are extended widely, supported on pillars, with a seat below; often there are benches actually in the boughs; sometimes the whole tree is surrounded by a barrier, as we see it still round the lime-tree at Michelstadt.'*

The elements of 'expectation and surprise' are regarded as

* Gothein (1928).

92

103 *'Garden of Love', with low brick benches and platform, turfed (1450).*

104 *Turf-topped bench, supported by planks and planted with flowers (1460).*

104

fundamental to good garden design, and are most readily ensured by making a number of small gardens separated by walls or hedges, connected by walks, steps, gates and bridges. We find this practised even in the Middle Ages, for in the *Roman de la Rose* the garden is of that kind. There is a flower garden with grass and a fountain feeding a stream flowing beneath a trellis, beyond which lies another garden, divided from a third by a rose-trellis, and so on.

The art of making rose-grown pergolas and arbours was also highly developed at this time. There is an account of an arbour and pergola covered with a single climbing rose of such a size that it could give shade to twelve knights together. Out of such arbours developed summer houses and pavilions of a more substantial kind.

The maze, a very ancient garden feature — exactly how ancient it is impossible to say — was revived in the Middle Ages. The outer hedge was planted in the shape of a circle or, more rarely, a hexagon, and the inner part laid out according to an ancient, stylized pattern. The ultimate origin of the garden maze was the Cretan maze. There is at Pompeii a trace of a garden maze: a sign which reads *Hic habitat Minotaurus*. But what was the origin of the Cretan maze itself? The Minotaur is clearly the cultural descendant of the Horned God of the famous (Palaeolithic) Ariège cave, and perhaps the ancestor of the Christians' devil. Like

many very ancient gods, this one may have taken to living in a grove; Pan, another of his epiphanies, is a grove-dweller. Very likely the maze is the oldest surviving feature of the garden. Two of the most famous mazes in Europe were planted at, respectively, Henry II's Woodstock, where he hid Fair Rosamund and where the maze was called 'The House of Daedalus'; and the maze at the Hôtel des Tournelles, likewise known as the 'House of Daedalus', which the Duke of Bedford, when Regent of France, destroyed to make room for a stand of elms. His reasons may have been quite other than aesthetic: if the maze is a stylized sacred grove, as I believe, it was a centre for the Old Religion. The Old Religion in Bedford's time was manifest in the Witch Cult; and Bedford's worst enemies, Joan of Arc and Gilles de Rais, were both said to be witches.

In Germany and France, but not, as far as I can discover, in England, some noblemen made hunting parks after the Persian style. That is, they enclosed as many acres as they could afford within a wall, planted it, park fashion, with trees, and stocked it with game which they could hunt at their leisure. These parks are the ancestors of the English deer park, but in them the kinds of game were diverse and might be kept separate by interior walls. In the most magnificent of such parks rare animals, such as lions and even giraffes, were installed — or so it is claimed by recorders and annalists. But as a rule the game, apart from large birds

105

106

107 *Raised beds and sparse planting 1580.*

105 *Railed and 'chess-board' garden of 1470. The sixteen beds are arranged in chess-board form and each is surrounded either by low trellis-work or by boards.*

106 *Meistersinger's garden of 1465.*

including peacocks, were various kinds of deer. Frederick Barbarossa made such a park in 1161. However, while interesting in our context, the making of such parks cannot properly be called gardening, although in many such a formal garden might often be included.

Contacts between West and East other than those in Saracenic-Norman Italy and Sicily had some influence on European garden design. There are traces of Byzantine influence on what little we know of Charlemagne's gardens. Frankish imperial embassies to the Caliphs, especially of Baghdad, brought home ideas for gardens. So, of course, did the Crusaders, and the few stands of naturalized *Lilium martagon* in England are locally and traditionally attributed to returning Crusaders. They are said to have introduced other plants, but we do not know which. Europe certainly had her citrus trees from the North African Moslem gardeners, by way of Spain and Sicily. Lesser garden plants are very seldom named, but there was a slow enrichment of our plant material throughout the Middle Ages. Other Oriental features, such as marble baths for bathing the feet, were introduced into gardens in Germany and Italy.

It is not easy to know how, if at all, English gardens differed

94

9. *Montreal. A botanic garden which continues the French spirit.*

10. *Schönbrunn, Vienna's great French garden.*

11. *Los Angeles Arboretum. American gardens continued the English rather than the French or Italian traditions.*

12. *Shalimar, Lahore. Italianate influence in late Islamic garden art.*

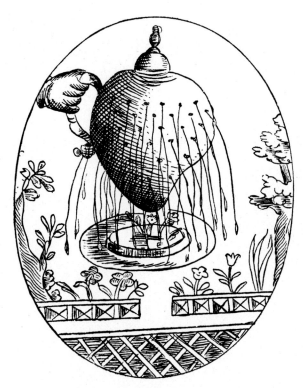

108 *Garden with outer lattice railing and inner dwarf railing of the Louis XI garden of 1470.*

In France and Italy, both of which borrowed the idea from Provence, which had it from Moorish Spain, Gardens of Love were made — not for erotic use, however, since the romantic love of the troubadour was supposed to be chaste. Love gardens were enclosed 'flowery meads' with a table for refreshment but no seats: the troubadour and his lady sat on the grass.

The earliest technical and therefore objective work on gardens in England was probably first published in 1400 or thereabouts. It is called *The Feate of Gardening* and its author was one Mayster Ion Gardener. It is in nine parts, including the Introduction. The second part deals with the raising and planting of trees, notably fruit trees, with something about grafting. There is a section devoted to grape-vines; sections on the time and manner of sowing seeds; on how to grow green vegetables; on herbs, above all parsley; and there is a part devoted to saffron-growing. Of the ninety-seven plants named, Miles Hadfield (1960) says that twenty-six were certainly alien introductions. Flowers mentioned are cowslip, daffodil, foxglove, hollyhock, honeysuckle, lavender, Madonna lily, orpine, periwinkle, hepatica, primrose, rose, scabious. Most of these were grown as medicinal herbs and not primarily as ornamentals.

from other European gardens in the fourteenth century. They were perhaps on a more modest scale in most cases, but not always. We have Chaucer's descriptions in several of his works, but unfortunately they are clearly stylized, romantic rather than objective, drawn from the same source as Guillaume de Loris's *Roman de la Rose*. De Loris borrowed his garden descriptions from the Latin and Greek authors, freshening them, it is true, by means of his own acquaintance with gardens. Other poets followed him, enriching their plant lists by lifting names from Ovid, Horace and above all Virgil, quite regardless of whether the trees and herbs in question really grew, or could grow, in the lands in question. Chaucer and Lydgate did likewise, and as a consequence their works are not worth much as documents;* but nor are they quite worthless, for if garden descriptions in poetry were stylized, so also were gardens. And there is much freshness in Chaucer's descriptions. The garden in his *Troilus and Criseyde* has gravel walks shaded by flowering trees, and turf seats. In other places we find much made of arbours and clipped evergreens with sitting places cut deeply into them.

Albertus Magnus, among all his other skills and learnings, was a great gardener, and certainly the finest European scientific horticulturist since Roman times. There is an extraordinary story of his receiving King William II of Holland, King of the Romans, at his monastery on 6th January 1249, and showing him, in the cloister garden, fruit trees bearing ripe fruits, and other plants in flower, despite the season. Albertus forced them by the use of 'mild heat'. There is nothing impossible about this: Roman gardeners had made forcing houses and forcing frames by using mica as we use glass or plastic film, and a cloister could fairly easily be turned into a sort of orangery, with wood-burning stoves as the source of heat.

In the fourteenth century interest in, and the making of, gardens began to spread down from the nobility to the class of burgesses, in Paris and especially in Germany, where some of the great cities were not far behind the Italians. But since the style of ornamental gardening used by the burgesses originated in Italy, that country must, as usual, be dealt with first. The example was set by Petrarch, almost as enthusiastic a gardener as he was a poet. There is, in the Vatican library, his own copy of Palladius's treatise on agriculture, and

* The poets are not the only culprits in this respect. When, in Tudor and Jacobean times, classic textbooks on horticulture such as the work of Conrad Heresbach began to be published in English translation, no regard whatever was paid to climatic conditions.

109 *Gate of garden;*
from The Romance of the Rose,
1481. (The Lover plucking the Rose.)

110 *The garden of* The Romance of the
Rose (*The Lover gathering the Rose*),
edition of 1538, showing
the changed idea of the later date.

111 *The Lover gathers the Rose; from*
a fifteenth-century edition of
The Romance of the Rose.

its margins are full of notes in Petrarch's handwriting on his gardening operations, successes and failures. Like our own, his vegetable and salad seeds failed to germinate. Like us, he was not discouraged. He laid out and planted gardens in a number of places in Italy, but the only one which is fairly well documented is his garden in Parma. There, in 1348, he took over what seems to have been a simple kitchen garden, and to it added a pleasure garden of his own design, with a lawn, which would in those days have been perhaps more like a little meadow of grass and wild flowers. There were fruit trees; and aromatic herbs including rosemary and hyssop. He received cuttings of good vine varieties from friends in other parts of Italy, and grafted them onto his own stocks. And as had been usual in some parts of the country since early Roman Republican times, and despite all attempts by such experts as Columella to stop the practice, Petrarch grew and trained his vines over his fruit trees. It is significant of his state of mind as a gardener that his preferred 'textbook' for gardening was Virgil's *Georgics*.

One of Petrarch's circle of friends and fellow-gardeners was Galeazzo Visconti, Duke of Milan, who was not only a gardener but a botanist. Although he was a great nobleman, the example of simple gardening, of making a garden as a pleasant place for a centre of sober family life, was one which the burgesses could imitate. He and Petrarch exchanged garden plants. The Duke made a garden about his new house, Pavia Castle. Its nucleus was a lawn surrounding a stone bath and surrounded by pergolas of vines, and for the rest regularly planted with fruit trees in the Roman manner. According to Georgina Masson (1961):

'Galeazzo also enjoyed taking his meals *al fresco* and he had a special balcony made outside the castle dining-room, overlooking the garden, where he and his family ate serenaded by the music of trombones, cornets and flutes.'

We shall presently see the Duke's garden balcony appearing on the houses, overlooking the new gardens, of many north German burgesses.

We know less than we should like about smaller gardens: they had lawns, at all events in the north; they were enclosed within walls or clipped evergreen hedges; they had beds of aromatic herbs and some flowers, certainly roses, lilies and

112
*Garden tent of
the fifteenth century:
'Louis XIII in his tent'.*

violets. They made much use of evergreens for boscage, arbours, bowers; and they also made use of topiary.

After Petrarch and Galeazzo Visconti the next man to stimulate horticultural activity in Italy was Cosimo de' Medici, who was born in 1389. He was another nobleman, but his boyhood acquaintance with gardens was with the small ones which rich Florentine citizens planted between the inner and outer walls which protected the city. In due course he gave practical expression to this early-acquired love of gardens by remaking the garden of the house at Careggi which he inherited from his brother. This garden was, in essence, a careful imitation of Roman models. Thus its most important elements were clipped or naturally grown evergreens — chiefly box, bay and myrtle — just as they were, and for the same reasons, in Islamic gardens. Layout was regular, aromatics were important, and fruit trees included quince and pomegranate. Some of Cosimo's flowers were relatively new to northern Italy — some new dianthus, probably carnations, for example, which had come from Persian to Sicilian gardens and thence into Italy. Citrus trees were grown in giant pots; they were doubtless taken under cover during the winter. There were several fountains, one of them adorned by Verrocchio's 'Boy with a Dolphin'.

After meeting and talking with some of the Greek scholars who came from Constantinople for the Oecumenical Council at Florence in 1439, and who were to take refuge there following the fall of their city to the Turks fourteen years later, Cosimo used Careggi's garden as a meeting place for the Platonic *academe* which he founded. This became the power-house of the Humanist movement and so of the Italian Renaissance — and so, in due course, of the whole European Renaissance. Thus the tremendous revival of the arts and sciences and of learning in general in the following three centuries could almost be said to have begun with the revival of gardening; and had its origin in a garden. The men who met to talk of philosophy, science and the arts in Cosimo's garden harked back, of course, to the Greek tradition, with the younger Pliny as their guide; and idealized it. But it was, after all, in their own terms that they expressed it, both in their gardens and in the other arts.

The architect who set the style and made the rules for these Humanist gardens of the late Middle Ages was Leone Battista Alberti. He not only created villas and gardens for various patrons — the palace he built in Florence for Giovanni Rucellai is his key work — but he also wrote a textbook on the art, *De Re Aedificatoria*, between 1445 and 1452, and presented it to Pope Nicholas V; it was first published in 1485.

Alberti considered that a villa, that is a combined house-and-garden, should be on a hillside commanding fine views. As in the classical villa, house and garden should be interpenetrating, the links being loggias which were half living-rooms, half garden-rooms; house at one end, garden at the other, so to speak. Paths ought to be lined with symmetrically-planted trees, including pomegranates, which the Italians valued so highly for their flowers and decorative fruits, and a cornus. Climbing roses should be set to clamber over the trees. Paths could also be lined with clipped aromatic and box edges, and the same plants should be used to make parterres of geometric design. Vine pergolas were important, their rafters to be borne on marble columns. There should be fountains, as many as possible. And Alberti also borrowed from Pliny the idea of a shady grove of cypress, juniper and myrtle, overshadowed by oaks. Ivy must be allowed to grow freely over the trees. As for flowers, they should be grown in big pots and amphorae.

In Humanist as in Islamic, and for that matter modern

97

113 'Garden of Eden'.

114

English, American, Russian and European gardens, the rose was by far the most important flower. The varieties available were apparently the same as those grown in Pliny's time — the Damascene, Prenestine, Paestine, Campanian, Lychnian and Milesian. These are all placenames, and must originally have been locally selected cultivars of a very few species. But now the number of climbing plants was increased: jasmine reached the north from Sicily; convolvulus and clematis were domesticated and honeysuckle became a garden plant. Groundlings included *Gladiolus byzantinus*, bluebells or hyacinth, narcissus, iris, buttercup, forget-me-not and, surprisingly, orchis. At least, these are the flowers named in Francesco Colonna's *Hypnerotomachia*, which was written in the late 1460s although not published until the sixteenth century.

Probably as good an example as any of the mid fifteenth-century Florentine garden is that of the Villa Quaracchi, which was laid out *c.* 1459. It is described with admirable felicity by Georgina Masson (1961), who uses, as her source, the *Diaries* of Giovanni Rucellai who owned the house:

'The house stood on a slight eminence and was surrounded by a moat and fishponds, but from the description of the tree-shaded and balustraded terrace that overlooked them it appears that there the water served a decorative rather than a defensive purpose. A simple axial plan already evidently existed in this garden, for its owner says that the chief pergola led from the front door that had a small loggia above it, down the centre of the garden, and that it was flanked by walks bordered by breast-high hedges of box, with the arms of the family suspended above as a festoon. The pergola terminated in the *giardino segreto*, which was a garden room, filled with sweet-smelling herbs and flowers such as marjoram, basil and sweet rocket, growing in terracotta pots placed round a small lawn. Topiary in the modern sense of clipped hedges and figures of box was one of the chief ornaments of this little private garden that must have been a truly delightful retreat, filled with the scent of flowers and the spicy aroma of herbs and also providing some much-needed privacy for the owner and his family, as it is evident that the garden lay open to the eyes and enjoyment of passers-by on the Pistoia road.

'The main axis of the Quaracchi garden was continued on the far side of the *giardino segreto* by an avenue of trees that led to the banks of the Arno. Apart from this there appears to have been no attempt to achieve a symmetrical layout

98

114 *Convent garden of 1490, with raised banks running round the walls.*

115 *'Garden of Gethsemane', enclosed by railings; 1495.*

115

and a large part of the garden was given over to hedged orchards divided by paths with seats shaded by evergreens. Except for a considerable amount of topiary, most of the main features of the garden were medieval — arbours of evergreens and honeysuckle, a mount planted with evergreens, an aviary and a rose garden. Already, however, it is evident that humanistic studies had revived an interest in horticulture and Giovanni Rucellai mentions with pride a sycamore and exotic fruit trees that he may well have brought back from his foreign travels.'

The outcome of this Italian revival of gardening in Italy itself will be dealt with in chapter 9. Meanwhile, what influence was it having on the rest of Europe? Spain and Portugal we can ignore in this context — they were out of the mainstream, still under Moorish influence and soon about to be dominated as to style by the influences of the new worlds they discovered. So let us look first at France.

Charles VIII of France invaded Italy in 1495 and marched triumphantly to Naples, from which city the king wrote to Pierre de Bourbon:

'You can never believe what lovely gardens I have seen in this town; for on my word it seems as though only Adam and Eve were wanting to make an earthly paradise, so full are they of rare and beautiful things.'

Naples was culturally Greek, of course, but on top of Romanization and Gothicization, it had also experienced some Sicilian Moorish influences. In any case, it was not from Naples alone that Charles and his people took their lessons, which began the education of France in the new gardening as in all the revived arts, for Charles took back to France twenty-two assorted Italian artists as well as four tons of artistic loot. The place which the king chose for his new artists to begin the work of transforming France into a paradise on the Italian model was Amboise. Charles himself lived only long enough to see this work begun, but his successor, Louis XII, pressed on with it and after seventeen years was succeeded by François I, whose passion for beautifying his country exceeded Charles's own.

The garden artist whom Charles brought from Naples was Pasello da Mercogliano, a priest. Again we have the ancient

99

116

association of clerics with gardens; nothing is more striking in the history of gardening than the huge debt which the art, and the science, owe to clergymen. We have seen that in most ancient Mesopotamia and Egypt, in China and Japan, the earliest gardens and the models for later ones were those laid out and planted by monks of various religions. In Greece gardens developed out of sacred groves and were often tended by priests. In ancient Iran the oldest gardens were shrines of one sort or another. In the Dar-al-Islam the earliest gardens were, like the Patio de los Naranjos in Córdova, often those made about mosques. The Jewish religion begins in a garden. In medieval Europe it was the regular clergy who set the gardening example, around their monasteries. Even in eighteenth- and nineteenth-century England, and into our own times, clergymen have played a disproportionately large part in garden development. The reasons for this are not, perhaps, obscure, for apart from the very ancient connection between gardens and sacred groves or shrines, the priesthood, in all countries, is almost the only corporation of men, other than the great landowners, whom their fellow-men have always been willing to exempt from following any gainful trade, to keep them provided with the necessities of life, and by so doing to give them time for the practice of letters, and of such arts as gardening. Moreover, excused military service at all times and in all places, and protected from violence by taboos more or less

117

116 *Garden with wattle fence, fruit trees, flowering plants, and grape vine; late fifteenth century.*

117 *Palisade garden with low and broad palisades, a fountain, trees, but no flowers. A circular brick-faced turfed seat runs nearly round the garden. End of fifteenth century.*

effective, the clergy have been able to study and preserve the arts of the past, carry them over periods of disturbance and into the next period of peace, and so replant them. Such, indeed, was Mercogliano's task in France when he started work at Amboise.

What he found there was a small and primitive medieval garden. He enlarged it by widening the terrace it occupied, and enclosed it with pavilions and fences of lattice-work. He then laid out, on a simple geometrical pattern, flower or herb beds surrounded by regularly planted fruit trees. That was all he could do in the available space; but elsewhere in the grounds Charles built and stocked the first orangery in France; his oranges were the bitter ('Seville') ones; sweet oranges were not introduced until much later.

Mercogliano's next job was for Louis XII at Blois. There he found a small, sunken, medieval garden at the foot of the donjon or keep. He enlarged it and made it the lowest of a series of three, sited on mounting terraces, but all different and unconnected. His flowerbeds were surrounded by low wooden trellis, and a magnificent Italian fountain by the Genoese Pacchiarotti was imported to be the glory of a central pavilion. The highest terrace, called the King's Garden, had a fine Italianate pergola added in Henri II's time, when the garden became famous for its fine fruit, especially for its

mulberries. The finished gardens were strictly rectilinear and geometrical in design; wide, spacious, foreshadowing Versailles, and by our standards rather bleak.

This royal example in garden making was soon being followed. Cardinal Amboise, Louis XII's minister, laid out a garden at Gaillon near Rouen, one of his bishoprics. Its special feature was a fountain presented by the Venetian Republic but made in a famous Genoese *atelier*; it was destroyed during the Revolution. The Gaillon gardens were characteristic of French medieval gardens in having no proper connection with the house. The main garden had a gallery down both side walls, pierced by a gateway leading into side gardens; and as was to become usual, the central feature was a vast rectangle filled by geometrically placed parterres, and subsequently called simply the parterre. Some of these square or oblong beds were planted with flowers or herbs, but most of them were laid out with patterns of coloured earths and gravels, slate and terracotta. I suspect, here, Persian influence reaching France by way of Sicily, Italy and possibly even Spain. These beds were first bordered with wooden fretwork, later with clipped box. There were two mazes, with an overlooking gallery so that visitors could amuse themselves watching one of their number getting lost. On a high terrace was a garden of trees. According to a rather late account, some of the parterres reproduced coats of arms. This garden

118 *Garden with wattle fence, a 3-tier fountain, bee-hives, four trees, a fruiting climbing plant, and two kinds of flowering plants. End of fifteenth century.*

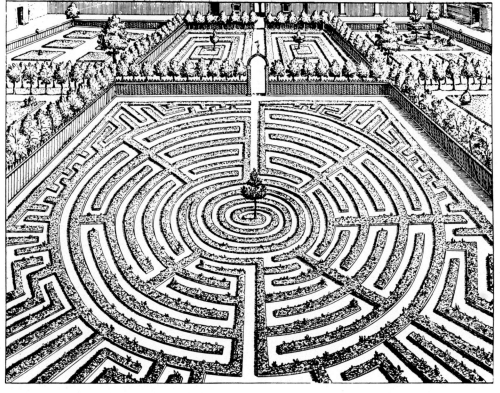

119 *Maze of unknown location; one of the set of engravings from which it is taken has 'Cock fecit, 1558*

120 *The labyrinth has no dividing hedges, but only flower beds; so it could be solved by a few steps across the beds.*

121 *Garden of G. J. Morosini at Padua (before 1714).*

121

was also decorated with a whole menagerie of fabulous and real beasts cut out of wood, foreshadowing a repulsive Dutch and English Jacobean fashion. Flowers were of little importance. To sum up, the Cardinal's garden was very much what many French gardens were to be for two centuries or more: a vast living-room out of doors, a decorated space for polite human intercourse rather than an exhibition of beautiful living natural objects.

From thus early, in fact, French gardeners and designers took their own way, stimulated but not ruled by the Italian masters and models. The Italians simply eliminated the medieval garden from their repertoire and took up their work at the point where the Romans had dropped it. The French stuck to the medieval garden scheme, so that house and garden had no connection with each other, and if they achieved a happy association, did so by accident. The Italians were ready to deviate on occasion from the rigid axial lines of the garden plan, and to connect terrace to terrace by stairways to create an integral work. The French did neither. But there was another, and in the event far more profitable, sense in

which they derived their garden plan from the medieval castle layout:

'The French adhered longer and with more conscious intention than any other country to that type of castle which is encompassed by a wide moat. And when at last these had lost their old use as a protection to the house, they remained simply as ornaments...'*

But not only 'remained'; new moated houses were built long after the military point had ceased to be even arguable. The moat is an expression of the Frenchman's deep distrust of his leaders and the 'times' — any 'times'. At all events, as a result of this retention of the moat the French came to use water in their great gardens as no other people used it. They used it, of course, *à l'Italien* too; but when François I made his garden at Fontainebleau out of an old hunting lodge in the midst of a forest, he dug a wide moat which completely encircled the complex of château and gardens, and he turned the nearby marsh into a lake which lapped one side of the château. This, incidentally, became (and still is) famous for

* Gothein (1928).

103

122

123

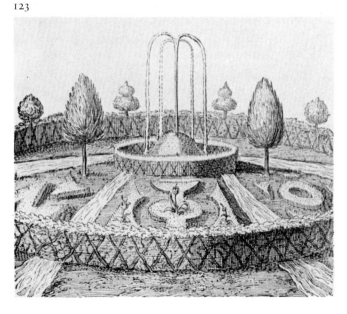

104

122 *Garden of Henri IV of France, 1608.*

123 *Enclosed garden of 1607. An early instance of the transition from the square beds of the Renaissance parterres.*

giant carp. Lesser canals were used to separate one rectangular enclosure from another, almost in the Persian manner. For the rest, avenues of fine trees, parterres, fountains; and a Jardin des Pins planted with pines or firs in straight lines, with box-edged beds symmetrically between them used either for vegetables, or for patterns made with coloured earths or gravels; or possibly for some flowers.

Again, when the Montmorency family rebuilt Chantilly at this same period they virtually stood the château in formal lakes, leaving very little room for anything else but some small parterres, a grotto, an aviary, a little pavilion or casino on an island in the principal lake; and a 'Real' Tennis court, a feature which was becoming fashionable in both the French and English gardens of the nobility. So here too water dominated the plan, used in a manner which clearly derives

124 *De Bry's garden, 1612, with raised beds in formal arrangement and sparse planting.*

from the medieval. This was to remain a feature of French gardens into the high Renaissance.

In England gardening remained very backward. From the mid to the late fifteenth century social conditions could hardly have been more unfavourable to an art which demands peace, plenty and time. Marauding armies and bands of political ruffians looting and wrecking are not exactly helpful to the work of the garden architect and gardener. A change came with the accession of Henry VII and the success of his peace-keeping, money-accumulating policy. The great men of the day, such as Wolsey, Colet and More, had the taste and inclination to patronize artists, including garden-artists. But to an even greater extent than in France the notions of the Middle Ages persisted, and the new Italian ideas, in any case slower to reach England, were not quickly or readily adopted. When Edward Stafford, third Duke of Buckingham, began to build Thornbury Castle in 1511, he included gardens in his plan. The one on the north side of the inner ward was overlooked by a gallery giving access to it, in the manner then fashionable in North Italy and Germany. It was enclosed in high walls, two of which were lined by a gallery to make a simplified peristyle. It was about forty yards square, and almost certainly laid out as a knot garden about a central fountain.*

'..."On the east side of the castle [that is, of the main mass of buildings] is a large and goodly garden to walk in, closed with high walls imbattled. The conveyance thither is by the gallery above and beneath, and by other privy ways." Along-

* See Hadfield (1960), as also for the following passage which he quotes in modernized English from the Royal Commission report on the Castle to the Crown in 1522 following Buckingham's execution for treason.

125

side this "is a large and goodly orchard, full of newly grafted fruit trees well laden with fruit, many roses and other pleasures; and in the same orchard are many goodly alleys to walk in openly. And round about the same orchard, covered in at a good height, are other goodly alleys with resting-places covered thoroughly with whitethorn and hazel; outside these alleys, the outer part of the orchard is enclosed with sawn palings, beyond which are ditches and quickset hedges." Then, beyond these ditches and hedges, and to the north and east of the buildings, lay the park newly taken-in by Buckingham, with "no great plenty of wood, but many hedgerows of thorn and great elms".'

Another garden-maker of the period was Cardinal Wolsey, whose taste for the Italian arts made him more likely to introduce into England the styles which Charles VIII and his successors brought into France. Yet even so his knot garden

at Hampton Court seems to have been very like Buckingham's at Thornbury. Sir Thomas More, Henry's favourite after Wolsey's disgrace, made a famous garden at Chelsea, of which we know nothing but that it was, by repute, full of lovely flowers and fine fruit trees, with a splendid view over the Thames; and that there rosemary was first grown in England. In reality rosemary had probably been grown in England since Saxon times. (We know nothing of Saxon gardens, but such Saxon nobles as the Godwinssons were much more civilized than their Norman conquerors and loved to build great houses and found monasteries.) In that fine film of More's life, *A Man for All Seasons*, King Henry VIII is shown admiring More's lilacs in the latter's Chelsea garden, and comparing them with his own in the royal gardens; but this was an anachronism, since lilacs were not introduced

106

126

127

125 *Spring garden of Crispin de Pass; 1614.*

126 *Garden with raised bed kept up by boards; 1542.*

127 *Garden showing the gateway of an 'Elizabethan Herb Garden'.*

128 *Arbour (about 1600) with an outdoor revel in progress. In the background, a man being chased away, his money having been spent.*

128

until half a century later. More's garden was laid out in regular, rectangular beds, his fruit trees were trained against walls, and there was at least one small summer house.

If a great man had so simple a garden, we can take it that other people's gardens, in so far as they had any, were even simpler, with the same vegetables and salads, and the same few herbs and flowers as had been grown during the past century. The time for England to become Europe's master in gardening was still a long way in the future.

The new Italian gardening reached Germany by means of such travelling, scholarly noblemen as Duke Eberhard of Württemberg, who was much impressed by Lorenzo de, Medici's Florentine garden when he visited it. But perhaps

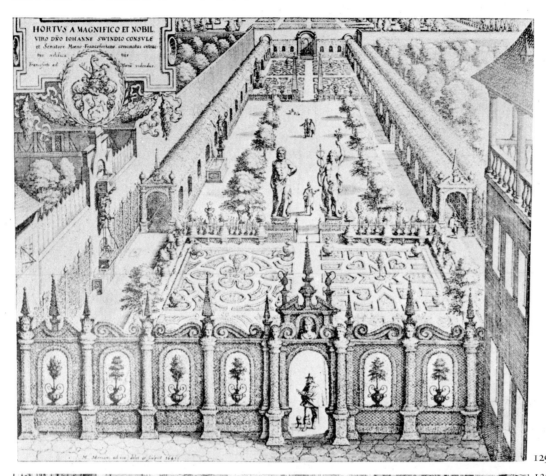

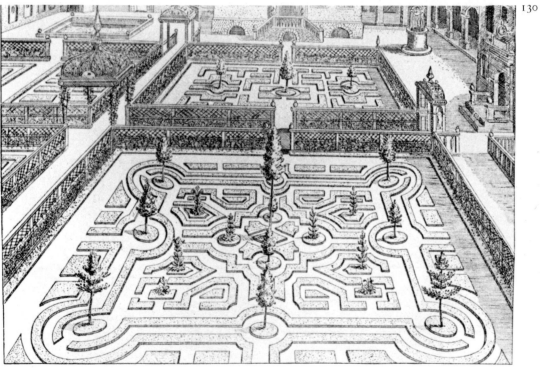

129

130

131

129 *Matthias Merian, Florilegium et Auctum (Frankfurt, 1641). Formal garden.*

130 *Place unknown. Date c. 1650.*

131 *Castle garden, Heidelberg, from an engraving of 1620.*

even more influential carriers of the new ideas were scholars of the burgess class, such as Henricus Cordus who, after taking a degree in medicine at the University of Ferrara, laid out a garden at Erfurt in 1525 and another in Marburg when he went there five years later to be that city's Professor of Medicine. Medicine and botany, then and later, went together, and indeed the gardens laid out by Cordus and his son, and by the great botanist Conrad Gesner and their like, were really physic gardens. They foreran the kind of botanic gardens which the Italians took the lead in planting in the mid sixteenth century (see chapter 9). True, such gardens were also for recreation. In the Netherlands, for example, Erasmus was probably describing rather than merely imagining when, in his *Convivium Religiosum*, he has the guests strolling before dinner in a well kept garden of which he says:

109

132

132 *Choir of Angels in Adoration by Benozzo Gozzoli.*

133 *A very late instance, at the end of the seventeenth century, of the sparse planting of the Middle Ages.*

134 *Garden with wattle fence, a fountain, a tree, and a few plants. From Boccaccio,* Decameron, *1509 edition.*

'This place is dedicated to the honourable pleasures of rejoicing the eye, refreshing the nose and renewing the spirit'.

Sweet-scented herbs were the principal plants of such gardens, set in regular order, each one labelled with its name and virtues. Erasmus's garden has also a kitchen garden, two summer houses, and a brook which divides the garden into two halves and drains into the decorated stucco basin. And once again there was a gallery, part of the house, from which the sight and scents of the garden could be enjoyed.

Because of the great wealth and importance of such cities as Augsburg, Germany had urban gardens before any other country in Europe except Italy. Certainly the first really grand garden in Germany was the one made by the Fuggers, the great medieval banking family, in Augsburg. A garden which could rouse the admiration and envy of the Emperor Charles v must have been remarkable; he visited it in 1439. It was apparently very large, and perfectly rectangular. It became larger and larger until the citizens of Augsburg complained that it was seriously encroaching on the people's *Lebensraum*. Laid out on the usual strictly geometrical plan, it was more remarkable for size than for originality. But the Germans and the Dutch were forward in the introduction of new plants to horticulture. The claim made for Clusius (*see* chapter 9) that he first introduced and flowered oriental tulips in Europe may be challenged by that of Councillor Johann Heinrich Herward of Augsburg, who flowered his tulips from Constantinople in 1559. Nor was Augsburg the only city distinguished by burgess gardens. Both Nuremburg and Frankfurt were famous as early as 1530, for gardens of the kind described by Erasmus.

As it happens we have a list of the kinds of gardens which were to be seen in Germany by the mid sixteenth century. I am leaving out of account the great Renaissance gardens, although the periods overlap, because they will be dealt with in chapter 9. The list was made by Gesner a year after he had travelled to Augsburg to see Councillor Herward's tulips so that he could include a woodcut of them in his *De Hortis Germaniae*. The list is as follows:

1. Ordinary gardens for the household, with vegetables, vines, orchard and grass for the nourishment of man and beast.
2. Medicinal gardens, containing in addition to these things various healing plants both foreign and native.

133

3. Miscellaneous gardens with not only healing herbs but also peculiar plants that attract attention and admiration.

4. Elegant gardens meant only for ornament, with arbours, pleasure-houses, and places to stroll about in, with fine evergreen trees and all the various designs which can be made by curving and weaving the branches. Such are the gardens of wealthy ladies and all wealthy people, especially monks.

5. Show gardens such as learned men or princes or the state itself may possess, with splendid buildings, ponds and waterworks, artificial mounds, squares for tournaments and for tennis.

It was in this last class that Austria was to excel. One might have expected imperial power to be forward in gardening, and it was indeed to become so. It is true that Clusius was laying out a physic garden for the Hapsburgs in Vienna in 1537, but it was no more than that. Doubtless Austria did have the same sort of gardens as were to be found in the other German states, but it was not until the Archduke

Ferdinand set the example of making a grand garden at Innsbruck in 1564 that Austria began to make her great contribution to the art. That story belongs to chapter 9.

134

PRE-COLUMBIAN GARDENING IN AMERICA

8

Owing to the destructiveness of the sixteenth-century Spanish conquerors of Central and South America, our knowledge of gardening in the two high civilizations which were native to the Americas is much less than it should be. However, we do know enough to make a chapter on the subject necessary in any history of gardening; the more so in that both the southern and central zones of civilized living contributed very substantially to the horticultural as well as the agricultural flora of the whole world. Maize and potatoes are field crops, yet both are grown in our gardens on an enormous scale; most of our beans, of the haricot kind, are American. Chocolate and tobacco are plantation, rather than garden, crops, although both are extensively grown in sub-tropical and tropical gardens; while pawpaw is to be seen now in every small garden of the tropical and sub-tropical zones. As to flowers, there is more difficulty in knowing which ones were grown in Inca and Aztec gardens, but we can, as will appear, name some with a measure of assurance.

America was peopled from Asia, probably in a series of waves of migration, the earliest being about 35,000 years ago in the Palaeolithic epoch. Either independently of the Old World, or stimulated by a much later migration from Asia, the Americans evolved a Neolithic culture. Towards the end of it, they invented or adopted agriculture and, in the Andes, stock-raising. As far as we know, their first essays in cultivating food plants instead of gathering them in the wild, and in herding instead of hunting the llama, began later than the similar movements in the Old World. Moreover, they developed differently: in the Central American zone there were no animals suitable for domestication comparable with the sheep or cattle, camels or horses of the Old World, so the civilizations from Mayan to Aztec were based wholly on plant husbandry, including horticulture. In the Andes the llama, guanaco and vicuña were first hunted; then the llama was domesticated; but even there animal husbandry for the provision of food was much less important than for the provision of wool and porterage. Plant husbandry was the real staple occupation, and consequently horticulture was developed.

At the time when the Spaniards arrived to destroy the great empires of the Incas in ancient Peru, and of the Aztecs in Central America, the most advanced American civilizations were, technically, emerging from the Chalcolithic epoch into the Bronze Age. This means, roughly, that they were still using many Neolithic-type tools and weapons of flint or some other stone; that copper was the most important technological metal; but that some bronze was being used. Gold and silver were fairly common and much used; it is

February

April

March

said that in some royal Inca buildings stone was bonded to stone with molten gold. Most of the horticultural and agricultural tools were still of stone or more commonly wood — e.g. the digging-sticks, hoes, etc. — although the shapes were sophisticated. The Americans had no plough and no wheel, and, in the central zone, no draught animals.

Pre-Columbian Peru was a vast empire extending 2,700 miles from north to south on the west coast of South America, composed of a number of ancient, and anciently civilized, formerly independent nations, and some new, still barbarous territory. It included all modern Chile and perhaps a bit of Argentina, all modern Peru, Bolivia, Colombia and Ecuador. It was ruled by the Incas, originally a mountain tribe from Cuzco, by means of an elaborate and very efficient civil service or bureaucracy whose members were nearly all of the Inca *ayllu* or clan and whose chief was the Sapa Inca, which means Unique Inca. The system was communist; there was no private property, nobody could own land, everything belonged to the people in common, embodied in the State. There was no poverty but there was privilege, since the royal, noble and high bureaucratic sections of the Inca *ayllu* were better housed, clad and fed than the common people. But the latter had a very effective, benevolent and efficient welfare state and were in no sense slaves or ill-treated or ill-provided for.

This (as it were) Divine Communism — for the Sapa Inca was a god — was based on an advanced and, by the fifteenth century, ancient system of agriculture and horticulture of a very special kind. The aridity of the narrow coastal strip of the central parts of the empire had forced the pre-Inca peoples to develop an elaborate system of irrigation; the system was perfected in early Inca times, and constantly improved. It entailed bringing water in stone channels, and distributing it in smaller channels, from the Andes foothills, down to the coast. Many of the channels are still in working order. It also entailed the greatest system of terracing the world has ever known, for as the population increased the small fertile side-valleys of the foothills did not allow enough room for adequate food production. Hundreds of miles, perhaps thousands of miles, of terraces were built on the west face of the mountains to an extraordinary altitude, with the hardier crops cultivated at the top, the tender ones in the warm levels below. The Inca farmers and their bureaucratic masters were the only people in the world until modern times to eliminate famine by adequate stock-piling and proper accountancy.

Andean horticulture began about 2500 BC. Techniques remained essentially horticultural rather than agricultural into the sixteenth century, if only because, for want of the plough, land was tilled by teams using digging-sticks and hoes.

114

May

July

June

Maize in some primitive form, probably a pod-corn, was the first crop; the potato was early important at high altitudes, and gradually came down to the plains. From analysis of material in the middens of what are called the Early Farmer cultures, we know that prehistoric Andean gardeners cultivated several kinds of gourds, squashes and beans, potatoes and other esculent roots. At a very early date they domesticated wild cotton (*Gossypium hirsutum* and *G. purpurascens*), but that can hardly be called a garden crop.

The earliest terracing and irrigation is in the so-called Cultist (Chalcolithic) period between 500 BC and the beginning of our era. To that period belongs also the domestication of a very important plant, *Coca*, which the ancient Andeans chewed with lime, as a stimulant, and which the Inca bureaucracy rationed very carefully in their day, so that only workers who needed it got it. It is, of course, the source of cocaine. We also know that to this period belonged the invention or discovery of the important horticultural technique of propagation by cuttings, since among the garden crops were certain sterile cucurbitaceous plants which could not have been propagated in any other way. The following 'Mastercraftsmen' and 'Classic' epochs (the names are those used by palaeontologists) were richer in horticultural developments. By 250 BC all, or almost all, the crops which the Spaniards found in cultivation when they arrived were

135-141 *Part of an Inca calendar.*

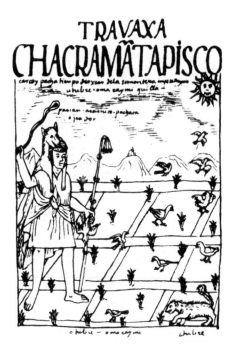

August *September* *October*

142-146 *Part of an Inca calendar.*

already in use. Not only had the potato been brought into gardens, but so, remarkably, had the pineapple, which must have reached the Andeans from Mexico, although the two great peoples seem to have known nothing of each other's civilizations. Two other exotics from remote sources had also reached the Andes and were being cultivated in gardens: the pawpaw and the sweet potato.

In the City Builder period which followed, horticulture, as well as agriculture, must have advanced and expanded greatly to support the huge populations of such cities as Chan-Chan, capital of the great pre-Inca state of Chimu, which covered eleven square miles of territory, far bigger than any European city of that time. There were probably market gardens within the cities as well as on the outskirts. Whether these cities also had pleasure gardens we simply do not know; but so advanced were the people in such arts as weaving and dyeing, ceramics — some of the most beautiful the world has ever known — and goldsmith's work, that it seems likely they would have embellished their cities with some kind of parks, and would have grown some flowers.

Some of the Sapa Incas, but notably one *qoya*, that is queen, were patrons of gardening. Chimpu Urina was the chief *qoya* of the Sapa Inca Mayta Capac and also, as was customary, his sister. She:

116

November   *December*

'seems to have been an outstanding woman, a zoologist, naturalist and inventor. She maintained a large menagerie of animals... she took an active controlling part in managing the women workers on the royal estates, telling them when and what to sow. She introduced several new plants to horticulture...'

Thus the chronicler Sarmiento, who also says that this lady made a thorough investigation of vegetable poisons for use as arrow-poisons in hunting and war.

At least two other *qoyas* took an active interest in gardening developments. Women had a disposition for the craft trained into them, for under the Inca system, although children of the one to nine age group, known as Playing Children, were given only the lightest of domestic tasks, after that they had, like everyone else, to make some small contribution to the imperial economy. Girls from nine to twelve years of age were responsible for the gathering of the flowers and herbs from which dyes for their incomparable cotton fabrics and drugs for their medicine were extracted. From twelve to sixteen, they had to weed gardens.*

The Incas and their associate peoples in the imperial communist state were certainly aware of flowers as such, and not simply as raw materials. This is manifest in some of the few fragments of their poetry, and of their various liturgies, which have survived. When the old Sapa Inca Pachacuti † knew that his death was near upon him, he composed a sad little poem and sang it:

> 'I was born as a flower of the field.
> As a flower I was cherished in my youth.
> I came to my full age, I grew old,
> Now I am withered and die.'

The Sapa Inca Pachacuti, great prince and poet, has been called by the historians and Americanists who know his work, the greatest man of the native American race who ever lived. But it was probably during the reign of his equally remarkable and brilliantly able son Topa Yupanqui that the arts, including the art of gardens, reached a zenith of sophistication, if not of the exquisite taste that had distinguished Chimu in the past. What do we actually know about such gardens? Many of the Spaniards who saw them rave about their wonders but tell us remarkably little about what those wonders were. We know that royal palaces and the great houses of the high officials were always set in gardens. The Incas had the same taste as the Islamic Persians (and after them the Mongol khans) for artificial trees, shrubs and even

---

* The authority for this and much else in these passages is Poma de Ayala (1580).

† Sarmiento says he was 120. He was certainly very old.

birds and animals, made of gold, silver and precious stones, but with the difference that in the Inca gardens these works of art were 'planted' among the real, living ones, the artists' models. Owing to the insatiable greed of the ruffian Pizarro and his officers, who tricked the last Sapa Inca Atahualpa into their hands, most of these gold plants were melted down; but a few reached Spain as a gift to the Crown, and their workmanship was there pronouced superior to anything Europe could show at the time. Flowering shrubs planted in Inca gardens almost certainly included the ones for which Quichua names survive (Quichua was the official language of the empire, the 'Latin' of ancient Peru). They include *Berberis darwinii*, the crinodendrons, eucryphias, embothriums. *Schinus molle* was used as a garden tree, possibly also as a street tree, as it still is even in California. Other, probably garden, shrubs were fuchsia and the Chilean myrtles (*M. luma* and possibly one other). I shall have a little to say about herbaceous plants below.

The Inca gardens included a number of exotics among the fruit plants. We know that they had the avocado pear (*Persea*), the chirimoya and the pineapple, all from Central America. These may not have been introduced until after the last of the imperial conquests, when Topa Yupanqui annexed what is now Ecuador, chiefly for its emerald mines. Capsicums were both ornamental and useful. *Solanum muricatum* provided the fruit called *cachun* in Quichua, *pepino* in Spanish. *Solanum quitoense* was grown for the fruit drink squeezed from its fruits. The absurdly named 'Cape Gooseberries' (*Physalis ixocarpa* and *P. peruviana*) were garden grown. Very important for its tubers was the lovely *Tropaelium tuberosum*: rightly or wrongly (I have never tried them), Inca physicians believed these tubers to be anti-aphrodisiac, and they were issued to the troops on campaign to solve a problem which in other times, including our own, has usually been solved by rape. Other drug plants in gardens were sources of belladonna, mandragora and henbane — this is what the Spanish called them, but they were presumably South American congeners of the plants in question. *Genipa americana* was grown in gardens for its fruit, from which a kind of wine was made; and in fields for the dye extracted from the fruit. The *Opuntia* cacti were cultivated as fodder for the cochineal insect, but perhaps not in gardens. *Jatropa* species, and *Justicia pectoralis* were grown as aphrodisiacs; *Stenomessum varietum* as a contraceptive.* There is good evidence that both

* A possible reason for the importance of contraceptives in the empire was that sexual relations between a woman of the Inca upper crust and a commoner was a capital offence in law. An effective contraceptive might help to avoid discovery.

Datura and *Thevetia* species were grown in gardens; is it possible that they provided the Inca surgeons with anaesthetics? *Sapullu*, gourds, were garden plants, and two kinds of guava; also something called *Ussu* and described as 'a kind of cherry' which I have not identified. Our own large-fruited strawberries derive from a Chilean species (*Fragaria chiloense*) and it seems likely that the Andeans grew them.

The Spanish and native historians and chroniclers are even more sparing in their accounts of Inca gardens than they are of the Mexican Aztec gardens to which we shall come presently. There is a passage in Prescott's *History of the Conquest of Peru* which is soundly based on the authority of the half-Inca historian Garcilaso de la Vega 'the Inca':

'But the favourite residence of the Incas was at Yucay, about four leagues distant from the capital. In this delicious valley, locked up within the friendly arms of the sierra, which sheltered it from the rude breezes from the east, and refreshed by gushing fountains and streams of running water, they built the most beautiful of their palaces. Here, when wearied with the dust and toil of the city, they loved to retreat and solace themselves with the society of their favourite concubines, wandering amidst groves and airy gardens, that shed around their soft, intoxicating odours, and lulled the senses to voluptuous repose. Here, too, they loved to indulge in the luxury of their baths, replenished by streams of crystal water which were conducted through subterraneous silver channels into basins of gold. The spacious gardens were stocked with numerous varieties of plants and flowers that grew without effort in this *temperate* region of the tropics, while parterres of a more extraordinary kind were planted by their side, glowing with the various forms of vegetable life skilfully imitated with gold and silver! Among them the Indian corn, the most beautiful of American grains, is particularly commemorated, and the curious workmanship is noticed with which the golden ear was half disclosed amidst the broad leaves of silver and the light tassel of the same material that floated gracefully from its top.'

The conditions of soil and climate in Anahuac, which we call Mexico, were very different from those which shaped the horticultural techniques of the Andean peoples. Neither terracing nor irrigation were necessary in the Valley of Mexico, with its string of five lakes around, and in which the Aztec cities were built. The ancient Mexicans lived a sort of half-aquatic life. The great capital city of Tenochtitlan, like other cities, was half built on piles out into the lake, so that as it grew it became a city with as many canals as streets, a sort of Venice.

The Aztec people, builders of this city and masters of a vast empire at the time when Cortés and his Conquistadors arrived among them to destroy what they had made, were not the inventors of the agriculture and horticulture which supported their economy. They inherited them at several removes and after thousands of years from the people who first made the move from a hunting, fishing and food gathering economy to horticulture and agriculture, and who became the Maya, one of mankind's great innovating races: master builders and mathematicians and astronomers of genius. But the Aztecs made excellent use of their cultural heritage, and in the matter of gardens they became some of the most inventive and successful horticulturists in the history of this art and science. Of the Aztec horticulture, Prescott had this to say:*

'It would obviously be out of place to enumerate in these pages all the varieties of plants, many of them of medicinal virtue, which have been introduced from Mexico into Europe. Still less can I attempt a catalogue of its flowers which, with their variegated and gaudy colours, form the greatest attraction of our greenhouses. The opposite climates embraced within the narrow latitudes of New Spain have given it probably the richest and most diversified flora to be found in any country of the globe. These different products were systematically arranged by the Aztecs, who understood their properties and collected them into nurseries more extensive than any then existing in the Old World. It is not improbable that they suggested those "gardens of plants" which were introduced into Europe not many years after the conquest.'

We know too little of Aztec social history to be able to follow the development of gardening. All we can do is to convey some idea of what the gardens were like at their zenith before the Spaniards lost, by neglect, what they had not destroyed by violence. Fortunately we have brief accounts written by people, including Cortés himself, who actually saw these gardens.

First there were the urban gardens. To put them in context, here is Cortés's own description of what Tenochtitlan was like:

'The principal streets are very wide and very straight. Some of these, and all the smaller streets, are made as to one half of earth, while the other is a canal by which the Indians travel in boats. And all these streets, from one end of the town to the other, are opened in such a way that water can completely cross them. All these openings, and some of them are very wide, are spanned by bridges made of very solid and well-worked beams, so that across many of them ten horsemen can ride abreast.'†

* In *The Conquest of Mexico*.
† Soustelle (1964).

The anthropologist Jacques Soustelle (1964), says that the majority of the houses, with windowless façades hiding a private life led in the courtyard gardens, must have been like an Arab town except that they were built along straight roads and canals. But the townscape was not dreary or monotonous. The crowded flat roofs, each with its roof-garden, were relieved by the towering pyramid of a temple here and there, and some of the streets were devoted, as in European and Oriental cities of the time, to particular trades — goldsmiths, feather-workers, jewellers. Others were filled with the warehouses of the merchants, who had such an honourable place in Aztec society. Nor was the city one of solid masonry standing in water, for apart from some vast public squares, there were still mixed flower and vegetable gardens round the simple peasant huts, built of reeds and thatched, which had been absorbed into the city as it grew.

We shall have occasion to mention these urban courtyard and roof gardens again, for they made a great impression on the Spaniards. But the real glory of the Aztec gardeners was the gardens surrounding the palaces of great men. The Aztec historian Ixtlilxochitl, in his *Historia Chichimeca*, describes the gardens of King Nezaualcoyotl of Texcoco, a nation independent of, and as advanced as, the Aztec Empire. It had, he says, many fountains, ponds and canals, many fish and birds, and the whole planted with more than two thousand pines...

'...and there were several mazes according to where the king bathed; and once a man was in he could not find the way out... and further on besides the temples there was the bird-house, where the king kept all the kinds and varieties of birds, animals and reptiles and serpents that they brought him from every part of New Spain. And those which were not to be had were represented in gold and precious stones — which was also the case with the fish, both those of the sea and those that lived in the rivers and lakes. So no bird, fish, or animals of the whole country was wanting here; they were there either alive or figured in gold and gems.'

That was the capital, Texcoco; in another city, Tetzcotzinco, the same king had more gardens, of which Ixtlilxochitl says:

'These parks and gardens were decorated with rich and sumptuously ornamented summer-houses with their fountains, their irrigation channels, their canals, their lakes, and their bathing places and wonderful mazes, where he had a great variety of flowers planted and trees of all kinds, foreign and brought from distant parts... and the water intended for the fountains, pools and channels for watering the flowers and the trees in this park came from its spring: to bring it, it had been necessary to build strong, high cemented walls

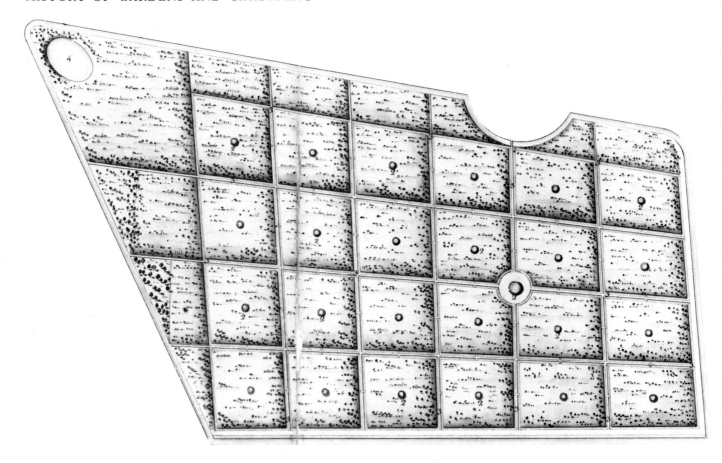

of unbelievable size, going from one mountain to another, with an aqueduct at the top which came out at the highest part of the park.'

This aqueduct supplied the water to a reservoir tank which had been embellished with historical bas-reliefs, and was barbarously smashed up by a friar called Juan de Zumarraga who became first bishop of Mexico. He was under the impression that the historical figures were idols. From the tank the water was carried by two channels, one flowing north and the other south, and these filled basins where sculptural steles were reflected in the surface of the water. From those basins, says Ixtlilxochitl, the water:

'...leapt and dashed itself to pieces on the rocks, falling into a garden planted with all the scented flowers of the Hot Lands, and in this garden it seemed to rain, so very violently was the water shattered upon these rocks. Beyond this garden were the bathing-places, cut in the living rock... and beyond them the castle that the king had in this park and in which still other rooms and halls were seen, and many of them; one was a very large hall with a court in front of it, and it was there that he received the kings of Mexico and Tlacopan

and other great lords when they came to enjoy themselves with him: the dances and the other spectacles and delights took place in this court... The whole of the rest of this park was planted, as I have said, with all kinds of trees and scented flowers, and there were all kinds of birds apart from those that the king had brought from various parts in cages: all these birds sang harmoniously and to such degree that one could not hear oneself speak. Outside the gardens and beyond a wall the country began, full of deer, rabbits and hares.'*

While we cannot be certain that the Aztec writer, himself a member of the Texcoco royal family, did not exaggerate, there is proof of his description still in reservoirs, aqueduct, steps, terraces — the parts of this great garden too massive for Spaniards or time to destroy. Perhaps even some of the Spaniards were ashamed of the vandalism, for the old soldier-chronicler wrote many years later, on a note of what sounds like remorseful sadness, 'Ahora todo está el suelo perdido, que no hay cosa'. — 'All that is now fallen, not a thing is now left'.

* The Spanish translator is responsible for the rabbits and hares. The animals in question were presumably native rodents.

The Aztec emperors and nobles could do things on a grand scale, but every small house had a garden of some kind. The lakeside suburb of Xochimilco, part of a conurbation whose population Soustelle estimates at about 700,000, was one vast market flower-garden supplying the city markets with cut flowers, and, possibly, seedlings and rooted cuttings for planting in the urban roof-gardens, courtyard gardens and terraced gardens which were the admiration of the Spaniards. But the first of the really grand gardens to astound the conquerors were those of Iztapalapan.

This was a royal residence which stood on a peninsula separating the lake called Chalco from the lake called, like the city, Tezcuco. At the time of Cortés's arrival the royal city had a population of between 12,000 and 15,000 households, by Cortés's own estimate, which is confirmed in the memoirs of Bernal Diaz. The city was governed by Moctezuma's brother Cuitlahua, whose palace was built of stone and roofed with 'cedar' (Mexico is rich in fine conifers but has no true cedar). The walls of its rooms were hung with painted cotton tapestries. Cortés describes the place as equal to anything Spain could show. Prescott, drawing on both Cortés and Bernal Diaz, says:

147 *Plan of the first Botanic Garden in North America: Chapultepec.*

The Aztecs and kindred peoples had a passion for flowers which far exceeded that of the Incas; the greater part of their lyric poetry was in praise, and sometimes almost in adoration, of flowers. When Moctezuma I, ancestor of the emperor who was betrayed and murdered by Cortés, had conquered the *tierra caliente* to the west of his dominions, so adding a tropical province to the empire, one of his first public acts was to found a botanic garden in which the plants of this new province and of all his other tropical provinces were to be grown and tended. There can be no doubt whatever that this botanic garden was the first of its kind in the world.* Imperial messengers who were plant collectors were sent to all the tropical parts of the empire to have flowering shrubs and trees dug up, their rootball wrapped in matting and transported back to Oaxtepec where the garden was being planted. Forty gardeners from various parts of the empire were moved, with their families, to Oaxtepec to care for the emperor's new garden, and Moctezuma himself 'opened' it at a special ceremony.

* The source for this and what follows is another Aztec writer, Tezozomoc (1853), vol. I, pp. 211-12.

'But the pride of Iztapalan, on which its lord had freely lavished his care and his revenues, was its celebrated gardens. They covered an immense tract of land; were laid out in regular squares, and the paths intersecting them were bordered with trellises, supporting creepers and aromatic shrubs that loaded the air with their perfumes. The gardens were stocked with fruit trees, imported from distant places, and with the gaudy family of flowers which belonged to the Mexican flora, scientifically arranged, and growing luxuriously in the equable temperature of the table-land. The natural dryness of the atmosphere was counteracted by means of aqueducts and canals that carried water into all parts of the grounds.
'In one quarter was an aviary, filled with numerous kinds of birds, remarkable in this region for brilliancy of plumage and of song. The gardens were intersected by a canal communicating with the lake of Tezuco, and of sufficient size for barges to enter from the latter. But the most elaborate piece of work was a huge reservoir of stone, filled to a considerable height with water well supplied with different sorts of fish. This basin was sixteen hundred paces in circumference, and was surrounded by a walk, made also of stone, wide enough for four persons to go abreast. The sides were curiously sculptured, and a flight of steps led to the water below, which fed the aqueducts above noticed, or, collected into fountains, diffused a perpetual moisture.
'Such are the accounts transmitted of these celebrated gardens, at a period when similar horticultural establishments were unknown in Europe; and we might well doubt their

existence in this semi-civilized land, were it not a matter of such notoriety at the time and so explicitly attested by the invaders.'

Next, from the same and some additional sources, we have an account of Moctezuma's remarkable zoological gardens of his palace in Tenochtitlan itself, and of the flower gardens adjoining, where, says Soustelle (1964),* 'The rarest flowers from all the regions had been planted in the gardens, and medicinal herbs; and there were great sheets of water with ducks, swans and egrets.'

Unlike the great men of the Old World, the Aztecs would not allow fruit trees in their pleasure gardens. Moctezuma, according to the memorialist Francisco Lopez de Gomara, and also to Toribio, considered them unsuitable in such gardens. Prescott describes the palace gardens as follows:

'Extensive gardens were spread out around these buildings, filled with fragrant shrubs and flowers, and especially with medicinal plants. No country has afforded more numerous species of these last than New Spain; and their virtues were perfectly understood by the Aztecs, with whom medical botany may be said to have been studied as a science. Amidst this labyrinth of sweet-scented groves and shrubberies, fountains of pure water might be seen throwing up their sparkling jets and scattering refreshing dews over the blossoms. Ten large tanks, well stocked with fish, afforded a retreat on their margins to various tribes of water-fowl, whose habits were so carefully consulted that some of these ponds were of salt water, as that which they most loved to frequent. A tessellated pavement of marble enclosed the ample basins, which were overhung by light and fanciful pavilions, that admitted the perfumed breezes of the gardens, and offered a grateful shelter to the monarch and his mistresses in the sultry heats of summer.

'But the most luxurious residence of the Aztec monarch, at that season, was the royal hill of Chapoltepec, — a spot consecrated, moreover, by the ashes of his ancestors. It stood in a westerly direction from the capital and its base was, in his day, washed by the waters of the Tezcuco. On its lofty crest of porphyritic rock there now stands the magnificent, though desolate, castle erected by the young viceroy Galvez at the close of the seventeenth century. The view from its windows is one of the finest in the environs of Mexico. The landscape is not disfigured here, as in many other quarters, by the white and barren patches so offensive to the sight; but the eye wanders over an unbroken expanse of meadows and cultivated fields, waving with rich harvests of European grain. Montezuma's gardens stretched for miles around the base of the hill. Two statues of that monarch and his father, cut in bas-relief in the porphyry, were spared till the middle

of the last century; and the grounds are still shaded by gigantic cypresses, more than 50 feet in circumference, which were centuries old at the time of the Conquest. The place is now a tangled wilderness of wild shrubs, where the myrtle mingles its dark, glossy leaves with the red berries and delicate foliage of the pepper-tree. Surely there is no spot better suited to awaken meditation on the past; none where the traveller, as he sits under those stately cypresses grey with the moss of ages, can so fitly ponder on the sad destinies of the Indian races and the monarch who once held his courtly revels under the shadow of their branches.'

A city equal to those of the Aztecs in culture, and its rival in politics, Tezcuco long kept its independence. There, too, were some very grand gardens. But the only other one of which we have an actual description was in Chalco on the lake of that name, where Cortés's lieutenant Sandoval, with Tezcucan allies, fought a major battle against Moctezuma's generals. After taking the city, Sandoval set up his headquarters in the Governor's palace, which was:

'...surrounded by gardens which rivalled those of Iztapalapan in magnificence and surpassed them in extent. They are said to have been two leagues in circumference, having pleasure-houses, and numerous tanks stocked with various kinds of fish; and they were embellished with trees, shrubs and plants, native and exotic, some selected for their beauty and fragrance, others for their medicinal properties. They were scientifically arranged; and the whole establishment displayed a degree of horticultural taste and knowledge of which it would not have been easy to find a counterpart, at that day, in the more civilized communities of Europe. Such is the testimony not only of the rude Conquerors, but of men of science, who visited these beautiful repositories in the day of their glory.'

Here again we have Cortés's own word for it that the gardens were indeed remarkable. Visiting them at a later date, he wrote:

'...gardens are the largest, freshest and most beautiful that were ever seen. They have a circuit of two leagues [six miles] and through the middle flows a pleasant stream of water. At distances of two bow-shots are buildings surrounded by grounds planted with fruit trees of various kinds, with many shrubs and odorous flowers. Truly the whole place is wonderful for its pleasantness and its extent.'*

A difficulty with all the descriptions quoted above is that we are not told how these gardens were laid out and on what plan. But if we consider the style and feeling of the pre-Columbian Mexican art in general, from Maya to Aztec;

---

* The sources are Cortés and Diaz; also Toribio in *Historia de los Indios*, in MS.

* Soustelle (1964).

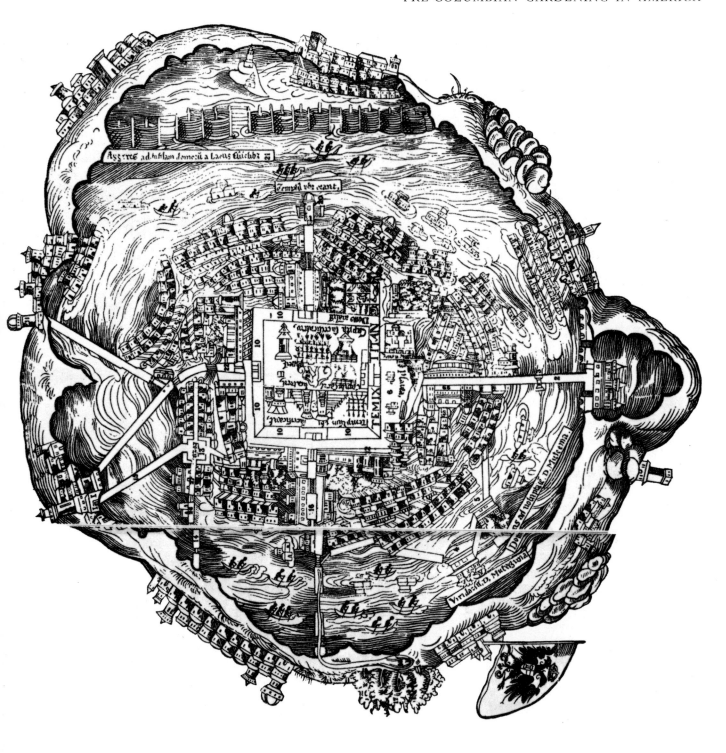

148 *Map of Tenochtitlán, 1519.*

and if we study the implications of the magnificent Museum of Anthropology in Mexico City with this problem in mind; and if we consider what remarkable mathematicians the Maya and their successors were; and take into account the implications of their building styles — then we can, I think, safely conclude that the Aztec gardens must have been on a rectangular and geometrical plan. There is one more item of circumstantial evidence in support of this hypothesis: I doubt whether Spaniards would have been so impressed and delighted with gardens which were anything but regular; their own taste would have rejected wild or disorderly gardens as evidence of barbarism.

We have a small amount of information about smaller, urban gardens in Tenochtitlan. Cortés and others who wrote accounts of their impressions on first entering that city were clearly deeply impressed by the residences of the Aztec nobility, which lined both sides of the great avenue from the end of the causeway, on which they were to fight one of the most extraordinary retreats in history, and which connected the lake-shore with the city. The houses were built of a porous red stone, easy to quarry and dress, and were one or two storeys in height, with flat roofs. These roofs Cortés describes as like parterres, so thickly were they planted with flowers. The terrace gardens, or what some of the writers describe as 'hanging' gardens, were between the houses. Gian Battista Ramusio, in his *Relacion del gentilhuomo*, says: '...e giardini alti e bassi che era cosa maravigliosa da vedere' — 'and gardens high and low which were a marvel to see'.

One thing emerges very clearly: unlike most of the gardening peoples with whom we have dealt till now, a principal object of the Aztecs was to grow flowers in profusion. Yet they were not the only garden subjects which mattered, even if fruit trees were, as a rule, banished to the kitchen garden. Here, to give some idea of the Aztecs' horticultural wealth, is a list of specifically kitchen-garden crops which were, during the century following the Conquest, introduced to Old World horticulture:

Beans, *Phaseolus*: four species and many cultivars. (These are our 'Scarlet Runners'/'French beans'.)
Gourds, melons and cucumbers, *Cucurbitaceae et alia*: six species or cultivars.
Sweet potato.
Arrowroot.
Capsicum, sweet peppers: two species and some cultivars.

Opuntia, prickly pear: several species.
Anona, pineapple: seven species or cultivars.
Carica, pawpaw: two species.
Persea, avocado: two species (?cultivars).
Psidium, guava: two cultivars, perhaps species.
Anacardium, cashew: one species.
Lycopersicum, tomato: many cultivars.
Physalis, 'Cape Gooseberry': two species.

This leaves flowers out of account (see below) and, of course, such agricultural crops as maize and such plantation crops as chocolate. The most important of the many Mexican drug-plants was probably the *Cereus* which yields mescalin, but it is not clear that this cactus was ever cultivated, and the withered flowers which were chewed may have been collected in the wild.

In addition to the kinds of gardening which were familiar in the Old World as well as the New, pre-Columbian Mexico had a kind of gardening which was, perhaps, unique: *chinapas* were floating gardens. The spectacle of these on the lake on which Tenochtitlan was built greatly astonished the Spaniards, who had seen nothing in the least like them. They are described by Prescott, drawing on his usual sources, as 'wandering islands of verdure teeming with flowers and vegetables and moving like rafts over the waters'. But what were they? They originated in land-famine. When the Aztecs first came from the north into the Valley of Mexico they were made slaves by their more powerful and civilized neighbours; even later, when free, they were at first poor and weak, and confined to the marshy lake shore which nobody else wanted. So they built on piles out into the lake because what dry land they did have was too valuable for the raising of crops to be used for building. Hence their cities in the water, and their great causeways. But they also *made* land: they built rafts of reeds and rushes lashed together with tough roots, and onto them they piled soil dredged up from the shallow bottom of their lake which, consisting largely of decayed vegetation, was very fertile. Raft was joined to raft and artificial, floating islands were formed as much as 200 feet long, and for the most part about four feet deep. The larger and older *chinapas* had small trees planted on them, as well as plots of flowers and vegetables for market and even a hut for the gardener to live in. By using a long pole the gardener could punt his floating garden from shade to sun or sun to shade, or nearer to his market. At times it seems that scores of these floating gardens could be seen gliding about the surface of the lake.

These *chinapas* remained in use for centuries after the conquest, although they steadily declined in numbers. They survived long enough to be described by Humboldt, and, indeed, much longer.

Although every eyewitness speaks of the marvellous flowers and gorgeous colours of Mexican gardens, nobody put names to them until long after the conquest, partly because it was a long time before they had any Latin names. However, it is fairly obvious what some of these flowers must have been. An important point is that the fact that European plant-collectors may have introduced a plant to Europe from the wild, does not mean that that plant had never before been in cultivation. In both Peru and Mexico a large part of the garden flora was lost by neglect, when the Spaniards became masters of those countries.

Mexican gardeners cultivated dahlias, of which their country has twelve species, long before Europeans did. They reached Europe by way of Spain and were not grown in England before 1790. Zinnia was another genus cultivated in pre-Columbian Mexico and introduced to Europe by way of Spain; it reached England in 1753. The huge, modern cultivars are of United States origin. *Alstromeria* was first grown in Inca Peru, as also were *Eucharis* and *Hippeastrum*, two of the most flamboyant flowers in gardens. It is probable that Inca gardeners were the first to use *Zephyranthes*; that Inca and Aztec gardeners used the ornamental bromeliads before we did; and that the Aztecs used yucca and cactus as garden plants. What shrubs the Aztecs grew is not clear, but perhaps *Choisya ternata* and some *Ceanothus* species were among them.

In the context of this history of gardening, the principal and considerable contribution of the South and Central American native cultures was one of material — useful and ornamental garden plants; and perhaps the idea of systematic gardens of plants.

149 *Part of the Vatican garden.*

9

150

THE RENAISSANCE

BOTANICAL GARDENS

No movement in the history of horticulture has contributed more to the enrichment of garden plant material than that of botanical gardening, which began half way through the sixteenth century. I have suggested in the last chapter that the idea of these gardens of plants may have reached Europe from Mexico, where such gardens had made a great impression on the conquering Spaniards. Whether this was so, or whether our botanical gardens developed out of the much older Physic Gardens and as a by-product of the growth of botanical science, it is impossible to say: no doubt all kinds of influences, including that of the Mexican gardeners, were at work.

The renaissance of botanical science which had such a strong influence on gardening was due to the rediscovery, by western Europeans, of the botany of classical antiquity; in other words, it was a part of the Renaissance. The old botanists whom men now read again for the first time for centuries were Theophrastus, who had published his *Inquiry into Plants* c. 300 BC; the elder Pliny, whose *Natural History* appeared about four centuries later; and the *Materia Medica* of Dioscorides (first century AD). The first and third of these writers had had physic gardens, and were interested in plants only in

so far as they were useful to man, not as objects of disinterested study. So the first botanical revival was confined to pharmaceutical botany: new herbals were written, based on Dioscorides — by the German Otto Brunfels in 1532; by two other Germans, Boch and Fuchs, in 1539 and 1542 respectively; and by the Italian Matteoli, the first empirical botanist of the new age, in 1544.

The first two botanical gardens for the study of botanical science were those of Padua and Pisa. As to which came first, there is a dispute which has continued for four centuries. The Florentines claim that Pisa's garden was started in 1543, but have no documentary evidence; whereas it is certain that the Venetian Senate passed a Bill founding the Paduan garden in 1545. What matters to us is that the Paduan botanical garden is still there, perfect and just as it was made in 1545 and the following years. The site for this garden, 20,000 square metres in modern measure, was ceded to the Republic of Venice and the University of Padua by the monastery of S. Giustina. The architect commissioned to draw plans for it was Giovanni da Bergamo, and the plan was carried out by Professor Pietro da Noale, the work being supervised for the Senate by the Patrician Daniele Babbaro, himself a considerable botanist. Their joint work is a masterpiece of design: a perfect circle eighty-four metres in diameter, it is defined by a handsome brick wall coped by a white marble balustrade. In the eighteenth century this balustrade was decorated with busts of all the garden's *Praefecti*. The first *Praefectus* was a botanist, Luigi Squalerno, called Anguillara. He laid out the interior of his garden in sixteen equal divisions each twice subdivided, so that the whole circle of 5,555 square metres (there is an area beyond this circle with a mount and other features) is a rigidly geometrical pattern of very small beds each devoted to a single genus or even species.

A feature of great interest in this enchanting little botanical garden is a greenhouse shaped like a lighthouse on an octagonal plan, built to cover a single plant which has been known since Goethe visited it in the eighteenth century as *La Palma di Goethe*. The plant is a *Chaemerops humilis* planted in 1585. It was the basis of the Praefectus Giulio Pontedera's establishment of the genus in 1720, and it was the origin of Goethe's *Metamorphosis of Plants* (1790).

The list of plants cultivated for the first time at Padua, that is for the first time in Italy and even in Europe, includes *Bignonia radicans*; a number of bamboos; *Cedrus deodara*; *Robinia pseudoacacia*; *Pelargonium cuccullatum*; *Cyclamen persicum*; *Jasminum nudiflorum* (1590)* and the potato (c. 1575). As for Pisa, its *Praefecti* introduced horse-chestnut in 1597;† *Juglans nigra*; *Ailanthus glandulosa*, *Cinnamonium camphora*, *Chaenomeles japonica*, *Magnolia grandiflora* and the tulip tree. The garden's first *Praefectus* was Luca Ghini, who was the teacher of such great botanists as Aldrovandi and Matteoli. But perhaps Pisa's most distinguished *Praefectus* was Andrea Cesalpino (1554-8) whose work on systematizing plant taxonomy set the example for Tournefort, Ray and Linnaeus to follow.

The example set by Pisa and Padua was soon being followed: in Florence, Ferrara and Sassari before 1554; and in Bologna in 1568, the prime mover being Aldrovandi whose *Tavola di piante, fiori e frutta*, written during his connection with that garden, is one of the most clearly observed and exquisitely illustrated of the sixteenth- and seventeenth-century *Florae*. The next important botanical garden was planted outside Italy, at Leipzig in 1580, but far more important in the history of gardening was the next in point of time. The Leyden Botanical garden in Holland was officially founded in 1587, but planting did not begin until 1594 because the

* Three centuries before Fortune's 'introduction'.
† Whether from Vienna or directly from Turkey is not clear.

151

University's medical faculty, responsible for the garden, were bookish men of the medieval type, unstirred by the new, inquiring, Italian spirit. But at last, in 1592, the *Curatores* of Leyden University made an attempt to get the greatest living botanist of the times as their *Praefectus Horti*.

Charles de l'Ecluse, better known as Clusius, was a French Fleming born in Artois in 1526. He read law and then medicine. In the course of his medical studies at Wittenberg he became interested in plants far beyond the limit of their medicinal uses; and at Montpellier, where he went to complete his studies and take his degree, this interest hardened into the passion of a lifetime. He spent the years 1565 and 1566 plant-hunting in Spain and Portugal, and as a result described and published 200 species until then unknown to science. His next work was to translate Garcia de Orta's Portuguese treatise on Indian plants into Latin. Later, during a visit to England, he came across Nicholas Monardes' book on American plants (published in England under the title *Joyfull Newes from the New Found Worlde*), and made that available to the learned in all countries by putting it into Latin. His work had made him known all over Europe when, in 1573, the Emperor Maximilian II invited him to Vienna to lay out and plant a Physic Garden. Clusius seized this chance to spend three years studying the *florae* of Austria

151 *The crafts of pruning, grafting and pollarding made great advances during the Renaissance. Pollarding for summer shade at Pallanza.*

152 *Padua's is the oldest surviving of the botanical gardens produced by the Renaissance. The greenhouse covers 'Goethe's Palm' on which* The Metamorphosis of Plants *was based.*

153 *Bust of Von Siebold in the botanical garden of Leyden University. The great plant collector sent many of Japan's plants to this famous scientific garden whose first Prefect was Clusius.*

152
153

and Hungary, and that was the basis of his *Historia stirpium per Pannonium* in 1583. After this Clusius settled in Frankfurt. There, in 1592, he had a fall which partially crippled him. It was thus that, old, tired and sick, he refused the offer made to him by the Leyden University *Curatores*; he wanted neither the responsibility for an important scientific garden, nor the labour of delivering lectures. However, Leyden's intermediary with Clusius happened to be an old friend and great admirer, Johan van Hoghelande, who would not take no for an answer. At last the old man accepted the appointment on condition that he be given a *Hortulanus* — i.e. head-gardener. The man appointed was a pharmaceutical chemist or herbalist called Dirck Outgaerzoon Cluyts, who, not seeing why he too should not have the distinction of a Latin name, insisted on being called Clutius.

If I have spent some time on Leyden and Clusius, it is because the combination of this garden and its two remarkable masters, Clusius and Clutius, was of the first importance for the future of gardening. Clusius made Leyden a great centre of plant introduction, study and diffusion, while Clutius found out how to grow exotics until then unknown in cultivation. From their records a later *Praefectus Horti*, Professor Doctor Baas Becking, was able, in 1931, to reconstruct the original Clusius-Clutius garden. It can be seen today, across the canal from the later botanical garden as it was remade again and again by Clusius's successors. Their names compose a roll of honour of great botanists and gardeners, of whom the greatest, after Clusius, was perhaps Boerhaave. Probably the most important garden plant which we have Leyden to thank for is the tulip; but because that very great plant collector Von Siebold used the Leyden garden for his Japanese collections, the list of what we owe to Leyden is a very long one.

The herbalist John Gerard's London garden near Holborn, planted in 1597, was not much more than a physic garden. France had her first botanical garden in 1635, probably as a result of the publication in 1623 of Gaspard Bauhin's *Pinax theatri botanici* in which he described 6,000 species of plants. This garden was the Jardin du Roi, later the Jardin des Plantes, in Paris. It was there that Tournefort, greatest of the taxonomists until Linnaeus, did his work. The eagerness of botanists like this Frenchman, the Englishman Ray, and the Italian Cesalpino, to have living as well as herbarium material on which to found their various systems of logical nomenclature had a great deal to do with the introduction of plants into our gardens from all over the world.

I shall in due course have to revert to the subject of botanical gardens, which continued to influence gardening until well into the nineteenth century and which, now, are beginning to do so again. But while the first plant scientists and garden scientists were busy founding their science, what were the garden artists up to?

ROMAN RENAISSANCE

If Florence was the centre of that Humanist school of gardening created by Petrarch, Rome was more important at the next stage. Influenced by the Florentines and led by such men of taste as Pope Nicholas v, half way through the fifteenth century the Romans began to discover that it was not enough to study and admire antiquity; one must emulate its artists and scholars. A new time of making began — the making, among other things, of gardens. Nicholas v projected, but did not live to accomplish, the Vatican garden; the man who 'changed the whole conception of gardening in Europe'* was Cardinal Giuliano della Rovere, later Pope Julius II, patron of Michelangelo and builder of Saint Peter's.

* Masson (1961).

Julius made his first garden in 1486 beside the church of San Pietro in Vincoli (he was its Cardinal). We know nothing of it except that it was walled, wooded, and was used to house the Cardinal's collection of antique statues, which included the Belvedere Apollo. Elected to the Papacy in 1503, Julius transferred his collection to the Vatican, found the old Belvedere garden an unsatisfactory setting for it, and resolved to connect it to the Papal palace by a garden in the manner of a Roman villa.

The architect he chose for this work, on the basis of similar works which he had already accomplished, was Donato Bramante. The Pope could hardly have done better. Bramante's masterpiece was said to be the Cortile del Belvedere, which survives only in disconnected vestiges and fragments; but the *atrio di piacere*, as it was then called, survives in numerous prints and drawings, and there is no doubt that this was the model and original of all the great Renaissance gardens. It was Bramante who set the fashion for shaping whole hillsides into gardens by making a series of terraces set in a framework of loggias and cloisters; who made an open-air theatre a part of every great garden; and who used spectacular staircases to link the parts of his garden together into a single monumental work in the manner which ultimately became a cliché. Was Bramante's Cortile del Belvedere entirely original? In so far as any work of art ever is, yes; its inspiration is said to have been either the ruins or legends of the gardens of Lucullus on the Pincian Hill; or the Temple of Fortune at Praeneste. What is certain is that he had an unequalled knowledge of what, in his time, remained of Roman villa architecture.

Another great garden created at this time, and one which had a very strong influence on the style of Italian and European gardens in general throughout the Renaissance period, was the so-called Farnesina; although the Farnese only acquired it by purchase and it was in fact built by the millionaire banker Agostino Chigi. Its architect was Peruzzi. Very little of this work survives, but the vestige is important since it includes the garden loggia whose frescoes were painted by Raphael, and the decoration of garlands of flowers and fruit by Giovanni da Udine. The latter, like few artists of his day, was a good botanist, naturalist and country-lover, with the result that his garlands (as Georgina Masson has pointed out) are composed of elements correctly drawn from garden flower models. They include 'cabbage' roses, Madonna lilies, violets, jasmine, periwinkle, daisies, convolvulus, poppies, iris, hemerocallis, wild roses, anemones, paeonies and cycla-

154, 155 *Aspects of the Villa Gamberaia garden. Started in the sixteenth century and twice remade, it is representative of a style which endured for three centuries.*

men. From this painter's work and from other sources we know that the big gardens of that time had both lemons and oranges, pomegranates and hawthorns; also cultivated was the elderberry, a shrub which the great Boerhaave, in the following century, was always to salute by raising his hat when he passed one, so highly did he esteem its manifold usefulness and its beauty.

Three artists had a hand in the design of the so-called Villa Madama, the villa and garden built in 1516 by Cardinal Giulio de' Medici on Monte Mario overlooking Rome: Raphael, his pupil Giulio Romano who was the chief architect, and Antonio Sangallo the Younger. They carried to its extreme expression the style of interpenetrating buildings and garden, for which the model was the Villa Adriana, and which we have seen developed quite independently in Japan; or so it would seem from their plans, for nothing but the *giardino segreto*, a Humanist feature, survives from the original, the rest being restoration. The villa was burnt when the imperial troops sacked Rome in 1527.

'The Villa Medici on the Pincian Hill is the only great Roman Villa of the sixteenth century whose garden layout has survived intact, though natural growth and the evolution of a taste for less and less severely disciplined planting has increased its *bosco* character.'

Thus Georgina Masson (1961). The *bosco* of an Italian Renaissance garden was a woodland area, survivor or descendant of the sacred grove, providing both shade and shelter. Built by Annibale Lippi for Cardinal Ricci in 1544, the villa was bought by Ferdinando de' Medici in 1580. It included a great courtyard decorated with regularly planted fruit trees behind the house; and a garden of geometrically designed parterres planted with flowers and enclosed in a wall or clipped hedge. This included fountains, statuary and fruit trees in big terracotta pots. It had cypress-shaded walks, a large *bosco*, and a terraced gazebo garden flanked by a long, walled walk. The garden was still very much as Lippi made it when John Evelyn visited it a century later; but half a century later still the floral parterres had been replaced by *ricami* — elaborately beautiful cursive designs carried out in clipped box. In Italy, again as in Japan, flowers tended to be fewer as garden design became more sophisticated, although for quite different reasons. In Japan it was a set of religious conventions which had this effect; in Italy the conventions were purely aesthetic. This garden was originally the setting for Cardinal de' Medici's collection of ancient statuary, but very little of that now remains.

To my mind and for my taste, the loveliest of the Italian Renaissance gardens and the most perfect as an accomplished work of art, and as such historically the most important, is the Villa Lante. But before coming to it, we must consider one which the greatest experts on the period hold to be the most 'typical' of the Italian Renaissance gardens, and more particularly of the Roman expression of that style. This is the Villa d'Este at Tivoli, created by Pirro Ligorio for Cardinal Ippolito d'Este.

Ligorio first enclosed a regular area of the hillside, completely separating it from the surrounding landscape, and within that enclosure he built up a connected series of rising terraces, creating as he did so vista after vista of great magnificence. Planted areas, walks, stairways, open spaces, fountains, statues: all are regular, symmetrical, ordered, antinatural. And all are perfectly combined into the unity of an accomplished work of art.

In no other garden in the world is water so variously and wonderfully used as in the Villa d'Este. At the bottom level are fishponds enclosed in finely dressed stone. They are fed from, and so connected to, the higher waterworks by various water staircases. At every crossway of the garden stand superb monumental fountains in colonnaded garden rooms

156
157

158

156, 157, 158 *Details of the Villa Garzoni garden, a magnificent example of Italian baroque gardening at Collodi, Italy. The garden dates from the second half of the seventeenth century. In the late Renaissance (baroque) gardens like this, with steeply tiered terraces linked by magnificent staircases, the garden was not abruptly separated from its surroundings, but merged into them by way of tree plantations.*

sheltered by trees now grown to an immense stature. Water grottoes and smaller fountains mark every junction and terminal of the higher walks. The waterwork of the greatest magnificence is the 'walk of a hundred fountains', a long transverse promenade with the falling vista of the garden seen between great trees on the one hand, on the other the raised bank of fine sculpture with its hundred jets of water. Originally some of the fountains made music, or at all events a noise: there was an Owl Fountain which hooted, and an Organ Fountain of which Montaigne complained (*c.* 1580) that it only played on one note. And there was a Dragon Fountain which, to John Evelyn's delight, made a roaring noise.

While the architect Vignola was engaged in making the great garden of Caprarola, another of the most magnificent gardens of Italy's high Renaissance, he was commissioned by Cardinal Gambara to build him a summer residence at Bagnaia, on a site which had been presented by the city of Viterbo to the Episcopal See for just that purpose. The name

by which Vignola's masterpiece is known was attributed to it later when it was let, by the See of Rome which inherited it from Gambara's successor, to the Lante family. The grounds of the Villa Lante are in two parts: the *bosco* which here for the first time in Italian Renaissance gardening merges into an unenclosed countryside to form a park; and the formal gardens. The long axis of the formal gardens is a steep hillside down which they descend in a series of terraces. From the tree-shaded fountain on the high terrace water is led down a marvellously wrought formal cascade which forms the backbone of a long staircase enclosed by clipped evergreens. This cascade is in the form of an elongated *gambero*, a crayfish, this being a play on the Cardinal's name and arms. At another level the water passes through a central channel cut in the surface of a great stone dining table, the centrepiece of an enchanting dining-garden. The channel was used either for cooling wine, or possibly to float dishes down the table from guest to guest. The fountain, feeding these water features and itself fed from a formal lake by gravity, is a glorious work of spouting dolphins, masks and urns.

133

159

160

159, 160 *A feature developed in the Renaissance and baroque gardens of Italy was the 'green theatre'; it has been repeated ever since, as at Bodnant, Wales, and in Longwood, Pennsylvania. This beautiful seventeenth-century example is in the Villa Marlia garden near Lucca.*

161 *In Renaissance gardens like that of the Villa Marlia, pools and lakes were formal and rectangular works of architecture, and often enclosed 'garden rooms' whose 'walls' were of clipped evergreens.*

Indeed, the whole Lante garden is alive with the music and glitter of water. The lowest terrace is a square formal lake, a basin made of the lovely golden-brown stone of the region, with another exquisite fountain on a circular base joined by four stone trelliswork bridges to the sides of the lake. Today the fountain is in the form of four bronze youths holding high above their heads the arms of Cardinal Montalto, surmounted by a great star of water jets.

The Lante garden as a whole is a perfectly accomplished work of art. Less magnificent than half a dozen other Italian Renaissance gardens, it nevertheless represents the zenith of Italian garden art, with every element, including the charming *ricami* parterres which flank the lake, in perfection; and in the perfection of proportion.

What was achieved at this period and in all its numerous masterpieces of garden art was the complete expression of the spirit in which Italians of the Renaissance approached the making of gardens. In the first place these gardens — using stone, water, trees, evergreen bushes and a very few flowers — were works of art which owed nothing but their raw materials to nature. The spirit was the antithesis of what the Chinese spirit of gardening had been and still was, and of what that of the English was to be. Italian gardens were, so to speak, unroofed *salons* for polite intercourse, recreation and contemplation; they were a setting for man and not for plants and flowers. Gardening in that spirit was to be carried even further by the French.

FRENCH RENAISSANCE

We have seen already that while the French learned the art of the new kind of gardens from the Italians, they still clung to their native medieval style, and in particular to the

161

practice of divorcing the garden from the house. But as the Renaissance made progress in France, the notions of formal elegance, and of the unity of house and garden, gained ground. One of the greatest artists of all time was responsible for the first move in this direction. About 1514 Leonardo da Vinci, old, sick and soon to die, drew a plan of a *château* and water-garden for King François I, in which house and garden closely interpenetrate in the Italian manner. This villa, for that was what, of course, it was, was never built; but as the thought and feeling of the Renaissance made progress by such means in France, others like it were. Florimont Robert, François I's most successful ambassador, apparently built one such near Blois. It is now a ruin, but the plans survive and they show progress towards the Renaissance ideals of elegance and unity.

Perhaps the garden which set the style for the great French Renaissance gardens was Dampierre, near Boissy-sur-Seine,

built by a banker but bought and lived in by Cardinal Lorraine. Here are all the elements of a grand French garden — house and formal, geometrical parterre of clipped evergreen *broderie* (*ricami*), enclosed in a balustrade and surrounded by a formal and perfectly rectilinear canal; an absolutely rectangular plantation of trees densely planted in rows; a raised terrace for promenading while viewing the parterre; and a very large and, again, rectangular formal lake.

Chenonceaux, one of the few French Renaissance gardens from which it is still possible to see what the early seventeenth-century garden artists were creating, is not a unity in the Italian sense, but only because the site made such unity impossible. The grand parterre was separated from the castle and from the park by canals. The raised terrace around it may once have been embellished with a pergola. The smaller, sunk parterre has flower-beds outlined with clipped box,

135

162
163

but we do not know what flowers were grown in them. Possibly none; coloured earths or patterns of small pebbles may have been used.

Anet, built by Philibert de l'Orme for Henri II who gave it to Diane de Poitiers, was the first great house-and-garden unity to be perfectly accomplished in France. It is true that the palace is surrounded by a wide canal of water, but this is no longer a dividing element. It serves rather to unite palace and garden: an ornament with a function, not a mere bastion. The drawbridge to the entrance lodge, and the lodge itself with the Benvenuto Cellini nymph in a lunette, are, again, all part of the whole.

There are coppices of trees casting dense shadows on each side of the portal. The foremost court also has its coppices, surrounding the fountains, one of these being Goujon's *Diana* (Diane de Poitiers enjoyed dressing up as Diana). The garden proper is surrounded on three sides by a *rustica* gallery. There are two fountains central to the flower-beds in the side gardens subtended by the wings of the palace. There is a large semi-circular pool and there were originally, beyond the flower-garden, two separate and enclosed hunting parks. The rule is clear: absolute symmetry, a sort of geometrical elegance which excludes any kind of natural disorder. This rule was followed by every great French garden thereafter: rectangles were not de rigueur, but geo-

162, 163, 164 *Details of the Vatican garden, a magnificent example of Renaissance garden design by Bramante. Many features of this garden inspired garden architects for centuries in the design of garden monuments.*

metry was, so that at Azay-le-Rideau we have triangles, at Maune a pentagon. The whole art was dominated by two architects, de l'Orme and du Cerceau. They had only one theme, though they might vary it. It was the theme implicit in Rabelais' vision of the garden of his Abbey of Theleme — a formal and perfect hexagon surrounded by water, and with not only the fruit trees but also the shade and ornamental trees drilled into regimented lines and geometrical figures.

A feature of all European gardens from the earliest time, the grotto, was given a new expression in Renaissance France by Bernard Palissy when his friend and patron the Duc de Montmorency commissioned him to make him a grotto for his garden at Ecouen. There had been grottoes and groups of grottoes in France before that, often used as open-air theatres. But Palissy was the master-artist in that field, and as a result of what he did at Ecouen, Catherine de' Medici sent for him to design the great grotto in her very stiff and very dull Tuileries garden. Thereafter he took to writing on gardens in general, and his designs exactly express French taste in garden design for the times. The site must be quite flat — evidence that the French never developed that Italian taste for using terraced hillsides, and the reason why no great French garden was ever quite as beautiful as the best that was done in Italy. Then, the garden should be an enclosed and isolated square — another example of the way in which French garden art was dominated by plane geometry. And

it continues in the same spirit: the garden must be divided into four equal squares by two avenues crossing at right angles. Each main walk terminates in a grotto and a garden house, the lower storey to be used for storing fruit, the upper as a recreation room. Palissy had the curious, and to our taste vulgar, notion of embellishing the upper storey balconies with life-sized models of human figures contrived so that they could be made to move and look real. These realistic figures became a feature of gardens all over Europe, except perhaps in Italy, during the seventeenth century. Palissy's grottoes also had a wide vogue. They were made to look like caves, but the mouths of those caves were supported by Herms or pillars, and the interiors were enamelled in brilliant colours. Another kind of Palissy grotto was more natural, built of rocks among shrubs and trees and with a stream of running water. Palissy also had a taste for pleaching carried to such lengths that it perfectly expressed the French inclination to keep garden design strictly architectural, and to use plants as if they were building material. His designs and notes show elms planted so as to make little halls of tree-trunk pillars with the branches so trained and intertwined as to form leafy walls in which windows could be cut. The higher branches are to be trained to form a pitched roof: an extreme expression of pleaching.

Although, according to Gothein (1928), the making of her-mitages in gardens began in Spain, it was certainly in France

164

that the fashion was really popular. The point should, however, be made that these hermitages were not, at least at first, merely frivolous ornaments and the resident hermit an elaborate joke, as in England later. The hermit incumbent was often a real holy man; in fact many hermitages were chapels. There were no less than seven such chapels in the grounds of Chantilly. Moreover, one Chantilly hermit was allowed by the Pope to grant indulgences; probably most of the hermits were in holy orders. The garden architect du Cerceau describes the chapel-hermitage built by the Cardinal Bourbon at Gaillon:

'You walk from the upper garden through the park partly by terraces, partly through avenues of trees, keeping your eyes fixed upon the beautiful valley, and you come to a little chapel and house and hermit's rock in the middle of a square basin of water; all round are narrow paths where you can stroll for pleasure. To get there you cross a swing bridge. Close by you find a little garden and in it are statues three or four feet in height, standing on a great plinth, depicting all sorts of allegorical subjects, and also several *berceaux* covered with greenery; the hermitage here is very pretty and attractive and as full of charm as any you will find anywhere.'

The great age of the French Renaissance garden begins with Henri IV. In a dedication to one of Boyceau's writings on gardens the King, by then dead (1652), is described as having himself '...planted and grafted, and so even now the great lords and princes of France take the utmost pleasure in doing the same...' Boyceau was one of three men whose writings and works had a decisive influence on the shape of the French garden. The others were Claude Mollet and Olivier de Serre.

Part 6 of Olivier de Serres's *Théâtre d'Agriculture* deals with gardens. His gardens are chiefly for the cultivation of vegetables, fruit and herbs; but there is a flower-garden, *bouquetier*, and in it, for the first time in French gardening, flowers become really important. The parterre ceases to be a pattern of clipped bushes and becomes an elaborately designed pattern of flower-beds edged with clipped aromatics such as lavender and marjoram — box only later, *c.* 1690 — with flowers so planted as to fill in the formal patterns of colour. The favourite flowers seem to have been violets, wallflowers and pinks, with lilies-of-the-valley and some spring-flowering bulbs. But taller herbaceous perennials were used beside walks, and always in mass-plantings of one kind. Clipped box was used to make the arbours, screens for seats and other

165

architectural features of the parterre. De Serres also introduced artificial mounds and hillocks into his gardens, with grottoes built into their lower levels.

Claude Mollet was Henri IV's head gardener, succeeding his father in that office. It was after retirement in 1613 that he took to writing about gardening. He seems to have had a proper sense of his own worth, for he wrote: 'God has granted me his Grace, so that for the blessed King Henri the Great I have made many beautiful things.' His two sons helped their father with his book, *Le Théâtre des Plants et Jardinages*, by making the plates for it, but the work was not published until 1652, long after Mollet's death. His son André Mollet, by the way, was to have much to do with the introduction of French gardens into England and Sweden. As a practical gardener, Mollet was a pioneer in the craft of keeping his borders always bright with flowers by bedding-out, and of planting herbaceous perennials for succession of flower against a background of tall shrubs. We can perhaps call him the inventor of the herbaceous border. Like Olivier

165 *Of the Villa Lante, whose cascade is shown here, Sacheverell Sitwell wrote, '...were I to choose the most lovely place of the physical beauty of nature in all Italy, or in all the world that I have seen with my own eyes, I would name the gardens of the Villa Lante'.*

166 *Topiary and sculpture in the Villa Gamberaia gardens.*

de Serres he used pleaching very elaborately to form 'windows, battlements, arches and pillars'; but also tall, clipped box. And under the influence of the Italianate-French architect du Perac, he made his parterres as a single unity; one grand pattern instead of several smaller ones.

Du Perac had lived in Italy, made a study of Italian gardens, become Henri IV's architect, and had been put in charge of Fontainebleau. He designed, among other places, the new garden of the Duc d'Aumale's Anet where, according to Mollet, '...each garden forms a single parterre divided by wide paths...' So, with du Perac, we come to the so-called *compartiments de broderie* French garden. It is curious, and strong evidence for the independence of French taste, that there is in du Perac's gardens very little sign of the Italianate, though he was such an enthusiast for Italian gardens. An excellent example of this kind of *compartiments de broderie* can be found in Boyceau's drawings of the Luxembourg gardens parterres in his *Traité du Jardinage* (Boyceau himself was the greatest of the new parterre designers). The Lux-

embourg and other *compartiments de broderie* gardens were planted not in geometrical patterns but in elaborate 'arabesques'.

Just as in Persian gardening there is a close connection between Persian floriculture and the designs of Persian carpets, in Japan between the fashions of flower-growing and the designs painted on china, and in Europe between English landscape gardening and Italian and French-Italianate landscape painting, so in the France of this epoch there was a very close connection between the designing and planting of garden *broderies* and the composition of parterres, and the new craft or minor art of floral embroidery for dressmaking and, later, for furnishing fabrics.

'So great was the growth of skill and the love of luxury that soon the ordinary flowers did not suffice; and people looked around for foreign plants which were eagerly copied by embroiderers with extraordinary effect, while men were also attempting to produce something equally beautiful in the parterres. The two arts were so closely allied that the

167 *Typical of the best in Tuscan Renaissance gardening, the Villa Muti garden has been a work of time but assumed its present perfection early in the 18th century.*

168 *Nikitsky Sad, Yalta. An 'English' landscape garden in the Crimea.*

169 *Water-stairway, Nikitsky Sad, Yalta.*

168

169

fashionable and profitable trade of embroiderer was often carried on with the gardener's business by the same person.'*

Jean Robin, the royal gardener, a major influence on gardening all over Europe, and a great introducer of new plants, planted *broderies* of exotics with the deliberate aim of supplying the embroiderers of fabrics with new elements and themes.

The first sign that the making of garden after garden by the rule of straight lines and a level plain was becoming wearisome was expressed in practice when Henri IV called in an Italian, Francini, to design and lay out his garden at his new palace at Saint-Germain-en-Laye. Francini gave the King an Italian garden, although there was a French element in the parterre by the river. In theory, the same discontent was voiced by Boyceau in his *Traité du Jardinage* written about 1635 (and published in 1638):

* Gothein (1928).

170 *Uppsala, Garden of Linnaeus.*

'It wearies me past expression to find every garden laid out in straight lines, some in four squares, others in nine or six, and no variety anywhere.'

He is supposed to have given practical expression to this complaint in his designs for the new Tuileries gardens. What, as far as one can judge from Evelyn's account, he did there was to relieve French flatness and regularity with some Italian elements. At Fontainebleau, too, another of Henri IV's gardens also attributed to Francini, the Frenchness was less rigorous. Curiously enough, although the revival of Italianate elements at this time was due to Marie de' Medici's influence on Henri's taste, she herself got, in the Luxembourg garden, not an Italian garden from her architect Salomon de Brosse, but a great parterre garden much more French than Italian. But it was soon to be considered the finest in France by all but her enemies — the friends and faction of Richelieu — who claimed that the Cardinal's garden at Ruel was even finer.

Those aspects of Ruel which particularly caught John Evelyn's fancy when he visited the place during his sight-seeing tour were the great vista avenues each ending in a magnificent fountain; the Citron Garden, with a painted *trompe-l'œil* Arch of Constantine so realistic that birds were apt to try to fly through it; the parterre embellished with fountains and statuary; the grotto of fine shell work, with its water-curtain; and above all the tremendous water-staircase cascade, with basins and fountains at regular intervals down the steep slope — a completely Italianate feature, this, to be imitated all over Europe including England (Chatsworth) and later in the United States.

Thanks to John Evelyn we know a little, too, about the smaller French gardens of the French Renaissance. In the case of the nobility — Evelyn particularly mentions the Comte de Liancourt's garden — the ancient Roman device of enlarging

13. *Birr Castle: the lake.*

14. *Gardening operations: from a Persian miniature in the British Museum.*

15. *The bridge over the lake: Hoare's masterpiece, Stourhead.*

16. *Vanbrugh's bridge over Capability Brown's lake, Blenheim.*

171 *Buenos Aires Botanical Garden.*

the perspective by painting landscapes on the garden walls
was used. By this means they made their little town gardens
seem 'to flow for some miles'. But there were other kinds,
and he visited one belonging to a retired professional gardener,
Morine by name. This was a perfect oval enclosed by dense,
close-clipped thuya to make green walls within which Morine grew a collection of flowers which were then rare in
cultivation, including tulips, crocuses and anemones.

ENGLISH RENAISSANCE GARDENING

It is an odd fact that the English passion for gardens and
flowers creates a great difficulty for the historian of gardens;
that and the fact that in the eighteenth and nineteenth
centuries the English gentry were rich enough to indulge
expensive fancies. The heirs or purchasers of houses with fine

143

gardens in France, Italy and Germany were apt to keep the garden as it was unless they simply neglected it. The English, on the other hand, were forever destroying old gardens to make new ones in some later fashion. So that what we know about old English gardens is hardly at all from actual surviving examples (although there are a few exceptions) but chiefly from contemporary accounts of them.

In garden taste, as in so much else, it was Henry VIII who pulled England into the Renaissance movement; but credit for introducing the king to the new style of Italian gardening belongs to Cardinal Wolsey. Just as the French gallicized Italian garden art, so the English anglicized it. Both these gifted peoples made something original out of what they borrowed in a way that the Germans, for example, did not.

Conditions for a boom in garden-making in England were good. Thomas Cromwell's dissolution of the monasteries, with its consequent enrichment in land and money of the epoch's new men, and the resultant building of fine country houses, meant that there was a call for hundreds of new gardens from people rich enough to spend money on them. John Leland, Henry's antiquary, who spent the years 1536 to 1542 travelling all over the kingdom, records the great number of new houses then in the building, new gardens in the making, new orchards in the planting. The king had set an example at Hampton Court when, in 1533, he had the mount, topped by a lantern-arbour, made there.* This mount was a feature which Olivier de Serres had tried, with very little success, to introduce into French gardens: the French did not like it, it disturbed that level plain which they so much preferred. Providing an interesting difference between the English and the French taste, de Serres seems hardly to have thought of the mount as an ornament at all. He suggests that the collection of native and exotic medicinal herbs, in short the private physic garden, be grown on artificial hills, thus saving space and giving a variety of aspect to suit the different kinds of herbs. Ornament or mere convenience, the mount reached both France and England from Italy where a fairly typical example, with the spiral path among trees, can still be seen in Padua's botanical garden (see p. 127) started in 1545. But its origin is very much more ancient: it is the last vestige of the Hanging Gardens of Semiramis style — in short, of the prehistoric *ziggurat*.

Henry's mount was a pile of a quarter of a million bricks covered with earth, planted with hawthorns. The shrubs

* Sands (1950).

threaded upwards by a spiral path to the lantern-arbour, a three-storeyed tower with many windows and a cupola roof topped by a heraldic lion in the form of a wind-vane. Some variety of this mount was thereafter to be found in every great English garden for the next couple of centuries.

The model for the great English Renaissance garden was almost certainly Nonsuch, started by Henry but not finished until it was taken over by the Earl of Arundel in Mary's reign.* Virtually all we know about the Nonsuch garden is that it was probably copied from the one at Fontainebleau; not the great Henri IV version but the earlier François I version. This fact could be taken as a sort of symbol of English Renaissance garden history: those gardens were Frenchified Italian, more or less anglicized and lagging about a decade behind Continental fashion, if not more, and sometimes much more. Thomas Platter (1599) gives a very few details of the Nonsuch garden during Queen Elizabeth's residence there. He says that it included a wood with rides and vistas — in short a gallicized *bosco* — a bowling green and a tennis court. There was a maze and, another French fashion, imitation animals so life-like that they could be mistaken for real ones. Nonsuch also had a grand banqueting hall in the garden, which Hadfield thinks must have been the first of its kind in England.

Gardening received, at this time, encouragement of a kind very different from that implied by the existence of a newly rich class with a readiness to follow the Court taste. Refugees from France and Flanders, fleeing Catholic persecution, included many professional gardeners bringing with them both skills and plants new to Britain. William Turner, 'father of English botany', published a herbal in 1548; the Lord Protector Somerset's physician, he had his own garden at Kew, and he left us some account of what was grown in English gardens in mid sixteenth century. Fruits include peaches, apricots and figs, medlars and almonds. Among the flowers were French marigolds, which seems surprising, for this is *Tagetes patula* from Mexico, and Cortés did not complete the Conquest until 1522. This may be something we had from Spain rather than France or Italy, but Turner's antirrhinums and jasmines came from Italy, and he also grew columbines, pansies, wallflowers, carnations and pinks, Madonna lilies and some daffodils. All these were in common garden use.

Partly because of temperament, and partly for climatic

* Hadfield (1960).

172 *Villa Cuzzano, Verona.*

reasons, the English were beginning, as early as Elizabeth's reign, to show a bias in favour of plantmanship over garden design, and with one interval of artistic greatness, this has been apparent ever since. There began a great flow of introductions from Europe, America and elsewhere. When, in 1587, William Harrison's new edition of Holinshed's *Chronicle* was published, there was a new passage by Harrison boasting of all the new plants which had reached and were reaching England all the time from 'India, America, the Canary Isles'. He had, he said, seen in many gardens three or four hundred or even more novelties, and nobody would even have heard their names forty years ago. He goes on to say that our gardeners are now so clever at enlarging flowers, doubling them and changing their colour, that they seem like Nature's superiors. All these

new plants, species from abroad and cultivars made at home, aroused more excitement and were given more importance in English gardens than anywhere on the Continent except, perhaps, in Holland.

Returning to the great houses and their gardens, there is a description in Paul Hentzner's *Travels in England during the Reign of Queen Elizabeth* of Lord Burleigh's garden at Theobalds in 1598, the year of Burleigh's death:

'...one goes into the garden encompassed with a ditch of water, large enough to have the pleasure of going in a boat and rowing between the shrubs. Here are great variety of trees and plants; labyrinths made with a great deal of labour;

145

173 *Germany, Grosssedlitz Schlosspark,
'Stille Musik'.*

174 *Potsdam; Sans Souci Park,
'Das Musenrondell'.*

a *jet d'eau*, with its basin of white marble; and columns and pyramids of wood, up and down the garden. After seeing these, we were led by the gardener into the summer-house, in the lower part of which, built semi-circularly, are the twelve Roman Emperors in white marble, and a table of touchstone; the upper part of it set round with cisterns of lead, into which water is conveyed through pipes, so that fish may be kept in them and in summer time they are very convenient for bathing.'

This says nothing of the several other gardens adjoining, and of the two miles of fine avenues; perhaps Hentzner did not see much, for his visit was on the day of Burleigh's funeral.

Some of the great gardens had parterres in the French fashion, for knot gardens were first made in England in Queen Elizabeth's reign and a knot is the English word for *broderie* or *ricami*. Patterns which have survived are simpler than the French, and it could be that the style reached Britain from Italy or Holland directly, and not by way of France. They were doubtless knots which Robert Laneham (1575) calls parterres in a brief description of Leicester's garden at Kenilworth. Laneham was a court official who accompanied the Queen on progress. Elizabeth had given Kenilworth, an old castle, to her favourite, and he had built onto it and made a new garden on the north side:

'Close to the wall is a beautiful terrace ten feet high and twelve feet broad, quite level and covered with thick grass, which also grows on the slope. There are obelisks on the terrace at even distances, great balls, and white heraldic beasts, all made of stone and perched on artistic posts, good to look at. At each end is a bower, smelling of sweet flowers and trees. The garden ground below is crossed by grassy avenues, in straight lines on both sides, some of the walks, for a change, made of gravel, not too light and dusty, but soft and firm and pleasant to walk on, like sands by the sea when the tide has gone out. There are also four equal parterres, cut in regular proportions; in the middle of each is a post shaped like a cube, two feet high; on that, a pyramid, accurately made, symmetrically carved, fifteen feet high; on the summit a ball ten inches in diameter; and the whole thing from top to bottom, pedestal and all, hewn out of one solid block of porphyry, and then with much art and skill brought here and set up. Flowering plants procured at great expense, yield sweet scent and beauty, with fresh herbs and flowers, their colours and their many kinds betraying a vast outlay; then fruit trees full of apples, pears and ripe cherries — a garden indeed, so laid out that either on or above the lovely terrace paths one feels a refreshing breeze in the heat of summer, or the pleasant cool of the fountain. One can pluck from their stalks and eat fine strawberries and cherries.'

Then there was the garden of Christopher Hatton's Holdenby. It was destroyed in the Civil War, but there seem to have been four gardens more or less disconnected, including a rose garden, orchards, lakes and two mounts. Now nothing is left but the two enormous gateways. In Surrey, at Beddington near Croydon, Sir Francis Carew had a great fruit garden and the first orangery in Britain. According to Aubrey he had imported the trees from Italy. Sir Francis, moreover, was good not only at forcing tender fruits in a cold climate, but also at retarding hardy ones. He was able to offer Queen Elizabeth fresh ripe cherries when she visited him late in August 1599. The fruit had been retarded by covering the trees with canvas cooled by constant spraying with water.

Francis Bacon's famous essay *On Gardens* was, no doubt, speculative, but it was based on what he saw about him as well as on what he thought it would be pleasant and practicable to do. He had the spirit and the temperament of a scientist. He planned a garden of thirty acres, very large indeed for that time. This was to be divided into three areas, and the first immediately adjoining the house was to be joined to it by 'stately galleries'. The Roman villa was here in his mind, for these galleries were specifically described as 'open'. In this area also he would have had a lawn ('Nothing more pleasant to the eye than green grass kept finely shorn'), and avenues and some covered walks. He would not have had a parterre or knot garden, for he writes of such knots that '...they be but toys; you may see as good sights many times in Tarts'. The principal garden was a perfect square enclosed by an arched hedge: '...Over the Arches let there be an entire hedge... and upon the Upper Hedge, over every Arch a little Turret with a Belly enough to receive a cage of Birds; and over every space between the Arches, some other little figure, with Broad Plates of Round Coloured Glass, gilt, for the sun to play on...' This kind of artificial ornament, so distasteful to ourselves, foreshadows the fantasies of Jacobean gardening which were to continue right through the century and into the eighteenth. Bacon would have had his walks hedged, with a mound at the end of each to afford an elevated point of view, and a diversity of trees. But he disliked topiary work: 'I do not like Images cut out in juniper or other Garden Stuff; they be for Children.' He would have had a mount topped by a banqueting hall, and he likes fountains and running water generally, but not ponds because the water gets dirty.

In at least three of his suggestions Bacon was an originator of a specifically English type of garden which was not to

147

come into its own until very much later: in his advocacy of lawns, his rejection of knots, and his dislike of topiary. But the most specifically English part of his garden was the third area. This was to be a wilderness: it probably derives from the *bosco*, but if so from the *bosco* anglicized, for it is to have no trees '...but some thickets made only of Sweetbriar and Honeysuckles and some Wild Vine amongst.' Here his groundlings would be violets and primroses and he would also have had '...little heaps in the nature of Molehills, set with thyme, pinks and germander... which gives good flower to the eye'. He named other flowers for this wild garden, forerunner of the shrubbery which has been an English garden fashion ever since, including periwinkle, daisy, cowslip and red roses, lily-of-the-valley, sweet william, '...and the like Low Flowers, being withall sweet and sightly...' On some of the little heaps he proposed to plant standard roses, hollies, junipers, red currants, bay laurels and rosemary '...but these standards to be kept with cutting, that they grow not out of course.'

Bacon was the only English garden designer of the epoch who had original ideas (even though he never made a garden such as he describes in his essay). He was, by a very long time, the forerunner of such English garden-makers as William Robinson. No Frenchman or Italian of his day would have used precious garden space as he suggests using it. There is no evidence that anyone ever made such a wild garden as Bacon conceived. But the influence on many practical gardeners of a much more popular writer of rather later date was direct. John Gerard, Lord Burleigh's head gardener at Theobalds was, as we saw above, owner of a physic garden off Holborn in London. In 1596 he published his *Catalogus arborum fruticum* etc. etc., a list of over 1,000 plants supposed to be growing in that garden. Later came his *Herbal*, a best-seller for centuries and still in the bookshops today. Gerard was one of those unscrupulous charmers who can persuade men of integrity that they too are honest scholars in their field. But in fact, although a clever practical gardener, he was a semi-charlatan, or at best a plagiarist, in botany. His book was respectfully received because Burleigh was his patron, and also because it had a preface by the great Flemish botanist Matthias de l'Obel who had settled in England after the assassination of his patron William the Silent of Orange. Only later did de l'Obel discover that Gerard's catalogue was thoroughly unreliable. And the *Herbal* was not Gerard's original work at all; it was filched from the botanical works of the Belgian botanist Rembert Dodoens. Still, it did introduce English gardeners to much new knowledge of plants, as

did de l'Obel's own work as *Botanicus* of Lord Zouche's famous garden in Hackney which '...was a rallying point of the growing band of Londoners interested in plants, and a link between them and the Continental schools'.[*]

King James VI of Scotland took an active interest in gardens. He, followed by his nobles, came under the Italian rather than the French influence in the art, perhaps only because the very steep hill-sites of many Scottish castles made terracing the best solution to the garden problem. When he became James I of England, the king persuaded Burleigh's son, the first Lord Salisbury, to give him Theobalds in exchange for Hatfield. Salisbury did not like it, but made the best of it by at once beginning to lay out a garden about his new house. By that time French influence was paramount, and the Hatfield garden had its parterres, one enclosed by pleached limes, its maze, bowling green and rose garden. The grand Neptune Fountain was erected by the French architect Salomon de Caus, who doubtless had a hand in designing the rest of the garden too. Salisbury included a vineyard in his garden — vineyards were fairly common in England from the seventh century and were still being planted in the nineteenth.[†] He also followed the king's example in planting mulberry trees, which had been introduced during Elizabeth's reign. The king wanted England to have her own silk industry.

Shakespeare, incidentally, was a planter of mulberry. Edmund Malone, the eighteenth-century Shakespearian scholar who wrote a supplement to Steevens' 1778 edition of the Works and in 1790 published an edition of his own, says of the once famous mulberry at New Place:

'That Shakespeare planted this tree is as well authenticated as anything of that nature can be... and till this was planted there was no mulberry tree in that neighbourhood. The tree was celebrated in many a poem, one especially by Dibdin, but about 1752 the then owner of New Place, the Rev. Mr Gastrell, bought and pulled down the house and wishing, as it should seem, to be damned to ever-lasting fame he had sometime before cut down Shakespeare's celebrated Mulberry tree, to save himself the trouble of showing it to those whose admiration of our great poet led them to visit the poetick ground on which it stood.'

Lord Salisbury's greatest contribution to gardening was his patronage of the elder Tradescant. He sent that great gardener, naturalist and plant-collector to fetch him new

[*] Hadfield (1960).
[†] Hyams (1953).

plants for Hatfield from Holland, Belgium, France and Italy. An East Anglian, Tradescant became Salisbury's gardener early in the seventeenth century, and he made his first foreign tour in 1609. After Salisbury's death in 1612 he worked for Lord Wotton in Kent. He had money invested in the Virginia trade, which enabled him to get plants sent from America. In 1618 he went to Russia — as naturalist attached to the Digges embassy — and returned with hundreds of plants and many crammed notebooks. He even braved and fought Algerian pirates to get plants from North Africa. He became head gardener to Charles I's favourite, the Duke of Buckingham, and as such was in a position to cause Royal Navy captains to be ordered to bring home new plants from overseas. His next post was head gardener to the king, and even after his retirement he maintained his plant-introducing activities. Tradescant was only one, albeit the greatest, of the gardeners who were enriching the English garden flora at this time.

Another man who had a major influence on the gardening developments of his age was John Parkinson (1567-1650). Little is known of his early years, but during the first decade of the seventeenth century he was an apothecary with a shop in London apparently well known for its rarities. Made Herbalist to James I, in 1629 he published the first great English gardening book. The title is a learned pun on his name — *Paradisi in sole Paradisus Terrestris*, and here, because it fully describes the work, is the sub-title:

'*A choice garden of all sorts of rarest flowers, with their nature, place of birth, time of flowering, names and virtues of each plant, useful for physic or admired for beauty. To which is annexed a kitchen garden furnished with all manner of herbs, roots and fruits, for meat or sauce used with us. With the art of planting an orchard of all sorts of fruit-bearing trees and shrubs showing the nature of grafting, innoculating and pruning them. Together with the right ordering, planting and preserving of them with their select virtues; all unmentioned in former Herbals. Collected by John Parkinson, Apothecary of London, and the King's Herbalist.*'

This great book earned Parkinson the title of *Botanicus Regius* to Charles. It was, as a consequence, to Parkinson that de l'Obel's papers were passed when the great Belgian died in 1616. And it was with their help that, after decades of work, Parkinson published his *Theatre of Plants*, in which over 3,750 kinds of plants are described, in 1640.

Although, by Jacobean times, the English garden was beginning to grow out of the Tudor mania for ornaments in the shape of wild beasts and diverse wooden structures strangely painted — in, for example, the gardens of Sir John Danvers as described by John Aubrey, or the garden which Isaac de Caus (Salomon's son) made for Lord Pembroke at Wilton — yet it was not until the influence of such Italianate artists as Inigo Jones, and of French rather than Dutch taste too, began to make themselves felt strongly, that garden art taste was purified in England of such excrescences and impertinences as even Francis Bacon had advocated. What it came to was this: that the gardens of the Commonwealth period and the reign of Charles II, as described by such authors as the great gardener Sir Thomas Hanmer, and by John Evelyn, were, in all but detail, already French, although the great period of French garden art was still to come.

THE RENAISSANCE IN NORTHERN AND EASTERN EUROPE

We noted in chapter 7 that in Germany, while the burgesses of the free cities were making small urban gardens, there as elsewhere the really great gardens were being made by the very rich. This, with one or two exceptions like that of the Fuggers, meant by the nobility.

Among the principal great houses which took an active interest in the art was that of the Hapsburgs — Maximilian I von Hapsburg, indeed, wrote one or two books on gardening — and the fact that Charles V was master of Spain and the Netherlands as well as of Austria led to many new plants being early introduced to Vienna and other imperial cities. But the first Hapsburg prince to create a great garden — at Ambras near Innsbruck — was the Archduke Ferdinand, second son of the Emperor Ferdinand I. He made this garden about his *château* (it was not a medieval castle) as a present to his morganatic wife Philippa Welser; and there the Archduke and his sweetheart lived together, disapproved of by the Emperor but in a love which became legendary all over Europe. As to what the garden was like, we have a brief description written by the Jesuit tutor of Prince Karl von Jülichsberg who in 1574 paid a visit to the Archduke on his way to Italy, Mecca of every civilized European of his day; and a later etching by the elder Merian. The garden had labyrinths, parterres with pergolas, grottoes, grand fountains, arbours of topiary work — in short, all the elements of a slightly gallicized Italian garden. Germany, unlike France and England, did very little to (as it were) naturalize Italian garden styles. This is not to say that Germany simply borrowed styles and contributed nothing; but the contribution was in small details and there has never been a specifically German garden, in the sense that there are Italian, French and English gardens.

The principal parterre at Ambras, for example, was wholly French, divided into nine squares centred on a circular, cupolaed pavilion on simple pillars. Another pavilion, in the park just outside the formal gardens, was set high to command a view; used for banqueting, it had a circular, revolving table.

Ferdinand's elder brother, who was in due course to become the Emperor Maximilian II, began work on his own great villa, the 'Pheasantry', in 1569. Of it, our great authority for this period, Gothein (1928) again, says this:

'There was a square exactly the width of the villa, which was enclosed by a wide wall with arcades; at its four corners it was topped with high two-storeyed turrets, whose dome-shaped roofs cased in copper commanded a distant view over the outer walls, while on the arcade roof itself there was a fine promenade. The square included the upper flower-garden divided into sixteen beds in a geometrical pattern, two of which showed the Austrian arms, the double eagle, and were provided with many fountains. The arcades and the pavilions in the corner turrets were finely painted.
'From the upper garden one passed next into a narrow court dividing the garden from the villa. This was enclosed on the valley side by a loggia in the real Italian style. Hence one could see over the lower gardens, which fell away towards the Danube in four terraces, first two narrow ones planted with trees, next a flower-garden in size and situation almost the same as the upper ones, and on the lowest of all a large pond — so at any rate it appears to be in the engravings. Bongarsius, a Swiss visitor, who saw the gardens when they were completed in 1585, speaks of two ponds, but this may not be quite accurate, for he makes no mention of the beautiful fountains adorned with statues which (according to the account of expenses) were set up in the lower gardens. Round the flower-garden of the highest terrace stretched the park within the great battlemented and tower-crowned walls: it was approached through two immense gates on either side. Bongarsius thus describes it: "Round the flower-garden there is a park of fruit trees planted well, and a fine labyrinth; in the middle of the whole park there is a trench three or four feet wide, marked out by stones and getting its water from a hill a mile and a half away"'

It is probable that the artist was an Italian, but if so he was influenced by French taste and he was not a major artist in the field.

In 1587, as we have noted elsewhere, Maximilian had Clusius working for him as his Inspector of Gardens, and as a result a good many new plant introductions were grown in the imperial gardens. But Clusius was, of course, a botanist, not a gardener, and he made no impression on the shape and design of Austrian gardens. However, the great Fleming's tenure of office in Vienna resulted in the first *Flora* of Austria and Hungary; in the garden cultivation of tulips in eastern Europe; and in the first appearance of the horse chestnut as an ornamental tree in European gardens.

The preference of the melancholy and misanthropic Emperor Rudolf II for Prague over Vienna, and his passionate love of his garden in the Hradschin, during the period before he withdrew altogether from the mankind he hated, had one positive result: the introduction of the art of gardens into Bohemia, now part of Czechoslovakia. Rudolf did not have to begin from scratch, for at the Hradschin he found a *château*, the Belvedere, built by a pupil of Sansovino, with a small Italian garden. This garden the Emperor took in hand. It became famous for its 'Singing Well'; for its grottoes lined with mirrors and music from some sort of concealed machinery (or possibly an orchestra, this is not clear); for its menagerie; and above all for its exotic plants which Rudolf introduced from Italy, Spain and Turkey. Although the credit for introducing tulips from the east into European horticulture goes to Clusius, as we have said, it is at least possible that it should go to Rudolf, and that it was by way of Prague that Turkish tulips reached Vienna.

The development of Dutch garden art and plantmanship at this time is documented by a certain number of paintings, and by the history of the Leyden University's botanical garden (dealt with at the beginning of this chapter) a little later, after Clusius had gone to Leyden. The Dutch and Flemish paintings of gardens should not be looked at as portraits of actual gardens, but as idealizations based on realities, so that they can be taken as representing Dutch and Flemish gardening as a whole. In design it did not differ importantly from that of French and English gardening — in fact, of course, much English garden design was of Dutch origin. Where it did differ was in the relative richness of the Dutch garden flora. Exceptionally, the Lille Breughel may have been an actual portrait of a real garden; for what appears to be the identical garden also appears in a painting by Abel Grimmer at Antwerp.

There is a still better source of knowledge of Dutch and Flemish gardening: in 1568, and again in 1583, Vredemann de Vries published a set of engravings depicting gardens, enti-

175 Oxford Botanical Garden.

tled *Hortorum Viridariorumque Formae*. Some are smallish town gardens such as the Dutch made in great numbers; others are grand Austrian gardens — Rudolf II was de Vries's patron and the artist lived and died in Prague. Some of the engravings are probably ideas for gardens, rather than actual gardens. There is remarkably little difference between them: it is as if the elements of the great gardens were identical with the small ones. For these big gardens are complexes of little ones, rectangular, flat, enclosed in hedges, each with a tree, a summerhouse or a fountain in the middle; and a geometrical arrangement of beds composing something approximating to a French parterre. Unity seems seldom to have been achieved, and at best the larger gardens are pulled together by containing pergolaed or arcaded walls. There is, however, often a lawn in the garden nearest to the house. Water played a rather small part in most Dutch gardens; there are no cascades, and fountains were not impressive.

There is a Flemish engraving of the garden which was laid out by Rubens at his house in Antwerp. It shows the house itself as a very handsome but rather peculiar mixture of Dutch and Italian styles. The garden, opening out of the principal room on the ground floor, is a flat, level and rectangular parterre, decorated with stone urns on pedestals at regular intervals, an Italianate-Flemish pavilion, and a sort of triumphal arch which is one of the gates into the garden. The use of the arch in gardens is of very ancient and probably prehistoric origin; one of the cleansing rites for both men and cattle practised by the people who built megaliths all over Europe and the Near East, was that of passing under an arch.* The rite crops up in Roman practice (victorious armies had to march under an arch, the vanquished under a yoke, another kind of arch). As we have seen in the cases of China, Japan and the ancient proto-civilizations, religious elements have always been important in gardens, and that this continued to be so is clear from the case of the hermitages in Renaissance gardens. Thus, the arch in Rubens's garden had, as it were, a very ancient pedigree.

As for Rubens's flower-beds, they are done in the French *broderie* fashion. The engraving conveys an impression of light and openness carried to such a point that it all looks rather bleak. The garden is, like all Dutch, German and Austrian gardens of the period, architectural, with plants used as the raw material for pattern-making rather than for their own sake.

* See Varagnac in Arambourg (1967).

It was not until late in the seventeenth century that the Dutch garden came into its own; the only style from Continental northern Europe to have a great influence on the gardening of other countries in this post-Renaissance period. The influence of Holland and Belgium was, again, botanical rather than architectural.

In Germany gardening reached a late Renaissance zenith between 1590 and the outbreak of the Thirty Years' War, which severely checked the growth of the art. Several influences contributed to this flowering. One was the translation into German of French and Italian books on gardening; more important was the publication of the first great German book on gardening, by Johan Peschel in 1597. Peschel makes a great point of garden plans; carefully drawn plans must be prepared before any practical work is done. The garden layout must be rigorously rectangular. There must be *stackets* or *gelender* (covered walks such as Francis Bacon made a point of) in every good garden. For the rest, Peschel's gardens are gallicized Italianate.

A number of German artists, notably Joseph Furttenbach of Ulm, were publishing copper-plate engravings of *broderie* designs for parterres, for the guidance of German gardeners. Furttenbach had travelled in Italy, and his published plans for whole gardens were Italian, modified by the prevailing German taste for certain French elements. Nevertheless, he was a great innovator in at least one respect: he realized the social and educational value of gardens. He was certainly the first European gardener to make a point of the value of garden surroundings for children: schools, he maintained, should all have gardens, and he designed suitable ones for that purpose. They were calculated, in his opinion, '...to rouse good thoughts in the children, of walking in Paradise, so practising them in the Christian faith and in other good, useful and honourable studies'. The pavilion in the children's garden would be used to hold examinations to discover what the children had learnt in the garden, and those whose answers were satisfactory would be rewarded by being allowed to pick a bunch of flowers.

An outstanding garden maker in Germany at this time was Marcus Sittich, Bishop of Salzburg, who created a long-famous garden at Mirabellschloss, and an even more widely celebrated one at Hellbrunn just outside the city:

'In the castle itself grottoes were introduced on the ground floor, not only on the entrance side but also on the garden

176 Florence, Villa Gamberaia.

side. By the garden below the terraces there is a great grotto construction; here we find the abundance of statues, water-plays and automata, which we recognise as like those in Italian gardens, and which are still mostly intact. There is the rain grotto, the mirror grotto, and another with a dragon coming out of a hole in a rock who drinks from a fountain and vanishes again. There are all sorts of birds singing, and actually the beloved "vault of ruins" is not wanting, with its stones threatening to fall.

'In front of this garden façade extends the large, deeply-sunken star-pond into which falls a cascade of three tiers, ending above in a semicircular theatre. The ibex, the Hohenem crest, is to be seen everywhere, and is a sure guide to the estates of Marcus Sittich. A long narrow canal passes out from this pond on both sides, beset with an inexhaustible supply of grottoes and little water-plays. Certain regions at the end of the canal hail from a later day, as for example the mechanical theatre, a costly toy with marionettes doing all sorts of things. The passion for grottoes is at its highest in this garden. An engraving by Merian shows a great number of small grotto-houses, which enliven the garden, sometimes open at the top and sometimes shut.

'On the other side of the walk of grottoes there stood near the house a small summer pavilion, which was oriented as

centre piece with four corner turrets and a tank in the shape of a trefoil. People were beginning to imitate Italian casinos by setting up unusual summer-houses in their German gardens. We find them still more varied in the seats of princes of Middle Germany, and it looks as though a peculiar style of central erection came about with this feature much emphasised. The chief parterre at Hellbrunn was a water parterre: there were four basins on small lawns, the middle one having a summer-house on a round hill which was approached by thirty steps. On the eastern façade of the house there was another water site, which, unlike the chief garden, is still for the most part preserved. It has three basins, one behind the other, the middle one oval, and the two others square; these are connected by narrow canals, and with each is a fountain group with a stone table and ten stone seats. In the middle water poured forth to fill the drinking-glasses; but woe betide those who sat down on the seats. They were driven off by water spurting out, and if they tried to escape back to the steps that led to the semi-circular theatre at the grotto, or to the pretty balustraded galleries on the side, they were met with a fresh shower of rain from many little pipes. From pedestals Democritus and Heracleitus — allegorical figures of tragedy and comedy — looked down upon this merry play; while above was Rome, placed in the broken gable of the semicircle, which was adorned with blue stones and shells above the arms of Marcus Sittich. On the right near this part there was similarly a small grotto-house, which contained Orpheus and a sleeping Eurydice and all sorts of animals; near by was a charming little menagerie.'*

But Sittich was only one of the princes of church and state engaged in making such gardens, exchanging new plants, bulbs, seeds and garden designs in the first decade of the seventeenth century. An instrument of importance in such exchanges was a much-travelled and always travelling gentleman art dealer, gossip, dilettante and toady to the nobility, who was also a lover of gardens, Philip Hainhofer by name. In 1612 he published an account of his travels and dealings with princes. It was from Hainhofer that Duke Philip II of Pomerania obtained drawings of princely gardens, and even plants from those gardens, when he came to lay out a garden at his castle in 1611. And Hainhofer was employed by the dukes of Bavaria, and by other nobles and princes, to bring them both garden designs and ideas, plants or seeds, from the greatest centre of early seventeenth-century German horticulture, the gardens laid out and planted by the prince-bishop of Eichstatt, Johann Conrad von Gemmingen, at Willibaldsburg. Hainhofer says that there were eight gardens in all, '...diverse in ornament, in area, in divisions, in order of flowers — all wonderful with their roses, lilies and other flowers.' Von Gemmingen set an example to other princes by financing the publication, with copper-plate engravings made by Basilius Beseler, of a *Hortus Eystettensis* (1613), so that at least a record was left after the Swedes had destroyed his gardens in 1634.

Hainhofer also has accounts of Duke William's three gardens in Munich—they were Italianate, with a shell-and-stalactite grotto housing a Mercury cast in gold; of the hermitage at Maxburg, '...made out of the living rock, with firs and wild trees all about it and water gushing out of the rock...'; of the beginnings of Maximilian of Bavaria's garden at the Residenz in Munich; and of several other gardens. They confirm our impression that German Renaissance and post-Renaissance gardens were Italian or French or both, but that until the later seventeenth century the influence of Italy predominated. In a few cases the German Italian gardens rivalled, and even surpassed, the best in Europe outside Italy itself. The enormous garden, a complex of parterres, at Heidelberg castle near Stuttgart, was a case in point. It included an orchard of orange trees, confusingly called an Orangery, which Olivier de Serres held up as a magnificent example to be copied. The trees, exceptionally large ones, were covered with wooden huts during the winter. The famous adventurer and traveller Michael Heverer says of it that he '...never saw the like either in Italy or Egypt', and he then goes on to describe the Count Palatine's other lovely garden on the Gaisberg outside the town. When Elizabeth, daughter of James I and VI (the 'Winter Queen'), married the wretched Frederick V of the Palatinate, she wanted a garden at the castle of residence itself, and she persuaded her husband to send to England for Salomon de Caus to lay it out for them. The Heidelberg castle garden was probably his masterpiece. One of the sources he drew upon in making it was the book which he himself had drawn and written, a collection of designs for fountains and grottoes dedicated (1615) to Elizabeth in memory of her beloved brother, Prince Henry.

'At that time he found outside the walls by the castle nothing besides a little level plot made in 1508, about two hundred feet square, with a wall. This ground was called the hare garden; and the few drawings show nothing at all of a real garden design, though we may assume that there were vegetables or something of the sort. Above this place, the mountain rose steeply, broken by the deep dip of the Friesenberg valley. The configuration could not have been worse for a garden site with terraces, such as de Caus desired; and it is indeed wonderful what the architect accomplished by hewing away the mountain side and filling up the valley. Even at the Villa d'Este there were no greater difficulties to contend with; in many places the walling amounts to seventy or eighty feet, so that the colossal niches which are visible in the great terraces are not by any means the least important of this earthwork. And in two years the completion of four and in some parts five terraces was accomplished, so that it could support the famous garden of Heidelberg Castle.'*

Among the horticultural feats which Salomon de Caus accomplished in the planting of this garden was that of moving all the old and very large orange trees to one of the new terraces, to form a sort of small avenue, without losing any of them.

Yet another German garden of this epoch which achieved European fame was that of Christian von Schönburg-Glauchau-Waldenburg at Rochsburg in Saxony. Largely responsible for its celebrated beauty was a very singular man

* Gothein (1928).

indeed, a Protestant fanatic named Andreas Harten. Originally an innkeeper, he had taken to gardening because he loved it, became a professional, and by mid century was head gardener at Rochsburg. Harten attributed the great boom in garden making in Germany to the Reformation: gardens were, in his opinion, a sort of heavenly reward for that incomparable blessing, and he practised gardening almost as an act of worship. Since the Reformation, he says, in his *Wordly and Heavenly Gardens* (1648), an extraordinary work entirely devoted to comparing the Bible to a pleasure garden, '...useful and necessary building of gardens and for the growing of herbs have again reached so flourishing a state, though after great expense, that there is hardly a townsman who keeps anything in the town but rather spends his all on garden building, to say nothing of potentates, lords and nobles.' Harten even blames the Thirty Years' War on the devil's determination to put a stop to garden-making: 'The devil is always at work to hinder the delightful and daily building of gardens... inciting the great princes one against the other so that they lose sight of all the peaceful pleasure of eye and heart which aforetime they took in their gardens...'

The devil did not always succeed in this fell work, for in the midst of the war one of its great warriors, Wallenstein, was not only calling on the people to make more gardens and to beautify their towns with planting, but also making a grand garden of his own at Gitschin in Bohemia. Later, after the war, he made a second one in Prague. Nor did he simply give the orders and leave the job to architects and gardeners; even when deeply engaged in political manoeuvring, and while his overthrow was being engineered by the princes at the council of Ratisbon, when he might have been supposed to have other things to think about, we find him writing to his bailiff at Gitschin:

'If I am not mistaken, there is no fountain in front of the loggia in the garden plan. Tell the architect that a large fountain must be put in the middle of the garden square before the loggia. All water is to run into it and then out of it, dividing into two streams right and left, making the

other fountains in the courts run in the same way. Send me the designs...'*

There were six fountains, an avenue of limes, plantations of rare and exotic trees, streams and a cascade.

To complete this impression of the state of garden art in northern Europe until the middle of the seventeenth century, we should glance at the garden works of Maurice of Nassau. His country, the Netherlands, sent him to their colony of Pernambuco in 1637. During his seven year term of service there he built three palaces in the form of fortified castles, and all three had gardens. From such accounts of them as survive, they had parterres in the French taste, although it is difficult to imagine the plants of the tropics being suitable, or at all events manageable, for that kind of gardening. Can Maurice have been a remote forerunner of Burle Marx (see chapter 16) in making formal, abstract gardens with tropical plants? At all events he carried European gardening ideas to South America. In 1644 Maurice returned to Europe, and it was at Cleves, in the service of the Great Elector, between 1647 and 1650, that he did his best work as a garden artist, turning a whole town into a garden in the manner advocated by Wallenstein, as well as making individual gardens. His taste was Italian, he liked terracing, amphitheatres, great fountains. But as a Dutchman, he was also a plantsman. The combination produced gardens which, if we can rely on his own reports to the Great Elector and the admiration of sound judges from Holland, were among the loveliest in Europe.

By the end of this period Italy, which had taught all Europe gardening, had passed her zenith and lost her primacy in the art; this was passing to France whose great century in garden art as in all else was beginning. England's great age was still far in the future; Holland and Belgium were teaching the world horticultural botany; and Germany, having borrowed her garden styles from Italy, was to go on borrowing, first from France, and last from England. She has yet to develop a specifically German style.

* Quoted by Gothein (1928).

One of the basins at Versailles.

THE FRENCH CENTURY

During the late sixteenth and early seventeenth centuries the specifically French garden, the kind which for a century was to be the great garden of Europe, was in the making. As we have seen, at first under Italian influence and often in the hands of Italian artists, the early seventeenth-century gardens of France were more or less Italianate. But, as we have also seen, an independent native style early asserted itself; some Italian elements were rejected and elements dictated by French taste and temperament put in their place. By mid seventeenth century the fully accomplished French garden was ready to emerge and it did so at Vaux-le-Vicomte, a masterpiece which was to be surpassed in its own school only by Versailles. The artist in both cases was André le Nôtre, son of one Superintendent of the Tuileries gardens and grandson of another. The patrons were, respectively, the brilliant financier Fouquet and Louis XIV.

Fouquet was Cardinal Mazarin's Finance Minister during the Regency. He must have been interested in gardens, as he was in all the arts, before Le Nôtre recreated his garden at Vaux; for the editor of Claude Mollet's *Le Théâtre des Plants et Jardinages* dedicated it to the rising Minister and in the dedication writes of how, in the wonderful gardens at Vaux, '...art is delightfully allowed to strive with Nature, and every day brings on fresh beauties and new treasures'. This was

certainly long before Fouquet's colossal building and garden-making operation, for it was apparently not until 1650 that he commissioned the architect Le Vau to build his new château. Le Vau's plans called for a great deal of space; it was in the spirit which at long last was to provoke bloody revolution that Fouquet bought and demolished three villages to get the land he wanted. He had secured the services of the painter Charles Le Brun to do the interior decorating of the house, and it was Le Brun who recommended Le Nôtre for the gardens. He and Le Nôtre had studied together in the same studio, Simon Vouet's; he knew of Le Nôtre's special interest in the art of gardens; and of the botanical knowledge which his friend had learned from his father in the Tuileries gardens, and from Claude Mollet to whom he had been apprenticed. What is remarkable is that so enormous a project as Vaux was entrusted to so young a man and one who, although appointed Designer-in-Ordinary of the King's Gardens about 1640 (through his father's influence), had yet to make a name. It was at Vaux that he did so. In doing so he, Le Vau and Le Brun spent sixteen million livres of Fouquet's more or less ill-gotten money; and employed up to 18,000 workmen.

All the arts of a country's great creative period give expression to one and the same dominant spirit and use the same

178

set of symbols, whatever they may be. The clue to Helle-
nism, whether in gardening or in physics, is solid geometry;
just as the clue to modern Western Europeo-Americanism,
whether in the amorphousness of its politics or the abstract
quality of Burle Marx's gardens (see chapter 16), is in our
anti-concrete mathematics. In seventeenth-century France
it was the spirit which has since been conventionally associated with French thought and arts, the spirit of order, logic,
discipline, polish and refinement, of plane geometry given
life by a thrusting curiosity and love of variety, which dominated. Le Nôtre realized or at least sensed intuitively, how
a garden could give expression to this spirit quite as well as
a painting, a building, a poem, an equation, a military strate-
gy or a political policy. The spirit of logical order could be
expressed in garden layout; the thirst for variety satisfied in
the elements of that layout.

If you stand on the terrace of the château of Vaux-le-Vicomte,
the whole of Le Nôtre's first masterpiece is before you.
Rather exceptionally, it is framed by woods and shrubberies
on both sides, a novelty first remarked on by Mademoiselle
de Scudéry in her novel *Clélie*. A moat crossed by a drawbridge separates the garden from the château. Long, straight
parterres to left and right lead the eye to the hill of grottoes
which terminates the work in the distance, but only after
it has taken in the great *broderie* parterre below. Outside
the parterres on both sides Le Nôtre laid out small rectangular flower-gardens of many beds and small paths, each
embellished with many fountains, one of which was the
grand *fontaine de la couronne*.

There were many other waters: the big parterre was de-
limited by canals still rather in the Renaissance style, and

178 *Vaux-le-Vicomte: Le Nôtre's masterpiece.*

179 *De La Quintinie, Versailles.*

179

by a grand circular fountain. Beyond are more formal flower-beds focussed on still more fountains. There is the great square formal lake, the terminal canal, and then the hill which closes the prospect and completes the framing of the garden which begins with the woods and shrubberies at the sides. In the hill itself Le Nôtre made grottoes and placed fountains and animal statuary all the way to the top, where he set up a great figure of Hercules and a mighty *jet d'eau*.

The side gardens, still within the framework of trees, differ from each other. On the left, where he had rising ground, Le Nôtre made a terrace — Italy was not yet forgotten — reached by a magnificent staircase and embellished with a magnificent cascade. The right-hand side, being flat, was planted with shrubberies, trellis-edged walks, and the amphi-theatre of fountains.

In short, at Vaux-le-Vicomte Le Nôtre brought *the* French Garden into existence; architectural, a vast, formal pattern sharply and clearly stated and framed; an expression of logical order, a defiance of nature's disorderly exuberance; grand, arrogant and cold. The elements of variety and fancy were in the diversity of the parterre designs and the *bro-deries*, in the fanciful shapes of fountains and cascades, the shrubbery walks, the virtuosity of both art and engineering. What is entirely absent is mystery, secrecy, the charm of the vague and seemingly unfinished. If Vaux commands admiration and even something like awe by its magnificence, and the simpler pleasure of delight in its detail, it has, in English and German eyes on the one hand, in Italian eyes on the other, a certain bleakness, a certain iciness of the spirit, laid so open to the pale sky. And whatever importance flowers may have had in it, it is in no sense (and cannot ever

159

180 *Fountains at night, Versailles.*

181 *The water parterre, Versailles.*

182 *Versailles, the grand vista with Fountain of Latona.*

183 *Versailles, main avenue.*

have been) a display of flowers. It is, above all, a grandiose setting for people, for social intercourse and for the ostentatious parade of assurance, taste, wit, wealth and fashion. As such it is as perfect an expression of France's golden age as one could hope for, more effective in that respect than any work of painting or literature, just as the great Renaissance gardens of Italy are the nearest to a perfect expression of that country's golden age.

Fouquet's tremendous garden was his downfall, or at least the occasion of it. Colbert, leader of the party hostile to his power, had been using Fouquet's extravagant parade of wealth — a lot of it had been spent splendidly on the arts, on libraries and patronage of the theatre, but it was his garden at Vaux-le-Vicomte which leapt to the eye — to turn the King against him. While he still seeemed unshakably powerful — he was made Intendant General of the realm in 1659 — his overthrow had been decided. In 1661, when château and garden were at last perfectly accomplished, he gave a grand garden party in honour of Henrietta Stuart, wife of Monsieur (the King's brother). The highlight of the party was the first performance, in a theatre erected in the garden, of Molière's *École des Maris*. Louis was not invited; egged on by Colbert, the King let it be known that if his Intendant General gave another such party, he would accept the invitation. Fouquet gave this second, command, garden party, on 17th August 1661. The King came, was furious at a magnificence he had been told that he himself could not afford, a brilliance with which he had not the talent to compete. There was a banquet, followed by a performance of Molière's *Les Fâcheux*, which was written for the occasion in fifteen days, in a temporary theatre erected at one end of a conifer avenue. The scenery had been painted by Le Brun, and Pélisson's prologue was recited by La Béjart, the greatest actress of her time. There followed a ballet produced by Giacomo Torelli. The success of the whole was somewhat marred by an accident: the Queen Mother's carriage-horses bolted and two of them were drowned in Le Nôtre's grand canal.* It was a portent: a month later Fouquet was arrested, accused of high treason, and imprisoned for life. 'The nymphs of Vaux are weeping', Lafontaine wrote to Fouquet; and the great fabulist began work on his *Dream of Vaux* in which, of the four muses of Vaux, Architecture, Painting, Garden Art and Poetry, Garden Art lost the laurel to Poetry only because Painting spitefully showed the judge, Fouquet himself, a picture of what Garden Art looked like in winter.

* Lafontaine, in a letter to Mancroi: 'I did not imagine that my account [of the party] would have such a sad ending'.

184 Parterre, Versailles.

Vaux-le-Vicomte is one of the quite literally 'epoch-making' gardens in the history of garden art, as are, for example, the Ryoan-ji garden in Japan, Stourhead in England, the Villa Lante in Italy, or the Burle Marx landscape garden round the Museum of Modern Art in Rio de Janeiro. Such gardens, by perfectly expressing a state of mind and taste in a people rising to the zenith of its powers, set fashions which endure until another garden of equal importance in some other national culture sets a new one. Not only in what Le Nôtre had made of Vaux-le-Vicomte, but also in the activities for which it provided and in its associations (Molière, Lafontaine, Louis xiv, Fouquet, Colbert, Le Brun and others), does it so perfectly express the spirit of seventeenth-century France that it has the status of a great work of art or literature. Versailles is more magnificent; it is not more important.

At Versailles Louis xiv possessed a favourite hunting lodge; he had spent happy days in childhood there and so had his

father. It was there that before he was ten he formed his lifelong passion for hunting. The garden had been laid out, doubtless on the site of an earlier one, by Jacques Boyceau, in the Renaissance style. Vaux made the King very dissatisfied with it; in 1662 he commissioned Le Nôtre, who was in any case the royal garden designer by appointment, to design for Versailles a garden to surpass anything the world had ever seen. It is important to realize that the garden came before the palace at Versailles and that its scale dictated the magnificence of that palace. The team was the same as at Vaux: Le Nôtre, Le Vau and Le Brun. The King was too attached to the old house to pull it down and Le Vau had not only the difficult task of incorporating it into the new palace, but also of keeping up with Le Nôtre in grandeur and magnificence: it is not too much to claim that we owe the splendour of the palace at Versailles, as well as the garden, to Le Nôtre. There is no justification for attributing to Louis himself any of the merit except that of accepting the plans made by Le Nôtre and Le Vau, and finding the millions

which their vision called for. The King had neither the imagination, the vision, the taste, nor the knowledge to be a Fouquet; but, determined to outshine his disgraced minister, he left the way of doing so to Fouquet's own experts.

But at least he backed his experts: when Colbert, who had engineered Fouquet's downfall and was in power, objected to the choice of Versailles, as part of a general policy of trying to check Louis' extravagance, on the grounds that this woodless, waterless, sandy marsh was a most unsuitable site for a great garden and palace (which it was), the King replied: '*C'est dans les choses difficiles que nous faisons paraître notre vertu.*'

The work took fifty years to complete, but of course Louis did not have to wait that long for his garden; there were stages of completion. Louis himself wrote the guidebook which was printed for the use of visitors; nor is that surprising, for Le Nôtre succeeded in expressing, in Versailles, precisely what Louis himself symbolized.

163

185

'The landscape has been completely subjugated to the taste of the seventeenth century. Trees are tonsured and pieces of water laid to lighten the cold perfection of the perspective with their glimpses of the sky, where we are almost surprised to see the still untutored clouds sail by. Statues of gods and goddesses themselves stand meekly by, like lackeys in stony servitude, deities no more, degraded by the architects of the king of France.'*

The nature of the ground entailed massive earth-moving operations: that vast plateau which is now the flower and fountain parterre before the palace, had to be made artificially. The engineering work entailed by Le Nôtre's endless ingenuity in waterworks, was very exacting. The Louis XIII/ Boyceau *rondeau des Cygnes* fountain was replaced by the much grander *bassin d'Apollon*. It was 1672 before the great water parterre was completed, but long before then Le Nôtre had finished the horseshoe sweep from the terrace to the

Latona fountain parterre, had made the 400-yard long avenue, had planted the *bosquets* with their own hidden beauties and surprises and had completed the great basin terminating the avenue. What, by then, his genius had accomplished was an immense theatre in which Louis, Hero of the Age, and a full supporting cast of grandees, could strut and preen and play their stately parts. By 1664 the garden was ready to be used as a theatre indeed; Louis, still aping the brilliant Fouquet, (not to mention his royal cousin in Madrid who had a mania for garden *fêtes*), gave a garden party at which theatrical performances, including Molière's *La Princesse d'Élide*, sports, fireworks, water games, entertained and amazed the guests, who, heaven knew, needed diverting since they had nowhere to sleep; the King had invited six hundred people but had not lodging for half so many. As Madame de Sévigné wrote to her daughter, 'The gentlemen of Switzerland and Elboeuf had not a hole to hide in'; the Swiss and Elboeuf gentry could safely be offended, but they were not the only ones.

* Coats (1963).

164

185 *Versailles.*

186 *Versailles, vicinity of the Grand Trianon.*

186

Not content with imprisoning Fouquet and then imitating him, Louis also robbed him, taking from Vaux not only La Quintinie, by far the greatest gardener of his time, but 190 of Fouquet's orange trees for the Versailles orange garden which was finished in 1664. La Quintinie kept the Court in prime fruit and flowers and vegetables, taught a whole generation of horticulturists, including John Rose, later the English king's gardener, and wrote a number of books on fruit-growing which are still of practical use.★

The Versailles garden as we see it now is not quite the same as it was in the late seventeenth century. As the palace grew, the garden had to shrink a little, and there have been many changes. For example, Le Nôtre had his Grotto of Thetis where the chapel is now: it was made by the brothers Fran-

★ The late Justin Brooke, one of the most successful fruit-growers in Europe, once told the author that his successes with figs and pears in Suffolk were due to his following not the modern theorists but La Quintinie.

cini who specialized in such fancies and whose family had been brought to France for work of this kind by Marie de' Medici. They built large reservoirs which there was great difficulty in filling, to supply their hundreds of streams, cascades and fountains. Three gigantic and gilded wrought-iron gates closed the way to this elaborate grotto, surmounted by a golden sun-disk and a relief sculpture of Helios descending to Thetis, welcomed by nymphs and tritons. The interior of the Sun King's grotto was elaborately decorated with shellwork, and in 1675 it was embellished with three groups of statuary.

The grand canal was started early in the course of the works, beyond the Apollo fountain, and the work went on for years. Le Nôtre's original inspiration for this canal was the one at Fontainebleau, and his first essay in such works the one at Vaux. But the canal at Versailles is by far the most magnificent of the French garden canals, nearly a mile long, 130 yards wide, with cross canals totalling over half a mile;

imposing, almost daunting in its geometrical severity. Its banks were lined with statues, its surface kept lively with boats, and it also served a very practical purpose since it drained the marshy part of the land and so made it better able to grow big trees.

The more enormous the scale on which Le Nôtre worked at Versailles, and of Le Vau's matching enlargement and embellishment of the palace, the better Louis was pleased and the more worried Colbert became about the expense involved. One day when Louis and Le Nôtre were walking in the garden and Le Nôtre was, as usual, making proposal after proposal for improvements, even the great garden designer seems to have wondered how far he could go. To each of his proposals the King made the same answer, 'Le Nôtre, I will allow you ten thousand francs for that.' Sometimes, when king and artist were particularly pleased with one of their schemes and with each other, Le Nôtre, who was warm-hearted and excitable, would spontaneously kiss the King.* But on this occasion he said: 'I shall not open my mouth again, Sire, or I shall be the ruin of Your Majesty.'

Expense was not Colbert's only objection to Versailles: anxious to keep the King under his guiding hand in Paris, he wanted what money there was to be spent, since spending there must be, on the Louvre. He wrote to the King: 'Your Majesty is well aware that except for brilliant feats of arms nothing shows the grandeur of spirit of a prince so much as monumental buildings...' So far so good, but then the Minister went on to deprecate Versailles, '...how deplorable it would be if the greatest and mightiest of kings... should be measured by the standard of Versailles...' In Colbert's eyes it must have been a case of too little on the palace, too much on the garden, and both in the wrong place.

This was not the opinion of four friends who visited the garden in 1668 — Lafontaine, Racine, Boileau and Molière, of whom two at least were doing work in the same stately, orderly and grandiose spirit as Le Nôtre's. Later Lafontaine incorporated a dialogue prologue into his *Psyche*, in which the four friends talk about the garden and praise it. Says one:

'It is only Jupiter who can rule the world without rest; human beings need to pause. Alexander gave over his leisure to debauchery, Augustus to games, Scipio and Laelius often

* Louis himself is the authority for this. He told the story when the Court were laughing over a tale that when Le Nôtre was received in audience by the Pope, he was so excited that he embraced him.

187

188

189

189 *Luxembourg Gardens. Le Nôtrian tree-planting.*

187 *Parterre, Villandry.*

188 *Restored seventeenth-century garden, Villandry.*

amused themselves by skipping flat stones over water. But our king is content to build palaces and that does him honour... and gardens so lovely are an honour to our country.'

It is not possible in a work of this scale, nor would it serve much purpose, to describe all of Versailles, or to recount the long history of its enlargements, improvements, shrinkings and other changes, but some idea of them must be given. Parts of it were changed repeatedly. The water theatre was made in 1688, with its water-stairways and arch-forming jets, its fountains, trees, clipped yews and turf auditorium. In 1674 Le Nôtre made the labyrinth, placing a fountain in the form of an animal from Aesop at every principal parting of ways in the maze; thirty-nine fountains in all, fanciful and amusing and inspired, of course, more by Lafontaine than by his ancient original. Madame de Montespan was responsible for fountains in the shape of trees made of bronze, spurting water from their leaves, a sort of practical joke; she had the notion from Spain, but as we know it was a much more ancient one. At one time Dutch sailors, at another Venetian gondoliers were permanently employed to keep the grand canal lively with boats. In 1674 the architect Mansart's Clagny was built in the park for Madame de Montespan, and so fast did Le Nôtre and La Quintinie work on the garden that when Madame de Sévigné visited it in 1675 she could write to her daughter:

167

190

'It is a palace of Armida; the building grows under one's very eyes, the gardens are already made. You know what Le Nôtre is. He has left standing a little dark wood which is very pleasing; and next comes a little wood of oranges in great tubs: you can stroll in this wood which has shady avenues, and there are hedges on both sides cut breast high, so as to conceal the tubs, and these are full of tuberoses, roses, jasmine and pinks. This novelty is certainly the prettiest, most surprising and ravishing that one could imagine, and the little wood is greatly liked.'

Clagny cost seventeen million francs and Louis gave it to Mme de Montespan as a *douceur* when, on with a new love, he was off with the old.

In 1670 came the Trianon de Porcelaine of which André Félibien (1674) wrote:

'It is regarded as a miracle by all, for it was only started at the end of winter and by the end of spring there it was,

as though it had grown out of the earth with all the flowers about it.'

Its decoration of Dutch faience instead of porcelain was the first European garden *chinoiserie*, inspired by French missionary accounts of Chinese garden buildings, and especially of the tower of porcelain at Nanking.

La Quintinie's work at Versailles was less spectacular than Le Nôtre's but not less exacting. For one thing, he had always to have ready in the nursery garden well-grown trees and shrubs in some variety, ready to carry out Le Nôtre's schemes, or the scheme for a new *bosquet* devised by a courtier and which Le Nôtre sometimes felt it wise to accept. La Quintinie was responsible for the winter garden, a movable wooden house stocked with oranges and lemons, myrtles, jasmines, hyacinths, carnations, tuberoses and other fragrant flowers. It contained a *cabinet de parfums* of scented

190 *Chenonceaux, sixteenth-century use of water.*

191 *The Sphinx Walk, Chenonceaux.*

191

flowers which made a great impression on the embassy of mandarins which the Greek adventurer Constant Phalkon, Chief Minister of the King of Siam, sent to Versailles.*

The influence of Versailles on garden making extended not only all over France but all over Europe. Every nobleman, said the *Mercure de France* in a leader (1686), had to have his Trianon, and even the burgesses built themselves little ones — though it might only be a hut decorated fancifully. But it was not only the elements of Versailles that were copied, it was the whole, and its style was dominant until the rise of the English garden in the late eighteenth century. Louis himself was first to try to repeat Versailles. True, at Marly, he began with modest intentions, a little lodge where he could escape the Court; but modesty was not in the King's nature. Louis, as Saint-Simon wrote in his *Memoirs*:

'...weary of being fine* and tired at last of the swarm of courtiers, persuaded himself that he needed from time to time a small place and solitude. He searched near Versailles for somewhere to satisfy this new taste, inspecting several sites and exploring the lovely banks of the Seine. At last he found a narrow valley near Louveciennes, unapproachable because of its marshes, shut in by hills on every side, and very narrow with a miserable village on one slope, which was called Marly. So the hermitage was built. The plan was to spend there three nights only... two or three times a year, with a dozen or so courtiers for necessary attendance. But what actually happened was that the hermitage was enlarged, building after building sprang up, hills were removed, and waterworks and gardens were put in. It is no exaggeration to say that Versailles as we saw it did not cost as much as Marly... It was the king's bad taste in all things, and his proud delight to force nature, and this could not be checked by the pressure of war or of religion.'

Elsewhere the duke says that if the cost of the continual

* Collis (1965).

* *lassé du beau.*

169

192-4 *Levens Hall, Westmorland.*

Court journeys to Marly be taken into account then the cost of Marly must be counted in hundreds of millions.⋆

Le Nôtre, whose last major work at Versailles was the laying out of the gardens for the new marble Trianon with which Louis replaced the Trianon de Porcelaine, was naturally consulted by all who wanted and could afford a garden in his manner. Condé was an early client, remaking the garden at Chantilly between 1660 and 1668; here Le Nôtre made a great cross canal as he had done at Vaux, a grand stairway up to the terrace from the parterre, avenues and *bosquets*. As usual the parterre had almost as many fountains as flowers. Then, at Fontainebleau, he remodelled Henri IV's old garden; at Saint-Germain he made the grand terrace; at Saint-Cloud he worked on the already beautiful gardens when the widowed Duc d'Orléans married Liselotte of the Palatinate. There he showed his quality by refusing to spoil

⋆ *'... on ne dira point trop sur Marly seul en comptant par millards.'* The principal expense was probably for reservoirs and aqueducts for the fountains and canals.

the beauty of one of France's best Italian gardens and confining himself to making some enlargements and throwing the complex of small gardens into one whole. And all over France his disciples were making gardens in his style.

If I name no other garden designer for this whole epoch it is for good reasons. Seventeenth-century gardening had become wholly French; French gardening was wholly Le Nôtre. Marie-Louise Gothein asks why his style so long and so completely dominated north Europe, and answers her own question by arguing that the style was particularly well adapted to the northern landscape, was easily taught and readily understood. There is little force in these arguments: under northern skies there is, especially in winter, a touch of sad bleakness about Le Nôtre's work, a defiant magnificence even when it is simple, as at Saint-Germain-en-Laye, which can be rather depressing. It is not more readily taught than English landscape gardening, and as for being readily understood, there is surely more of the Latin than the Nordic feeling in Le Nôtre's austerely beautiful living geometry

however it be relieved by baroque or rococo ornament. No; Le Nôtre dominated the gardening of the late seventeenth and early eighteenth centuries simply because his was the French century in European culture and even the remote Swedes and remoter Russians had to try to be French, just as all Europe in the sixteenth century had to try to be Italian.

One of Le Nôtre's disciples was the painter and architect Alexandre Jean-Baptiste Le Blond. Not only had he, by his own account, read all there was to read about garden art, he had also laid out and planted a number of gardens in the region of Paris. When, in 1709, the first and long standard work on French gardens, later pirated, translated, re-edited and plagiarized all over Europe, was published anonymously, it was widely attributed to Le Blond.* This was the man

* The author of *La Théorie et la Pratique du Jardinage* was almost certainly A. J. Dezallier d'Argenville. Why this well-known naturalist did not put his name to the work which does its author so much credit is a mystery. It was published in an English translation and edition by John James in 1712, and even James did not know who the author was.

who was taken by Peter the Great from Germany, where they met in 1716, as Architect-General of St Petersburg, then being built. The Russians owe to Le Blond the Nevski Prospekt and much else, including Peterhof. The general plan of this great garden is pure Le Nôtre: 40,000 trees were planted in straight lines, to make a wood penetrated by broad rides offering tremendous vistas in precisely the manner of the great Frenchman. True, the two garden pavilions, *Mon Plaisir* and *Marly*, were, to please the Tsar's mania for Holland, more Dutch than French, but all else was French touched with Russian orientalism, as in the gilding of the statues. The famous Oak Tree Fountain, which pleased Peter's slightly mad taste for rough practical jokes, was a copy of Madame de Maintenon's, which had been a copy of a Spanish original derived from classical Persian garden practice. The golden-lead statues of Aesop characters — Peter's own notion — were copied by Le Blond from the maze at Versailles. As for the magnificent fountains and other waterworks, they were such as Le Nôtre himself might have planned; moreover the best of them were the work of

195

195, 196 *Levens Hall, Westmorland.*

Nicholas Pineau, a pupil of the sculptor Coysevox who made many of the Versailles fountains. Peter's garden was copied, of course, by nobles in various parts of Russia; but Le Nôtre's style was hardly calculated to make much impression on a more or less barbarous people whose excessive conservatism is still so troublesome to the rest of the world.

In England and Scotland, although French influence was paramount in design for a while, it did not really last long. For a time during the Restoration the flower-loving English turned against flowers in gardens; they carried this anti-flower movement further than love of French gardening

196

obliged them to do, and came to confuse flowerlessness with Frenchness and so, when they returned to their old love, rejected the French style. But in fact the French attitude to flowers in gardens never went to the lengths implied in Pepys's famous conversation with Hugh May, recorded in the *Diary* (22 July 1666):

'Then walked to Whitehall where saw nobody almost, but walked up and down with Hugh May who is a very ingenious man. Among other things discoursing of the present fashion of gardens to make them plain, that we have the best gravell walks in the world, France having none nor Italy; and our green of our bowling allies is better than any

they have. So our business here being ayre, this is the best way, only with a little mixture of statues, or pots which may be handsome, and so filled with another pot of such or such flower or greene as the season of the year will bear. And then for flowers they are best seen in a little plat by themselves; besides, their borders spoil the walks of another garden; and then for fruit the best way is to have walls built circularly one within another, to the south, on purpose for fruit; and leave the walking garden only for that use.'

By 'our business being ayre' Pepys means, of course, that the garden was a place in which to get fresh air and gentle walking exercise, not to enjoy flowers. May's boast of the superiority of English lawns — 'our green of our bowling

173

allies'* was clearly justified: Francis Bacon was perhaps first to make a point of it. But d'Argenville's *La Théorie et la Pratique du Jardinage* advised the French that they could not do better than follow the method of cultivation of lawns used in England, '...where their lawns are of so exquisite a beauty that in France we can hardly hope to come up to it'. As for English indifference to flowers, almost hostility, it could not last. It was against the feelings of ordinary people; and the naturalist Rea protested against it in his *Ceres, Flora and Pomona*, declaring that, '...a choice collection of living beauties, rare Plants, Flowers and Fruits are indeed the wealth, glory and delight of a garden.' He hopes that what he calls this newfangled, ugly fashion will soon be over. It was not, not immediately, for it was favoured by the taste for French gardens even if, under Dutch influence, the English went further than the French in keeping flowers in their place — outside the walking garden. It may surprise some readers to learn that the Dutch gardens were eschewing flowers; but we shall see that, barring certain bulb flowers, this was, for a time, the case.

When Charles II was restored as king he appointed, as royal gardeners, the two sons of the Claude Mollet who had been Henry IV's gardener and author of *Le Théâtre des Plants et Jardinages*. Claude was, of course, just pre-Le Nôtre; but his sons André and Gabriel were Le Nôtreists, and André Mollet's own book, *Le Jardin de Plaisir* shows the author perfectly familiar with the new principles. Where Gabriel had been working is not clear. André first came to England just before the Civil War, left that country when the war broke out and went to Sweden, where he had been in the service of Queen Christina, to whom his book was dedicated (it was published in Stockholm in 1651). He had made a big garden of *compartiments de broderie*, lawns and *bosquets*, statues and fountains, at Jakobsdal; it was more Renaissance than Le Nôtre in style. It included a grotto, and an Andromeda Fountain showing the lady bound to a rock and Perseus coming to her rescue. There was also the inevitable Orange Garden. Presumably Mollet made other gardens in Sweden; certainly the influence of Le Nôtre, of which he may probably

---

* Pepys's bowling allies, for which another term was, of course, bowling green, led the French under d'Argenville's and Le Blond's influence to fall in love with English lawns; they have remained in that state ever since. In France lawns, of a kind, became known as *boulingrins*; a *boulingrin* had nothing to do with bowls, however, but was usually a sunk garden with a grass parterre centred on a fountain or statue. Incidentally, this word, clearly a corruption of bowling-green, has given French philologists a lot of trouble, and it is highly entertaining to read some of the fanciful but learned derivations they have devised to explain what requires not erudition but only an ear.

197, *Munich, Nymphenburg garden.*

have been an instrument, is very apparent in, for example, Dahlberg's *Views of Swedish Castles* (1735).

Now to return, with the Mollets, to England. Charles set them to work altering St James's Park in the French style. What else they did is not known for certain; by 1666 they were both dead, and their successor was John Rose; Rose had been gardener to the Earl of Essex, who had sent him to Versailles to study under Le Nôtre.* Charles went even further in his taste for the French way of making gardens; he asked Louis XIV to lend him Le Nôtre and Louis agreed to do so, but there is no evidence that Le Nôtre was ever in England, unless the legends of his having personally designed this or that English garden be evidence. Who cut the avenues through the park woods at Hampton Court in the French manner, which John Evelyn (1661) mentions as im-

---

* Cf. Hadfield (1960). But Gothein (1928) says it was the King who sent Rose to France. I prefer Hadfield; but it is just possible that Rose went more than once.

17. *The Palm House at Kew: designed by Hooker and Turner but attributed to Decimus Burton.*

18. *Camellias at Bodnant.*

19, 20. *Kitchener's Garden on Elephantine Island in the Nile.*

21. *The Botanical Gardens, Sydney. English paradise styles are superbly expressed in Australian gardens.*

198 *Munich, Nymphenburg garden.*

proving the beauty of the place? It could have been the Mollets.

Rose is known not as a garden architect but as a gardener; under his influence interest in flowers was quite restored. Sir Thomas Hanmer (*The Garden Book of Sir Thomas Hanmer*), himself a very great plantsman, whose garden had an astonishingly wide range of species, refers to Rose's special skill with auriculas, the 'Bears Ears' which became a mania with the English gentry at this time. But Rose was better known for his fruit-growing; he was the first gardener to grow pineapple in England; he cultivated a royal vineyard and wrote an excellent little book on viticulture in England (1666) which was still of practical use to myself and others when experiments in viticulture were being made in England in the late 1940s, experiments which have resulted in at least two English-grown wines being now on the market. But if Rose did indeed study under Le Nôtre (and possibly learn his pomology from La Quintinie at the same time), his

influence would have favoured the French style even if he designed no gardens. What is certain is that the English gardens remodelled at this time and for the next few decades were Le Nôtre gardens with English modifications. In some cases the owners themselves were personally responsible: they returned from a visit to France and set about remaking their gardens in the new way, or more or less so. Melbourne Hall in Derbyshire is a case in point and can still be seen in nearly its original shape. So — but they are no longer as they were, having later been 'improved' out of existence — were the Woburn gardens as remade for the dukes of Bedford by John Field during the sixteen-sixties: Celia Fiennes saw this garden when it was mature, in 1697, and what she describes is a Le Nôtre garden. From Evelyn's references too it seems clear that Cassiobury, as remade by the Earl of Essex and his gardener Moses Cook between 1669 and 1680, was in essence French. Moses Cook was a dendrologist: his *The Manner of Raising, Ordering and Improving Forest Trees* (1676) was an important textbook for half a century; but if

175

199 *Moritzburg, Dresden, May 1895.*

200 *Moritzburg, from the north.*

his choice of trees was his own, his manner of planting them was Le Nôtre's. Consider, too, this passage from Dr C. Leigh's *Natural History of Lancashire, Cheshire and the Peak* (1700):

'Chatsworth, like a sun in an hazy air, adds lustre to those dusky mountains, and attracts a general congress to be spectators of its wonders...

'The gardens, very delightful, pleasant and stately, adorn'd with exquisite water works; the first we observe is Neptune with his sea-nymphs from whence, by the turning of a cock, immediately issue forth several columns of water, which seem'd to fall upon sea-weeds: Not far from this is another pond, where sea-horses continually roll; and near to this stands a tree, composed of copper, which exactly resembles a willow; by the turn of a cock each leaf distils continually drops of water, and lively represents a shower of rain; from this we passed by a grove of cypress, upon an ascent, and came to a cascade, at the top of which stand two sea-nymphs, with each a jar under the arm; the water falling thence upon a cascade, whilst they seem to squeeze the vessels, produces a loud rumbling noise, like what we may imagine of the Egyptian or Indian cataracts. At the bottom of the cascade there is another pond, in which is an artificial rose, by turning of a cock the water ascends through it, and hangs suspended in the air in the figure of that flower. There is another pond, wherein is Mercury pointing at the gods and throwing up water; besides, there are several statues of gladiators, with the muscles of the body very lively displayed in their different postures.'*

The examples of the gallicization of English gardens are numerous — Eastwell Park in Kent, Kirby in Northamptonshire — but perhaps above all, Hampton Court as remade by John Rose's pupils London and Wise for William and Mary, while Christopher Wren was building their new palace:

'...In front of the lately erected east wing they cut off a large semicircular piece of the park, and laid it out as a flower-garden; for this the walks which led up to the old castle had to be put back, and then other walks, and also a canal, were made round the semicircle on the outside. On the inside it was laid out with *parterres de broderie*, the paths being kept in the form of a star which led to the castle. There were thirteen fountains, some large, some small, and a great many statues. By the side of the house ran a gravel path, 2,300 feet long, following the whole length of the house and its side wings, and this path had to serve instead of terraces.

'Although William had large plans, he could not see his way to making those enormous earthworks which sunk gardens would have involved, and this was the only way of getting a terrace. His contemporaries, and writers of a later date, all bewail the want of a terrace to give a general view...'†

* Quoted by Hadfield (1960).
† Gothein (1928).

For this garden the great French smith Jean Tijou wrought the magnificent grille and twelve gates which closed off the back of the semicircular garden where the Mount had been. There was, again under French influence, a general levelling of Mounts at this time. But in some respects the English gardener remained very English; and at Hampton Court, as in many other gardens, a Baconian Wilderness was retained or planted. Still, despite such English touches of nature, the new gardens made in the late seventeenth and early eighteenth centuries, as well as the old ones made over, were — the point has been sufficiently laboured — French. And when Henry, Duke of Beaufort, built his Badminton (Gloucestershire) in 1682, the great garden he laid out, with its twenty avenues starring outwards from a single *rond-point*, its flat parterres, and its trees in soldierly ranks, might have been designed for him by Le Nôtre.

If, in Britain, there was some small resistance to the new fashion in garden art, in Germany the dominion of the French garden was so absolute that it is rare to find anything native in the scores of great gardens made in this French century. In Germany there was a void to be filled: not only had the Thirty Years War so devastated the Germanies that there was enormous physical destruction and neglect to be made good; it had also left Germans with a longing to be surrounded with the symbols of peace, and of these the garden is the most potent. So high stood the reputation of Le Nôtre and the French gardeners in general that it was natural for the Germans to turn to them at once, more especially since there really was no native tradition to which they might turn.

The example was set by Ernst Johann Friedrich, Duke of Hanover, who, having secured an Italian to build him a château at Herrenhausen, commissioned Charbonnier, a pupil of Le Nôtre, to lay out the garden. Later, this garden was doubled in size but only by repeating Charbonnier's pattern. It was a vast rectangular, perfectly flat and level parterre, divided into triangles by paths; there are the usual central fountains, four square pools, two pavilions, *bosquets*, a formal circular lake. The whole was contained within canals bordered by avenues of limes. Herrenhausen was, in short, an elementary Le Nôtre textbook garden. This sort of thing happened all over Germany. Exceptions, such as the Landgrave Karl's garden near Cassel, Italianate and made by the Italian Guernieri, prove the rule, especially as this grand cascade garden was never completed.

201

Originally, and this again shows the strength of the French influence, the great Nymphenburg and Schleissheim gardens in Bavaria were to have been Italian, but were finished as French. Work on them was hardly begun when it was interrupted, first by the death of Adelaide of Savoy who conceived them; then by that of her husband, the Duke, who was willing to pay for them; still later, by the defeat of Bavaria in her war with Austria and the consequent enforced exile of the new Duke, Max Emmanuel, in Paris. When at last Duke Max was able to return to his country and throne, he was full of French ideas and brought with him a French architect, François Girard, to make his gardens. That artist's Nymphenburg was doubtless the greatest French garden ever made in Germany: as described in 1781 by a visiting connoisseur, the Graf von Rothenstein, it had nineteen fountains emitting 285 jets of water and, says the count, such a number of water devices, vases, statues met the eye as could be better imagined than described. The principal flower parterre, centred on one big fountain and with four lesser ones, was over 300 yards long, its arabesques outlined in dwarf, clipped box, its flowers changed from month to month. Of its forty-six statues, twenty-eight were gilded — an abomination either invented

201 *Plan of park, Grosssedlitz (eighteenth century).*

202 *Dresden, Palace in the 'Grosser Garten'.*

203 *Dresden, Palace in the 'Grosser Garten', 1719.*

178

202

203

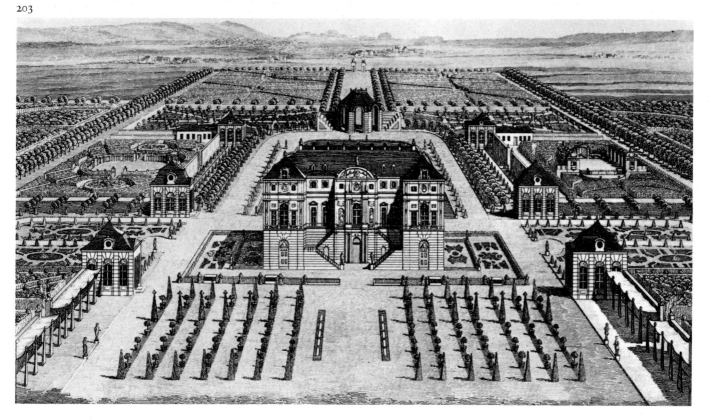

204

in Germany or copied from the Dutch. The great Fountain of Flora was made of white marble and had a basin 100 feet in circumference. Needless to say there were canals and a grand cascade. Among the numerous pavilions in this garden, the Amalienburg was, according to Peter Coats (1963), hailed as the one 'immortal creation of Bavarian rococo'. Nymphenburg had a hermitage with a real priest as hermit, in the old Hispano-French style. The park was full of small houses for members of the royal family, each with its own French garden.

Girard was kept busy making gardens for other German princes, notably at Bonn and Brühl for Clement Augustus, 'nephew' of the Prince-Archbishop of Cologne, although in both places much of the work seems to have been done by another Frenchman, Robert de Cotte. At his Bonn château, Poppelsdorf, Clement Augustus instituted a Brotherhood of Florists whose business was to keep a chapel of Christ the

Gardener permanently decorated with fresh flowers. Another Prince-Archbishop, Lothar Franz von Schönborn, Elector of Mainz, made a whole series of French gardens, decorated with German rococo ornament; but of these the only trace left to us is in the engravings of Salomon Kleiner, published in 1728. The best of them, with a magnificent cascade or water-staircase from the front of the house down to the Rhine, was called 'a little Marly'. Lothar Franz had seven 'nephews'; four of them became rich and powerful princes of the Church, and all made French gardens famous in their day, the most important of these being Würzburg, of which Salomon Kleiner published an album of engravings in 1740. The second owner of this garden was the Prince-Archbishop Friedrich von Seinsheim who, in 1770, appointed as his garden superintendent the Czech botanist Johann Procopius Mayer, who there wrote his book in defence of the Le Nôtrean garden, which was being shaken in its hegemony by the new English landscape style.

205

204 *Brühl, near Cologne.*

205 *Dresden, 'Grosser Garten'.*

In Austria garden making was halted or at least severely checked by that country's preoccupation with the task of saving herself and all Europe from the Turks. But no sooner had the enemy been halted, defeated and driven to retreat than the hero of the victory, Prince Eugene of Savoy, began to set the example by starting buildings and garden making. His estate in what were then the outskirts of Vienna was called the Belvedere. The garden which he made there was on two levels, the upper a big French parterre centred on a fountain, the lower a simpler parterre, the two linked by a grand cascade. The lower parterre was surrounded by a raised terrace. There were the usual *bosquets*, wide lawns and tall, rigorously trimmed evergreen hedges of the kind still to be seen at their impressive best in Vienna, although at Schönbrunn rather than the Belvedere. Today, incidentally, the Belvedere grounds include one of the half-dozen best alpine gardens — the Alpengarten im Belvedere — and collections of alpine plants in the world, superlative at least as regards

206

quality, although there are doubtless larger collections.*

The Belvedere was one of the first of the great gardens to be made in Austria between 1700 and 1750. They are of particular interest because they show the beginning of a tendency to break the French rules and to revert to the earlier, Italian style. Kleiner's engravings, and those of another garden illustrator, Delsenbach, show a few canals but many cascades; few level gardens, but many terraced hillsides; and simpler parterres and *bosquets* than the French fashion favoured. There are several possible explanations of the fact that Le Nôtre's grip, still so firm everywhere except in England, was relaxing in Austria: France and Austria were at daggers drawn; Maria Theresa introduced and favoured Italian

* Salomon Kleiner published an album of engravings of the Belvedere in 1731. It is grandly entitled: *The Wonderful Home of the Incomparable Hero of our Time in Wars and Victories; or the actual presentation and Copy of Gardens, Court and Pleasure Buildings belonging to His Most Serene Highness, Prince Eugenius Franciscus, Duke of Savoy.*

182

styles in all the arts and crafts, including cooking, dressmaking, furnishings and garden design; the two leading Viennese architects of this period, Hildebrand and Fischer von Erlach, were Italian-trained and enthusiastically Italianate.

Nevertheless, in the grandest of all imperial Austrian gardens, Schönbrunn, the influence of Le Nôtre's Versailles reasserted itself. It is true that when, early in the first decade of the century, von Erlach drew the first plans for the new palace, what he designed was an immense and very grandiose Italian garden which would, had it ever been made, have surpassed anything of the kind in Italy. But the Court could not afford the cost; the architect had to re-do his work, putting the palace at the foot of the hill instead of on top of it, and the garden sloping up the hill instead of terraced down it. This alone dictated the kind of garden it was to be. The garden as he replanned it was an immense parterre surrounded by canals and with corner pavilions, pure Le Nôtre, and quite different from the Schönbrunn we see now, so that we can know it only from Canaletto's paintings.

The canal plan was never accomplished; and the *gloriette* was not added until 1771, at which time also the Archdukes started a botanical garden, later moved to the Belvedere, on the slopes below it. There were two flower-gardens, sunken in the manner beginning to be thought of as Dutch although it did not originate in that country, and separated from the great parterre by pergolas.

Thus, despite the Austrian taste for the Italianate in gardens, the principal garden at Schönbrunn was French. However, in the park a new Italiante element made its appearance: artificial classic ruins. Gothein attributes these to the influence of the archaeologist Winckelmann. But although these ruins were a relatively late addition to the park, they were not that late: as far as we can ascertain, Winckelmann did not visit Vienna until 1786. And in any case there are more probable reasons for the appearance of this new element: English landscape gardening based, as we shall see on the 'classical' landscape painting of Claude, Poussin and others; or, perhaps, the same landscape school acting directly on garden design.

Saxony was a great garden country in the late seventeenth and early eighteenth centuries, for not only her prince and nobility, but also her burgesses, were making remarkable gardens.

The burgesses, more conservative than their betters, retained a great many Italian elements. The two gardens made by the brothers Bose in Leipzig were half-Italianate and were so remarkable that even the Pope asked to see the plans of Kaspar Bose's gardens. When Goethe, as a very young man, visited them in their maturity (1761), he wrote to his sister:

'These gardens are so beautiful I have never seen anything like them in my life. I may send you a view some time of the entrance into Apel's garden. It is glorious. The first time I saw it I thought I was in the Elyssian fields.'

The Bose gardens were especially famous for their Orange Parterres; for their fans of avenues; for their elaborate *bosquets*. One admiring visitor was Saxony's king, Augustus the Strong; his visit was perhaps the inspiration of his intention to make a garden to rival Versailles. His intention was never realized; but Augustus did make a grand French garden at the Moritzburg in Dresden, and in the Zwinger created one of Europe's loveliest Orangeries.

The Oranienberg and Charlottenberg gardens, made in Berlin by Frederick I of Prussia, were wholly French. But in Prussia it was Frederick the Great who showed the keenest taste for gardening and who, while still Crown Prince, had made Rheinsberg, his residence, locally famous for the beauty of its garden: its vineyard was in the form of a labyrinth centred on a statue of Bacchus. At Neuruppin he planted orchards and vineyards, calling the place Amalthea. His

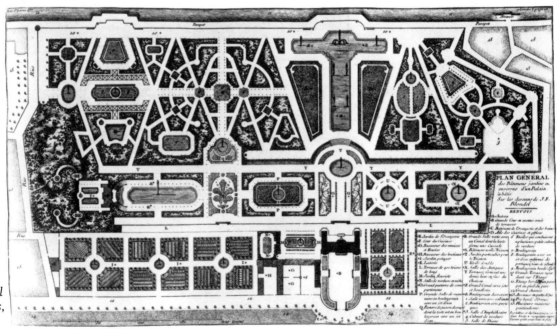

206 *Oranienbaum, near Dessau.*

207 *Plan by Jacques-François Blundell for a palace and gardens, possibly the Trianon.*

208

first inspiration as a gardener, however, was not classical literature, but his mother's beloved garden which she called Mon Bijou. She, by the way, must have been among the first Germans to complain of a certain roughness of the Russians as guests. In 1717 Peter the Great and his suite spent a few days with the queen at Mon Bijou. Knowing what to expect, she had as many breakables as possible stored in safe places; even so, after her guests had departed, she complained that her precious garden looked like Jerusalem after the sack. Her experience was not unlike John Evelyn's with the same party: he let his Deptford house, with its famous and treasured holly hedge, to Peter when the Tsar was studying shipbuilding in London. Peter wrecked it by having himself wheeled through it in a barrow.

Frederick laid the foundation stone of his *Sans Souci* in 1744. He left the palace to the architects, but supervised the laying out of the garden himself. What is remarkable is that the

208 *Vienna, Schönbrunn.*

209, 210 *Schönbrunn: 'after' Le Nôtre.*

211 *Pleached walk at Schönbrunn.*

king made the nucleus of the garden a vineyard terrace.* The Prussians of the eighteenth century developed, like the English before them, a sort of *nostalgie du midi* and yearned to surround themselves with the symbols of Mediterranean culture. Frederick's vine terrace also had orange trees and pomegranate trees, so that in winter it had to be covered with glass. Below the vineyard was a big French parterre, and beyond that an equally French canal. Beyond the canal a long, straight avenue led to two pavilions. According to a letter written by Biefeld,† friend of Frederick's youth, the king himself drew the first rough plans for the *Sans Souci* garden, had them put into professional shape by his architect, Knobelsdorf, but then acted as his own overseer of works. In course of time the gardens were extended on both sides, the extensions including a cherry garden, more pavilions, a new terrace garden, a 'Dutch' sunk garden, and a *parterre d'émail* made chiefly of glass beads and Dutch faience. Lower was the Grotto of Neptune. But the elaborate and very gallic water-works, including a grand cascade, never worked properly for want of sufficient water.

Holland was as much influenced by France, in garden art, as was Germany; but she did more to modify the Frenchness of her seventeenth- and eighteenth-century gardens with native elements. The Dutch were ahead of the rest of Europe in horticultural botany, which made some difference to her gardens, although not as much as one might have expected; however, the botanical progress of this period is dealt with separately below. Holland was, in several respects, particularly suitable for the Le Nôtre garden: for one thing, she had canals ready made; for another, Dutch farmers developed the modern methods of orderly farming, and it was second nature to them to apply strict rules and geometrical design in their gardening. As for the manner, Holland had more comfortable burgesses than any other country in Europe, people who were not rich but had money to spend on the decencies and small luxuries of life; so the Dutch were first to develop the small suburban garden. But even this was a modified French parterre, its patterns outlined in clipped dwarf box and then filled with coloured earths. There were alternatives; flowers were used, and particularly

* Berlin, lat. 52° 32′ N., is more than 2 degrees too far north for viticulture by the standard accepted among specialists, but its relatively hot summers make viticulture possible. In this connection, see e.g. Slicher van Bath (1963). He shows that wine was successfully grown at even higher latitudes in Germany at various times in the middle ages, vineyards being often planted when wheat and oats prices were falling. Cf. Hyams (1965b).
† Quoted by Gothein (1928).

209
210

211

those tulips which became the object of the collecting mania and boom in tulip bulbs, the story of which is too familir to be repeated here, but which ruined many middle-class families and made one or two fortunes for clever speculators. When the tulips and hyacinths were out of season, then Dutch gardens were filled with the kind of glittering ornaments which Francis Bacon had favoured. Moreover, the Dutch had their own way of using garden statuary, reviving Bernard Palissy's notion of using lifelike human figures made as realistically as possible and which in some cases were made to move, and even to emit sounds, by using some kind of clockwork contrivance. Here is a brief description (late for our period, but the Dutch long clung to their style against the strong current of English influence), written by Johanna Schopenhauer, of what these small Dutch gardens were like:

'The gardens in front of their houses are wonderful to behold. You find everything there except nature. There are trees which no longer look like trees, so clipped are their tops, and whose very trunks are painted with white oil paint to make them ornamental. There are all kinds of possible and impossible animals from the known or unknown worlds, cut out of box, and columns, pyramids and grand gates carved out of yew trees. In the middle of the garden stands

212 *Schönbrunn.*

213 *Montreal Botanical Garden.*

the choicest decoration, perhaps a Dutchman sitting on a tub and very highly coloured, or perhaps the figure of a Turk smoking his pipe, or an enormous flower basket with the figure of a gardener looking out of it roguishly, painted white with gilt extremities. The ground is covered with countless scrolls and flourishes, as neat as though they were drawn with a pen; the spaces are filled in with coloured glass beads, shells, stones, and pots in all manner of colours; and in their perfect symmetry they resemble embroideries of colossal size and the very worst taste.'*

Probably, at another season, there might have been tulips and hyacinths in place of the gewgaws; but not necessarily, for the Dutch loved their *jardins minéralogiques* — another French import.

It is often written that the Dutch had a great influence in shaping European garden style; in horticultural botany, certainly. But in design? Hardly: her own great gardens of the period, the Haus Neuberg near Ryswick, Het Loo, Houslaerdyk, the great Heemstede near Utrecht, the Haus Petersburg, and others, were wholly Le Nôtrean, and, unless in the architecture of their garden buildings, merit no particular description on grounds of originality. Where, in England or Germany, a garden of this period was said to be 'Dutch', one of two things was meant: that the garden buildings were Dutch in style, or that the garden was sunk and planted as a parterre with tulips or some other bulbs. The plans for parterres, no fewer than two hundred of them, in Van der Groen's *Den Nederlandischen Howenier*, published in 1668, and by far the most successful Dutch gardening book of the century, are decadent, simplified French.

This very brief sketch of French influence on German and Dutch garden art can best be concluded with a few lines on the Schwetzingen garden made by the French architect Pigage for the Elector Palatine Karl Theodor of Bavaria. The Elector was very much a man of his time, that is a man of taste: patron of Verschaffelt, founder of the Alte Pinakothek in Munich, he made not only Schwetzingen, but also the Englischer Garten in the city. By this time the new English garden was becoming so fashionable that Le Nôtre gardens were no longer being made and some were even being swept away to make room for English gardens. As a result, Schwetzingen was a transitional garden; for Karl Theodor had too much taste and respect for the principles of *La Théorie et la Pratique du Jardinage* to turn to England for his garden plans.

* Quoted by Gothein (1928).

187

214 *Schloss Benrath, near Düsseldorf.*

215 *Sans Souci, Potsdam.*

Schwetzingen, then, began as a French garden, with a trace of the new licence in that the parterres were not given sharp rectangular outlines. But hardly had Pigage completed his patron's little Versailles — *tapis vert* margined by *bosquets*, and decorated with lines of statues; grand canal, rococo fountains, cascade, avenues, and strictly aligned clipped hedges — than the Elector lost his nerve, gave way to the new landscape school, and commissioned Ludwig Skell to make him an English landscape garden set like a girdle round Pigage's French garden, and separated from it by the canal.

It was not only in North Europe that French gardens were being made during the second half of the seventeenth and first half of the eighteenth century. In Italy, if there were any attempts at a French garden as far south as Rome, they must (with one exception) have been very few, very timid and quite unremarkable. For some reason the Villa Albani is quoted in some works as 'French'; it is ineluctably Roman Renaissance. But in the north the case was different, and although there are no good French gardens left in Italy today, Da Costa's *Delizie del Fiume di Brenta* and Dal Res' *Ville e De-*

lizie di Milano (1773) show that both the Venetians and Milanese made French gardens. The Villa Castelazzo, the public gardens laid out in Parma by Carlos III of Spain in 1731, and the same Bourbon prince's Caserta near Naples, were all French gardens.

Caserta was yet another attempt to make a Versailles. Nothing need be said about it, except that its immediate model and inspiration was not Versailles itself, but still another imitation of Le Nôtre's masterpiece, La Granja at Idelfonso, north-west of Madrid. This great 'French' palace and garden, built round a farmhouse and hermitage by the melancholy Philip V of Spain, was where Carlos had spent his childhood and it was natural that he should try to reproduce it when he started building at Caserta. The greatest beauty of La Granja is its fountains, cascades and other water devices. Its principal parterre was simpler than was fashionable in France, and its maze was a poor one, but the enormous Andromeda fountain was admired all over Europe. In time, as the trees which Philip had planted grew into exceptionally fine specimens, and the garden's maturity

216-18 *Sans Souci, Potsdam.*

219 *Grosssedlitz, looking towards the castle.*

220 *Grosssedlitz, looking towards the 'Stille Musik'.*

221 *Grosssedlitz, orangerie.*

222 *Salzthalen, by Peter Schenk.*

allowed it to settle into the splendour of the mountain site, the beauty of La Granja was enhanced by nature; and by nature given a touch of the wildness which was to be the clue to the new, English, style.

All over Europe during this period of the French Garden, advances of two kinds were being made in the knowledge of plants, knowledge which was greatly to enrich garden material in the following epoch, and which, indeed, had already done so in England and Holland: botanical knowledge and horticultural knowledge.

In the first place, this is the epoch of the great taxonomic botanists, based on the botanical gardens founded, as I

VUE ET PERSPECTIVE DE SALTZTHALEN AVEC SES ENVIRONS DU COTE D JARDIN

222

have explained, early in the Renaissance period and thereafter, and growing the material with which these scientists worked. At the *Jardin Royale des Plantes*, originally the *Jardin du Roi* physic garden, Tournefort, Vaillant, the first of the de Jussieu dynasty of botanical scientists and their helpers were trying to find a satisfactory system for the systematic classification of plants, while Jean Robin, and his son Vespasien Robin after him, were introducing new plants and trying to discover how best to cultivate them. In England John Ray and (at the Oxford University Botanic Garden) his scientific opponent Robert Morison, an Aberdonian who had studied under Tournefort in Paris, were working to the same end, while the *Praefectus Horti* at Oxford, Bobart, and such amateurs associated with his garden as Robert Sharrock, were advancing the techniques of pruning and grafting. In Padua,

Cesalpino laid the foundations on which both Morison and Linnaeus worked; and Linnaeus' own work, much of it done in his late 'teens, which led to the system of classification and binomial nomenclature all were soon to accept, belongs within this epoch. At the Leyden University Botanic Garden, Everard Vorstius, third *Praefectus*, was introducing new plants from the East Indies; while Outgaers Cluyts, old Clutius' son who had studied under Clusius, first taught botany at Montpellier, and then went plant collecting in North Africa where, like Tradescant before him, he was roughly handled by Barbary pirates. Also under Vorstius, and his successor Florens Schuyl, Leyden introduced asters, oenotheras and some species of *Rhus* from North America; pelargoniums, mesembryananthemums, and gladiolus from South Africa. Paul Hermann, Schuyl's successor at Leyden, had himself

193

collected plants in the East Indies and at the Cape. He re-planted the Leyden garden on the lines of Morison's system at Oxford and still continued his plant introductions, including 'nasturtiums' from South America, arums (*Zantedeschia*) and agapanthus from South Africa. It was the Leyden garden which made Holland so much richer in new plants than most countries, although England was soon her equal and was shortly to surpass her. Leyden's activity reached a zenith towards the end of this period when, beginning in 1709, the great Hermann Boerhaave became *Praefectus Horti*; the catalogue of Leyden plants which he published *c.* 1711 has 3,700 kinds; Boerhaave's activity can be gauged from the fact that when in 1720 the University Press published his *Hortus Brevis Historia et Index Alter*,* the plant list had grown to 5,846 and included such rare and difficult exotics as the Cape *Proteas*. In the single year 1725 Boerhaave received 1,416 different kinds of seed from overseas.

Linnaeus studied at Leyden and Boerhaave was to be the first to read the twenty-three-year-old scientist's *Introduction to the Floral Nuptials*. The great Swedish botanist did not finally settle in Uppsala until 1728, whereafter that university became a world centre for all botanists. His garden there is still lovingly maintained as a monument.

If one had to choose a single year of this 1650-1750 'French' period as a botanical *annus mirabilis* it would probably be 1670:

'Robert Sibbald was founding Edinburgh's first botanic garden.† At Oxford, Robert Morison, the University's first Professor of Botany, had just published his *Praeludia Botanica*, based on the work of the Italian botanist Cesalpino. John Ray had just made his first experiments on the movement of sap in trees, thus laying the foundation on which de Jussieu and de Candolle were to work at the *Jardin des Plantes*, and published his *Catalogus Plantarum Angliae...* Marcello Malpighi submitted his first work on plant anatomy to the Royal Society in London on the day that the Society also received Nehemiah Grew's *Anatomy of Vegetables Begun*.'+

If the botanists were busy, so were the practical gardeners. The way was shown, appropriately enough in the century of Le Nôtre, by the French: it was Jean Robin's nursery garden on an island in the Seine near Nôtre Dame that supplied the garden makers of Paris with exotics, and for

* In this *Index* the Angiosperms and Gymnosperms were correctly separated for the first time.
† To be the most important in the horticultural world for two genera, *Rhododendron* and *Primula*.
+ Hyams (1969).

223

whom *Robinia* ('acacia' in the vernacular) was named. I have already mentioned his son Vespasien Robin; and La Quintinie, of course, whose work on the cultivation of such fruits as figs, pears and peaches in cold climates was fundamental. Cluyts, too has been mentioned above. What is curious is that we know very little about the gardeners who produced the enormous number of tulip varieties which, by this time, were being grown (see below) in European gardens. Moses Cook's work on trees, so valuable in an era when trees were the predominant garden plants, was followed by a very much more important one, John Evelyn's *Sylvia, or a Discourse of Forest Trees* (1664), the standard work till the end of the eighteenth century. The diarist also published a *Pomona*, as an appendix to his *Sylva*, about apple trees; and in 1693 came his *Aceteria, a Discourse of Sallets*.

223 *Queluz, Portugal.*

224 *Rio de Janeiro Botanical Gardens.*

224

In England the two greatest flower-growers after the Tradescants* were probably John Rea (d. 1681) and Sir Thomas
Hanmer. Rea's flowering shrubs were roses, usually grown as
standards, in thirty-one varieties; the ornamental, double-
flowered pomegranate; the Strawberry Tree, *Arbutus unedo*,
and such climbers as jasmines, honeysuckles and clematis.
His border flowers were auriculas, primroses and other primulas, hepaticas, rose campion, violets, wallflowers, stocks,
paeonies and, surprisingly, yuccas; his bulbs were lilies in
several species, fritillaries, and an enormous number of

* In much of the literature and especially the correspondence for the
later part of this epoch, used by garden historians, Elias Ashmole receives
respectful attention. Ashmole was a crafty solicitor who more or
less swindled the Tradescants out of their collection and should be
remembered as infamous rather than famous.

tulips, the best being Sir Thomas Hanmer's 'Agate Hanmer'
which, in a poem on the genus, Rea called '...queen of all
delights'. It was a striped purple, white and scarlet tulip.
Rea describes almost two hundred tulip cultivars, a very few
of them being English, ('Rickett's Fine Agate' for example and
'Chimney Sweeper'), a great many French, and even more
Dutch. As well as this extraordinarily large number of tulips,
the European gardeners of this epoch had many daffodils
and other narcissi, hyacinths, gladioli, ornithogalums, cyclamens, anemones and still others. In short, Europe's garden
flora had been enormously enriched.

In his *Ceres, Flora and Pomona* Rea describes a score of apples,
as many kinds of pears, five kinds of quince, fourty-four plum
and twenty-five cherry varieties, six apricots, a nectarine and

thirty-five peaches, nine varieties of grapes, three mulberries, figs, nuts and some fruits we no longer cultivate, such as edible haws and sorbus berries.

The bustling activity in the cultivation of new plants, in letter-writing about new plants, in plant exchanges and in garden visiting is described in admirable detail by Miles Hadfield (1960). A very large number of the new plants reached Britain from France and from Holland, and certainly in Holland and some parts of Germany horticultural activity was no less. There is some evidence, however, that by the end of this epoch England was already becoming supreme in plantmanship (partly as a matter of climate), and in her market-gardens, where great skill was developed in the production for market of fine vegetables such as asparagus and artichokes, cucumbers and other salad fruits, and melons grown on hotbeds.

The Dutch contribution was in new bulbs, in plants from the southern hemisphere and the Far East, in the arts of pleaching and topiary which the Dutch first learnt from the French and then carried to extraordinary lengths. Jan Commelyn's *Nederlantze Hesperides* (1676; English Translation 1683) taught other gardeners how to grow oranges and lemons and suggests that in this branch of pomology the Dutch had also become supreme.

The Dutch, finally, were carrying European horticulture into other parts of the world. So were the English, of course. But that story must have a chapter to itself.

225 *Memorial plaque to André Parmentier, Brooklyn Botanic Garden.*

226

11

EURO–AMERICAN BEGINNINGS

The first people to introduce Old World plants to the Americas were, of course, the Spaniards. Their Mexican introductions naturally had some influence on the garden flora of the rest of North America, but much less than one might expect. The reason for this is obvious. For a long time there was, between the Spanish settlements in the Central American lands and in Mexico, and the settlements later made by other Europeans in the north, a vast area inhabited by Indians who were less and less sedentary in their ways the farther one got from the Mexican area, and who were, therefore, not very likely to adopt new farm or garden plants. It was not until later that European settlements in this area, the area now occupied by the southern United States, formed a link between the Spaniards in the south and the old English, Dutch and French colonies in the north. Furthermore there was deadly enmity between the Spaniards and all the European settlers in North America. Thus it was that, on the whole, the Spanish introductions of European cereals, grape vines, fruit trees and vegetables did not spread north. The northern colonists had to introduce these plants, and the ways of using them in gardening, for themselves. There were some exceptions, notably the peach tree, as we shall see. But although Cortés certainly brought wheat and the grape vine to the Americas before the end of the 1520s, as well as (probably) salad plants, they never moved north of

the Mexican frontier; or, if they did, they failed to survive for want of care.

Following the Spaniards in introducing plants and garden techniques to supplement those of the native Americans came the English, the French and the Dutch; later the Swedes and the Germans. But before we glance at what these peoples brought with them, it will be as well to give a brief account of what they found in the way of Indian gardens and gardening when they arrived.

There was, in the northern half of the newly discovered continent, nothing to equal the grand and sophisticated gardens of Peru and Mexico. But many of the Indians of the North did have gardens of a kind; and among some of these peoples, the Cherokees and the Iroquois for example, horticulture was the principal source of food. These people were, in short, in the late Neolithic phase of culture, when hunting has become secondary to food raising, but when true agriculture has not yet developed out of horticulture. The four basic crops were maize, beans, pumpkins and squashes, all of which had reached the northern Indian nations from Mexico during the course of the Neolithic revolution and some of which must originally have reached Mexico from Peru. Maize is not really considered a garden crop, but the primitive method

197

of growing it was horticultural rather than agricultural. Early accounts of the Indians say that as well as these vegetables some grew such fruits as the native grapes, plums and mulberries,* a few flowers including roses and sunflowers and other wild flowers found within their range; and, of course, tobacco. In what is now Texas the fruits of *Opuntia* were valued, as they still are in Mexico and elsewhere, but it is not clear that this plant was ever cultivated.

Drawing upon the accounts of John Smith in his *Description of Mexico*, Ulysses P. Hedrick† concluded that the best native gardeners in the south-east of North America were the Cherokees, the best in the north-west being the Iroquois. Both peoples cultivated the same small range of crops, and both retained and valued shade-trees in their village gardens. Where did they learn the craft? For the Cherokees the question is hard to answer. The Iroquois belonged to that group of American people which anthropologists call Apalachid; they derived from a mixture of the continent's most archaic people and newcomers who crossed into America from Siberia during the second millennium BC, bringing the art of primitive gardening with them. Thus the garden craft of the northern tribes of America was an Asian heritage; yet it is curious (if — and it seems to me a large IF — the anthropologists and archaeologists are right about this) that the incomers brought no Old World crops with them.

As to the Indian manner of managing their gardens, we know something about this, at least in the case of one people, the Senecas, from the accounts of Arthur Parker (1926).+ The Seneca Indian gardens belonged to the people in common and were cultivated and managed by the women of the tribe. A senior matron regulated the work, laid down and supervised the rest periods which were filled with singing, games or story-telling. The principal tool, if not indeed the only tool, was the hoe. The Senecas grew ten different varieties of maize, several kinds of squashes or melons, and about a dozen kinds of (haricots) beans. The same crops, in more or less variety, were grown by most of the North American tribes. By the sixteenth century few were still in the Palaeolithic stage of being entirely dependent on hunting and food-gathering for their living.

Although garden tools and techniques were very limited, the Indians of some tribes had made interesting technical advances: Huron women, for example, knew how to force seeds into quick germination. They made a special seed compost by powdering rotten wood into flat boxes made of bark; the seeds, say, of gourds, were sown in these and the boxes hung in the smoke of the cooking fire.* They also knew that, if they wished to preserve a pure strain of some crop or other, it was important to grow it in isolation from others of its kind. They had so improved on the wild prototypes of some of their crop plants, for example the sunflowers which they cultivated for oil seed, that nothing quite like them could be found in the wild.

When European settlers began to introduce Old World plants, the first which the Indians adopted and cultivated were, naturally, those which somewhat resembled their own: peas which were, by some accounts, planted on Isabella Island by Columbus himself as early as 1493,† were soon thereafter to be found in Indian gardens; and the Indian women readily adopted the melons and cucumbers which were so like their own gourds and could be grown in the same ways. But some complete novelties also appealed to them: the peach, for instance, spread northward so fast following its introduction by the Spaniards into Mexico, that some later Dutch, English and French settlers in the north thought that it might possibly be native to the Americas which, of course, it is not. The author, for his part, is not entirely satisfied that the peach may not have been naturalized in North America before the Discovery. As scholars such as P. Bosch-Gimpera+ have very clearly shown, it is no longer possible to question the archaeological and anthropological evidence that the Far Eastern civilizations were trading with North America and South America in prehistoric times and into their own early historic times. It is likely that the Far Eastern traders brought at least some dried fruit with them; and it is at least possible that one or two of the species, thus unwittingly introduced, survived in America. There is one difficulty in the matter of the peach which seems to have been so widely diffused among the North American Indians when our settlers began to arrive: it is questionable whether the Far Eastern civilizations themselves had it early enough to fit in with the present theories about this prehistoric trade. But it is certainly possible.

European gardening began in North America on 7th March 1621 when, following their first and almost lethal winter

---

* *Vitis*, several species; *Prunus nigra*; *Morus rubra*.
† (1950); and numerous other works.
+ Parker himself was part Seneca. The Senecas were an Iroquois people.

* Sagard-Théodat.
† Arber (1885).
+ In Arambourg (1967).

227 *A portion of the Bodleian plate showing buildings, flora and fauna of the Governor's Palace, Williamsburg, Virginia, 1732-47.*

in the New World, the *Mayflower* Pilgrims of the Plymouth colony planted 'garden seeds'. Almost as soon, they allotted garden plots* to each of the nineteen founding families. And they also began to look about them at once for native plants which might be worth planting alongside their European crops. They found:

'...grapes, white and red, very sweet and strong, also strawberries, gooseberries, Raspas, Plums of three sorts white, black and red, being almost as good as a Damson. Abundance of Roses, white, red and damask, single but very sweet indeede...'†

The Massachusetts Bay Colony founded by the Puritans near Salem in 1628 had better land and better gardeners than did the Pilgrims of 1620. 'Governors Winthrop and Endicott', says Hedrick (1950), 'set examples so remarkable that they have come down to us as America's most notable gardeners of the seventeenth century.' By 1630 the Colony had its vineyards of native grapes and its orchards of native fruits. When William Wood visited the Colonies in 1630 and 1631 he found many gardens well planted+ and familiar garden plants growing there as well as they did in England. Less than four decades later gardens had become very numerous

and simple flower-garden plants of Europe had been introduced. Oddly enough, however, the colonists did not at once introduce European techniques. For example, they did no fruit-tree grafting, but relied for their stocks on seedlings and suckers, with the interesting result that they produced a whole range of new cultivars peculiar to the Americas.* European fruits grew so vigorously and well that soon crops of all kinds, but especially of apples for cider, were greatly in excess of what was usual in the Old World.

A curious character in early New England horticulture was a clergyman, William Blaxton, described as a bookish man and a recluse, who arrived in the colonies in 1625. He at once set about planting a garden and an orchard, for he had a passion for growing fruit and flowers. His house and garden were on the slope that is now Beacon Hill in Boston, near the corner of Charles Street. Blaxton trained a bull to the saddle, instead of using a horse; and from its back he used to distribute fruit and flowers freely to his fellow colonists. In 1635 Blaxton moved to Pawtucket, Rhode Island — the first white settler and the first gardener in that State. He produced the first named apple cultivar to be raised in what was to become the United States, originally called 'Yellow Sweeting' but now grown (if at all) as 'Sweet Rhode Island Greening'. Gardeners cannot accomplish much until they have a nursery from which to buy plants. In an authoritative paper on

---

* Said to have been laid out along both sides of what is now Leyden Street, Plymouth.
† Edward Winslow quoted in Young (1846).
+ Wood (1633).

* Josselyn (1674).

228 *John Bertram's garden, near Philadelphia, 1758.*

229 *View of the Botanic Garden of the State of New York, established c. 1812.*

229

the origins of the garden nursery trade in America, Dorothy S. Marks (1967) says that for two hundred years the colonists continued to import stocks from the mother country; and she gives the Prince Nursery, on Long Island, 1737, as the first commercial nursery*. Nevertheless, Hedrick (1950) quotes George Fenwich of Saybrook, Connecticut, as maintaining a commercial nursery in 1641; also one Henry Wolcott (1648 and later), whose Account Book is now owned by the Connecticut Horticultural Society. He sold fruit trees and stocked several varieties of each kind. The colonists seem to have concentrated on fruit in their gardens; or perhaps they did not consider lesser plants worthy of record. The same is true of the New Amsterdam Dutch and their gardens and orchards in Connecticut. But it was perhaps the French who set this fashion, at their (1604) Saint-Croix settlement, whose orchards actually lasted into the nineteenth century; and at their Castine settlement where the Baron de Saint-Castine planted apples and pears at least ten years before the Pilgrim Fathers landed in Massachusetts.

* See *Boston News Letter*, 5 April 1745.

Not only were named cultivars of fruit trees still being imported from Europe two centuries after the first settlements, but (anyway until the middle of the eighteenth century) this was also true of vegetable and flower seeds. Advertisements for seeds in the *Boston Gazette* and the *Boston News Letter* always announce that the seeds have been imported, usually from London. Typical advertisements list the herb, salad and vegetable seeds by cultivar names or at least by specific names; but they treat the flowers as less important in some such phrase as, '...also a parcel of curious flower seeds'.

New England gardens during the first century following the settlements were very like English cottage and farmhouse gardens. Like them they had mixed flowers and vegetables, herbs, and salads, usually in front and usually fenced or walled. Walling was exceptional; the fence was of whitewashed wooden stakes or pickets. The early Euro-Americans seem not to have had the distaste for privacy which makes the modern American gardener often dispense with any

201

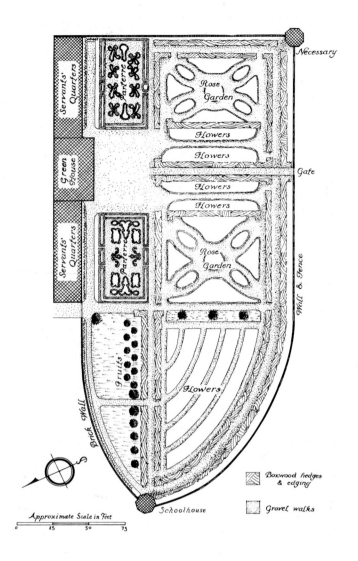

Boxwood hedges & edging

Gravel walks

230 *Plan of flower garden, Mount Vernon, Virginia.*

231 *French-Italianate at Mount Vernon.*

kind of fence or hedge. The town gardens were much the same as the village or farmhouse gardens. There would be a shrub on each side of the gateway in the fence; small flower-beds edged with box (if near enough to the sea for winters to be relatively mild), or with pinks where a hardier edging was needed; the flowers grown were a small selection of those chiefly grown in England, including lilies, paeonies, a few bulbs, gillyflowers and hollyhocks. Marigold, poppy and saffron crocus were grown more for medicinal or culinary reasons than for ornament. There might also be some native flowers, especially native lilies. Roses were the shrubs most commonly planted.

The first flowering shrubs, other than roses, to be intro-duced from the Old World were lilacs (*Syringa vulgaris* and other species), probably about 1700, possibly earlier.

The New Hampshire tradition that the first lilacs in America were those planted by Benning Wentworth in 1750 is a legend. John Bartram, the Pennsylvanian botanist, wrote to the English botanist John Collinson in 1737 saying that lilacs were well established in the colonies*, and stating that they were at their finest in Colonel Custis's garden in Virginia.

There appears to have been little in the way of great-garden-making in America until after about 1750. Doubtless there may have been exceptions, but not enough to discredit this statement. Consequently, there was no question of the formal, Le Nôtre garden being represented in the colonies. The real beginning of gardening as an art belongs to the epoch of the English landscape garden and so to a later chapter. For a very brief time, in the first flush of slave-based wealth in

* Hedrick (1950).

202

231

the south, there were some formal gardens: we shall come to them presently. The earliest extant letters to an English nurseryman from the owner of a grand 'place' in America, are those of the Bostonian Thomas Hancock to James Glin of Stepney, near London; and they were written in 1736.*

A little more than twenty years after the English were first settling in New England, Dutch Protestants and French Huguenots, flying from persecution in Europe, were beginning to arrive and to settle in what is now New York State; at first on Long Island, and then up the banks of the Hudson as far as Albany. The first of the great gardeners in this early wave of settlers was Peter Stuyvesant, who reached the colony of New Amsterdam in May 1647.

* 'The Hancock House and its Founder', *Atlantic Monthly*, XI.

Here, a digression is in order: the Dutch were, at this time or a little later, transplanting the European garden not only to America but also to South Africa. This came about for practical reasons. The Dutch East India Company needed a source of fresh vegetables for the crews of their ships bound to and from the East Indies: the Cape was a suitable place to plant a vegetable garden. That garden became, then, the nucleus of the Dutch colony planted at the Cape, whose first Governor, an enthusiastic gardener, was Jan van Riebeck. Later, when the old garden was placed in the care of the Van der Stels, father and son, it became one of the most remarkable botanical and display gardens in the world. Paul Hermann, the Prussian botanist, named above as *Praefectus Horti* at Leyden, was plant collecting at the Cape in 1672 and he made use of the garden as a sort of depot for his plants. In 1685 another visitor, the botanizing missionary Father Tachard,

232 'Landscape' at Mount Vernon:
North Grove.

233 Mount Vernon: Washington's garden
restored: South Grove.

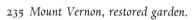

234 'Gardenesque' at Mount Vernon.

235 Mount Vernon, restored garden.

describes the garden as one of the most beautiful and curious he ever saw. According to Sir William Temple (1680), the Van der Stels' garden was a collection:

'...of fruits, trees, flowers and plants that are native and proper to each of the four parts of the world, so as in this one enclosure are to be found the several gardens of Europe, Asia, Africa and America... There could not be in my mind a greater thought of a gardener nor a nobler idea of a garden, and may pass for the Hesperides of our age.'*

I do not know the source of Temple's information; I doubt if he had ever been to the Cape himself, but if what he says be true, this was the first botanical garden planted on the geographical plan later so much favoured by the great botanical institutions, especially in Germany and Russia. At all events, the seventeenth-century Dutch were planting gardens not only in their American colonies, but also in other parts of the world newly settled by Europeans.

A Dutch word for *farm* is *bouwerij*; Peter Stuyvesant's farm was not quite on the site of the New York Bowery, but north and east of it, and until 1866 one of the pear trees which he had brought from Holland in tubs was still flourishing near the church of St Mark's-in-the-Bowery. This Stuyvesant *bouwerij* was particularly important, for from the gardens of fruit, vegetables and flowers which Stuyvesant planted there, seeds, roots, cuttings and scions were distributed to the new Dutch, French and German settlements on Long Island and up the Hudson River.

Just as in New England fruit-tree stocks were grown from seed or suckers, so too in New Amsterdam and New Netherlands, and although the Dutch were the most advanced and skilful garden craftsmen in Europe at this time, grafting was the exception rather than the rule. Adriaen van der Donck, who visited those colonies in 1655, had this to say: 'But in general grafting is not as necessary here as in the Netherlands, for most of the fruit is good without it.'†

This can only mean that some of the seedling trees raised thus early in American horticulture had turned out to be good ones, and had perhaps already been selected. As to flowers in the Dutch gardens, the same author tells us:

'The flowers which the Netherlanders have introduced there

are white and red roses of different kinds, the cornelian roses, and stock roses; and those of which there were none before in the country, such as eglantine, several kinds of gillyflowers, jessoffelins, different varieties of fine tulips, crown imperials, white lilies, the lily fruitularia, anemones, baredames, violets, marigolds, summer sots etc. The clove tree has also been introduced, and there are various indigenous trees that bear handsome flowers, which are unknown in the Netherlands. We also find these same flowers of native growth, as, for instance, sunflowers, red and yellow lilies, mountain lilies, morning stars, red, white and yellow maritoffles (a very sweet flower), several species of bell flowers etc., to which I have not given particular attention, but *amateurs* would hold them in high estimation and make them widely known.'

The Dutch and English were not the only people contributing to the foundation of European gardening in the northern half of America. In the 1670s and 1680s French Huguenots were settling in several parts of what is now New York State, at New Paltz on the Hudson and New Rochelle, Long Island. So that one of the remoter consequences of the infamous Revocation of the Edict of Nantes was the enrichment of early American horticulture. In both these French colonies the gardens and orchards were famous, the principal orchard fruits being peaches and apples.

In 1655, a peach orchard in New Amsterdam was the cause of a massacre. Hendryk van Dyck, a town councillor, was infuriated by the cool way in which the Indians stole his peaches. The fact is, of course, that the American Indians could not conceive of any individual owning land; the earth was for the people's use. So they had no idea of such an immorality as a *private* orchard: orchards, like fields and other gardens among them, were communal property, open to all. Van Dyck caught an Indian woman eating a peach in his orchard and shot her dead. Retribution was swift: on the following day something like 1,000 of her tribe raided the town and killed, or carried into slavery, 200 of Van Dyck's fellow-townsmen.

The Dutch also founded colonies and planted gardens in New Jersey. So did the Swedes, whose colonial centre was at Wilmington; they seem to have concentrated on vegetables and fruits, and had little interest in flowers. Even a century later, when Linnaeus' friend the botanist Peter Kalm visited the Swedish colony, he found much more to interest him in the woods and fields than in the gardens to which his countrymen had introduced so few native plants. He took home more than he brought with him, being particularly interested

---

* This garden, in the heart of Cape Town, which the author saw in 1968, is still beautifully maintained.
† Van der Donck, A., *Description of the New Netherlands*, Old South Leaflets No. 69. Boston.

24. *Carpet bedding at Withersdane Hall, Wye College.*

23. *Longwood Conservatory. Chrysanthemum borders and 'cascades'; a twentieth-century revival of a Victorian style.*

22.   *The scientific garden at Berlin-Dahlem owes much to English landscape tradition.*

236 *Monticello. In restoring Thomas Jefferson's English garden, the plans and plant lists which he made in his garden books were followed.*

in the native grape vines, like his remotely ancestral fellow-Scandinavian Leif Ericson*, North America being very rich in *Vites*. But it was not the Dutch, or, surprisingly, the French, but the English who first realized the potentialities of the American native grapes. The first man to have them planted on a big scale and argue that they would be better in America than the imported Old World grape (which was invariably killed by *Phylloxera* in North America), was Lord Delaware.

The Pennsylvanian Quakers were, perhaps, the most active

* *The Saga of Vinland the Good*. Leif the Lucky is said to have landed in Massachusetts Bay *c*. AD 1001. He is said to have taken home a cargo of grapes; if he did they were perhaps *Vitis labrusca*.

237 *The gardens on the east and west lawns of Monticello, neglected for many years, were restored in 1939 and 1940 according to Jefferson's plans. Several drawings were found amount his papers showing the scheme he projected and ultimately executed. On one is indicated the long gravel walk with its borders that circumscribes the west lawn.*

of the colonists in bringing American native plants, including ornamentals, into cultivation, and adopting the Indian cultivars. William Penn sent professional gardeners from England — Andrew Doz, Ralph Smith, and a third, known only as 'James' whom, even if the poor fellow had no surname, Penn recommended in a letter to his steward as especially able:

'...a good gardener, counted a rare artist at it, let him have at least three hands for he will put things, I hope, in a very good method, thou wilt have the tryall of him.'

And in October 1686 the steward reported back to Penn:

'The Gardiner is brisk at work. The Peach-Trees are much

broken down with the weight of fruit this Year. All or most of the Plants that come from England grow (being about four Thousand). Cherries are sprung about four and five Foot. Pears and Apple Grafts, in Country Stocks, and in Thorns, are sprung three and four Foot. Raspberries, Gooseberries, Currans, Quinces, Roses, Walnuts, and Figs grow well. Apricocks from the Stone fourteen or sixteen Inches sprung, since the month of April.'

The Pennsylvanians seem to have been the first colonists systematically to offer a return for the garden plants sent to them from home. One letter (quoted in Myers, 1912) asks the Bishop of London's gardener to send over trees, shrubs, flowers and seeds, '...and we will furnish them from these places'. Penn, moreover, was, after the Incas and Mexicans, the first town-planner in the Americas to include public gardens in his projects. Philadelphia was to have five squares planted as gardens, and, at the centre, an open space of ten acres. Furthermore, he directed that every house '...be placed, if the Person pleases, in the middle of its place as to have the brea[d]th of it, so that there may be grounds on each side of it, for gardens'.

The Americans owe their first botanical gardens to the founder of the Quakers, George Fox, who was in the colonies in 1671 and 1672. At his death he bequeathed land to the Pennsylvania Quakers for various purposes stated in his will, including that of a Physic Garden, 'for lads and lasses to know simples...' The second such Physic Garden was, according to Hedrick (1950), planted in America some time after 1694, on the Wisshakon river by a colony of Rosicrucians settled near Philadelphia. Next, and far more important, was Christopher Witt's garden in Germanstown, established in 1708, four years after he reached America from England. Witt grew not only medicinal herbs, but also plants which interested him as a pure botanist, some of which he sent to England to his botanist friend, the Quaker Peter Collinson already mentioned. Still later, in 1728, came the Bartram Botanic Garden at Kingessing on the Schuykill river. This Bartram, a physician and herbalist, did a great deal of plant-collecting in the colonies and beyond. A friend of Benjamin Franklin, and through him a correspondent of many European botanists and scientists, Bartram was described by Linnaeus as the greatest natural botanist in the world. His garden became a depot for the raising and acclimatizing of European plants in America; and for the propagation of American plants to send to Europe. The correspondence, maintained for over thirty years, between Bartram and Collinson is a wonderful record of the plant exchanges of that period between the two continents, by which the garden florae of both were much enriched.*

Although Virginia was the first of the English colonies, the 'Old Dominion', and although the younger Tradescant was plant-collecting there for King Charles I as early as 1637, gardening there got away to a late start. On that rich soil, in that mild climate, and with the woods still teeming with game, it was easier to live like an Indian than to bother with cultivating gardens. Later, it was the extraordinary predominance of a cash-crop, tobacco, instead of the usual subsistence crops, which inhibited gardening. John Smith, reporting to the Virginia Company in London in 1629, wrote that gardens in the colony were 'prospering exceedingly', but that the people let them be spoilt by the cattle while they gave all their attention to the tobacco crop. This crop, taken over from the Indians with the practice of smoking, was forbidden in Britain, King James himself even writing a pamphlet against it as a filthy weed the smoking of which was most injurious to the lungs. He was not to be vindicated by the medical profession for three centuries. Meanwhile, tobacco was the one crop which the colonists could grow without fear of home competition and which was, albeit perishable, easy to ship. Not until the Virginian planters were emancipated from field labour would they be able to turn their attention to gardens. That happened when in 1619 a Dutch ship arrived in the colony with twenty Negroes for sale as slaves. As Hedrick (1950) says:

'Without the aid of Negroes, a plentiful supply of which began coming in, Virginia and the colonies to the south could hardly have planted and maintained the fine estates built on the profits from tobacco, indigo, rice and later cotton which brought wealth to the south.'

Until they thus became rich on slave labour, so reluctant were the southern colonists to bother with gardening that the Company had to pass a law (1629) compelling the Jamestown settlers to plant gardens. This was not immediately effective but in due time it must have become so, for the fine quality of Virginian and Maryland gardens figures largely in late seventeenth- and early eighteenth-century accounts of both colonies.† Similar attempts by the Company to enforce the planting of vineyards failed time after time, simply because they insisted on the Old World vine which was invariably killed by *Phylloxera vasatrix*. This aphis, which attacked the leaves of the native American vines, doing little

---

* See Darlington (1849).
† See, e.g., Hammond (1656), the first of these encomia.

harm, attacked the *roots* of Old World vines; it was not discovered as the cause of the trouble for more than two centuries. The Old World vines were also very seriously damaged by both downy and powdery mildews to which the New World vines were resistant since they had evolved with them as their parasites.

This colonial gardening we have been discussing was, as I have said, all of the cottage and utilitarian kind, which was very natural in a new country. But it seems likely that a beginning was made in real garden art, in sophisticated ornamental gardening, late in the seventeenth and early in the eighteenth century, in both Virginia and Maryland. It cannot have been much of a beginning even then; at all events very few accounts written by European visitors to the colonies have anything to say about a subject which in Europe was as important in cultivated conversation and correspondence as, say, painting or the newest book of poems. Yet some fine gardens there certainly were, about the homes of such old Virginian families as the Byrds, Eppes, Carys, Carters, Beverleys and some others; and at such Maryland manor houses as Evilinton, Great Oak, Kent Fort, Susquehana Manor and others. It was in such places that topiary was introduced to America: even today ancient yew and box hedges survive from this period, gnarled and misshapen. Knot gardens in the Elizabethan manner were made in Virginia thus late; and, evidence of growing sophistication, they were, by the early eighteenth century, being called parterres. The garden maze reached America in the third or fourth quarter of the seventeenth century. The Governor's palace at Williamsburg, as described by Hugh Jones (1724) who speaks of its fine gardens, even had a Le Nôtre-style canal.

Among the places where the French Huguenots founded colonies in the sixteenth century were Florida and Georgia, and of course they brought with them some of the gardening techniques and garden plants of their own country. In Florida, however, they had no time to make gardens or

anything else, for in 1565, only three years after their settlement, the colony was wiped out by the Spaniards who massacred every man, woman and child in defence of their Spanish Main monopoly. The Spanish themselves then founded a colony, St Augustine, and from it others, or rather a number of missions, as far out as South Carolina and Alabama. Gardens were planted, and among the new introductions were oranges, pomegranates and figs.* We are not told whether the figs succeeded.† Quite possibly they also introduced the olive and the lemon, for when an English colony was founded in Georgia in 1733, Oglethorpe, its leader, found abandoned plantations of olives, figs and oranges, some of the trees being very old and of immense size. But the English, too, introduced Mediterranean plants into the southern United States at least as early as 1670 when the Charles Town (Charleston) colony on the Ashley River was settled. They planted, among other things, oranges, lemons, limes and pomegranates; and the same fruits were planted by the people of the Cape Fear colony founded in 1664.

* Letter from Bartolomé Martinez to Philip of Spain, 1577, quoted by Hyams (1965a). Martinez, commander of the Colony, tells the King that he planted these trees with his own hands.
† When, much later, the first attempt was made to establish large-scale fig plantations in California, the venture failed. No scientist, but the observant peasantry of Italy, told the American investigators of this disaster that figs cannot set fruit *as a rule* without the intervention of a pollinating insect, the fig-wasp *Blastophaega psenes*. This insect having been introduced into California, the California fig industry became successful, to the lasting discomfort but, doubtless, health of millions of costive children. There is no record of earlier introducers of the fig running into this difficulty. Why? Partly, no doubt, because figs introduced from England and France would have been of the very few long-selected parthenocarpic varieties which do not need the service of this wasp. But what of the earlier, Spanish introductions into (for example) Mexico? I do not know the answer.

238 *Bronx Botanical Garden.*

The Charleston colonists were quicker than most to plant ornamental knot gardens hedged with clipped box or yew. A little later came topiary, and artificial ornament in the Franco-Dutch style.

By the time there were colonists rich enough (and of the social class) to make great gardens, Le Nôtre formal gardens were out of fashion in Europe, and on the whole the great gardens of the Carolinas were made in the landscape style. But because of the time lag between taste and manners in Europe and the same vogue in the American colonies, one which might be as much as two decades or even more, there were some exceptions. As for small gardens, there is evidence in such plans and descriptions as we have that the influence of the French Huguenots on these was very considerable, in Charleston and elsewhere. In the plans for the town of Savannah which Oglethorpe drew in 1733, the houses are given each a garden of 90 feet by 60 feet. There is a brief account of what these were like when planted, quoted by Hedrick (1950) from *The Garden History of Georgia*★:

'The home, if a mansion, was set back from the street. A strip of formal planting or a small formal garden enclosed by a wrought iron fence constituted the front yard. In the rear, between the residence and the servants' quarters and the barns, lay another garden enclosed by high brick or tabby walls. In this back garden were flowering shrubs, figs and citrus fruits with grapes or roses sometimes led from one building to another.'

Some of the native plants to be found in southern gardens were first introduced into cultivation there, and also sent to Europe, by the English botanist Mark Catesby who worked in Virginia from 1712 to 1719, and later in the Carolinas.† Not primarily a gardener, Catesby had an eye for a good garden plant. Even more important in this work of introducing new garden plants was a rich merchant and nurseryman named Henry Laurens. He could afford to indulge unprofitable whims, and had, in his English gardener, Watson, an enthusiastic and skilful ally. But his contribution and Watson's, including the reintroduction of the olive, lime, ginger and several kinds of fruits, really belongs to a period which will be the subject of another chapter.

* For which, exceptionally, he gives no bibliographical detail.
† His *Natural History of Carolina, Florida and the Bahamas* was published in London between 1731 and 1733.

239 Persian book-cover with garden scene.

240

LATER ISLAMIC GARDENS

It has commonly been the case that once a culture perfects a garden style which suits it, giving expression to its artistic and social axioms in terms which are proper to it, innovation stops. Perhaps all arts are, within a cultural frontier, finite. It is possible to spot the moment at which a state which it would not be proper to call perfection but which can be defined as satisfactory, is reached. Before that moment, foreign influences may be accepted, will be digested, and may modify the native style, but will not damage its integrity, will, rather, add to its richness of texture; the art is still growing, the ideas and feelings which inspire it and the terms in which it can be expressed have not been exhausted. But after that moment foreign influences, if sufficiently strong, are not absorbed, and the native style is quite corrupted by them, loses its integrity, ceases to express the native feelings and ideas. In garden art, the perfect example of this can be found in Japan: from the Nara Period to Late Edo, that is from the seventh to the nineteenth century AD, Japanese garden artists made all the styles which reached them from China and Korea, and even from India, their own; but the deliberate westernization of Japan after the fall of the Shogunate, letting in European garden styles, was the death of garden art in the one country where it had been raised to the high level of one of the fine arts. Modern Japanese gardens are pretty, but they are not fine art.

In China, once a style and manner which gave expression to Taoist nature-worship, Confucian gentlemanliness and Buddhist mysticism had been accomplished, no real change occurred in many centuries: finite, the art had ceased to grow. The same thing happened in both Italy and France: a perfected style could be repeated indefinitely; or 'English' gardens (or some other alien gardens) could be made on Italian or French soil; no new syntheses were possible, at least for the time being. Why? I don't know; it is for social historians to discover why cultures lose impetus and energy and so the power to use and digest alien material.

The point is that, *historically*, there is nothing to say about an art which has ceased to grow. So that a world history of a particular art, in this case the art of gardens, has to look, for its own progress, to the growing-points. During the late sixteenth and early seventeenth centuries there was one such growing-point which has not yet been considered: Iran.

If we want a convenient starting point for the new period in Persian garden making, we might do worse than take the spring of the year 1598 when the Safavid Shah Abbas decided to build a new city between the old town of Isfahan and the Zayandeh river. The site was an area of open fields, orchards and gardens, some of which were retained, for the city which

213

Shah Abbas conceived was to be what we should now call a garden city. Seventy years later, when the French jeweller Chardin visited Isfahan, it had a population of over half a million people, 162 mosques, 48 schools, 273 public baths, 1,800 caravanserai, each with its garden, and all built round a nucleus of palaces with a maidan on one side and a magnificent avenue of elms down the other.*

To say that the buildings of the new Isfahan stood in gardens is inadequate to describe the close union of building and garden. We have already noted that the Islamic gardens of Spain and to a lesser extent those of Northern India, which were remote copies of the Western Islam gardens, derived in plan from the Roman villa-palace; the new Persian gardens were a new and original expression of that ancient style of which the type is the Villa Adriana. Perhaps it is not necessary to add that there is here no suggestion of conscious imitation, of an art which knew its own derivation. Artists adopt and diffuse the chief elements of styles often without even realizing what they are doing. Burlington and William Kent brought Palladian to England, but, with a few exceptions, English Palladian houses were not mere copies of Italian villas; they were so English that even so great a French historian of art as Hippolyte Taine totally failed to understand their beauty.

At all events, in the new Persian works of architecture, buildings and gardens so interpenetrated that they cannot be considered apart. The many inner courts, for example, were rooms without ceilings; and many of the covered parts were open at the sides, were, so to speak, roofed gardens. Shah Abbas's new palace was a complex of such works. Central to it was an inner enclosure; this was a formal garden of pools and canals lined with blue tile, fountains, and parterres of flowers. But the outlines which would otherwise have been rather too hard for Persian taste (however well

* Chardin (1711).

240-2 *Persian garden miniatures.*

243, 244 *Persian garden miniatures.*

they might have suited the French) were everywhere softened by the random planting of trees, both as specimens and in boscages; and some of this tree planting was cleverly used to give an effect of distance and expanse. Set among trees were four pavilions — a Guest-house, the Paradise Pavilion, the Sea Pavilion and the Hall of Mirrors. These, or some of them, were, it seems:

'...made expressly for the purposes of love. The furnishings

245

245 *The Persian Shah's 'Loggie Terrene' or pleasure walk, Isfahan.*

246 *Palace of Chehel Sutun ('Forty Pillars Palace'), Isfahan.*

of each part are the most magnificent in the world and the most voluptuous, with retreats which are nothing but an entire bed.'*

The most famous palace-cum-garden of this complex of gardens and pavilions and palaces was the Chehel Sutun. Its porch was founded in white marble and supported by fluted cedar pillars; its ceiling, painted in blues, greens, golds and reds, dominated and was reflected in a long, formal pool. The woodwork was inlaid with innumerable, diversely-shaped mirrors. At the centre was a fountain with four lions spouting water into a basin of white marble. It is extremely difficult to tell from contemporary engravings of such court-yard gardens as this one, or of the Chahar Bagh, the Avenue of the Four Gardens, what plants were used. One can see that hedges were clipped evergreen, that trees were often

* Quoted but not identified by Wilber (1962).

216

kept to formal shapes; but not what kinds they were. How-ever, it is quite obvious that cypress, plane and poplar were favourites, that myrtles were used, and that citrus and roses, both grown as standards, were used in regular plantings; and that jasmines were the usual climbers. For the rest, records are unfortunately wanting. It does not really help much to learn that Shah Abbas was guilty of the vulgarity of planting gold and silver coins under his trees, by way of manure. Some of the gardens of the Chahar Bagh give us a clue to what they were like in their names, e.g. the Mulberry Garden; the Garden of the Vineyard; and the Garden of Barberries. The same complex included still more gardens. Two poems dating from the reign of Shah Abbas, *The Rose-Garden of Prosperity* and *The Secret Language of Sweet-smelling Flowers* are in part descriptive of the imperial gardens in the Sa'adatabad area across the river from the Chahar Bagh and connected with it by a bridge. From a plan and an en-

246

graving one can deduce something of the layout, a series of maze-like walks between tall, clipped evergreen hedges, and with the trees planted with almost Le Nôtre-like regularity. Persian gardens were enclosed, secret, shady and cool; the whole garden might, by its site and terraced shape, command a view; but within the garden the prospect, except across water, was deliberately limited, near, forcing the eye to look at detail.

Still part of the new complex at the heart of the new Isfahan was a garden called the Hazar Jerib. The Chevalier Chardin says that this was about a mile square, probably an exaggeration. It was made in twelve terraces rising from the river bank, and its walks or rides formed a regular grid of twelve avenues at right angles to the river and three parallel with it. Three of the avenues had stone-lined canals running on either side of them, each canal having a big central basin;

the fountains were 'innumerable'. Chardin names five pavilions as integral with and penetrated by the garden, adding that in spring it was a carpet of flowers beside the canals and basins. He describes himself as astonished at the number of fountains which were to be seen on every side as far as the eye could reach, by the beauty of the scene whichever way one looked, by the scent of flowers and the flights of birds, some kept in aviaries and some among the trees. It is important to bear in mind that avenues in Persian gardens were planted so close, and under-planted with fruit-trees, that the trees formed into impenetrable walls. This garden was made about 1650, but an even larger one, Far-ahabad, was laid out in 1700. Nothing is left of it today, but apparently it had two very large lakes (*daryache*) each of which had its islands and pavilions; there were extensive woods, formal orchards and numerous palace-pavilions.

217

247 *A view of the Chehel Sutun Palace gardens, Isfahan.*

What were the flowers of such gardens? Chardin says that all the flowers grown in Europe were common and he specifically names the following: tulips, anemones, ranunculus, crown-imperial, eight kinds of narcissus in several colours, pinks and jasmines, mallows, white and blue hyacinths, red and yellow stocks, and various kinds of pinks. He mentions roses in five colours and these include what he calls 'yellow-red' roses, clearly the originals of the very popular HTs and Floribundas of the 'Masquerade' type. The *Rosa foetida* from which all these derive is, of course, a native plant of Iran.

But the Chevalier's list is not complete; we can supplement it from other sources with several kinds of iris and notably the miniature ones, primroses in variety, *Muscari*, wallflowers and carnations, delphiniums, tuberoses, and about fifty more besides, not always identifiable. And the gardens of the Caspian area were all remarkable for 'whole forests of oranges and lemons'.*

These Caspian gardens were, by reason of the warmer, wetter climate, virtually tropical or at least sub-tropical, rather different from those of the high plateau. Jonas Hanaway,† who visited the coastal strip known as the Mazanderan in 1744 and who wrote about the long-established gardens which he saw there, says that the region benefited by having a long spring when '...Their lawns and meadows are strewn with flowers and their bushes with honeysuckles, sweet briars and roses'.

Among the fruits of these gardens he names peaches, oranges, lemons and pomegranates; also, '...here are an abundance of grapes... growing wild in the mountains with great luxuriancy...'+

The principal gardens of the Mazanderan were, like those of Isfahan, made by Shah Abbas, who built lodges at six-mile intervals along the coast road of three hundred miles, which he also built; they were to make his journeys by the seaside more comfortable and for the use of other travellers. Off that road he made six great palace-cum-garden villas. Noth-

ing of these remains, but Wilber (1962) says that the Shah's garden at Amol was, by tradition, remarkable for its size and for the height of its famous cypresses; it was almost certainly a great terrace garden like Farahabad. The same author, who visited and studied the sites of all these Caspian 'villas' late in the nineteen-fifties, has this to say about another of them:

'Near the settlement of Barfurush, now known as Babol, Shah Abbas ordered a garden laid out which did not conform to the customary types. South of the town a stream was led into an area enclosed by an embankment, so that a lake of nearly two miles in circumference was created. In the lake was an artificial island of some acres in size, and brick pillars supported a long wooden bridge from the mainland. Other pillars within the lake indicate that at least one pavilion stood by itself in the midst of the lake so that it could be reached only by boats. This garden was known as the Bagh-i-Shah (Royal Garden), or as the Bahr ol-Eram (Sea of Paradise). Today the Safavid buildings have all vanished and there are remains only of two nineteenth-century brick structures, a residence, with *anderun* (women's quarters), of Mahmud Quli Mirza. Even in the absence of the early buildings, it is possible to visualize the garden of Shah Abbas as a variation of the daryacheh, or "little sea" gardens, common to the plateau proper. In those gardens hillside springs flow down into a vast pool, but on the Caspian slope water is so much more abundant that the pool, as at Amol, becomes a real lake.'

We know a little more about two of the gardens made by the Shah near Sari because Xavier Hommaire made some drawings of them in 1847.* In one of them a single-storey pavilion with an open porch supported on pillars overlooks the long, formal pool of a walled garden of lawns, crowded with trees and palms, and one can see other such enclosed gardens in what is a villa-like complex of gardened courts and buildings. Yet another of Shah Abbas's Sari villas was visited by the English envoy, Sir Thomas Herbert, almost as soon as it was finished in 1628.† Sir Thomas begins well:

'It [the palace] has two courts comparable to the Fountain bleaus [Fontainebleau] either of them which express an elaborate art in the skilful gardiner... the spreading Elms, Chenores and sicamores surrounding...'

But the poor man was so horribly shocked by the interior decorations:

'...the Walls varnisht and painted in oyle, but by an uncivil pencil, the genius of some goatish Apelles; such Lavaltoes

* Wilber (1962).
† Hanway (1753).
+ This Caspian mountain area is the original home of *Vitis vinifera*, or rather one of them, and certainly not far from its original place of domestication, so that the careers of the vine of history, and of wine, begin there or near there. See Hyams (1965a). Academician Negrin of the Leningrad Institute of Applied Botany, who made a thorough study of these wild vine populations, found that while some are in fact wild, others originated in 'escapes' from vineyards so ancient as to be prehistoric.

* Hommaire de Hell (1854-60).
† Herbert (1638).

248

of the Persian Jupiter are there, such immodest postures of men and women, nay of Paederastyes, as makes the modest eye swell with shame...'

that his eye, thus put out of commission, saw nothing more of the gardens. Chardin, too, visited this palace of the Jehan Numa (1666), but of the garden says little but that its Jasper Fountain was covered with sheets of gold.

Beginning in the year 1612 Shah Abbas built another enormous, villa-like complex of palaces, pavilions and gardens farther along his Caspian corniche, at Beshahr (then called Ashraf), on a site five miles inland but with a fine view over the Bay of Astarabad. The new garden palace was called the Bagh-i-Shah and there, too, Xavier Hommaire made some drawings. The principal garden element was the Garden of Forty Columns — Bagh-i-Chehel Sutun — and it was another terraced garden dominated by the palace which, from a portal at the other, lower extreme, was approached by a broad avenue mounting from terrace to terrace. From Hommaire's drawing the trees of the avenue seem to have been cypress, plane and poplar. In front of the palace-pavilion on the highest terrace was a formal pool about fifty yards square; the name Forty Columns must have derived from its many-pillared porch, although only twelve can be seen in Hommaire's drawing. The canals associated with the pool and

with waterfalls down the terraces were pebble-lined. Travellers' tales say that the cypresses of this garden attained a height of sixty feet and that its orange trees were twenty-five feet tall.

The Bagh-i-Chehel Sutun was apparently linked not only by ride or walk but also by canal to another garden, the Bagh-i-Sahib Zaman, which means Garden of the Lord of Life, in whose single, six-halled pavilion Sir Thomas Herbert was received by the Shah. The British envoy was so overwhelmed by the wealth and luxury of the gorgeous interior decoration and furnishings, that he says nothing whatever about the gardens of either this or the adjoining courts which comprised the Spring Garden. This was yet another garden of descending terraces, water-stairways and fountains, topped by the Pavilion of the Fountain whose walls were of Dutch tiles and which was further decorated with paintings by one John Duckmann, a Hollander or Fleming in the Shah's employment. Herbert calls him John the Dutchman and describes his painting with contempt:

'...The solemnity with which we were conducted struck me with a kind of religious awe; but this was soon changed to contempt; for I was surprised to find the room adorned with paintings such as could please only a voluptuous Mahommedan. Here also were portraits of Shah Abbas first and

second, and of some other persons, all by a European hand, but meanly performed.'

Hanway was another visitor to this magnificent mountain-sited garden; he enthuses over the views, the birdsong and, above all, the cascades and fountains. And Wilber (1962) quotes a contemporary Persian account which '...was lyrical over the baths, mansions and open pavilions and "orchards and gardens resembling Eden and comprising these various edifices and water reservoirs of perfect beauty, filled with pleasant and salubrious water"'.

The Persian gardens of this period, which is more or less coincident with Le Nôtre's in Europe, can, although they were original works and peculiar to Iran, be connected with two other periods and styles in the history of garden art. Their most ancient derivation is clearly from the Hanging Gardens of Semiramis. On the Caspian, hillside sites were not wanting, and there the terraces-with-falling-waters manner almost imposes itself; on the high plateau, rising ground

248 *Bagh-i-takht, Shiraz, Persia. Formerly Palace of the Governors of Shiraz.*

249 *Palace of the Shahs at Isfahan, sixteenth century.*

249

250- *Spain, Seville. Courtyard of Casa del Pilatos.*

25. *The Iris border at Withersdane Hall, Wye College.*

251 - *Spain, Seville. Courtyard of Casa del Pilatos.*

had to be contrived, so true is it that a garden designer inspired by the feelings and ideas which govern the art style of his particular culture will, if necessary, work against the grain of nature. The seventeenth-century French were capable of levelling hills to get a flat garden; the seventeenth-century Persians were capable of creating hills to get a 'vertical' garden. The second affiliation of seventeenth-century Persian garden art is with Italian Renaissance and ultimately, therefore, with Roman, garden art. This is manifest in the similarity of an overall plan which united a number of gar-dens and buildings in a villa-like complex, so that I have not hesitated to call the Shah Abbas creations 'villas' despite their Oriental gaudiness; it is manifest, again, in the delight in rising terrace gardens and long cascades. It is important to stress that there is, here, no suggestion that Italian artists actually had a hand in the designing of Persian gardens. The garden designers of western Islam had long since made the villa style their own, and transformed it; Shah Abbas and his successors produced an original manifestation of garden art in the same spirit.

223

252

Although this and the subsequent period saw the making of still more gardens in Iran, with the distinctions which make it meaningful to speak of 'the Persian garden' as we do of 'the Italian garden' or 'the Japanese garden', that is to say making it a generic term, those gardens seem all to have been much the same in shape if diverse in detail. The final period in the art of the garden in Persia came a good deal later; but it will be convenient to say a little about it here, out of chronological order, so that we shall have finished with the subject of Persian gardens.

This last wholly 'native' period in the art begins with the transformation, starting in 1788, of Teheran from a village into the country's capital city, by Aqa Muhammad Khan, founder of the Qajar dynasty. This Shah was not himself a builder or garden maker; but his successor Fath 'Ali Shah, who came to the throne in 1797 and reigned almost half a century, built palaces, mosques and public buildings, and made many gardens. Fath 'Ali Shah needed plenty of accommodation for the royal family, since his children and grandchildren are said to have numbered two thousand. Among the famous garden works of this period are the Gulistan palace, the Qasr-i-Qajar, and the Negaristan.

A good account of the Gulistan as it was at the beginning of the nineteenth century was left by a French traveller, Jaubert, who saw it in 1806.* From an elaborate portal called the Dar-i-Sa'adat, Jaubert looked along a long, narrow pool set in faience to the Divan Khaneh (Reception Hall). The pool

* Jaubert (1821).

224

253

was surrounded by a paved court lined with tall trees. The Divan Khaneh was used for receptions whose magnificence and costliness of decor completely staggered European visitors.

The inner court of the Gulistan as painted later but still unchanged (c. 1862) by Mirza Khan Malek esh-Sho'ara, was a vast, formal pool reflecting the long, low palace pavilion, surrounded by regular parterres and irregularly planted trees, mostly cypress and pine. A gallery along the top of the façade overlooked the garden. Later the pavilion was built into the Hall of Audience, and the court, as painted (1875) by Muhammad Ghaffari Kamal-al-Molk, became even more beautiful. The principal open garden was made to the east of the main complex; it was not large, about an

252 *An inner courtyard of the Gulistan Palace, from a painting.*

253 *Another painting of an inner courtyard, Gulistan Palace, Teheran, 1862.*

254

254 *Inner courtyard
of the Gulistan Palace,
northern section, containing
the Great Hall of Audience;
1875, from a painting.*

255 *The Gate of Happiness
to the Palace,
c. 1860, from a painting.*

acre in extent, but it was brilliant with tulips in season, with daffodils and anemones in spring, and with various kinds of pinks or carnations in summer. All these flowers were planted in grass, somewhat after the manner of the 'flowery mead' of the medieval gardens in England.

Many other gardens were made in and about Teheran in the first half of the nineteenth century. They were almost invariably in courts entirely enclosed by the house, and contained a pool, more or less large and always rectangular. This pool was flanked by beds of flowering shrubs and fruit bushes or trees, defined by light, painted fences. They also included trees, chiefly plane, poplar and cypress. Sometimes, as at the Negaristan (1810) the garden of tall trees undergrown with roses, lilacs, myrtles and fruit bushes, was centred on a pavilion with an open, pillared hall or vast porch containing the garden pool and fountain. Two elements of this great Negaristan villa-type garden particularly delighted European visitors; and they, again, serve to make the point that Persian garden villas were contrived, like the

Roman ones, to enable the owner to live in and out of doors at the same time, and to conduct his business as much in the gardens as in the halls and chambers. One of these elements is described by the traveller Robert Ker-Porter:*

'At the upper end of the garden, is a small and fantastically built palace, enclosed in a little paradise of sweets. The Shah often retires thither, for days together, at the beginning of summer... and accompanied by the softer sex of his family, forgets, for awhile, that life or the world have other seasons than the gay and lovely spring. The building was of a light architecture, and, with its secluded garden, presented altogether a scene more congenial to the ideas I had conceived of one of these earthly imitations of the Houris' abodes, than any I had yet met in the East. The palace was nearly circular, full of elegant apartments, brilliantly adorned with gilding, arabesques, looking-glasses, and flowers natural and painted in every quarter...'

The other element of this grand garden which so pleased

* Ker-Porter (1821).

226

255

the Europeans who saw it was the Taj-i-Doulat, the Summer Bath, which the same author describes as follows:

'This bath-saloon, or court, is circular, with a vast basin in its centre of pure white marble, of the same shape, and about sixty or seventy feet in diameter. This is filled with the clearest water, sparkling in the sun, for its only canopy is the vault of heaven; but rose-trees, with other pendant shrubs bearing flowers, cluster near it; and, at times, their waving branches threw a beautifully quivering shade over the excessive brightness of the water. Round the sides of the court are two ranges, one above the other, of little chambers, looking towards the bath, and furnished with every refinement of the harem. These are for the accommodation of the ladies who accompany the Shah. They undress or repose in these, before or after the delight of bathing; for so fond are they of this luxury, they remain in the water for hours; and sometimes, when the heat is very relaxing, come out more dead than alive. But in this delightful recess, the waters flow through the basin by a constant spring; thus renewing the body's vigour, by their bracing coolness; and enchantingly refreshing the air, which the sun's influence, and the thousand flowers breathing around, might otherwise

render oppressive with their incense. The royal master of this *Horti Adonidis*, frequently takes his noon-day repose in one of the upper chambers which encircle the saloon of the bath; and, if he be inclined, he has only to turn his eyes to the scene below, to see the loveliest objects of his tenderness, sporting like naiads amidst the crystal stream and glowing with all the bloom and brilliancy which belong to Asiatic youth.'

There is something remarkably odd about the rose trees, *nastaran*, of this Taj-i-Doulat garden. Both Ker-Porter and other travellers say that the rose trees grew to a height of twenty feet and that some of them had trunks two feet in circumference. The flowers of these trees are described as single, pink and large, and as completely covering the trees in the flowering season. There are no such roses in Persia today; were there ever? It is true that rose trees grow to a great age there and attain a great size, but the dimensions given by these travellers are surely impossible. The word 'rose' was often carelessly used. What were these flowering trees, then? I have no plausible answer. Ker-Porter says it

227

was recognized that in Persia the rose grew to a perfection never attained elsewhere, and that it was nowhere else so highly prized:

'Their gardens and courts are crowded with its plants, their rooms ornamented with vases filled with its gathered bunches, and every bath strewn with its full-blown flowers plucked from their ever-replenished stems...'

Numerous other royal gardens were made still later; but by the mid nineteenth century European influences began to corrupt the integrity of the Persian style; such famous gardens as Shabrestanak, the Qasr Farahabad palace, or the royal gardens at Shimeran, while they did, of course, have many Persian features, had so many European ones that, in our present context they are less interesting, if only because the styles and elements which Persian garden designers increasingly borrowed from France and England, often by way of Russia, but failed to digest, are best studied in their native lands.

There is, however, another centre of Persian garden art which we should glance at before we leave the subject: Shiraz. But as Wilber (1962) points out, there is much disagreement between visitors and travellers who saw and described them as to the real merit of the Shiraz gardens. Chardin, on whose knowledge of the Isfahan gardens we have already drawn, says:

'The most beautiful things at Shiraz are the public gardens, twenty in number, which contain the largest trees of their kind in the world... cypresses, plane-trees... and pine.'

The gardens to which he refers lay on either side of a broad avenue which led out of the city towards the road to the Allahu Akbar pass. Each garden had its portal surmounted by a pavilion and dome. Chardin also admired the royal garden called Bagh-i-Firdaus (Garden of Paradise), in which the *pièce de résistance* was a formal pool 125 paces square, that is about four acres in extent.

On the other hand, here is what the English traveller Edward Scott Waring, who was in Shiraz in 1802, says* on the same subject:

'The gardens about Shiraz are much celebrated; but the striking uniformity of long walls and narrow alleys is sure to displease the European taste. You may, perhaps, walk quarter of a mile and on either side will not have a view of

* Quoted by Wilber (1962), who gives no bibliographical reference.

256 *A royal garden like Tamerlane's.*

a few yards. Yet the Persians delight in visiting these gardens; anything delights them; and a running stream makes them frantic. Nor is this to be wondered at; it is here that they rejoice themselves from the anxiety and drudgery of business and enjoy their sohbuts*. The day is passed in smoking, in the amusement of fishing, or in listening to the odes of the various poets...'†

The first two sentences express the judgment of a man already accustomed to the 'improved' gardens of England, the grand landscapes of which Stourhead was the prototype. But at least they serve to confirm the point that the Persian garden was a style on its own. And in Shiraz it was an ancient tradition, going back to the tenth century. Unfortunately, such very old gardens as that which was made about the Masjid-i-Maw mosque, probably in the fourteenth century but possibly earlier, have long since vanished, and we do not know what they were like. Then there are the garden tombs of two of the greatest Persian poets, which are gardens. Sa'di, born at Shiraz in 1181, and whose *Gulistan* ('Flower Garden') is concerned with flowers of virtue and is of no use to us as a source book, was given a garden tomb which was replanted as the Sa'diya in the eighteenth century; it was a small garden of cypresses and pines about a fish-pool, but as it was again modernized in the nineteenth century it is no longer wholly Persian. Hafiz, born at Shiraz in 1389, wrote generally in praise of his city, '...and the bowers of Musalla where roses throng' but not specifically of its gardens. His tomb, the Hafiziya in the Musalla, is also a garden of fine shade trees, green lawns and a pretty, seventeenth-century marble kiosk.

A famous Shiraz garden in the early eighteenth century was the Bagh-i-Dilgusha, Garden of the Heart's Ease, created by Karim Khan Zand; by the beginning of the nineteenth century it had been ruined by neglect. It was famous above all for its pool and fountain, and for its star of avenues underplanted with orange-trees. Karim Khan Zand made other gardens, notably the Bagh-i-Vakil, of which we know only that it was very large, walled, laid out as a grid of walks and avenues of cypress, plane and pine, and remarkable for its cascades and its marble-lined pools; and also for its many charming pavilions.

The Bagh-i-Naw, one of the gardens drawn by the French traveller Flandin in the first half of the nineteenth century[+],

257 *Persian gardeners at work.*

* sherbets.
† Quoted by Wilber (1962).
+ Flandin, E., and Coste, P. (1854).

258 *Bagh-i-Sheidh, rose garden, Shiraz, Persia.*

259 *Tomb of Hafiz, the great mystic poet, at Shiraz.*

and which was laid out by the Qajar prince Nawab Vala Husayn 'Ali Mirza Farman Farma in 1810, was on the site of an older, perhaps much older, garden, the Bagh-i-Firdaus, described by John Baptist Tavernier (1678):

'Without the City, upon the North-side, at the foot of a Mountain, is a Garden belonging to the ancient kings of Persia, called Bagh-i-Firdaus. It is full of fruit trees and rose trees in abundance. At the end of the Garden upon a descent of a Hill stands a great piece of Building and below a large Pool affords it water.'

The descriptions of later travellers show that this garden was remade a number of times; yet it would seem to have retained, in each period, the specific lines and character of a Persian garden, that particular combination of regular, formal pieces of water with fountains; lavish use of roses; grass planted with spring bulbs; trees which, unless they were in dense avenues, were planted with a pleasing irregularity; everything shut in, secretive and private; and elaborate and gorgeously decorated pavilions, which were the distinction of the Persian garden and entitle it to a special place in any history of garden art.

260 *Stourhead,*
   Wiltshire, part of the
   lake.

261

13

THE ENGLISH GARDEN

PICTURESQUE

In his *Upon the Gardens of Epicurus* (1685), Sir William Temple, whom I quoted on the subject of the Van der Stel garden founded by Jan van Riebeck at the Cape of Good Hope, wrote a passage on Chinese gardens. As far as I can discover, Sir William knew nothing about Chinese gardens at first hand; but he had no doubt read Father Matteo Ricci's description of a Chinese garden*, and perhaps those of the plausible but unreliable Johan Neuhof of the Dutch East India Company's 1653 embassy to the Chinese emperor. Sir William wrote:

'What I have said of the best forms of gardening, is meant only of such as are in some sort regular, for there may be other forms wholly irregular that may, for aught I know, have more beauty than any of the others; but they must owe it to some extraordinary dispositions of nature in the seat, or some great race of fancy or judgement in the contrivance, which may reduce many disagreeing parts into some figure, which shall yet, upon the whole, be very agreeable. Something of this I have seen in some places, but heard more of it from others who have lived among the Chinese; a people, whose way of thinking seems to lie as wide of ours in Europe as their country does.

* Published in French in 1610 and responsible for chinoiseries in some seventeenth-century gardens.

'Among us, the beauty of building and planting is placed chiefly in some certain proportions, symmetries or uniformities; our walks and our trees ranged so as to answer one another, and at exact distances. The Chinese scorn this way of planting, and say, a boy, that can tell a hundred may plant walks of trees in straight lines, and over-against one another, and to what length and extent he pleases. But their greatest reach of imagination is employed in contriving figures, where the beauty shall be great and strike the eye, but without any order or disposition of parts that shall be commonly or easily observed: and, though we have hardly any notion of this sort of beauty, yet they have a particular word to express it, and, where they find it hit their eye at first sight, they say the *sharadwadgi* is fine, or is admirable, or any such expression of esteem. And whoever observes the work on the best India gowns, or the paintings on their best screens or porcelains, will find their beauty is all of this kind (that is) without order.'

And here, from another source*, is a gloss on the word *Sharadwadgi*:

'This word is not Chinese, it is gobbledegook; but Temple and others used it, seemingly to mean (in Sirén's words in *op. cit.*) "unsymmetrical or gracefully careless patterns or decorative arrangements, i.e. something that corresponded to or could be combined with the concept of the picturesque". For Temple, and therefore after him for others, the word

* Hyams (1964).

233

262

262 *Stourhead, the Eleanor Cross.*

263 *Gardens at Stourhead; the Temple of Flora, Eleanor Cross and the bridge, seen across the lake.*

was used as if it were descriptive of the spirit of Chinese gardening; but, I insist, on what they conceived Chinese gardening to be, not what they knew about it which was nothing. *Sharadwadgi* may (see the *Architectural Review*, December 1949) derive from *Sa-to-kwai-chi* (careless or unorderly grace); this is according to Mr Y. Z. Chang. Mr F. V. Gatenby, however, says it may derive from *sorowadji*, a Japanese word meaning an unsymmetrical design. Mr Ch'ien Chung-shu says the word is probably a corruption of *San-lan-wai-chi*, a widely scattered or disorderly composition or arrangement. Presumably the garbled word was brought back to England as sailors' jargon and seized upon: but seized upon for what purpose, as descriptive of a new, imported idea? Or, rather, of a new but native state of mind in need of a name? The latter, surely.'

And that is the point which it is important to make: the English broke away from Italian and French styles and made one of their own, not in imitation of the Chinese — a theory unfortunately adopted by Oliver Goldsmith and subsequently by Marie-Louise Gothein and therefore by lesser writers ever since — but because it was in their nature to do as they did. At the very beginning of the eighteenth century both

Addison and Steele were making fun of the formal Anglo-French garden and particularly of topiary and all such excesses of artificiality; and Addison was calling for a 'wilderness garden in which art was used only to conceal art'. Moreover such influences as Alexander Pope's celebration of the natural beauties of Windsor Forest were powerfully at work persuading the English that the time had come when their own countryside was sufficiently, but not too much, tamed to be loved instead of feared.*

Poets and men of letters were the first to suggest that it was time to make a change from Italian and French geometry. Pope, above all, was as important to the beginning of the English movement away from architectural geometry

* Cf. Hadfield (1960). 'Instead of Marvell's earth-deforming and heaven-affrighting mountains we have John Dennis (who mixed with all the best persons in the literary world), writing in 1717 of the view from Leith Hill in Surrey, "*The sight of a mountain is to me more agreeable than that of the most pompous edifice; and meadows and natural winding streams before the most beautiful gardens, and the most costly canals...*"' Leith Hill is rather a *small* mountain; which is the point – in England, by 1700, nature was nothing to be afraid of.

234

263

in the garden, and towards a freer expression, as Petrarch had been to the Italian Humanist movement in garden design in fifteenth-century Tuscany; or as the poet-Shogun Hideyoshi to the art of gardens in Japan. Not that Pope was altogether the originator of the new manner:

'The origins of the movement, as we have seen had long been latent. According to Loudon, even the serpentine form of pool had been described, and perhaps constructed, long before Lord Bathhurst made his celebrated winding stream at Riskins, near Twickenham, or the forgotten Charles Withers joined a string of ponds to create the rather inflexible Serpentine, now the chief feature of Hyde Park and Kensington Gardens, in 1731. He tells us that Bishop Wren, who died in 1667, wrote in his copy of Wotton's *Elements of Architecture*:

"For disposing the current of a river to a mighty length in a little space, I invented the serpentine, a form admirably conveying the current in circles and yet contrary motions upon one and the same level, with walks and retirements between, to the advantage of all purposes, either of gardenings, plantings, or banquetings, or aery ground, without any sense of their being restricted." '*

* Hadfield (1960).

Lawrence Whistler, as historian of Stowe and its gardens, attributes* the great English break-away to Charles Howard, Earl of Carlisle, who in 1700 or thereabouts summoned George London† the royal gardener, to lay him out a garden at Castle Howard and then... but the outcome is described by Stephen Switzer:+

'Mr London designed a star which would have spoiled the wood, but that his Lordship's superlative genius prevented it, and to the great advancement of the design, has given it that labyrinthine diverting model we now see it.'

This Stephen Switzer was one of the first practitioners of the new kind of garden design. He was, despite his name, a Hampshire man and, by his own account, a gentleman reduced to professional gardening by financial ruin. He became a horticultural journalist and author, and a profes-

* Whistler (1954).
† Of the famous firm of nurserymen and market gardeners, London and Wise.
+ Quoted by Whistler (1954) and by Hadfield (1960).

235

sional garden architect. The secret of his art is summed up in a few lines:

'...as many twinings and windings as the villa will allow, will endeavour to diversify his views, always striving that they may be so intermixed, as not to be all discovered at once; but that there should be as much as possible, something appearing new and diverting, while the whole should correspond together by the natural error of its natural avenues and meanders...

'And to the end that he may know the better how to make the best use of natural advantage, he ought to make himself master of all rural scenes. And the writings of the poets on this subject will give him considerable hints, for in design the designer as well as the poet should take as much pains in forming his imagination, as a philosopher in cultivating his understanding.'*

A bolder exponent of the new manner was Arthur Bridgeman, who was connected on the one hand with the theorists in his acquaintance with Pope and his set, on the other with the practical men in that he is believed to have worked as a young man for the firm of London and Wise with which he was later connected. We know, however, very little about him except as a garden architect and, incidentally, garden economist, for he helped Wise to prepare a report on the cost of maintaining the royal gardens. He became Wise's partner in the management of those gardens, and, when Wise retired in 1728, his successor. Meanwhile, he was one of the first professional 'improvers' to work on the remaking of a number of great gardens, and if little or nothing of his work remains it is chiefly because it was obliterated by the work of later 'improvers', notably that of Lancelot 'Capability' Brown.

But Hadfield, by far the best historian of English gardening, judges Pope to have been the prime mover in promoting the practice of the new English gardening. The poet's work as a pratical gardener began in 1718 when he moved into the Thames-side villa at Twickenham where he lived for the rest of his life; like Petrarch, he did not confine himself to garden design but was interested, and even learned, in plants. Again like Petrarch, he did not confine his attention to flowers and shrubs, but was a keen kitchen gardener and fruit grower. That he had the best spirit of a gardener is clear from a letter which he wrote to Lady Mordaunt, in which the following passage is revealing:

'...My trees and shrubs will, indeed, outlive me, if they

* Quoted from Switzer's *Iconographia Rustica* (1718), by Hadfield (1960).

264

do not die in their travels from place to place, for my garden, like my life, seems to me every year to want correction and require alteration. I hope, at least, for the better. But I am pleased to think my trees will afford shade to others, when I shall want them no more.' (1736)

Pope's gardener, John Searle, later the great Ralph Allen's gardener at Bath, left a plan of the poet's garden as it was at the time of his death: from this the complete disappearance of French formalism is obvious. Perhaps a single line from his poem *Of Taste* gives a clue to what guided his design:

'In all, let nature never be forgot.'

Pope was active as a designer of gardens for others as well as for himself, so that the new style was spread by his own efforts. In collaboration with Bridgeman he helped to design and plant gardens for the Countess of Suffolk, the Earl of Oxford and others. In the meantime his influence on the shape of English gardens was working in still another way, through his friendship with William Kent.

264 *The Temple of the Sun at Stourhead.*

265 *Rhododendrons by the portico of the Temple of Flora.*

265

'Mr Pope undoubtedly contributed to form Kent's taste. The design of the Prince of Wales's garden at Carlton House was evidently borrowed from the poet's at Twickenham. There was little affected modesty in the latter, when he said, of all his works he was most proud of his garden. And yet it was a singular effort of art and taste to impress so much variety and scenery on a spot of five acres. The passing through the gloom from the grotto to the opening day, the retiring and again assembling shades, the dusky groves, the larger lawn and the solemnity of the termination of the cypresses that led up to his mother's tomb, are managed with exquisite judgement; and though Lord Peterborough assisted him to form his quincunx and to rank his vines, those were not the most pleasing ingredients of his little perspective.'★

The picture which Walpole paints in these words is that of a garden very different from anything which had ever been seen in Europe before, although perhaps one could find parallels with some Japanese garden styles (e.g. *Roji*).

This brings us to William Kent; but it will be convenient

to drop him for a moment and work our way back to him by another route. That way begins with the publication in 1570 of *I quattro libri dell'architettura* by Andrea Palladio; it continues with the adoption of that work and all it implied, as their aesthetic canon, by Inigo Jones and other English architects; and it proceeds to the patronage of William Kent, one time coach and sign painter of Bridlington in Yorkshire, by Richard Boyle, third earl of Burlington. Kent, helped by some local gentlemen, had managed to get himself to Rome to study painting; he was a great success there, and much patronized as *their* painter and a new Raphael by the English *virtuosi*, although he was not, in fact, a very good painter. In Rome he met Burlington†; the earl was no mere patron of the arts and architecture or a drawing-room prophet of Palladio, but an architect of great talent himself. He 'adopted' Kent and brought him back to England to practise all the arts, from painting and architecture to designing fashionable clothes and, above all, gardens.

★ Walpole (1785).

† Gothein's claim that Burlington sent Kent to Rome is not supported by any other document.

266

'One could claim rather crudely that Pope was a gardener of genius manqué and that Kent was a painter without it who turned to architecture and decoration and whose pictorial sensibilities were devoted to garden design. His purpose can perhaps over simply be stated: to recreate round Burlington's (or his own) buildings:

"Whate'er Lorrain light touched with softening hue
 Or savage Rosa dashed, or learned Poussin drew." '*

This by no means signifies that Kent's object was to make, in his gardens, living copies of the paintings of Claude Lorraine, Salvator Rosa or Poussin, or of any other landscape painter. For although these three were paramount, others, Everdingen for example, or Ruysdael, also had their influence. There was no more question among the new English garden artists of copying French, Dutch or Italian paintings than there had been among Japanese garden artists of repro-

ducing particular landscape paintings by Sung masters. No: but the landscape painters showed the gardeners how to make a great work of art out of the elements of a landscape. Thus Kent, and the garden artists who came after him, were *paysagistes* who, instead of using paint on canvas to create their works, used trees, shrubs, rocks, water, bricks and mortar and, as their canvas, a countryside. There is one other thing which, it is important to notice, they were not doing: they were not going all the way 'back to nature'; they were going to nature for elements and shapes (unlike the French, who went to architecture and geometry); but they were firmly of Addison's opinion that 'nature is at her happiest when she comes nearest to art'. Trees might no longer be pollarded, pleached or clipped; but they were to be planted according to rules. Paths were no longer to be straight; but they were still to lead somewhere and have a deliberately chosen terminal. Water was no longer to be used in canals and elaborate fountains; but there was still to be art in the shaping of streams, the placing of water-

* Hadfield (1960). The couplet is from J. Thomson's *The Castle of Indolence*.

267

266 *Stourhead, the Pantheon.*

267 *The River God in a grotto at Stourhead.*

falls and the design of irregularly shaped lakes.

Horace Walpole said of Kent that 'he leaped the fence and saw all nature as a garden'. Kent did nothing of the sort, even though he did use Bridgeman's device of the ha-ha in order to avoid the ugly, hard line of fence between garden and countryside. He made, or helped to make, at Stowe, at Chiswick for Burlington himself, above all at Rousham, landscape-gardens which were neither natural nor English; they were garden-pictures of the ancient, man-made Italian landscape, or at least that was what they tried to be. Philip Southcote, who came after Kent and was perhaps inspired by Ruysdael if by any painter, came much nearer to getting his landscape-gardens back to nature; but it was still not 'natural' nature, it was a poet's nature, an idealization.

The first landscape gardener who showed, in a single work, genius of the highest order, was not a professional garden architect or even an aristocrat-aesthete: he was a banker,

Henry Hoare by name, and of the great masterpiece which he created at Stourhead this is what one considerable art critic has written:

'The purely visual aesthetic of Stourhead, free of sentimentality and allusion, is what puts it into the class of European masterpieces, plus a controlling sensibility that combined toughness of conception with tenderness towards "the genius of the place" (Pope again, of course), in a manner that escaped Capability Brown for most of his life.'[*]

Henry Hoare's grandfather was a goldsmith-banker and Lord Mayor of London; his father, Henry Hoare, bought the ancestral estate of the Stourtons, pulled down the old house[†]

[*] Dr Rayner Banham in a review of *The English Garden* by Edward Hyams, in *The New Statesman*, 7 Dec. 1962.
[†] John Aubrey (1847) described the old house as follows: 'A gothique building which standeth in a great deal of ground, and this and Farleigh Castle are almost entirely the same as they were in the time of the old English barons. Here is an open-roofed hall and an extremely large and high open-roofed kitchen'. Antiquarians may regret the destruction of such a place; but it is worth remarking that only the heirs to a culture which has lost its nerve and vigour worship the old works to the extent of refraining from destroying even to build again.

239

268

268 *Stourhead, the hermitage.*

269 *Trees and part of the lake.*

and had the fashionable architect Colin Campbell build him a Palladian villa. He died before he had time to touch the grounds, leaving a widow and a son of twenty. This son, the Henry Hoare we are concerned with, succeeded to the property when his mother died in 1741. For the next thirty years he worked on the layout, planting and perfecting of the garden at Stourhead, leaving a masterpiece in the 'school' of Poussin more beautiful than any landscape ever put on canvas.

That Henry Hoare was, in fact, the 'onlie begetter' of this superlative work of art is unquestionable. That he had professionals to draw some plans and projects is probable, so that when Sir Richard Colt Hoare, Henry's grandson, wrote that his grandfather 'had the good taste and, I may add, the good sense, not to call in the assistance of a landscape gardener'*, he was mistaken. But any plans which were drawn were rejected, and the final work was Hoare's own:

* Quoted by Hyams (1964).

240

'The focus of Stourhead garden is the three-armed lake. This had to be made: originally the valley held a chain of fish ponds. Henry Hoare built a dam across the south-west corner of the valley which was thus flooded to form the lake. The shores of this were planted with beech and fir. The beech planting is now in decline nor have the firs survived as originally planted. The fringes of the water are today a mass of rhododendrons. They were planted by Sir Henry Hoare (1894-1947) the sixth baronet and this planting greatly upset the horticultural aesthetes. But it was inevitable that an attempt should be made to develop even this perfect garden in the direction of the whole gardening movement; I agree that in this case it was a pity. You cannot turn a Poussin into a mystery, a secret paradise, it is too "Greek". But as evergreens the rhododendrons seem to me unexceptionable and in no way to interfere with the creator's vision; it is true that in spring and early summer they transform the whole picture by spreading a flame of orange, mauve and white, with splashes of both red and crimson, over the lake shore. This was certainly not what the Henry Hoare who made the garden could have conceived; nor, probably, would he have liked it. During the time when the rhododendrons are in flower Stourhead is not the picture which Dr

269

Banham describes; it is a different one, one on the way to the later English garden. The fact is that because the English are plantsmen, as well as being driven to attempt the realization of their dreams, they find it very difficult to do what, for example, the Italians do, leave a garden as much alone as a satisfactory house; leave it as much unchanged as they leave their pictures unchanged instead of repainting them in a later taste. An English garden can be a masterpiece of art for a generation; but almost inevitably if the next heir be a gardener, it will be changed.'*

Like so much landscape painting of the school in question, Stourhead has its architectural foci; there is the Bristol Cross, originally erected at Bristol in 1373 and rescued from the crypt of Bristol Cathedral where it had been dumped as so much lumber, by Henry Hoare; a 'Turkish Tent' which was removed, however, some time after 1779†; the

* Hyams (1964).
† It appears in a drawing made a Swedish visitor, F. M. Piper, in that year.

Temple of Flora; the Grotto; the Pantheon; the Temple of the Sun and the Watch Cottage. None of them was for use, of course; they were simply elements in a picture in the manner of Poussin. Where, one wonders again, did the nonsense about plagiarizing the Chinese gardens begin?

The garden work of Kent and his school, of Hoare, and of Shenstone* and others of like mind and taste, can fairly be called 'classical' to differentiate it from that of later garden artists. Its first professional exponent on a really large scale, the man who made it replace the earlier styles all over Britain, was Lancelot 'Capability' Brown. Brown was born at Kirkharle, Northumberland, of humble people, in 1716.

* 'The poet William Shenstone, in his *Unconnected Thoughts on gardening* suggests an artifice by means of which an avenue can be made to appear longer than its true length: "An avenue that is widened in front and is planted there with yew trees, then firs, then with trees more and more fady, till they end in the almond, willow, or silver osier, will produce a very remarkable deception". True, it will. As we have seen the method

241

He received an adequate education at Cambo School which he left at sixteen to be taken on as a gardener by Sir William Lorraine, on whose estate he learned the elements and techniques of horticulture. He stayed there seven years, and then, in 1739, went south to make his fortune. He got a job as gardener to Sir Richard Grenville at Totton, but

was used and had long been used in Chinese gardening. But Sir William Chambers did not publish *A dissertation on Oriental Gardening* until 1772, did not include in it this trick for playing with the perspective, and was a throughly unreliable source of information in any case. The first account of lengthening an avenue by arboricultural *trompe l'œil* appears in Staunton's *Authentic Account* etc. [of the Macartney embassy to China], and that account was published after 1793. Shenstone died in 1763, at forty-eight. His own garden, Leasures, was a masterpiece by all accounts. The Chinese no more taught English gardeners perspective rules than how to make lakes. That art has too often been credited to Capability Brown because of the lake at Blenheim, his work. In fact, of course, Hoare was the originator here as in so many other respects, (Hyams, 1964).

a year later he changed it for one at Stowe, with Lord Cobham, Sir Richard's brother-in-law.

There Brown met, and was soon learning from, William Kent. After a year or two Lord Cobham was allowing Brown to go out and advise other landowners on the improving of their estates, so that by the time his employer died in 1749 Brown, now 33, had a new profession at his finger-tips. Self-confident, pushing and bustling, in 1751 he went to London and set up on his own. As well as transforming gardens and parks by landscaping them in the new manner, he taught himself architecture and was soon designing houses and garden pavilions.

Brown's success as a landscape gardener was largely due to the fact that he had worked out a formula which, while it simplified his task, was sufficiently flexible for application to a wide variety of sites and conditions. He used whatever water was available to make a lake or lakes which were given 'natural', irregular outlines; his paths were all

serpentine but their curves smooth and shallow. His land-scapes were certainly after nature, but can hardly be described as natural; for example he liked to put clumps of trees in isolation on top of hills, than which there could hardly by anything more unnatural. But, becoming ever more fashionable as he became ever more successful, he was called in by so many landowners that he was finally responsible for sweeping out of existence over a hundred old gardens, and replacing them with his picture-gardens. He had more to do with the transformation of the English countryside than any other man ever had, for he was widely imitated. In the course of this triumphant career he became the royal gardener, Sheriff of Huntingdon, a friend of George III, of William Pitt and of Lord Bute, and a man of consequence in more than one circle of important people engaged in shaping their age.

Since Brown's gardens were landscape pictures, they could not be changed without losing their integrity.

'Moreover, the gardens created by Brown were peculiarly

270, 271 *Two views of the bridge over the lake at Stourhead.*

unsuitable for development along the lines which lay in the future and which were determined by the advances not of gardening as an art, but of gardening as a science, and also by the activities of the great plant collectors. You could not have introduced any of the vast range of new flowering shrubs — scores of rose species, literally hundreds of rhododendron species, more than fifty genera unknown to science in Brown's day, twenty or thirty new evergreens, several hundred new kinds of trees, and many thousands of lesser plants — plants which poured into Britain by way of Kew and the R.H.S. in the century following Brown's death, you could not I say have introduced these or even one of them into a typical "Brown" garden without turning that garden into something quite else. If the English garden as it now is, the English garden as envisaged by William Robinson, was to develop without too much of a violent change out of the English garden as Robinson and his contemporaries found it, then it was necessary that the firm classic line of Brown's work, the "picturesque" but Italianate line, be softened and broken by someone who came after him to prepare the way for the new gardening of the post-Loudon epoch.
The man in question, the forerunner, was Humphry Repton.'*

Repton, son of an excise officer, was born in 1752, attended grammar school in Bury St Edmunds from his fifth to his tenth year, and when his family moved to Norwich, did two more years of grammar school there. When he was twelve his father took him to Holland to learn Dutch in preparation for a career in trade. There he lived in the house and became one of the family of Zachary Hope, the great English merchant banker of Rotterdam. In one sense this unfitted him for trade, for although he may have learned Dutch he also learned the tastes and taste, the ease and manners, of a gentleman, for the Hope household was remarkable for love of the arts and the society of men of taste. Not surprisingly, during his seven years' apprenticeship in the textile business in Norwich, Humphry gave more of his attention to poetry, music and above all to drawing, than to cloth, though at least he was interested in the cut of his own clothes, becoming a notorious dandy.

When he married at twenty-one he was set up in business by his father. Succeeding as a husband and father (his wife bore him sixteen children but only seven lived), he failed as a merchant, and when the death of his parents left him with a small fortune, he set up as a country gentleman at Sustead, where he had a pretty house and a nice little farm and garden. He was happy with these, spending much of his time and money improving them, making drawings of landscapes, and meeting such interesting men as the famous naturalist and

* Hyams (1964).

272 *Blenheim Palace, Oxfordshire.*

botanist Joseph Banks, and the dendrologist Robert Marsham, at the house of a friend and neighbour, William Windham. In his landscape drawing and painting he was particularly interested in '...the picturesque disposition of trees and water, of buildings in relation to their settings, and the effect of light and shade'.*

Again in financial difficulties, he went with Windham, as his private secretary, to Ireland where his friend was appointed Chief Secretary to the Lord Lieutenant in Dublin. On his return, more penurious than ever but with a full portfolio of landscape drawings (it is curious how he seemed to have been preparing himself for a profession he had no idea of adopting), he moved his family to a smaller and cheaper dwelling, a cottage in Romford, Essex, tried his hand at various works and failed in them all. It was during a sleepless night of anxiety in 1788 that he had the idea of turning landscape gardener:

'...Capability Brown had been dead for five years. There were a number of lesser artists at work but none of Brown's

* Stroud (1962).

stature. Repton was well acquainted with many of Brown's major works and Miss Stroud finds plenty of evidence that he based his own on them. But, as will appear, he did not imitate Brown; he had his own ideas and ideals, and it so happened that by giving expression to them in the jobs which were entrusted to him, he prepared the way for the more richly furnished, less classically austere gardens which were to come when the plant collectors and scientists had done their part.'*

Repton's rules as a gardener were much less strict and formal than Brown's, from whose son he borrowed many of the latter's plans and drawings for study. Instead of lawns right up to the house, he favoured balustraded terraces and even parterres in the immediate vicinity of the house.† He tried to get rid of hermitages, grottoes, sham ruins and other 'follies'. In his tree planting he scattered instead of clumping, getting nearer to what looked like a natural disposition of trees. But as he himself wrote:

'No groups will appear natural unless two or more trees are planted near each other, while the perfection of a group

consists in the combination of trees of different age, size and character...'*

Repton's method of working was to visit and study the grounds he was called upon to improve, driving and walking all over them and making notes and sketches. He would then prepare for his client a scheme in the form of a Red Book, as these documents were called: the Red Books are slim bound volumes containing a map or maps of what he proposed, with plans, drawings and water-colours. At the height of his enormous success his charges were £ 5 a day; that can hardly be considered as less than £ 50 ($ 120) of our debased money.

'Miles Hadfield (1964) has a very enlightening passage on the subject of Repton's contribution to the English garden: "But the most important development propounded by Repton was 'the proper distinction between *Painting and Gardening*' — the difference between a scene in nature and on canvas. The principle may be summarized thus: first, the spot from whence the view is taken is in a fixed state to the painter; but the gardener surveys his scenery while in

* Hyams (1964).
† Repton (1794).

* Ibid.

245

273-5 *The bridge and lake at Blenheim.*

motion: secondly, the field of vision in nature is much greater than in a picture; thirdly the light which a painter brings to a picture is fixed as he wishes it at a certain time of day — in nature it varies from hour to hour".'*

Repton was transforming the English garden from a classical to a romantic landscape. But not fast enough or thoroughly enough for his critics of the extreme romantic school. Even while his *Sketches and Hints on Landscape Gardening* was in the press and he at the zenith of his fame (1793) his work was attacked† by two country gentlemen, aesthetes, amateur garden artists who had ideas of their own about what a landscape garden should look like. They were Sir Uvedale Price and Richard Payne Knight, and their prophet was the Rev. William Gilpin whose *Observations Relative to Picturesque*

Beauty had appeared in 1789. Gilpin held that a landscape, to be beautiful, must be wild and rugged, trees gnarled and blasted, preferably even dead, and buildings ruined. Lovers of Jane Austen's novels will recall the argument between Marianne Dashwood and Edward Ferrars as to the relative merits of a healthy, flourishing oak tree, and a blasted dead one, Marianne's extreme sensibility favouring the latter, of course; and Catherine Morland's triumph as a quick student of taste when, from the top of a hill near Bath, she dismisses the entire city as spoiling the view. Such were the consequences of the Gilpin-Price-Payne notions, which can themselves be related to the taste for and enormous success of the 'gothic' novels of Anne Radcliffe.

Repton was in time to work an answer to his critics into the proofs of his book. Reviews and magazines took up the row and turned it into a national controversy which later spread to the Continent. Although Repton did not have things all his own way, for the movement of taste was towards extreme romanticism, he was not harmed by the criticism

* Hyams (1964).
† Chiefly in R. Payne Knight's didactic poem *The Landscape* (1794) in which Capability Brown, albeit in his grave, was the primary villain, but in which Repton too is slated. Uvedale Price's views were published in his *On the Picturesque compared with the Sublime and Beautiful* (1794-8) and his *Dialogue on the Distinct Characters of the Picturesque and the Beautiful* (1801).

and his practice continued to grow. Meanwhile the Gilpin-Price-Payne theories did something which they had not been intended to do: by still further transforming the English garden away from the purely picturesque and towards the 'natural', however romanticized by the taste for scowling crags and dead trees, they unwittingly prepared it for yet another revolution, to be wrought by an Irishman named William Robinson after a long transitional phase.

TRANSITION

The transitional phase in English gardening, which intervened between the early nineteenth-century romantic landscape artists and the creators of what I have elsewhere called paradise gardens,* was presided over by a man of genius with a wife who was almost as brilliant and quite as hardworking as himself.

John Claudius Loudon was a Scot, the son of a farmer, and

Hyams (1964).

his achievements in the art of gardens were two: he successfully married the swiftly growing science of horticulture to the now mature art of garden-making; and he popularized both, conveying them from a relatively small upper class to a vastly more numerous middle class. To Loudon we really owe the literally millions of pretty, suburban gardens of Britain which are world famous. In order to accomplish these ends, Loudon made himself into a garden designer, a nurseryman, a landscape artist, an encyclopaedist, a journalist and editor, a natural historian, botanist, agronomist and architect. Unlike most Jacks he mastered all trades. He was also the founder of *The Gardeners' Magazine*.* His wife, Jane Webb, whom he met and married when he was forty-seven and she twenty-three, was the successful author of a science-fiction novel, *The Mummy*, a vision of life in the twentieth century. When Loudon died in 1843, Jane Loudon worked herself to death carrying on most of his projects and some

* 'We had two grave objects in view: to disseminate new and important information on all topics connected with horticulture, and to raise the intellect and character of those engaged in this art.' J. C. Loudon in the Preface to the first completed volume.

276, 277 Blenheim gardens and Palace.

new ones of her own. Their most important joint achievement was the writing and publishing of *The Suburban Gardener and Villa Companion*, which had an enormous and long-continuing influence on gardening in the new and rapidly rising middle class.

The Loudons were forerunners of an era of common sense and eclecticism in the garden. But they had aesthetic as well as social vision, manifest in Loudon's definition of his own neologism *gardenesque*. Gardenesque garden design was the production of that kind of scenery best calculated to display the individual beauty of trees, shrubs and plants in a state of nature; the smoothness and greenness of lawns; and the smooth surfaces, curved directions, dryness and firmness of gravel walks. When the principal object of the gardener was to display the beauty of plants and flowers, then the end of the picturesque seemed to be in sight; but this gardenesque style is not yet, not by any means, the paradise garden which was to come.

If the Loudons were the heralds and first makers of the

kind of semi-formal and semi-natural garden in which, at long last, flowering plants began to be not elements in the decoration of an outdoor living-space, or materials for the making of a picture, but the actual objects of gardening for their own sake, there were also other powerful influences at work promoting this new kind of gardening. There was the rise in number and economic power of the middle class with small or medium-sized gardens which, if they were to be more than mere cottage gardens, needed a style of their own. There were also the swiftly growing success and importance of two institutions which together composed a sort of academy of garden arts and sciences: the Royal Botanic Gardens, Kew; and the Horticultural Society, later Royal Horticultural Society.

In 1730 Frederick, Prince of Wales, a good gardener for all his faults as a prince and a politician, leased Kew House which had long been in the hands of enthusiastic gardeners and amateur botanists. He had the garden there landscaped by William Kent, and with the help of his wife, Augusta of Saxe-Gotha, an even greater lover of gardens and flowers and plants than her husband, the prince collected and planted exotic plants into the Kent framework until his death in 1751. Thus the Loudons and the Prince and Princess of Wales were the people who began that process of enriching the plant material of landscape gardens which was to result in the emergence of the English garden in its final, 'paradise' form.

For the next twenty years, until her death, Augusta continued work on the gardens at Kew, and it was she who gave them their scientific character. In this work her guide, philosopher and friend was John Stuart, third Earl of Bute, who later became her son's Prime Minister and who, what is more,

278 Blenheim water gardens.

was a considerable botanist, with a collection of three hundred works on botany in his library.* By 1760 the gardens at Kew merited a *Hortus*, and the first *Hortus Kewensis* (although it was not so called), a *Catalogue of Plants Cultivated in the Gardens of H.R.H. the Dowager Princess of Wales at Kew*, was drawn up by Sir John Hill and published in 1768.

Since we are here concerned only with the influence of Kew on the plant material of English gardening, nothing need be said about such contributions to the beauty of the gardens

* His own contribution to the science, *Botanical Tables containing the different families of British plants distinguished by a few obvious parts of fructification ranged in a synoptic method*, with engravings by Johann Müller, is one of the rarest books in the world. Only twelve copies were ever printed, at a cost of £10,000. Bute's enemies in the anti-royalist Wilkesite party put it about that this was not really his own work; but there is every reason to believe that it was, and that the imputation was simply a part of a political campaign and, like all elements of such campaigns now as then, totally unscrupulous.

as a work of art as that of Sir William Chambers, designer of Kew's follies such as the Pagoda and the Orangery.

Kew's first Director was William Aiton, a Scot who had worked under Philip Miller, Curator of the Chelsea Physic Garden and author of a *Gardener's Dictionary* which remained a standard work for a century. Aiton was appointed in 1759, and in 1789 published the second *Hortus Kewensis* listing 5,500 species grown at Kew. When he died in 1793 he was succeeded by his son William Townsend Aiton who held the job until his death forty-eight years later and who, during his term and helped by his scientific Superintendent Sir Joseph Banks, published another *Hortus Kewensis*, this time with 11,000 species.

When George III inherited Kew from his mother he combined the grounds with those of his wife's residence, Richmond Lodge, had the whole re-landscaped by Capability Brown, and appointed Sir Joseph Banks Superintendent over the Aitons. Banks was a landowner and a rich man by birth, but far too brilliant and far too active to content himself with simply looking after his property. He had made the round-the-world voyage with Captain Cook; had made known to the scientific world the exciting newly discovered flora of Australia; had paid a long, scientific visit to Iceland; and had become the most distinguished botanist, naturalist and biologist in Britain. At Kew he began the long work of introducing to the Gardens and greenhouses plants from all over the world, in a systematic way, sending trained plant-collectors everywhere, enlisting the help of the Navy and the diplomatic corps, and giving generously of his own money as well as his time. As a result of Banks's work over 7,000 new species of plants were introduced into Britain during the reign of George III alone. Banks remained in charge of Kew Gardens until 1820.

This, then, was one great institution, to become even greater of course, upon which gardeners in England could now draw for knowledge and for plant material for the rapidly expanding public interested in gardens. The other, the Horticultural Society, was founded in 1804 by seven men: Sir Joseph Banks; John Wedgwood, son of the great pottery manufacturer Josiah Wedgwood; Charles Greville, the politician and man of fashion, who had a taste for the arts and sciences which included plants and flowers; William Forsyth, head gardener to George III; the botanist R.A. Salisbury; and a nurseryman and seedsman named James Dickson, who was also a good amateur botanist. Their Society

279

'...was chartered in 1809; started its first experimental garden in 1818, and by the end of the century was a rich, respected and rather solemn learned society which had entered the company of those national institutions which includes such diverse bodies as the House of Commons, the Athenaeum Club, the London Library, and the Zoo.'*

But Wisley, the great R.H.S. Garden which today inspires and guides tens of thousands of Fellows of the R.H.S., and indirectly millions of other gardeners, was not planted until 1904.

PLANTS AND PLANTSMEN

After the influence of the Loudons in transforming English

* Hyams (1964).

gardening, and after that of Kew Gardens and of the Horticultural Society, the next in order of importance was that of the newly introduced plants themselves. Something has been said about this in chapter 1, but we must take another look at the subject here.*

As we have seen, the first travellers who were sent out deliberately and primarily in order to collect new plants were the Tradescants. To them we owe lilacs and hypericums, gladioli and lupins, many crocuses and other bulb flowers, michaelmas daisies, the handsome shrub *Rhus continus*, the 'Tulip Tree', a number of maples, the 'Swamp Cypress', and

* Much of the information for the following short section will be found, in greater detail and at greater length, in Lemmon (1968) and in Bean (1914).

279 *Sheffield Park, Sussex, famous for its rhododendrons and autumn tints, but essentially 'picturesque'*

280 *The top lake, from the bridge.*

280

other plants from North America and Europe. Something has also been said about the work of such men as Bartram and Collinson in sending American plants to Europe and obtaining European plants for America. André Michaux, to whom I shall have occasion to refer again, was collecting in North America from 1785, and again in 1796. His plants went to France and from there most of them ultimately reached Britain, for in the introduction of New-World and other exotics by way of other European countries, such nurserymen as James Gordon of Mile End and the Lee and Kennedy firm whose gardens were where Olympia now stands, and above all the great Conrad Loddiges of Hackney, were very active.

In 1772 Sir Joseph Banks sent Francis Masson to fetch home new plants from the Cape of Good Hope, and in 1780 John Fraser began his twenty years of plant collecting in North America, bringing to Europe several magnolia species, azaleas and other rhododendrons including *Rhododendron catawbiense* from which spring almost the whole large race of hardy, garden hybrids. W.J. Bean estimated that during the eighteenth century 500 woody, hardy species were first introduced into Europe, to say nothing of the many more hardy herbs, and the great number of tender species.

Another collector in North America was David Douglas, whose patrons were Sir William Hooker, Director of Kew Gardens, and the Horticultural Society. Douglas was responsible for the introduction of scores of new species and especially coniferous trees between 1825 and 1834 when, while plant hunting in the Sandwich Isles, he was gored to death

253

281 *Bodnant, Denbighshire.*

by a wild bull caught in a pit-trap into which Douglas, too, had fallen. In a sense Douglas transformed the whole land-scape of Britain, for England has no native conifer, unless you count the yew as such, and Scotland only one. Yet today it would be difficult to find an extensive piece of countryside without its conifers.

A scion of the Bavarian nobility was one of the greatest planthunters of this epoch. In 1823 Philip F. von Siebold went to Japan, and for the next twenty-seven years he was introducing Japanese and Chinese cultivars and wild plants into Europe by way of the University's botanical garden at Leyden, and his own nursery garden near to it. At the same time he was making European medicine available to the Japanese, to such effect that Japanese parties visiting the Leyden garden today never fail to perform a little ceremony of respectful gratitude in front of Siebold's bust in the garden. The first collector in China itself, however, was Banks's man, John Kerr; he was there in 1803 but does not seem

to have accomplished much, and more Chinese plants reached Europe in Siebold's Japanese collections than directly.

The first and greatest collector of Indian and Himalayan plants for European gardens was Joseph Dalton Hooker. He was sent there by Kew, where his father was Director, in 1847 and spent four years botanizing, mostly in the mountainous north. To him we owe the Sikkim rhododendrons; his work must have enlarged the genus, as known in Europe, by at least fifty species, material for hundreds of new cultivars. But not even Hooker did as much for the enrichment of the European and American garden flora as did the great nursery firm of Veitch, for whereas Hooker's interests were primarily botanical, Veitch's were specifically horticultural. In 1840 Veitch sent William Lobb to Chile for new trees, shrubs and herbaceous plants suitable for British gardens and greenhouses. Lobb worked in South America until 1844 and made a second trip there in 1845. In 1849 he was collecting for Veitch in California and Oregon.

Robert Fortune, trained as a gardener and botanist in the Royal Botanic Gardens, Edinburgh, and in the Horticultural

26. *Paradise restored in Edinburgh: the Royal Botanic Gardens.*

27. *The formal garden made by the Earl and Countess of Rosse at Birr Castle.*

28. *Part of the Burle Marx Garden, Museum of Modern Art, Rio de Janeiro.*

29. *Burle Marx Garden, Rio de Janeiro.*

282 *Bodnant, Denbighshire.*

Society's garden at Chiswick, was sent to China by the Horticultural Society in 1843. In the course of many years' work there, and many adventures, some of them extremely dangerous, he sent home a very large number of both wild species and Chinese cultivars which were new to Western horticulture. During a second term in the East (1848) he founded the Indian tea industry by introducing the Chinese tea-plant *Camellia thea*, in quantity, to Northern India. He made two more collecting trips to China, in 1852 and 1858.

In North America, again, John Jeffrey took over where Douglas and his lesser successors left off, while Richard Pearce was plant hunting in Chile and Peru and John Gould Veitch in Japan where he was followed, during the 1870s, by Charles Sprague Sargent, first Director of the Arnold Arboretum, who also did much collecting in North America. Charles Maries was also collecting, for Veitch, in Japan, in the 1870s.

The first botanists to send home herbarium material and seeds from the florally very rich provinces of Central and Western China were French missionaries, notably Delavay and Farges, their plants being raised either in the Jardin des Plantes in Paris or by the famous nursery firm of Vilmorin. After them came the great Irish amateur Augustine Henry, an excise officer who subsequently became a great dendrologist. Henry began his plant exploration of the Yangtse Kiang gorges in 1885, and the exciting wealth of herbarium material which he sent home inspired Veitch to send a collector, Ernest Henry Wilson, to those provinces in 1899. There he worked with immense success until 1902, making a second trip in 1903-5. Sargent then procured his services, by offering him far better pay than he was receiving, for Harvard University and the Arnold Arboretum. For them Wilson made two more collecting trips in China. During the course of his work as a plant hunter, Wilson introduced into Western horticulture twelve hundred new plants, among them being four genera and four hundred species new to science. He also collected for the Arnold Arboretum in Japan.

We have already overshot the date we had reached in the

283

history of the English garden, but the subject may as well be disposed of here. Reginald Farrer collected plants in China for Veitch and the Arnold Arboretum jointly, principally in Kansu which was not rich in unknown plants. William Purdom, to whom we owe the lovely winter-flowering *Viburnum fragrans*, worked in the same field, and E.H. Cox in Central and West China. But there the most successful of collectors, to whom we owe literally hundreds of rhododendron species, was George Forrest (1873-1932). Harold Comber collected plants in the Chilean Andes, and later in Australasia, for a syndicate of British gardeners (1925-7 and 1929-30). Joseph Francis Charles Rock worked in China and Tibet for the United States Department of Agriculture in 1923-4 and 1927-30. Finally, last to date of the really great plant hunters, Francis Kingdon-Ward collected in China and the Far East from 1909 to 1913, and from 1919 to 1932, and yet again in the late nineteen-forties.

These, then, were the men chiefly responsible (but there

283 *Bodnant: formal design filled in with rich plantings in incomparable diversity.*
284 *The ultimate expression of 'wild' gardening at Bodnant.*

were others of lesser note) for enriching the garden flora of Britain, Europe and the U.S.A. with literally thousands of new and beautiful species of flowering plants. The point here is that the mere availability of such a wealth of beautiful new material was bound to alter gardening styles, as it began to be shown in the botanical gardens, in the Horticultural (later Royal Horticultural) Society's shows and gardens, and in a few of the big private gardens.

The greatest artists in garden making have never needed and do not now need a wealth of plant material: masterpieces of garden art such as the Ryoan-ji have been made with no plants whatever; and other masterpieces, such as the Villa Lante, the Gulistan, Stourhead or Versailles, with an ex-

256

284

tremely small range of plants. But the English, a flower-loving and romantic people, were quite unable to resist the temptation which botanists and nurserymen were putting their way, and one result was the making of gardens which were 'a riot of colour'. Carpet-bedding and the massing of enormous numbers of brilliantly coloured flowers for a time reduced the art of gardens to a mere *tour de force* accomplished by

skill and money without taste. The real problem, of course, was how to absorb the new material into the framework of the English garden without either turning the garden into a mere collection of flowering plants or into a vulgar and hideous display which was merely spectacular. It was not solved at once but it was to be solved by yet another modification of the landscape garden.

257

285 *Schloss Benrath, near Düsseldorf. The 'English' garden.*

286 *Villa Taranto, Lake Maggiore.*

14

THE ENGLISH GARDEN ABROAD

The delay in communicating European garden fashions to America was very considerable, often as much as half a century. Two things are, for example, significant about Judge Richard Peters's once famous place, Belmont, in Pennsylvania: that, at the very end of the eighteenth century, it was decidedly Le Nôtrean; and that it was considered to be the most elegant (to use Hedrick's word) in the northern states. It is described as having formal beds, mazes, clipped evergreen hedges, and a great deal of topiary, with statues, balls, pyramids, obelisks and suchlike ornaments. In short, Belmont was several decades out of date although not, apparently, an old garden.

It is true that by that date, *c*. 1800, landscape artists were arriving from Europe with the new fashions in garden art, and some gardens in the English taste were being made; but as the European specialists did not properly understand either the conditions of American horticulture, climate, soil, etc., or the behaviour of the American plants which were often substituted for Old World ones in, for example, evergreen hedges, the most successful gardens seem to have been those designed and planted by their amateur owners. One may also suppose that, until the arrival of Parmentier (see below), the garden designers who went to America were not those who had been good enough to make any consid-

erable success at home; for men of real talent such as A.J. Downing, the United States had to rely on native Americans.

But the fact seems also to be that in the North landowners and smallholders alike were, on the whole, still more interested in fruit orchards and kitchen gardens than in ornamental gardens. There was now great activity in introducing named varieties of esculents from Europe, although they do not appear to have flourished as well as the American cultivars of seedling origin. Certainly American apples and peaches were better, in America, than the European cultivars imported as scions for grafting; the only marked improvement resulting from the new trend was in cherries. What is remarkable is that as late as 1800 there was still much activity in importing the seeds of vegetables from Britain, Holland and France, and so very little home-production of market garden seeds. Advertisements of the period show a dozen for imported seed for every one which implies any home production.

A garden which was apparently typical of its class in the Northern states is described by Manasseh Cutler, well known in his day as botanist and gardener as well as preacher and politician, as follows*:

* Cutler (1888).

287 *Tropical waterlily pool in front of the Linnean House at Shaw's garden, St Louis, Missouri.*

288 Nymphaea *'Missouri'; the white flowers open at night.*

289 *Rose Garden with the Linnean House and Shoenberg fountain, Missouri Botanic Garden.*

287

288

'It contains four acres and has a grand circle in the middle. Near the middle is an oval surrounded with espaliers of fruit trees, in the center of which is a pedestal on which is an armillary sphere with an equatorial dial. On one side of the front is a hot-house containing orange-trees, some ripe, some green, some blooms, and various other fruit trees of the exotic kind and curious flowers. At the lower end of the aisle of trees is a large summer-house, a long square containing three rooms, the middle paved with marble and hung with landscapes. On the right is a large private library adorned with curious carvings. There are espaliers of fruit-trees at each end of the garden and curious flowering shrubs. The room on the left is beautifully designed for music and contains a spinet.'

To this can be added what Hedrick (1950) has to say about the furnishings of such gardens, that is, the gardens of the well-to-do. Each garden had its urns or vases of marble, pottery or lead (in the gardens of the less prosperous these ornaments were of cast iron), and they were usually planted with a stiff evergreen of some kind, often a dracaena or a centaurea.

THE ENGLISH GARDEN ABROAD

289

Who designed such gardens? Commonly, as I have said, the owner himself, but there were professional landscape gardeners working in the country as early as the seventeen-sixties. One Theophilus Hardenbrook, for example, who was advertising in the *New York Mercury* in 1758, is probably representative of a small but growing profession:

'Theophilus Hardenbrook. — This is to give notice that Theophilus Hardenbrook, Surveyor, Designs all sorts of Buildings, well suited to both town and country, Pavilions, Summer-Rooms, Seats for Gardens, all sorts of Rooms after the taste of the Arabian, Chinese, Persian, Gothic, Muscovite, Paladian, Roman, Vitravian, and Egyptian; also Water-houses for Parks, Keeper's Lodges, burying Places, Niches, Eye Traps to represent a Building terminating a walk, or to hide some disagreeable Object, Rotundas, Colonades, Arcades, Studies in Parks or Gardens, Green houses for the Preservation of Herbs with winding Funnels through the Wall, so as to keep them warm, Farm Houses, Town Houses, Market Houses, Churches, Altar Pieces...'

Nevertheless, in America as in Britain, the initiative in chang-ing the rules for gardening from architectural to picturesque was taken by the gifted amateurs, and the professionals then had only to standardize a set of clichés and, by generalizing from a few particular examples, to provide themselves with a working theory of garden design. Typical of such creative amateurs was Colonel André de Veaux who, in 1790, laid out an English landscape garden at Annondale in Dutchess County, which became famous for its beauty, and therefore a model. But he was by no means the only American country gentleman with such a garden; Downing* mentions a number of seats in the same part of the country which had good English gardens — Rose Hill, Ellersie, The Locusts, Glenhurst, Netherwood, Highcliff, Linwood were among them.

It is perhaps significant that Colonel de Veaux was a South-erner (he was a native of South Carolina), for it seems

* Downing (1841).

261

to have been the South that set the example. There were, in the first place, two great models which were widely imitated by great Southern landowners: Mount Vernon and Monticello. But although these two were models, they were not forerunners; there were scores of good English-type gardens in the Atlantic South as early as, or even earlier than, either of these. Still, their influence was very great, and

'...before Washington and Jefferson died there were a hundred and more estates notable for horticultural arts in Tidewater Virginia; up the rivers of the Old Dominion; up the Carolina rivers; and in the valleys and uplands on both sides of that indefinite range called "the Mountains". Many of these great estates showed in their treatment of food plants and ornamentals quite as much individuality as that displayed by Washington and Jefferson.'*

George Washington kept a diary from 1748 to 1799, and in it his gardening plans and activities were entered in considerable detail. He did a great deal of manual work in his garden, and he was particularly successful in grafting large numbers of fruit trees. He experimented with varieties of grapes and peaches; indeed, as a gardener, he seems to have been chiefly interested in fruit-growing until about 1768, the year in which his career as a landscape garden artist began. And it began with very hard work, for he set about making a ha-ha in the manner of Bridgeman, and he seems to have done some of the labouring work himself,

* Hedrick (1950).

290 *Interior view in climatron showing* Washingtonia *palm,* Philodendron *and* Papyrus.

291 *Looking south towards the portico with* Alsophila *ferns and* Monstera deliciosa *in foreground.*

'...tho' it was exceeding miry and bad working'. But maybe the complaint is on behalf of his slaves rather than himself. Thirty years later he had made Mount Vernon one of the most beautiful 'English' gardens in the world. For his tree and shrub garden, Washington favoured natives, and his diary names ash, locust, sassafras, service trees, catalpa, crab, magnolia, elm, holly, cedar, pawpaw, various pines and other conifers, poplar, yew, aspen, evergreen-oak, horse-chestnut, box, mulberry, willow, walnut, buck-eye, several thorns, lilacs, honeysuckles, guelder rose, jasmines and wild roses. Washington himself found many of the plants he wanted in the wild. Others were sent to him by other worthies and notables who were interested in landscape gardening. He met and entertained André Michaux when the great French botanist was in America, and he experimented with scores of new crops and ornamentals. As a garden artist his great achievement was to adapt the English landscape style to the Virginian scene. After his enthusiasm for fruit-growing had waned, landscape work remained his principal garden interest; true, Mount Vernon had remarkable kitchen gardens and fruit gardens, but they were left to the slaves and their overseers. As for flower gardening, the fifty-one years of his diary contain not a single mention of herbaceous ornamentals. But that is perfectly in the character of the landscape gardener; he was not interested in flower-growing.

Thomas Jefferson began gardening at Monticello in 1766. As a gardener he had exceptional advantages, one of them

292 *The Villa Taranto. Italian elements in a Scotsman's 'English' paradise garden on Lake Maggiore.*

being that he was a very considerable naturalist and botanist. He kept a garden book which is a good guide to his horticultural taste and ideas.* Jefferson experimented for years with the Old World grape vines (*Vitis vinifera*), even bringing experienced vine dressers from Italy to take care of his vineyards. But, like hundreds of other gardeners, he failed with them and was driven to plant some of the native species instead. These produced wine which his patriotism rather than his palate declared to be as good as anything Europe could make.

While Jefferson was United States minister to the French Court (1784-9) he sent home hundreds of parcels of seeds and roots for raising at Monticello. He also took the opportunity to go to England, and there to make a thorough

* Edited by E. M. Betts, it was published at Philadelphia, by the American Philosophical Society, in 1944.

study of the principal landscape gardens, using Thomas Wheatley's guidebook (1770). In this he marked certain passages, and on the basis of these and his notes he was later to reshape Monticello, at the same time extending the landscaped area to 300 acres. Nor was it only as an ambassador that Jefferson found time to maintain his interest in his garden; as President also he was still writing letters to his steward at Monticello, Edmund Bacon, giving instructions about planting, and even sending whole cartloads of young plants from Maine's Nursery in Georgetown. Typical of the influence which his English visit had on him as a gardener was the Memorandum he wrote in 1804 and entitled 'General Ideas for the Improvement of Monticello':

'...Jefferson, in 1804, made a memorandum of plans to eliminate the aspect of a farm in the grounds about the house. There were to be lawns and plantings of trees, diversified by thickets, "all so arranged as to give advantageous prospects" from the roads and paths that circled the little mountain on which Monticello stood. On the lower slopes of the mountain there was to be a park, orchards and a riding ground. A fish pond was to be built where it could be seen from the house. The park was to be broken by clumps of oaks, elms, maples and other native trees "as the open grounds of the English are broken by clumps of trees". There were to be thickets of dogwood, guelder roses, magnolias, azaleas, rhododendrons, and honeysuckle; there were to be recesses in which to build a "temple or seat".'*

Like the North, the South was beginning to be provided with professional landscape gardeners by the turn of the century, witness the following advertisement from the *Charleston Gazette*, 6th June 1795:

'The Subscriber, well acquainted with the European method of gardening, being a native of England, and likewise well

* Hedrick (1950).

293, 294 Villa Taranto gardens.

acquainted with it in this state, having been in constant practice for some years, — takes this method of informing his friends and the public in general, that he purposes super-intending ladies and gentlemens gardens in or near the city whether intended for pleasure or profit — he also plans and lays out gardens in the European taste on moderate terms. He likewise imports on commission, all kinds of trees, shrubs and seeds, either useful or ornamental, from England, Philadelphia or New York. Any person desirous of employing him in the above branches, by leaving a line at No. 131 King Street, — at 26 Queen street, — will be duly attended to.'

The *South Carolina Gazette* was carrying a similar advertise-ment for one Michael O'Brian who claims that he has 'been thoroughly brought up to the undertaking and practiced for several years in Europe'. These and other professionals were making picturesque rather than gardenesque gardens. And although plant material was being enriched by the active interest which hundreds of southern gentlemen took in the native flora, and by the work of such men as the visiting French botanist André Michaux who himself started at least two botanic gardens in the United States, it was still too early for England's new plantmanship to affect America. Not until the time of Sargent and the Arnold Arboretum did United States gardens start to be as rich as Britain's in plant material.

Nevertheless, that material was enormously richer than it had been early in the century. The nurseryman Bernard M'Mahon's *The American Gardener's Calendar*★ lists sixty-seven kitchen-garden vegetables, some in several varieties: sixty varieties of apple tree; twenty kinds of cherries; twelve apricots; three almonds, and a great many other fruits. He

★ *The American Gardener's Calendar* was first published in Philadelphia in 1806; 643 pages. Between 1806 and 1857, eleven editions were pub-lished. M'Mahon was, so to speak, America's Philip Miller.

mentions fifty-five varieties of Old World grapes cultivated in his nursery; of these Hedrick says that none of them could have survived long in North America, but he may here have overlooked a curious fact, that M'Mahon found the obvious solution to the problem of *Phylloxera vastatrix*, that of grafting the Old World vines onto native *Vites* roots. Most unfortunately the whole viticultural world made the same mistake as Hedrick, that of overlooking M'Mahon's discovery (which had at the time no economic importance) when the great *Phylloxera* crisis nearly wiped out the European wine industry almost a century later.† M'Mahon names 442 species of hardy deciduous trees and shrubs as growing in his nursery, and ninety-nine species of hardy evergreens. He lists 1,500 tender species of trees, shrubs and herbaceous plants suitable for Southern gardens only. M'Mahon was, says Hedrick, who doubts whether the lists were altogether based on practice and therefore doubts their reliability, unwilling that Americans should be behind their European fellow-plantsmen in the field of tender exotics which were then being introduced into British horticulture in bewildering number, but could only be grown in greenhouses of a quality that was not yet to be found in the United States. M'Mahon's hardy perennials and biennials number 392, his bulb species 116.

Seedsmen and nurserymen actually raising plants and growing seed in America, instead of importing from overseas, began to flourish towards the century's end. Thus material for landscape gardening in the English manner became easier to obtain; good native substitutes for the trees, the evergreen bushes and the few flowers used in such gardening were found; and plants introduced from the Old World were raised in nurseries in increasing numbers. Outstanding among the new nursery firms was the house of Landreth, which was started by an Englishman in Philadelphia in 1784; under the founder's son, David Landreth the second, this house became the leading seed and plant nursery in the United States, stocking in quantity such useful landscape material as camellia, rhododendron and magnolia, as well as many kinds of roses. Other important nursery firms founded at that time were Thorburn and Co. of New Jersey, and the great Prince Nursery on Long Island, whose proprietors, the Princes, were, for several generations of American gardeners, what the Veitch family were to generations of British gardeners, or the Vilmorins to the French.

Perhaps the most powerful and effective influence in popu-

† Hyams (1965a).

295

larizing the English landscape garden in America was that of the Frenchman whose name has been mentioned above, André Parmentier, who reached the United States in 1824 and died there only six years later. Hedrick (1950) expresses surprise that a Frenchman should have been so great an advocate of the 'naturalistic' garden, when French gardening was dominated by the Le Nôtre type of formal garden. Here the best historian of American horticulture overlooks the fact that by 1820 Le Nôtre's day was done; his gardens remained and would remain as masterpieces of a school; but gardens were by this time being made in a different taste in France. Helped by Rousseau's writings, the English garden was making its way in that country, and Parmentier, in preferring Repton to Le Nôtre as his master, was not really in advance of his time.

Parmentier began by founding a botanical garden which was also his nursery. It is still to be seen, near the Brooklyn Terminus of the Long Island Railroad. There he had 400 species of ornamental trees and shrubs, 200 rose cultivars and a great number of herbaceous and bulbous species. The gar-

296

297
298

295 *Wistaria by a formal pond at the Villa Taranto.*

296-8 *Villa Taranto gardens.*

dens which he designed were pure English landscapes, with traces of reversion to formalism such as Harold Peto was to reintroduce into English gardening nearly a century later. In that respect, Parmentier was an innovator. He liked an occasional statue in a niche as the terminal to a walk, and other, similarly Italianate 'embellishments' as Downing, Parmentier's disciple, called them. But despite these touches of Italianate, in his essay on landscape gardening published in his own nursery catalogue for the year 1828, Parmentier showed himself almost as great a 'naturalistic' extremist as Sir Uvedale Price and his friends. Despite his short working life in America, Parmentier had, according to Downing, a greater influence than had any other artist in persuading the Americans to make English landscape gardens.

Again according to A.J. Downing, the work which Parmentier did at Hyde Park, in a region of the Hudson river which became famous for its fine landscape gardens, was his masterpiece and 'justly celebrated as one of the finest specimens of the modern style of landscape gardening in America'. Hyde Park had originally been granted to a Huguenot

settler, Pierre Fauconnier, but it was first developed as a farm and park, a gentleman's seat, by his great-grandson, John Bard. That was in the 1760s. From him it passed to his son Samuel who sold it to a friend, David Hosack, and it was he who, towards the end of 1826, engaged Parmentier to landscape or, as the English would have said, to 'improve' it. From what little one can discover about it, the landscape garden seems to have been more or less in the manner of Humphry Repton; but it is quite possible that Parmentier had never seen a Repton garden and that the models he worked from were, in fact, French.

For France, outgrowing Le Nôtre meant being converted to the English garden: true, it was called the Anglo-Chinese garden, perhaps to deprive the English of any claim to leadership in one of the arts. There would have been no need for that had the French themselves understood exactly what was

happening, for the way into France for the English garden was opened by a Frenchman.

In a novel which every Frenchman and Frenchwoman of education and sensibility was reading in the year 1760, the heroine Julie takes her lover-to-be, Saint-Preux, to a garden which is a kind of wilderness in which art has been most wonderfully used to conceal art: flowers seem to be growing naturally in the meadow-like lawns, brooks wander and tumble over little waterfalls, paths are shaded by climbing plants which appear to have planted themselves in just the right places. That novel was, of course, *La Nouvelle Héloïse*; its author, Jean-Jacques Rousseau, whose gospel of Nature as sublime and sacred was as unwittingly artificial as the same feeling manifest in the English landscape gardeners from William Kent to Humphry Repton and its theorists from Alexander Pope to Sir Uvedale Price and his friends.

299, 300 *Villa Taranto water stairs and the lotus and lily pool.*

But if Rousseau's notion of a garden was a very powerful influence in opening the way for the English garden into France, we can still not call that influence wholly French. For Julie's garden in *La Nouvelle Héloïse* is virtually the kind of wild garden which Addison had called for, and there is no reason why Rousseau should not have taken it from Addison.

At all events, Rousseau's fictitious garden was realized in practice, a unique case no doubt, when the Marquis de Girardin, his friend and last patron, had it laid out at Erme-nonville, having first had paintings of it made by an artist so that his gardeners should know what was aimed at. Its flora consisted chiefly of native species, although doubtless cultivars rather than wild specimens were used. Its buildings included a temple dedicated to the *philosophes*. And in the wild garden, based on Saint-Preux's at Meillerie, was the lovers' hut-like cottage on a hillock dominating the very pretty lake. There, too, was a *tour de Gabrielle*, a romantic version of the castle of Henri IV's mistress; and finally, Rousseau's tomb, surrounded by poplars on an island in the lake.

In the classic French garden, a setting for social intercourse and recreation and not a picture, the pavilions were for use. In the English landscape garden, what the French came to call the sentimental garden, they were elements of the picture, not to sit in but to look at. This was so even in the rather mongrel gardens such as the Parc Monceau laid out for Philippe d'Orléans when he was Duc de Chartres (*c.* 1780) by the painter Carmontelle. True, the principal pavilion was for use, Philippe liking to give parties there; but it stood in the centre of the French parterre garden. The buildings in the surrounding landscape garden, with its artificially-made hills and valleys, its meadow-like lawns, its brooks, clumps of trees and contrived vistas, were in the extreme of picturesque taste, including a gothic sham ruin, and the so-called Naumachia which was a classic sham ruin in marble with a big marble tank or bath.

In England the purpose of such buildings, the evocation of a mood, was implicit, and in the earlier examples of the picture landscape garden it seems to me doubtful whether one can properly use the word 'purpose' at all; the buildings were elements in the picture, like the trees, the bushes, the water and the few flowers that might be used. But in France the purpose did become explicit: each building was deliberately designed and placed to evoke a particular mood or state of mind, as self-consciously as the placing and shape and relationship to each other of the rocks in a Japanese garden were deliberately designed to evoke certain specific feelings or suggest certain specific ideas. Marie-Louise Gothein has a penetrating and amusing comment on this:

'From the union of Rationalism and Emotionalism there had naturally sprung Sentimentality. Every impression was to be clothed in feeling, but man must always have an explanation and a sort of justification of the feeling, and this was most easily to be found in the so-called "animated nature" form. It was understood by people of the late eighteenth century that they must feel melancholy at the sight of a ruin, that a hermit's retreat incited to silence and solitude, that a Greek temple stimulated the *joie de vivre*. And if this was not enough, surely the Mood would be helped by a suitable inscription! The oddest part about it was that they never needed to be alone, but were sure to be seized upon by this Mood (which was produced by external things) when they were in a large company of people.'

Henry Home, in his 'Essay on Gardening'* gives expression to the kind of feeling which inspired French picturesque gardening so much more explicitly than it inspired the original English garden artists. The garden as a work of art must, he claims, inspire feelings of greatness; it must charm by giving rise to surprise and wonder, but also to both melancholy and mirth. To these ends the artist should juxtapose scenes quite different in kind (cf. the woods beside the vineyard in the Parc Monceau), rough and uncultivated areas beside the smoothest of contrived vistas. There should be nothing altogether and manifestly artificial, no fountains, for instance, no pagodas or triumphal arches.

The French, unlike the English, did not destroy the old

* In Home (1770).

301, 302 *Bagatelle; the English garden and the rose garden.*

303 *Munich: the Nymphenburg Garden.*

gardens in making the new. One does not destroy such masterpieces as Versailles or Vaux unless very sure that one has something better to put in their place, and the French were far from sure at first. The Abbé Delille (1782), poet and garden writer of the period, although an enthusiast for the English garden, does express the fear that Le Nôtre's masterpiece of Versailles may fall into ruin by being neglected for the new landscape gardens. But at the same time he fails to see in that masterpiece, in its flat monotony, anything which could possibly inspire a poet: such gardens are, after all, mere works of architecture, whereas the new ones are the work of philosophers, painters and poets. And if the new garden artists seek a master, let that master be Poussin, 'for he paints the merry dance of shepherds, and beside it sets a grave with the inscription, "I, too, was a shepherd in Arcady".' Despite which the French persisted in making their 'sentimental' gardens beside or even around their formal gardens. The Petit Trianon was an example, with its lake and woods and pretty round temple, but also its toy dairy and its mill. At Chantilly, too, an English garden was made adjoining the old French garden; and there were scores of such twin or even mixed gardens in the general neighbourhood of Paris and beyond.* But quite early, earlier than in England, they tended to have in some part of their extent, often near the house, a flower garden of mass carpet-bedding of the kind which was to afflict England also in due course, and which must, from descriptions of them, have been hideous.

In Germany the English garden was accepted much more wholeheartedly, the new movement finding its advocates in a circle of Swiss poets:

'The circle of Swiss poets around Bodmer had eagerly seized upon Spence's first principle, *ut pictura poesis*, but had also accepted Shaftesbury's and Thomson's gospel of the greatness and ennobling effect of untouched Nature, and had developed the idea at the same time as their compatriot at Geneva, if not perhaps so violently. And so we find in the poets of this school, Kleist and Gessner, the first expression of ill-will and actual revolt against the "cleverly laid-out gardens with their green walls, and labyrinths, and obelisks of yew rising in stiff ranks, and gravel paths, so laid that no plant may annoy the foot of the stroller". "Too bold man," Gessner cried, "why strive to adorn Nature by using imitative arts? What I love is the country meadow and the wild hedgerow." But in his pictures (which this poet-artist paints in the utmost sympathy with his idylls) he seems quite happy with lattices

* See, e.g., in Hirschfeld (1779). His other works on gardening were *Observations on Garden Art* (1773) and *Theory of Horticulture* (1775).

304

and bowers; and in the graceful idyll, *My Wish*, he depicts the garden behind the house "where simple Art assists the lovely fantasies of Nature with helpful obedience, not endeavouring to make her the material for its own grotesque transformations" — though all the same this garden is enclosed by walls of nut-bushes, and in each corner stands a little bower of wild-currant.'*

Almost at the same time, but in North Germany, another circle centred on the poet Gleim were beginning to garden in the manner of Pope, or perhaps I should rather say in the spirit of Pope. Their prophet was Christian Hirschfeld, Professor of Philosophy at Kiel University, popular landscape painter, and indefatigable historian of gardening, whom I have already quoted. Hirschfeld had soaked himself in the theories and literature of English landscape gardening, and Goethe said of him that he 'lit with his own fire the emulation and enthusiasm of the rest'. Hirschfeld's talk, his

lectures rather than his published writings, must have inspired the first and one of the finest of English landscape gardens in Germany, laid out and planted by Duke Franz of Dessau at Wörlitz.*

This Wörlitz landscape garden was based on a lake: artificial bays and inlets were cut into its banks, and some of these were then joined by canalizing streams, so as to form a number of islands. Each island had its carefully landscaped woods, its plantings of shrubs and a few flowers, and each had its ornamental building. The garden was celebrated in an essay by the Prince de Ligne, who was, among other things, a friend of Mme de Staël and Benjamin Constant, and of half a dozen 'sets' of intellectuals, aesthetes, politicians

* While it is very difficult to be sure, the Duke's garden seems to have antedated Hirschfeld's first essay on horticulture. In his encomium of the Wörlitz garden in *Dichtung und Wahrheit* Goethe dates the garden a good deal earlier than is acceptable; but he had a personal reason for doing so, and in that respect his date is unreliable.

* Gothein (1928).

272

304 *Longwood, Pennsylvania.*

305 *The Huntington Garden, Pasadena, California. Italianate ornament in an 'English' landscape garden.*

306 *The Japanese garden, Gothenburg, Sweden. An 'English' garden with elements of other styles.*

305
306

and what we may call (and what, alas, no longer exist) 'men about Europe'. The prince presents the garden as a play in five acts of seven scenes each, each act an island, each scene an aspect of that island. One island, which he calls the Elysian Fields, had an evergreen maze enclosing statues or busts of Lavater and Gellert; on another there was a gothic house; and one was a copy of the Rousseau island at Ermenonville.

A grotesque feature of Wörlitz (not to denigrate it, for it was unquestionably a magnificent work) was an extension of the grotto idea which might fairly be described as Wagnerian. The Prince de Ligne calls this feature Vulcan, and it was intended to be an artificial volcano of sorts. Inside was a chamber with light-effects achieved by the use of coloured glass; as to the outside, it looked, in Gothein's words, 'uncommonly like a baker's oven'. But it is important in our context because it foreran the Germanization of the English landscape garden, a Germanization that led to romantic excesses which German critics were the first to deplore.

307
308

307 *Strybing Arboretum, San Francisco.*

308 *The Rock Garden, Gothenburg, Sweden. English influence shaped this garden.*

309 *The Strybing Arboretum, San Francisco.*

Hirschfeld's writings brought the greatest living German to become an enthusiast in gardening with, as one might have expected, interesting results. Goethe, as soon as his attention had been called to the artistic possibilities of gardening, began the reshaping and replanting of the park at Weimar which ended in the creation of one of Germany's greatest landscape gardens. Goethe himself described the origin of this 'improvement' of the garden or park at Weimar in *Das Luisenfest*, which appears in his autobiography. The gardens with which the great poet started were in the old, formal style and did not comprise any kind of unity. The garden he made, the new 'aesthetic' garden to use the term he preferred for such landscape gardens, had its sham ruins, with a baroque campanile; paths which 'wound about, now over rocks, now under arches, now passing out into the light, with their empty and wild aspect, and here and there a hollow place for a seat, they gave some idea of the famous rock paths of Chinese gardens.'* All this change had its

* *Das Luisenfest.*

309

origin in the dressing up of a part of the garden for the *Luisenfest* in question, an improvised *fête* on the name-day of Princess Louise. The later features of this landscape garden, one after another, also came into existence on the occasion of some similar *fête* or pageant. They included a Knights Templars' house, another ruin, a temple and some lesser ornaments. In the case of the new garden at Ermenonville we saw how a real landscape garden was based on one in a novel, *La Nouvelle Héloïse*. In this case of Weimar the process was reversed; not only does Charlotte's landscape garden in Goethe's *Elective Affinities* grow part by part, as Weimar did; but Goethe also makes the growth of the garden a reflection and a symbol of his hero's and heroine's progress towards a unity composed of their complementary qualities. It is of the most particular interest that Goethe had made a very thorough study of English engravings of landscape gardens. And at least one remark of his, concerning the kind of book in which one found 'a picture of a landscape, and then on another page a picture of what had been made of it, so as to use the good points it already had and make the most

of them', suggests that he may have had one of Repton's Red Books in his hands, or at least one of Repton's published works.

From Hirschfeld's writings two things become clear: that there was a great deal of making of English gardens in several parts of Germany; and that want of nerve and taste led to the making of many monstrous hybrids between the old French and the new English garden, most of them remarkably ugly. I have already told how, just when the French garden at Schwetzingen was nearly complete, the architect Skell, fresh from England, was commissioned to surround it with an English garden. Hirschfeld arrived on the scene in 1784 and was appalled at what was being done. Not only was the English garden to have a 'Turkish Mosque' (one must remember, before laughing, that Kew had its 'Turkish Tent'), but also an Egyptian quarter, centred on a copy of an obelisk of the Pharaoh Sesostris, and all to be brand, spanking new and shiny — no ruins. Aesthetically, the Mosque was a success; Skell abandoned the Egyptian part of the project, perhaps at Hirschfeld's insistence. Skell, thereafter,

275

310

311

312

313

310, 311 *The Huntington Garden; compare this with Stourhead.*

312 *Detail of the Anglo-French garden, Livadia Palace on the Black Sea.*

313 *The shade house, Peradeniya, Ceylon. The plant growing over the iron structure is* Ficus stipulata.

became Germany's best and certainly most successful landscape garden artist. His finest work was in a much purer taste: the 'English Garden' in Munich is a good example; the master he seems to have favoured was Repton.

Skell and Hirschfeld notwithstanding, it was very difficult to keep German exuberance in hand, and perhaps the most extraordinary example of what that spirit could make of an 'English' garden was one created by a certain Graf Hoditz, at Rosswald, near Troppau in Silesia.

'Everything was heaped together there that people had thought of for hundreds of years. Beside a Chinese garden and a temple, there was the Holy Grave; after Christian hermitages came Indian pagodas; here a picturesque hill, there a little town for dwarfs, including a royal palace, church, etc.: for want of dwarfs the count for a time had children to live there. Next came Druid caves with altars; then an antique mausoleum to which sacrifices for the dead were brought.'*

Can such a circus be identified as 'the German Garden', a new category? Not really; the Germans were only overdoing what had been done in England and in France. Moreover, although many admired these excesses, including Frederick

* Gothein (1928).

the Great who wrote Hoditz an admiring letter and gave him a pension when the Graf had ruined himself in making this extraordinary garden, there were more Germans of consequence deploring than applauding. German critics, indeed, led the movement against cramming landscape gardens with fanciful buildings, if only because it was in Germany that the abuse was at its worst. For Hoditz's extravagances were not by any means the most outrageous. In the Hohenheim garden, for example, the theme was a ruined Roman town in the process of being reoccupied by a colony of settlers. That is to say, the garden consisted of an eighty-acre landscape into which literally scores of ruined houses and temples were built, scattered all over it, as if the wilderness had taken over an old ruined town. But that was the outward seeming, contrived to evoke a mood of melancholy reflection on the past and on the theme of *Eheu, fugaces...* Enter one of those ruined huts, and you were apt to find yourself, as the Prince de Ligne did, mysteriously in a suite of magnificent rooms all sumptuously furnished. The Prince himself, when he laid out his landscape garden at Hennegau in Belgium, put into it a Tartar village complete with mosque, incongruously occupied by a colony of 'shepherds' and 'shepherdesses' who, when they were not tending the real cows in the, presumably, Tartar dairy, were playing on

314

simple musical instruments collected by the Prince's agents in the Swiss Alps.

Goethe was not the only German poet of this *fin de siècle* to take an active interest in landscape gardening. It is hardly too much to say that most of the poets were involved in it. Schiller, although indeed he did no actual gardening, wrote didactically on the subject; he seems to have been confused in his opinions, for while he was enthusiastic about English landscape gardens, he deplored the taking of landscape painting as a guide, on the grounds that it had 'no reduced scale'. (It has, of course, as the Japanese garden artists had shown, but Schiller had never been to Japan.) Yet it was Schiller who coined the phrase 'nature exalted by art' to describe such picture gardens. And while there were many German critics to claim that in no circumstances could a landscape garden properly be called a work of art, there were others of equal stature to maintain, as did the poet Herder,⋆

'To separate harmony from discord, to know and to make

⋆ See the second part of his *Kalligone* and cf. Gothein (1928).

use of the individual character of each locality [Pope's "genius of the place"], to cherish an active desire to exalt the beauties of nature; to gather them together, if this be not a fine art then there is none.'

What was, as far as I can discover, altogether peculiar to Germany was the building into landscape gardens of Knightly Castles, ruined or otherwise, and then, quite logically, holding chivalric sports and pageants about them. It was, of course, Germany that led the Romantic Revival and had, *avant la lettre*, an ardent taste for Walter Scott. The Landgrave Wilhelm of Hesse commissioned (*c.* 1787) the elder Tischbein to paint him an imaginary landscape including a mighty Knightly Castle in partial ruins; and then executed the painting in his park, calling the result first Felsenburg, later Löwenburg. It had drawbridges, entrance towers, sallyports, glacis and moat; and for its chapel windows the Landgrave coolly confiscated some of the finest antique stained glass from the churches of his country. His example was followed in several, even in numerous, landscape gardens in other provinces, and in some of them jousting and other medieval games were revived. Austria followed suit, and at the Laxenburg near Vienna, in 1810, there was a tournament of ar-

315

moured 'knights' in which all the archdukes took part.

The cult of Nature on the one hand and of an imaginary or grossly idealized medieval chivalry on the other were at last uneasily united in a Lodge of the Rosicrucian Brotherhood centred on Frederick William II's court at Potsdam. There, in the 'English' garden of the new marble palace, these Brethren of the Rosy Cross (who, as we have seen, played a part in the introduction of European gardening into North America), held their meetings in a grove of pines and firs about a statue of the many-breasted Cybele. This Potsdam garden was, perhaps, the masterpiece of what we may call the Bogus School. There, a half buried and half ruined Greek temple concealed a modern kitchen; a sort of Egyptian building with guardian sphinxes (it reappears in the *Istituto Botanico* building at Palermo in Sicily) turned out to be the Orangery; the ice-room was masked by an Egyptian pyramid; an apparent hermitage of tumbled rocks concealed a luxurious bath.

There had, of course, to be a reaction against this kind of thing; Goethe, repenting of a youthful admiration for this

314 *Entebbe Botanical Garden, Uganda, on Lake Victoria.*

315 *Perth Botanical Garden, an 'English' garden in Western Australia.*

316

317

318

316, 317 *Bogor Botanical Garden, Indonesia — Kebun Raya is an 'English' landscape garden.*

318 *The Presidential Palace with its 'English' deer-park, at Bogor.*

excessive romanticism, poured scorn on it. It will be appropriate to conclude this brief account of the English garden in Germany by noticing a masterpiece created by Prince Pückler, prophet of the reaction, at Muskau. He set forth his intention, formed as soon as he came into his vast estate in the Neisse valley, in his *Hints on Landscape Gardening* (1834). His purpose was to create a landscape garden that would surpass the greatest of the English masterpieces of the art. He did create a masterpiece, although whether it surpassed the English ones must be a matter of opinion. In the course of this work the prince entirely changed the scenery of the Neisse valley and, despite his immense wealth, spent so much that he went bankrupt. He set about the work in the same manner as the Marquis de Girardin at Ermenonville; he engaged Schirmer to paint the landscapes which he, the prince, had envisaged; then he realized each of them in turn, all down the Neisse valley, so that one after another was opened to the view in the course of an hour or two's walking. In the immediate neighbourhood of the house Pückler followed Repton, or Loudon, rather than Brown, with a measure of formal flower-gardening and a touch of Italianate.

America, France and Germany were by no means the only countries in which the art of gardens was modified, or entirely transformed, by English feeling and English style, not to mention English horticultural science, in the garden. In Italy to this day one can occasionally find the whole or part of a municipal park laid out in the English manner; and the Contessa Bonacossa's Villa San Remigio at Pallanza, in which the Anglo-Irish romantic and Italian classical are perfectly blended, is topographically, structurally and florally one of the loveliest gardens ever made. English gardens were created, more or less badly, in Spain and in Russia; and rather better but later, in the paradise style we have yet to discuss, in Portugal. Among basically English botanical gardens are the *Hortus Bogoriensis*, one of the most beautiful landscape gardens in the world, made by the Dutch in Indonesia; Peradeniya in Ceylon; the South Yarra garden in Melbourne; the lovely garden of lawns and trees on Lake Victoria at Entebbe in Uganda; the magnificent *Botanichevski Sad* at Yalta; the garden of the palace at Livadia, on the Black Sea, which is now a clinic; the superb botanical garden at Tashkent in Uzbekistan; the Moscow botanical gardens and those at Minsk and at Kiev; and the gardens made by Carlos Thays in so many provinces of Argentina. It is certainly not too much to claim that between 1750 and 1850 the English garden conquered the world of garden art and garden science.

319 *Savill Gardens,
near Windsor,
named after their
maker.*

15

320 *Sissinghurst, Kent, the castle garden.*

PARADISE RESTORED

In the period of what, on the analogy of 'high farming', can fairly be called 'high gardening', which began about the middle of the nineteenth century, the science of horticulture was greatly advanced. Mechanical aids such as lawn mowers were invented or improved, the new and embarrassing wealth of plant material provided through botanical gardens and nurseries was fully exploited, and the many garden styles of the past were combined in various, mostly unsuccessful, syntheses, until, at last, what I have called the paradise garden emerged as the dominant form. The leading gardeners in this epoch of garden history, as in the last, were British; but important contributions were made by French, Belgian and Dutch plant breeders, German garden designers and American landscape artists. The labour of bringing the new kind of garden into being was long, hard and confusing, and the period here in question is so crowded with horticultural events that it will be necessary to try to convey some idea of it by picking out the work of a few individuals and a few institutions only for notice. In their works the nature and direction of what was happening to gardening during four or five decades is implicit.

The key to any understanding of the period, from the gardener's point of view, is Joseph Paxton. He was born to poverty in 1801, somehow contrived to educate himself, and began his gardening career as a very young man in the Chiswick gardens of the Horticultural Society. By 1824 he was foreman of the Society's Arboretum there. The Society's landlord in Chiswick was the Duke of Devonshire; he often visited the gardens and he got to know and like young Paxton. Finding himself without a head gardener for Chatsworth just before leaving England for a foreign tour, the Duke offered Paxton the job — wages 25s. a week and a cottage free. Paxton accepted.

The Duke was not interested in gardening (until Paxton converted him); the gardens at Chatsworth had long been neglected and were in bad shape. In twelve years Paxton brought them to such a height of perfection — of a kind — that he had made them and himself famous and was offered the post of royal gardener at Windsor, salary £ 1,000 a year. He refused it. Playing Le Nôtre to the Duke's Louis XIV, Paxton was able to obtain immense sums of money for what he wanted to do. He made Chatsworth a garden of mixed styles, partly a grand, Italianate architectural garden, partly picturesque landscape, partly gardenesque. His style was marred, in the eyes of men of taste, by excess. He made everything at Chatsworth bigger, more spectacular than anything of the kind elsewhere: the waterworks were breathtaking, he massed flowers in enormous numbers and the most vivid colours. He was without doubt a man of genius, but a vulgar one; vulgarity is a manifestation of vigour, and Paxton had enough of that for ten men. He advanced the sciences and crafts of horticulture by giant strides, inventing, adapting, innovating. He turned architect to design and build for Chatsworth the largest greenhouse the world had ever seen, basing the metal structure on a study of the structure of the leaf of the great waterlily *Victoria amazonica* which he was the first gardener to flower. On the model of this huge conservatory, he designed the Crystal Palace to house the Great Exhibition of 1851. In the course of this extraordinary career, in which he became the prototypical successful executive of our own time, Paxton made himself into an architect, a town planner, a building contractor, a company director and a Member of Parliament; and he was knighted in 1851. As a gardener he was great in every field but one;

he was no artist. When he had succeeded in everything he set out to do, he died, apparently for want of more worlds to conquer. In Chatsworth, he left a model which for all its faults was part way along the road to a kind of garden which would have the qualities of the picturesque garden, the Italian garden and the French garden combined, and would accommodate, without loss of line or perspective, the enormously richer plant material of the nineteenth century and later. He also left in it a vast laboratory of plantmanship and horticultural techniques.

Paxton left more than that: one of his most important contributions to gardening in general was the foundation, with the help of Bradley the publisher of *Punch*, of *The Gardeners' Chronicle*, with Professor Lindley, the distinguished botanist, as editor of the horticultural part. (The paper carried ordi-

321

nary news as well.) Both in Britain and elsewhere the horticultural press was to become a large and flourishing industry; but no single paper has been nearly as important in publishing new gardening techniques, descriptions and assessments of newly introduced plants and new cultivars, news and assessments of new tools, machines and devices. *The Gardeners' Chronicle* was the professional's paper, but it was soon being read by advanced amateur gardeners and it opened the way for the foundation and growth of the popular gardening press which has advanced the craft of gardening and the quality of gardens among tens of millions of people all over the world.

The most outstanding garden artist in Britain for this period was William Andrews Nesfield. (Charles Barry, with whom he often worked, was almost as important but will be dis-

cussed later in the present chapter.) Born in 1793, he was educated as an engineer, became a soldier, fought in the Napoleonic wars. But he was by vocation a painter, whose work was highly praised by Ruskin.* His novice work in garden designing, the joint gardens of two villas in Muswell Hill, received the accolade of a description in Loudon's *Gardener's Magazine* in 1840. It was partly landscape in little, partly gardenesque; in any case it was very simple and unspectacular, and was perhaps a relief from the fashionable 'Lawrencian' villa-garden, so called after a spectacular example of its kind.

'The garden in question, whose owner Mrs Lawrence was also its designer and maker, and the greatest amateur of her day, showered with Horticultural Society awards and medals,

* E.g. in *Modern Painters* (1843-60)

322

321 *Savill Gardens — the woodland 'paradise'.*

322 *Wild gardening in London. A corner of Holland Park.*

323

324

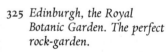

323, 324 *Melbourne Botanical*
Garden, exquisitely landscaped.

325 *Edinburgh, the Royal*
Botanic Garden. The perfect
rock-garden.

326 *The Botanic Garden*
of Copenhagen
— an 'English' garden and
a botanical collection in one.

had 3,266 varieties (not botanical varieties) of garden plants; it had greenhouses, forcing pits, compost and manure pits, and representations of every kind of gardening. No doubt it was admirable; it must also have been appalling, an early version of that "riot of colour" which, to my mind, is the ruin of a garden.'*

Nesfield made his name as a garden artist in very few years, and when the Royal Botanic Gardens at Kew were to be enlarged and landscaped in 1845, he was called in. The great new Palm House, still far from finished, was the focus of his work and we still have Nesfield's grand Syon vista towards it, and also his Broad Walk.

The Kew Director who employed Nesfield was Sir William Jackson Hooker, another man who had a great influence in shaping the English garden to come. His appointment was due to the recognition of his quality as a botanist and naturalist by Sir Joseph Banks, and to the reputation he had made as Professor of Botany at Glasgow and editor of *The Botanical Magazine*. As Director of the greatly enlarged Kew Gardens, which had been transformed from a Crown to a national institution in 1840, Hooker was responsible for the introduction, acclimatization and distribution of an enormous number of new plants, and also, by employing Nesfield, for a measure of restraint in garden art. His son and successor, J.D. Hooker, the great botanist of India and collector of so many new plants, including fifty-four species of Himalayan rhododendrons, succeeded him and carried on the work at Kew in the same spirit.†

Like Kew, the Royal Botanic Gardens in Edinburgh, the Glasgow Botanic Gardens, and the Botanic Gardens at Glasnevin, Dublin, were making important contributions to the science of plants and helping to popularize new genera, new species and new cultivars. The early moving spirits at Edinburgh were the botanical gardener James McNab, who became Curator in 1849, and Professor John Hutton Balfour. Edinburgh was to be pre-eminent in the study of the genus *Rhododendron*, the genus *Primula* and the genus *Meconopsis*. At Glasnevin, the key men were David Moore, and after him his son Frederick (later Sir Frederick) Moore. All of these scientists or gardeners took as much interest in popularizing the results of their work and making it available to gardeners as in the work itself.

It was in the second half of the nineteenth century that the

* Hyams (1964).
† For an admirable account of the lives and works of W. J. and J. D. Hooker see Allan (1967).

325

326

327

plant-breeding nurseries, the firms whose skilled gardeners were continually making new cultivars in the struggle to capture the best of the rapidly expanding market for good garden plants, rose into prominence. The craft of plant breeding was an empirical one, owing nothing to science. The discovery of the basic principles of genetics was made between 1856 and 1874 by the monk Gregor Mendel working in the monastery garden of St Thomas, Brunn. But his discovery remained unknown for many years; even after it was published it did not for a long time have any effect on the methods of practical plant and animal breeders, and has only became useful to them during the last couple of decades. It was therefore without benefit of science that in Britain many nurserymen were flooding the horticultural market with new cultivars and the progeny of species which plant hunters were sending from all over the world. Among them were John Standish (1814-75) of the Bagshot Nurseries (*Fuchsia, Calceolaria, Rhododendron*); Lucombe & Prince (*Cinneraria, Calceolaria*, and alpines); Thompson & Morgan

(aquilegias and a vast range of herbaceous plants); George Jackson and Sons (famous above all for clematis); William Jackson and Son (rhododendrons again); and the great house of Veitch, these and many more. Meanwhile great Dutch firms, such as De Graaff, were augmenting the number and variety of tulips, narcissus and other bulb cultivars at an ever-increasing pace. The French nurseries, headed by Vilmorin, were taking the lead with roses, lilacs, syringas and hydrangeas. In Belgium, new azaleas and camellias were being created.

In the United States progress was being made in the study of garden pests and diseases, based on the work of such entomologists as Asa Fitch, T.W. Harris and W.D. Peck.[*] This work was stimulated by the great importance which fruit-growing had assumed in American horticulture. As in Europe, so in America, nurseries producing new cultivars had an

[*] *Bulletin of the Brooklyn Botanic Garden, New York*, vol. 23, No. 3, Autumn 1967.

288

328

increasing influence on garden styles. The Mount Hope nurseries, centred in western New York State, had a nation-wide business through their agents. Another outsanding firm was Ellwanger & Barry, with 500 acres of nursery stock by mid-century. Their stock of cherry trees alone was 120,000; they also carried thousands of magnolias, 4,000 young sequoias, and twenty-four acres of evergreens for hedging and topiary work. Moon's Nursery in Buck's County introduced many plants into gardening, including two which were to be of the first importance, *Rhododendron obtusum* var. *amoenum* and *Exochorda racemosa*. Buist of Philadelphia became famous for his roses and camellias, and for giving a job to the young English immigrant Thomas Meehan who later set up in business for himself and became celebrated among gardeners all over the country for his stocks of native American ornamentals; he was editor of *The Gardener's Monthly* for thirty years and founded another gardening journal, *Meehan's Monthly*.

In 1831 American landscape gardening received a boost of

327 *Melbourne Botanical Garden; exotic material but an English composition.*

328 *Meisse, Belgium. The English-type botanical landscape garden.*

329

an unusual kind when the Massachusetts Horticultural Society established the first of those landscaped burial grounds of which Evelyn Waugh made savage fun in *The Loved One*. This early prototype of 'Whispering Glades', the Mount Auburn Cemetery, was landscaped as an English 'park' of rolling lawns and carefully placed trees, by Dr Jacob Bigelow, a well-known botanist and physician. It was widely imitated and had an improving influence on public gardening in general:

'Seldom has there been more universal acceptance of a new form of art and seldom has progress been more rapid in making a change. Within 20 years nearly all the cemeteries in towns and cities, and many in rural burial grounds, were laid out in naturalistic landscapes. In a very few years Green-Wood in New York, Laurel Hill in Philadelphia, and Spring Grove in Cincinnati rivaled Mount Auburn in beauty and adaptability. These new burying places were spoken of at the time as "open cemeteries", since railings and hedges were not permitted about individual plots. The kinds of monuments and markers and plantings of trees and shrubs were regulated.'*

Downing's importance as a landscape gardener has been mentioned. At the time of his death when he was engaged on making 'English' landscape gardens for the Capitol in Washington, the White House and the Smithsonian Institute, his style was paramount in America, and his masterpiece, Blithewood, in the Hudson River valley, was a model for lesser artists.† It was as a result of Downing's writings that the laying out of Central Park, in New York City, was started

* Hedrick (1950).
† A picture of this garden was used as the frontispiece to his *Treatise on the Theory and Practice of Landscape Gardening* (1841).

330

331

329 *South vista of a 'paradise' type garden made in Devonshire by the author.*

330, 331 *Rhododendron walk and hydrangea walk in the same garden.*

332 *A hybrid between* Vitis vinifera *and an American* Vitis *in the author's garden.*

332

(1858); and it was to his *Rural Essays* (1853, posthumous) and to his editorials in *The Horticulturist*, that the first movement to found city parks all over America owed its start. In 1851 Downing was visiting England and studying English landscape styles. While there he met a young landscape garden artist, Calvert Vaux, and persuaded him to return with him to the United States. Vaux became Downing's partner, completed the works which Downing left unfinished at his death, and, joining with Frederick Law Olmsted, won the contract for landscaping and planting Central Park, New York City. Vaux's partner in both the design and the business, Olmsted, an engineer, a farmer and an agricultural journalist, had studied the masterpieces of landscape gardening during a walking tour of England in 1850, and he turned landscape gardener as a result.* In the second half of the century

* See Olmsted (1852).

Olmsted became America's greatest landscape garden artist.

The rapid development of the public parks movement in the United States, in which Philadelphia took the lead, was not left solely to municipalities. Private entrepreneurs laid out and planted gardens which were opened to the public who paid an entrance fee.* There would be a flower garden, greenhouses showing a display of exotic flowering plants, an aviary, a bowling green, and either a tavern or a coffee-room. Some of these gardens were made from the start as a business undertaking; but in other cases private gardens were opened to the public, for pay, by owners who had fallen on evil days.

There is very little information about the smaller, private gardens of this period, except what is implicit in the editorials of the gardening magazines and their advertisements. They seem for the most part to have been smaller versions of the 'Lawrencian' or riot-of-colour gardens, where there was any ornamental gardening at all. Small householders tended to concentrate on the kitchen-garden and fruit-garden; there was certainly less flower-growing than in Europe, except in the deep South. At a rather higher social level, or income bracket, gardening was very good but not yet into the gardenesque epoch. Of the best of many gardens which she noticed on Manhattan alone, for example, Mrs Frances Trollope says:

'The loveliest is one Woodlawn situated in the beautiful village of Bloomingdale. To describe all its diversity of hill and dale, of wood and lawn, of rock and river, would be in vain, nor can I convey any idea of it by comparison, for I never saw anything like it.'†

In America, as in Britain at this time, there was great development in greenhouse building. There was, it is true, nothing to equal Paxton's great conservatory at Chatsworth or the huge and very beautiful Palm House built by Turner, Hooker and Decimus Burton at Kew; or even to equal Decimus Burton's less spectacular greenhouses at Kew. North American greenhouse building and technique had its chief growing-point not in the United States but in Canada, doubtless a case of response to the challenge of climate. In 1858 the editor of *The Horticulturist*, America's leading garden magazine for professionals, paid a visit to Canada. He found gar-

dening very backward in Ontario and Quebec, but more interesting in Montreal where there was an active and popular horticultural society subsidized by the government. He described a score of fine landscape gardens and flower gardens; and he considered that gardens generally in Montreal compared favourably with those of American cities. As for greenhouses: 'There are probably more glass structures for fruit and flowers in Montreal than in any city of the same population in our Continent.'*

Before the great railway development which put sub-tropical fruits from the South and from California onto the north-eastern markets, grapes, citrus fruits and even peaches were much grown under glass in the north-eastern United States, and Orangeries were common. Fruit houses were often quite large. Henry Winthrop Sargent, a pupil of A.J. Downing but a rich man with a superlative garden famous for its orchards and its avenues of fruit espaliers — Wodenethe, at Fishkill, N.Y. — had a greenhouse for exotic fruits which was 70 feet long and 20 feet wide by 12 feet high. Heated by hot-water pipes, it accommodated 250 citrus and other fruit trees in pots, and the trees were brought up from a cellar beneath it, so as to provide for a succession of fruit. Sargent claimed that this was the cheapest, and indeed the only good, way to grow even such hardy fruits as peaches, nectarines and apricots.

Maybe it was, but English landowners would hardly have agreed that this was a cheap way to grow fruit, at least when it came to the more difficult kinds. Readers familiar with Jane Austen will recall General Tilney's complaint to Catherine, in *Northanger Abbey*, touching the difficulty of getting a good crop of pineapples from the pine house: he had had barely a hundred fruits that season. A little later than that gardeners at the great English houses were growing not only pineapples but also bananas, mangos and custard-apples, superb melons and almost every kind of tropical fruits. America was not so forward, but greenhouse building there received a great boost in 1858 when William Saunders, a Scottish immigrant, began building fixed-roof greenhouses instead of houses with movable sashes; and in the following year Frederick Lord of Buffalo successfully built a greenhouse with large panes of glass instead of the tiny ones which had been used until then.

In America, as in Europe, there was great activity in the breeding and selection of new garden plants. It began fairly

* See *The American Gardener's Magazine*, July 1838.
† Trollope (1832). Mrs Trollope, mother of Anthony Trollope, was an admirable writer and the originator of the modern department store. Her book was severely critical of the Americans and gave great offence.

* *The Horticulturist*, XIII, 395-9.

early in the first half of the nineteenth century. There had been some, but not much, earlier work,* notably by the Prince Nursery in 1790, and by the Coopers of New Jersey who produced a range of new vegetables and salad hybrids at the very end of the century. Even earlier, the great Bartram, who had been reading Linnaeus and Camererius on the subject of sex in plants, had written to his friend William Byrd (1739):

'I have made several successful experiments of joining several species of the same genus, whereby I have obtained curious colors in flowers, never known before; but this requires an accurate observation and judgment tok now the exact time.'†

On the whole, American plant breeders concentrated on fruit and vegetables and by far the greatest activity was in grape breeding. The famous, and commercially very important, Catawba vine, origin unknown, was put into commerce by John Adlum, a celebrated viticulturist, in 1849. The first known successful cross between *Vitis vinifera* and the American species *V. labrusca*, the 'Alexander', was even earlier, and was introduced into gardens in the first few years before and after the Revolution. The very valuable and still widely planted 'Concord' grape was a seedling of a

* See Zirkle (1935). Cotton Mather recorded the first known hybrid in cultivation in America in 1716.
† Darlington (1849).

333 *Elizabethan features are retained in Montacute's Victorian garden.*

334 *The garden of Withersdane Hall, Wye College, Kent.*

335

chance seedling, breeding unknown; it bore its first bunch of grapes in 1849.

Between 1800 and 1850 strawberries, raspberries and all other kinds of soft fruit were greatly improved in size, quality and number of cultivars; the American native gooseberry and (in Missouri) American blackcurrants were first domesticated; and the commercial cultivation of cranberries was begun. All the fruit-trees were improved by breeding work,

and most of the vegetable and salad garden crops as well. But by and large ornamentals were left to European gardeners and breeders.

A few more examples of these will be in place here. The Dutch now began to exploit and improve Japanese and pompom chrysanthemums as popular garden plants in the West. Youell & Co., the nurserymen of Great Yarmouth, put these new Dutch cultivars into British garden commerce, and from Britain they reached America. In France, the rose-breeder Guillot produced the first hybrid tea rose, forerunner of a noble race, and called it 'La France' (1887). The British National Rose Society was founded and was to have an enormous influence in promoting the growing of roses and their continual improvement. The principal British rose nursery was A. Paul and Son of Cheshunt, later continued as William Paul and Son of Waltham Cross; William Paul's *The Rose Garden* (1848) was for long the most popular handbook for amateur gardeners. This firm's 'Paul's Scarlet' and 'Paul's Lemon Pillar' are still widely grown, but its staff did much work in the hybridization of other genera of shrubs. Hadfield (1960) cites the firm of John Bell of Bracondale for their pansies; Miller of Ramsgate for pelargoniums and fuchsias; Maule of Ramsgate for 'Japonica' (*Chaenomeles japonica*). Peter Barr, of Barr and Sugden, popularized new daffodils and some lilies. James Kelway, a name which today means paeonies to most British gardeners, first popularized the big gladiolus cultivars. The growing wealth and garden importance of plants with colourful foliage, for bedding-out and for shrubberies, is attested by the publication in 1852 of William Barron's *The British Winter Garden: a pactical treatise on Evergreens*. The house of Veitch, already named as active in the introduction of many new species, was equally so in the hybridization and selection work which resulted in scores of fine new cultivars.

Among the forerunners of the late nineteenth- and early twentieth-century paradise gardens in Britain were the first gardens to be made on picturesque landscape lines but in which an enormously increased range of plant material was used. Biddulph Grange, on the Staffordshire and Cheshire border, was a case in point, a garden created by James Bateman who began his lifelong interest in and collection of tropical orchids while still an undergraduate at Oxford. His *Orchidaceae of Mexico and Guatemala* (1837-41), illustrated by Walter Hood Fitch, is one of the masterpieces of botanical and horticul-

336

337

335, 336 *Ilnacullin, West Cork, Ireland. A part of the wild garden planted with southern-hemisphere exotics and English-Italianate by Harold Peto.*

337 *In the paradise garden Italianate and English are integrated at Ilnacullin.*

tural publishing. He began, with his wife's help, to make the Biddulph Grange garden in 1842, and he made it as a garden of many diverse parts and styles which, by all accounts, achieved unity. Bateman was perhaps the first gardener to plant rhododendrons, especially azaleas, in dense masses, in what he called his 'Rainbow garden'; he had a pinetum, a parterre garden and an arboretum.

'...This pinetum walk ended in a mountain of evergreens,

behind which lay, on the one side, a pond furnished with a rich variety of rushes and ferns, on the other an archway in the manner of a Cheshire half-timbered cottage, through which one entered a long, gloomy corridor and emerged into the Egyptian court. This, with some ornaments in the Egyptian style, gained its effect from the bastion-like masses of clipped yews. Emerging from Egypt, one returned to the parterres near the house by way of the decorative cherry orchard.'*

In addition to all this there was an extraordinary 'Chinese' garden; it included a sham-ruined 'Wall of China' that would have delighted some of Bateman's German contemporaries. But the real importance of the garden was its enormous range and diversity of plants of almost every family, hundreds of genera, thousands of species and cultivars.

Some of the forerunners of this garden-of-plants style have already been named; another was Augustus Smith, who now began the planting of the Tresco Abbey Garden of sub-tropical plants from Australia, New Zealand, South Africa and South America. It was at this time that the horticultural advantages of Britain's west coast and that of Ireland were realized: their mild winters and humid summers made possible the cultivation of a much greater range of plants than was possible in the east, or in Continental Europe north of the Mediterranean. The since famous Scottish garden of Inverewe, with its Australasian shrubs and South African bulb plants, was first planted by Osgood Hanbury Mackenzie in 1862, on Loch Ewe. In 1868 Edward Walpole, first of a long and unbroken family line of great gardeners, started the Mount Usher garden in County Wicklow. Two years later Surgeon-Major Samuel Thomas Heard began planting the Rossdohan garden in the far west of Ireland:† some of the great rhododendron and camellia gardens were being planted in Cornwall and in Devonshire.

But the introduction into gardening of the new exotic flora was not the only major change belonging to this period. There was also a partial return to a measure of Italianate formalism: parts of many great landscape gardens, untouched by the new plantmanship at first, were cut out and used for the making of 'Italian' gardens. The architect of this change and of many such gardens was Sir Charles Barry, most of whose work was done between 1840 and 1860, just before the first of the new proto-paradise gardens. There was no actual abandonment of

* Hadfield (1960).
† Hyams (1967). Some of his tree-ferns and true acacias have naturalized there.

picturesque landscape garden making; as I have mentioned above, Barry and the landscape garden artist Nesfield often worked together on one estate.

Barry had travelled and studied in Italy and he loved everything Italian, so that despite his skill in neo-gothic (e.g. his Houses of Parliament), some of his English villas look like Italian villas. Where Barry had to work on a place which had a landscape garden, he cut out a corner of it close to and usually on one side of the house, and there laid out a sunken parterre with box-edged beds into which the gardeners could bed out some of the new exotic cultivars; begonias, fuchsias, pelargoniums, calceolarias and lobelias were all very fashionable, raised in numbers in the greenhouses for planting out in due season. (This kind of gardening survives still in muncipal gardens and in such great American gardens as Longwood.) These gardens were certainly colourful but excesses often made them visually shocking. Where Barry was working on a larger scale, where he had to make an Italianate garden while Nesfield did the landscape work, for example at Trentham Castle which these two artists remade for the Duke of Sutherland, Barry built a series of grand, balustraded terraces descending from the foot of the house to a lower level, so that the landscape garden and the countryside beyond were all visually part of a whole. The terraces themselves were then carpet-bedded. A number of these semi-formal, semi-picturesque gardens were made before they went out of fashion again; the principal Barry-Nesfield garden was Shrubland Park near Ipswich, where Barry made an architectural garden of terraces reminiscent of several sixteenth-century Italian gardens, and of imposing magnificence. The broad terraces were carpet-bedded in vivid colours; but the vistas contrived by Nesfield opened to the view as one mounted towards the house, one after another.

The Barry-Nesfield garden was imitated by others. Thus when the fifth Lord Powerscourt planned the garden at his grand house near Dublin, c. 1840, he seems to have thought in the same terms; and when his successor actually made the great garden there, beginning in 1855, it was such a garden that he created.

I pointed out above that carpet-bedding began in France before it was ever practised in England, so that the English mid-century style was soon very much at home in France. Even Vergnaud (1835), who detested any kind of artefact or architecture in the landscape gardens he loved, does not condemn carpet-bedding for all its incongruousness with pure

338 *Birr Castle, Ireland. The river walk.*

landscape. The carpet-bedding style had its greatest French exponent in Édouard André, who called such gardens *jardins fleuristes*. In Germany also the style became very fashionable: Frederick William IV of Prussia, when he removed the old Orangeries from Sans Souci, replaced them with a sunk 'Sicilian' garden, which was in fact a *jardin fleuriste* enclosed with a wall in which there were niches containing statues, which presumably made it 'Sicilian'. And although Peter Lenne, Director of the Potsdam gardens, was a strictly 'picturesque' man inside those gardens, outside them he designed a number of *jardins fleuristes* for those parts of his clients' gardens which were nearest to the house. In Germany, France and Britain alike, this carpet-bedding style, or more or less poor imitations of it (for it called for the greatest

297

339

professional skill and a lot of expensive greenhouse work in advance), was taken up by small, amateur urban gardeners, and a trade in greenhouse plants sprang up to provide the material.

Despite the fashion for mixed Italianate-picturesque-carpet-bedded gardens, it is impossible to find in Continental Europe at this time any clearly dominant style. The wildest fancies in gardening were to be found cheek by jowl with the dullest respect for this or that old convention. Ludwig II of Bavaria made a fantastic garden in which, by Gothein's account, he

'...combined the flora of India with the architecture of the Moors. However, the lake, which he put on the roof of the house, proved to be insecurely supported from below.'

She does not tell us whether the whole building collapsed, but at all events this garden disappeared quite soon. The same king built a huge terrace garden in the Italian Renaissance manner at Linderhof; he also tried to build an imitation

Versailles near Oberammergau in a remote mountain valley. The French meanwhile, and the Dutch, were making gardens in the old, formal, geometrical style; in the sunk-garden style called Dutch; in English gardenesque; and in all styles, mixed. Only in the making of public parks, in which there was much activity in and just after mid-century, did the English picturesque manner still predominate; but even there it did not prevail entirely, and most parks had their bedded-out parterres of highly-coloured exotic plants.

Two remarkable gardeners were responsible for the next step towards the late nineteenth- and early twentieth-century paradise garden. They were William Robinson, an Irishman, and Gertrude Jekyll who was English. A point of some importance should be made here. It might be suspected that the author, being English and writing from an English point of view, is giving more than their proper importance to British gardeners and garden styles. But considerable pains have been taken to refer to French, German and American authorities, and the fact clearly emerges that at this time, while gardens were being made increasingly by the

340

339, 340 *Great Dixter, Sussex, by Nathaniel Lloyd and Sir Edwin Lutyens.*

middle-classes as well as by the gentry, in every civilized, prosperous country in the world they were being made in one, or a mixture, of the styles perfected in the past. Only in Britain and Ireland was the art of gardens still growing towards a conclusion which was by now in sight. In France, Germany, Holland, South Africa, Japan, and above all in the United States, advances in scientific horticulture were great; but there were none in the art of composing a garden except in Britain.★

William Robinson was born to very poor Protestant Irish parents in 1838 and nothing is known about his childhood; he first appears on the scene as gardener's boy in the gardens of the Rev. Sir Hunt Henry Johnson-Walsh, a clerical baronet of the Anglo-Irish Establishment. From the fact that later in life he was an admirable writer, Robinson must have managed to educate himself. By the age of 21 he was head gardener in the Johnson-Walsh gardens. One bitterly cold night

★ So true is this that when so good an historian of gardens as the German M.-L. Gothein comes to the end of the nineteenth century, she confines her attention to Britain.

two years later, in the very hard winter of 1861, Robinson opened all the lights in the hothouses which sheltered his employer's large and valuable collection of tender exotics, raked out the boiler fires, and ran away to Dublin.★ Whatever real or fancied wrong Robinson was avenging by this act of sabotage, it reveals the passionate and quarrelsome temper which was to trouble him and his associates for much of his life.

Robinson went to see David Moore, then Director of the Royal Botanic Gardens, Glasnevin. Either he told him nothing about his escapade or he had Moore's sympathy in the quarrel, for Moore advised him to go to England and gave him an introduction to Robert Marnock, Curator of the Royal Botanic Society's garden in Regents Park. Marnock, a friend of the Loudons and a lover of gardens, gave Robinson a job in the herbaceous section.

'The plants in it were all natives and one of Robinson's tasks was to collect specimens. In the course of so doing

★ Taylor (1951).

299

he conceived a passion for the English countryside and above all for the simple cottage-type garden. Out of this passion arose his vision: he saw a garden in which nature, so mild and lovely in England, should not be coerced and deformed, but aided and abetted to do her best by the planting of suitable exotics not merely in but, as it were *into* the native scene. The result, at its most glorious, and beyond Robinson's own achievement, can be seen in such gardens as Mount Usher, Castlewellan, Caerhays, Lochinch, Bodnant, Knights-hayes, Garinish Island and Trengwainton.'*

Meanwhile Robinson was continuing his self-education. He taught himself French so that he could go to the Great Exhibition in Paris as representative of *The Times* and also of Veitch. He gave up his job in the garden at Regents Park and began to live and prosper by his pen. He travelled and studied plants in the French Alps. He taught himself botanical Latin, and he was elected a Fellow of the Linnaean Society. In 1870 he published his first book, *Alpine Flowers for English Gardens*, very aptly since the special craft of rock-gardening with alpines was becoming more and more important. In the same year he went to America and also, at the end of it, published

* Hyams (1964).

300

his second book, *The Wild Garden*. In that book he described how a wild garden could be made by planting hardy exotic plants into an English natural landscape.

'In these early years, Robinson was working up his campaign against bedding-out, "pastry-work gardening", the subjection of gardeners to "decorative artists", and everything to do with the Crystal Palace. Generally, except in small matters such as plant names and the imagined sins of the authorities at Kew, he was not intolerant. An opponent of terraces and "railway embankment" gardening, he saw the rightness and beauty of steep, falling terraced ground at Powis Castle; scornful of fantastic topiary, he delighted in the neatly cut yews of a Cotswold garden. His watchword was Pope's: *Good Sense*.'*

Robinson launched two journals to propagate his ideas: *The Garden: an Illustrated Journal of Horticulture in all its Branches* (1871), which was a financial failure although a *succès d'estime*, and *Gardening* (later *Gardening Illustrated*, and much later incorporated with *The Gardeners' Chronicle*). He was quarrelsome, apt to be rude and excessively didactic;

* Hadfield (1960).

341-4 *Sissinghurst Castle, Kent. The white garden; view from the tower to the rose garden; one of the walks; and the tower from the white garden. Rosa Nevada.*

but he was a success, even at making a fortune by playing the markets. He did a great deal to get rid of the bedding-out and riot-of-colour kind of gardening. He created a style for the middle-class garden — broad, preferably undulating lawns round the house, beds of shrubs and roses mixed with herbaceous plants, much use of climbing plants to cover walls and trellises and even trees. For both the small and large garden, Robinson's style was just what was needed to make use of the new wealth of plant material pouring into the country from plant collectors, and into thousands of gardens by way of the botanical and nursery gardens, especially such hardy plants as rhododendrons, camellias, magnolias, barberries and paeonies. But in the process of making his wild gardens, as distinct from his round-the-house gardens, he was very apt to abolish all line, all shape, and to create simply a richer and more colourful wilderness.

But in 1875 Robinson met Gertrude Jekyll, a gentlewoman of old and prosperous family. Educated in music, literature and the other arts, she had a taste for fine craftsmanship and a love of the countryside and of flowers. She became a

345 *Sissinghurst Castle. A synthesis of three great styles. The Irish yews were planted in 1934.*

346 *Spring border under limes.*

painter, travelled quite widely, and learned various old crafts, in which she took a particular interest, including that of gilding, which she studied in Italy. Then came the meeting with Robinson; she liked his ideas, and she designed and planted her first garden, for her mother, in Surrey. She began to write articles for Robinson's papers, soon made a name for herself in the gardening world, and took up garden designing as a professional. In the remoter parts of her gardens she followed Robinson, making wild gardens with woods and waters, and planting exotics into them; in the garden near the house she adapted the old English cottage garden, giving it a more sophisticated expression. In both she imposed a greater measure of careful order than did Robinson, but the latter was soon being influenced by her, so that he too accepted a measure of discipline and form. What Gertrude Jekyll excelled in was the choice, placing and juxtaposition of herbaceous plants to create a perfect floral and foliar harmony; she was not a painter for nothing. Her influence, soon very great, was, like Robinson's, hostile to the riot-of-colour and carpet-bedding or *jardins fleuristes* schools. She was less hostile than Robinson to architectural features in a garden, and by her influence softened his hostility to such elements.

Gertrude Jekyll's influence on Robinson and on the gardening of her times was important because Robinsonian enthusiasts were tending to abolish the garden altogether, replacing it with untutored countryside into which exotics were planted. One of the greatest practitioners of Robinsonian gardening was the wealthy candle manufacturer George Fergusson Wilson, who planted many species of rhododendron and other shrubs, irises, and above all great numbers of lilies, into his woodland at Oakwood, near Ripley in Surrey. He is said to have replied to a criticism that what he had done was beautiful but not gardening, that he had envisaged a place where plants from all over the world would grow wild side by side. In short, an ideal of paradise.

When Robinson and Jekyll had done their work, a reaction against it was needed if a garden successfully integrating all the great styles which had by then been perfected, and which could absorb the new wealth of plant material without losing all form and harmony, was to emerge. It should be said, of course, that there was no question of the nineteenth-century garden makers consciously working towards a clearly envisaged ideal; but it is easier to describe what actually happened as if it had been a conscious process.

The most effective exponent of the reaction towards a mea-

30. *Burle Marx uses plants as an element of architecture, Sao Paulo.*

31. *Munich Botanic Garden. Here Italianate, French and English styles are mingled in a modern garden.*

32. *Longwood. English but also French and Italian styles are reproduced.*

33.   *Fountains at Longwood.*

sure of formalism in the garden was an architect, Harold Ainsworth Peto. He was not, however, the first in time. John Dando Sedding (1891) and Sir Reginald Blomfield (1892) both called for a restoration of some architectural element, some firm outlines, in English gardening. Another influence in the same sense was that of Sir George Sitwell who, both in the making of his own Italianate garden at Renishaw in Derbyshire, and in his *Essay on the Making of Gardens* (1909), pointed the way to a return to form and a measure of formalism. Moreover, when in 1896 Gertrude Jekyll built herself a house, Munstead Wood, employing Lutyens as her architect, their joint work on the design of the garden showed a marked return to formalism, but on the other hand taught Lutyens a great deal about gardening in general, knowledge of which he was to make use at Great Dixter (see below).

But Peto was the man who mattered more than any of them. Once again, as with Barry, it was a case of Italy and Italian gardens re-establishing their hold on the imagination of an English artist. It was Peto who, above all, and using Italian models, restored line and form to the English garden. He used, albeit quite sparingly and with discretion, Ionic colonnades, balustraded terraces, paving, handsome stairways, statues, urns. He made himself an entirely successful garden in his own style, Iford Manor near Bradford-on-Avon, and a number of other gardens both in England and on the Italian and French riviera. In our present context, however, his most important work by far was, for a reason which will appear, the garden of Ilnacullin, designed for Mr Annan Bryce on Garinish Island in the bay of Glengariff, Co. Cork, Ireland. But before coming to that very remarkable garden it will be as well to look a little longer at what some makers of large gardens were making of Robinson's principles and of the great wealth of plants which nurserymen were now offering.

Robinson himself tried to realize his own ideas at Gravetye in Surrey. He failed, finding he had to do a great deal of earth-moving and tree-felling, both of which were against his strict principles. Many of his exotic herbaceous species and cultivars, planted into English woodland, died. He worked on an enormous scale, planting for example one hundred thousand daffodil bulbs, and he did accomplish a remarkable wild garden; but others did better. I have already mentioned Inverewe in Scotland. At Caerhays, in Cornwall, J.C. Williams, by planting into the natural landscape great numbers of Sikkimese and Chinese rhododendrons, as well as the choicest hybrids (many of which he bred himself), camellias, magnolias and other woody, flowering plants, created the

347, 348 *Cottage garden, Sissinghurst, and the rose garden.*

349

loveliest wild garden in the world. Because Williams helped to finance plant hunters, besides being a brilliant hybridizer and a learned plantsman, and because the mild climate of south Cornwall is so very favourable to semi-tender exotics, it was at Caerhays that many of the most exquisite of the new introductions were grown.

'No one knows the number of rhododendron species eventually planted at Caerhays; it must run into many hundreds if not thousands. [It can hardly have been 'thousands'; there are between 800 and 900 species known to science. — E. H.] Mr Williams made very careful notes of them; he had a marvellous power of concentrating upon a difficult and complicated subject and becoming master of it... He himself was not content until he knew not only the height at which collected plants grew as well as their position, but also the geology of the district... He was keen on experimenting but once satisfied that a situation was wrong he took the line that there was always some other plant that would do there and would look well...'*

And again:

'...the sights that suddenly meet the eye are unforgettable. The visitor bursts in upon not one or two but a whole group of great rhododendrons, trees rather than bushes, blazing with large trusses of magnificent flowers, white or pink or red...'*

And yet again:

'It is perfectly possible to see as many as eighty, and perhaps a hundred species of rhododendrons from sub-shrubs a few inches tall to plants the size of trees, in flower, each represented not by one but by scores of specimens, on the same day. Of the Caerhays hybrids now planted in gardens all over the world, at least twelve are incomparably good in their class.'†

But rhododendrons did not fill Caerhays: scores of other

* Bishop Hunkin of Truro. *Journal of the Royal Horticultural Society*, January 1943.

* Ibid.
† Hyams (1964).

304

349 *Sissinghurst Castle: the Tudor entrance (built about 1490). A property of the National Trust.*

350 *Bodnant, Denbighshire. Part of the woodland garden.*

350

genera were treated in the same way, notably *Camellia*, planted into the Cornish scene to create a paradise wilderness which is certainly not a garden.

'The gardens are rich in tree heaths, in primulas, exotic oaks and beeches, in maples, in enkianthus, in... but what is the use? I am in precisely the same difficulty as that French gardener who came over to see the Cornish gardens and whose case is recounted by Bishop Hunkin: the Frenchman's host had noticed that as, day after day, his guest came back from a visit to some garden he sat down to write notes on it; but on the day he returned from Caerhays he wrote nothing. He was asked why, and he gave this despairing answer: "Because it is impossible. They will no longer believe me".'

This was wild gardening at its magnificent best. Ignoring chronology for the moment, for the style survived the coming return to formalism, similar gardens were made at Crarae in West Scotland by Sir George Campbell; at Glenarn, Rhu, by the Gibson family with their incomparable col-

lection and knowledge of rhododendron species, and elsewhere in Scotland; on Lake Maggiore — the Villa Taranto — by Neil McEacharn; in the south of France, in Portugal, all over the Commonwealth, and above all in Ireland. Of the Irish gardens, Mount Usher is in many ways the most remarkable.

Mount Usher garden was made by succeeding generations of Walpoles at Ashford, County Wicklow, and is still maintained by the same family. It was started in 1868, as mentioned above, and later developed with the advice and encouragement of Sir Frederick Moore, Director of the Royal (now National) Botanic Gardens. Here, again, a natural landscape based on a pretty, placid river was planted full of hundreds, perhaps thousands, of exotic species. Particularly remarkable are the magnificent southern-hemisphere trees, the splendid exotic conifers, the groups of enormous Australian and Chilean eucryphias. The garden is rich in rhododendrons, crinodendrons, camellias, magnolias and roses,

351 *Bodnant.*

352, 353 *Bodnant: from the high terrace, and the dell garden.*

in fact in every kind of flowering shrub and tree from all over the temperate and sub-tropical zones of the earth.

Another Irish garden of this kind, but which also includes a walled, quite formal area in the gardenesque manner, Anne's Grove, County Cork, was the creation of Mr Richard Grove Annesley. There the wild woodland garden, precisely in the manner of Robinson, is a sort of jungle paradise which, in June, is almost incredible. Andean embothriums flame scarlet above the gentler colours of rare Chinese rhododendrons; camellias grow in natural groves; and the woodland trees, superb specimens, are from every quarter of the globe. The riverside garden, too, is a fine example of wild gardening with exotic herbaceous plants, notably tens of thousands of Asiatic primulas of many species.

Among other such Robinsonian gardens in Ireland are the woodland parts of the beautiful garden made by the Earl and Countess of Rosse at Birr Castle, which also includes parts done in the formal French and Italianate styles; the remains of Rossdohan, a garden of tree-ferns and true acacias gone wild; a great part of Glenveagh Castle in County Donegal, where a whole hillside has been planted with exotics, the top of the hill having a simple belvedere from which can be viewed the lower gardens of lawn and shrubbery and the walled formal garden, a revival of a much older one. These are in the Republic; in Ulster, parts of Mount Stewart,

354
Fountain at Longwood Gardens, Kennett Square, Pennsylvania. The pool lined with blue tiles is the central focal point of a long brick walk through the old flower gardens.

355
Italian water garden at Longwood Gardens. The distant pair of pools is twenty feet longer than the closer pair, creating an illusion that all four pools are the same size, when viewed from the terrace.

356
View from the terrace across the fountain garden towards wooded hillside and the chimes tower, Longwood.

356

Castlewellan and Rowallane are done in the Robinsonian style. In each case the gardens include a more formal part. But it was with the Peto-Bryce work on Garinish that the deliberately planned picturesque-Italianate-paradise garden was at last accomplished.

In 1910 Annan Bryce bought from the British War Office the naked, rocky island of Ilnacullin which had been an outpost of coastal defence, with a Martello tower, for nearly a century. His idea was to build a house and make a garden on it, and while top-soil (of which it had almost none) was being shipped across from the mainland, he consulted Harold Peto who was chosen to design both house and garden. Peto decided to garden the whole island, but to do so on a framework of Italianate architecture. It was a long time before the house was built, but from 1910 to 1914, and from 1919 to 1924 when Bryce died, the two men

'combined their ideas and resources in the creation of this formal architectural garden with beautifully placed colonnades, flights of steps, terraces and pools, all of which blend in remarkably well with the natural setting and with the surrounding informal plantings. An Italian tea-house of Bath stone, and an Italian temple; columns of "Rosso Antico" taken from a rediscovered quarry and of a beautiful red colour; marble slabs, white and thickly veined with a rich yellow, from the island of Scyros; Carrara marble balustrading; a floor of green Connemara marble done in scagliola, the work of Italians brought over for the purpose, these are some of the architectural features.'*

Bryce's contribution and that of his friends, notably Richard Grove Annesley, was plantmanship. The garden has flowering shrubs and trees from Australia and New Zealand grown to an enormous size; it has all the best South American flowering shrubs, including the Chilean myrtles; it has all the finest Chinese and Himalayan rhododendrons, including the giant-leaved primitives and the species which grow into large trees; it has South African heaths in great variety. It has, in fact, the best from every one of the world's florae.

* Fletcher, Dr R. H. *Journal of the Royal Horticultural Society*, January 1966.

But because of Peto's influence the garden also has shape, interesting form imposed on the natural topography. And since the site is magnificent, with innumerable views of blue-green sea, well covered with golden seaweed, and purple mountains, Ilnacullin is indeed a paradise.

Happily, Bryce's son, Roland l'Estrange Bryce, was as interested in this garden on a rock as his father had been. He continued planting and caring for it, built the long-delayed house, and when he died left the whole work to the Irish Republic, for the use of its Prime Minister as a country house.

Wittingly or not, Bryce and Peto had accomplished for the art of gardening precisely what, at the end of the nineteenth and beginning of the twentieth century, it needed: given it a style which would accommodate, in a unity, the picturesque, the Italianate, the architectural, and plantmanship.

The most successful British gardens of the twentieth century have been those made more or less in the Bryce-Peto manner, or at least in that spirit. They were, in their flora, by far the richest gardens the world has ever seen, and in their use of this plant material they were 'natural' in the sense in which Robinson used the word; yet they revived in England the architectural beauty and sometimes magnificence of the best Italian models. Moreover, in the regard paid to the effect of landscape vistas and panoramas, they were also picturesque. The three principal elements of style were present in different proportions in different gardens. The garden of Great Dixter in Sussex, made by Nathaniel Lloyd and his architect, Sir Edwin Lutyens, is far more architectural than picturesque, but its plant material is very rich indeed.

In some ways the most remarkable of these new gardens was Hidcote Barton Manor, made by the American Lawrence Johnston in the Cotswolds. It combines and unites the three elements, but is original in its use of them; in the wonderful diversity of plants used for hedging the many enclosures; in the manner in which grand picturesque vistas were accomplished despite subdivision and enclosure which ensured 'expectation and surprise'; and in the firmness of the shape achieved by an architectural skeleton perfectly reconciled with Robinsonian planting. Almost every element of garden art and craft was used, yet Hidcote Barton is an integral work of art.

In the Sissinghurst Castle garden made by the late Sir Harold

and Lady Nicolson, there is, again, a union of the three elements; but here architecture imposed itself, since the fine old brick walls, the tower and archway, and the cottages, were all there before the garden was started and had therefore to be part of the design. Here as at Great Dixter, the range of plants is very great; Victoria Sackville-West, like Gertrude Jekyll, applied an artist's (in her case a poet's) judgment to the choice of plants, and especially of colours and juxtapositions.

The most spectacular of these great twentieth-century gardens of the three stylistic elements is Bodnant, in North Wales, largely the creation of the late Lord Aberconway, of the present Lord Aberconway and of Mr Charles Puddle. Architecturally the garden is Italianate, with its great terraces, each with its formal sheet of water, its balustrades and stairways, its Pin Mill garden, with the Pin Mill pavilion, the formal lawn and long, formal pool. There is a touch of Charles Barry in the way the balustraded terraces are built, and in its command of fine vistas the garden is picturesque, a great landscape garden. But the Glen and other parts, richly planted with thousands of exotic, flowering shrubs, is an entirely Robinsonian garden. Other English styles from the past have their echoes at Bodnant — gardenesque, for example; there is a reminiscence of the Biddulf Grange Rainbow Garden in one part of the rhododendron gardens.

Smaller gardens were made in the same manner; one can even find the three elements, reduced in scale and strength, in the best small suburban gardens. A superlative example of the three-element garden on a smaller, though not a small, scale, is Withersdane Gardens at the hall of residence, Wye College (University of London), in Kent. There a series of formally planned gardens separated from each other by hedges, one a lawn with a scree garden on a raised bank, one a sunk par-

357

358

357 *Waterlily pools, with many species and varieties of tropical waterlilies and aquatic plants, feature giant leaves of the South American water platter; Longwood Gardens.*

358 *Naturalized narcissus and muscari line the large lake at Longwood.*

terre, one a rose and herbaceous garden, one a herb garden centred on the formal fish-pool, compose a unity which is not, yet which has the essential quality of, a picturesque garden; and in at least one part the garden is almost in the manner of Capability Brown, for the distant landscape has, by the disposition of groups of trees, the air of being part of the garden.

But perhaps the most perfect garden in this twentieth-century school, in which the styles and traditions of the past are assimilated, is that of Dartington Hall near Totnes in

311

Devonshire. Two professional landscape artists worked on it: the American Beatrix Farrand at various times between 1926 and 1939, and Percy Cane after the Second World War. He was responsible for the more landscape-cum-architectural features such as the magnificent flight of stairs from the lower to the higher level, flanked by splendid plantings of tree heaths and magnolias; for the round belvedere which commands fine views of the countryside cleverly brought into the garden by the contrivance of vistas and by thoughtful tree planting; for the very clever use of the old Tiltyard; and for the splendid vistas, rather in the manner of Repton but making use of trees and plants Repton had never heard of. Beatrix Farrand was responsible for the gardenesque work round the ancient house, for the lovely flower garden, and for the rhododendron, camellia and magnolia walks. But in a sense the creator, and certainly the guiding eye, of the whole garden was the late Mrs Dorothy Elmhirst. Like Victoria Sackville-West and Gertrude Jekyll, she imposed on her gardeners a severe restraint in the choice of herbaceous plants, in the choice of colours and in their juxtaposition.

The distinctions of the Dartington Hall garden are these: perfect tact and a high degree of skill in the exploitation of the natural topography of the site; perfectly successful combination of the architectural and Italianate elements — mason's work, statues, urns, and picturesque landscaping, so that the garden is given just enough firm line to hold its elements together; a range of exotic plants which is comparable only with a botanical garden, yet which is always subordinated to the overriding consideration of design.

In the United States the late nineteenth and early twentieth century did not, as I have said, see any original work in design of gardens. Horticultural science and technology made giant strides there, notably in gardens which had been private but became State or even national institutions. Shaw's Garden, in St Louis, Missouri, is a case in point: from the beginning a garden where original work in horticulture and floriculture was done, it became particularly famous for the breeding of new water lilies. The tradition has been maintained, for its Climatron was, when built, far more advanced than any other large greenhouse in the world.

The grand Huntington Garden at Pasadena, California, is a good example of the manner in which almost all the styles of Europe were borrowed but were not, as in Britain, integrated. The Huntington Garden has much that is French seventeenth-century, something that is Italian sixteenth-century, much that is English eighteenth-century; it has an exquisite Japanese garden; and in its ten-acre cactus garden it has one element which is entirely original. It is very impressive and in parts superlatively beautiful, but it is not an integral work of art.

A more spectacular case in point is the Longwood Garden, in Pennsylvania. It out-Italys Renaissance Italy in its enormous complex of fountains and waterworks, which at night are illuminated with changing patterns of coloured floodlighting. The maker of this garden, Pierre Du Pont, was an engineer, and the numerous devices of this garden would have delighted the Renaissance princes or the German garden makers of the romantic epoch. Likewise, the use of masonry, statues, urns and pavilions is Renaissance Italian. But in the layout, disposition, management and flora of the flower gardens, Longwood is a *jardin fleuriste*, perhaps the only garden left in the world where carpet-bedding is carried on in the high Victorian manner. On the other hand, in the use of topography, tree planting and water, this extraordinary garden is Le Nôtreau in the near neighbourhood of the house, English picturesque in the more remote parts; and there are other parts where the words 'gardenesque' and 'parterre' are not out of place. Thus Longwood is very nearly a paradise garden, falling just short, however, of the difficult accomplishment of unity.

359 *Modern Art Museum, Rio de Janeiro. Garden by Burle Marx.*

TODAY AND TOMORROW

'Roberto thinks, as do the English, that a landscape is made up of melancholy, and, perhaps, like the hero of Huysmans' *A Rebours*, Des Esseintes, that *rien n'est moins poetique que la nature*. Nature is a dishevelled wench, and so he grooms and proceeds to subtle artificial experiments before introducing us to her as quite another person. Nature, as she is, is an object, not a work of art — a marvellously unruly, incoherent object that needs to be ordered and adjusted before she can lay claim to status in artistic circles. The topiary artist, in substance, wants to see a tree as material to be carved into a statue, and the result is a surrealist's joke; nevertheless it has been realised that nature requires artifice, corruption and correction, and these are the province of man.'*

The Roberto here in question is, of course, Roberto Burle Marx who, to the best of my knowledge and belief, is the only landscape-garden artist of original genius (though there are some of great talent) now living and practising. He is a Brazilian; and because his gardens are tropical gardens some may argue that his works cannot be considered as lessons to which we in the high latitudes should attend, however we may admire and enjoy them. This argument, to which I shall revert presently, could derive only from a misconception; for the art of the garden lies not in its materials, but in how they are used. As in other arts, style, design, purpose and intention can be given expression in any physically suitable material.

Still, a good artist studies the material he is to work with. The Italian Renaissance painters invented pigments; Wren spent many months in the quarries from which his stone came. The artist is the better for knowing his material thoroughly, and he may, if his overall concept so requires, seek different ones. Roberto Burle Marx, in order to use plants that will achieve the results he desires, has made so thorough a study of them that he has become an excellent scientific botanist and a skilled practical horticulturist. And from time to time plants he has himself discovered in the forests, the first man to do so, have suggested to him new refinements of his art, have opened up new possibilities in design.

Roberto Burle Marx was born in São Paulo of a German father and a Brazilian mother in 1909; his family removed from São Paulo to Rio de Janeiro in 1913. At the age of nineteen he went to Germany to study art at the Berlin Academy, but by then he had already discovered and revealed his talent not only as a painter but also as a botanist and a practical gardener. Many hours of his leisure time in Berlin were spent in the great Dahlem Botanic Garden, where he not only

* Bardi (1964).

313

360

361

became increasingly interested in plant physiology and ecology but also discovered in the hothouses the possibilities, for garden art, of plants native to his own, rather than to Berlin's, latitude. In 1930 he returned to Brazil and continued to study painting at the National Academy of Fine Arts, this time under Brazilian masters, notably Leo Putz and Candido Portinari. But his interest in plants was as strong as ever, and in 1933 be brought together his talent as a painter and his knowledge as a botanist to design his first garden, for a house in Rio. This was a success and two years later he was designing the new gardens for the Praça da Republica, the water garden in the old Casa Forte square and the Benefica cactus garden, all three in Recife, the State capital of Pernambuco. We are not here directly concerned with Burle Marx's career as a painter, but in 1937 he was awarded the gold medal for painting by the National Academy of Fine Arts.★

Between 1935 and 1951 Burle Marx designed about ten gardens of importance, three of them roof gardens, usually working in co-operation with some well-known architect; they included the Pampulha Park in Belo Horizonte (Minas Gerais). His paintings were now being shown internationally, and he himself travelled widely, chiefly in England, Portugal, Italy, France and Germany. In 1952 his landscape garden

★ London saw Roberto Burle Marx's first paintings at the Brazilian Exhibition at Burlington House in 1941.

designs were shown, together with his paintings, in an Exhibition at the Museum of Art in São Paulo; and in the same year he laid out the gardens at Rio's Santos-Dumont Airport.

The next two years were very productive. In 1953 Burle Marx won the prize for Landscape Architecture at the second international Exhibition of International Architecture, and landscaped the grounds of Galeão airport, as well as the new grounds of the University of Brazil. He also made gardens for the United States Embassy in Rio and a number of others; meanwhile he was designing sets for stage and ballet, and painting murals. Like so many of the great landscape garden artists before him, in Europe, China and Japan, he was a good gardener because he was a painter (or poet). In the following year he accepted the Chair of Landscape Gardening at the University of Brazil's School of Architecture, thereby adding teaching to his other work; lectured in the United States and in Cuba; had a one-man show in Washington, which was thereafter travelled about the country by the Smithsonian Institution; and laid out the Botafogo Bay gardens in Rio.

Burle Marx's first one-man show in London was in 1955. There is no point in citing all the gardens he was making and has since made; I shall have something to say about some of them below. But two of the most important public ones were the great Parque del Este in Caracas, Venezuela; and his share of the Beira del Mar gardens, started in 1962 and still

360, 361 *Pebbles and plants: details of Burle Marx work on the Rio de Janeiro waterfront garden.*

362, 363 *Dr Candido de Paula Machado's residence, Rio de Janeiro. Garden and walls by Burle Marx.*

362

363

far from complete, which are to cover the reclaimed land of Rio's waterfront from the Santos Dumont airport to Botafogo.

Professor Bardi has written of Burle Marx:

'...Architect, painter and sculptor, he expresses himself in landscape gardening, which harmonises these three arts and integrates them. To master that compendium it is necessary to possess technique or, rather, a technical feeling for nature, which is attained through science. Roberto has devoted himself to acquiring this, and it is an important aspect of the personality of this artist who has developed his knowledge not so much in the greenhouse and the laboratory as beneath the often perilous canopy of the Brazilian forest, in the thrilling search for flora that are unknown to those latter-day floral decorators who content themselves with utilizing the species easiest to obtain and disseminate.'*

The first paintings that Burle Marx made as a boy were of trees; from his boyhood he had collected, studied and propagated plants. As a botanist he has discovered during his forest expeditions many plants until then unknown to science, plants which he has named, or which have been named for him. In his intimate relationship with the living material of his art he is extraordinarily thorough, not only in exploring and hunting for new plants to carry out some project of a public or private garden, but in cultivating the

* Bardi (1964).

315

364, 365 *Brasilia. State Ministry terrace, Foreign Office. Garden by Burle Marx.*

society and friendship of scientific botanists and keeping himself up-to-date in their science. To quote Professor Bardi, his biographer, or rather the principal student and publicist of his work:

'...all this instills in the character of the new poet of *canticum botanicum* the joy of creation, together with the veiled melancholy that belongs to temperaments which endeavour to weld the ephemeral ventures of the day to the eternity surrounding them.'

Even in his work as a plant hybridizer Burle Marx shows himself a painter: one of his earliest undertakings in that field was, for instance, his attempt to obtain a particular shade of red in the leaf veinings of certain Aroids because that was what he needed for a design he had in mind. Probably no garden artist before him has ever tried to work in quite that way, create new plants not for the sake of doing so or for monetary profit, but to realize designs in which the plant was to be a mere component element. It suggests an entirely new art form, almost in the realm of science fiction: the artist uses the science of genetics in the service of his artistic concept, creates living artefacts which are works of abstract art. As a very young man Burle Marx made himself an experimental garden, a sort of laboratory, in his father's garden at Copacabana; and it was indeed his intense interest

in and skill with plants that, by impressing his architect-teacher Lucio Costa at the Fine Arts Academy, led to his first commission as a garden artist.

Naturally, Burle Marx also studied past works and artists in his chosen field. A few of these were under his nose. There was what remained of the works and teaching of François-Marie Glaziou, a Frenchman who in 1858, under the patronage of the Emperor Dom Pedro II, created the garden of the Quinta da Bôa Vista, and who, as botanist, collected and introduced into cultivation scores of plants discovered in the course of expeditions into the forests; and there was the earlier waterfront landscape work of Mestre Valentin da Fonseca e Silva.* Both men had worked in the English picturesque style, making romantic landscape gardens with tropical material; but their work was only one of the many sources of Burle Marx's art. Another was what he had seen in England; he himself has said that in planning the water garden of the old Casa Forte square in Recife, he was inspired for his group of three ponds by certain aspects of Kew Gardens.† But although he learned much from his study of English, French and German gardens, there can be no doubt that he very early realized that in order not only to suit the tropical scene, but also to match contemporary painting, sculpture and architecture, an original style, a new manner was needed, which, like the English eighteenth-century garden art, should be derived from nature, not from geometry; but nature 'corrupted and corrected' by artifice.

Burle Marx does not work single-handed; like an Italian Renaissance artist he has what is virtually a workshop of apprentices or disciples — architects, botanists, gardeners. He directs or guides a sort of school of younger practitioners who look to him for original designs, then carry them out and look to him again for the finishing touches of the master. His work in California, in Cuba and in Caracas has often been done with the help of this 'school'. As to how he and his followers approach their work, I cannot do better than to quote Professor Bardi once again, for he was the first to make a clear and explicit connection between the spirit in which Burle Marx attacks his works, and that of the English landscape gardeners of the eighteenth century:

'...As regards gardens, the world remains romantic: once the theme has been found it must be developed by the spiritual, sensitive and at the same time mechanical pursuit

* Bardi (1964).
† Ibid.

366

of the same thrilling — perhaps even more thrilling — venture of recomposing the landscape that the Pre-Impressionists achieved with an infinity of detail in form and coloring limned from life in the English countryside. These artists sought to represent in painting the nature of the ideal landscape; by a similar process Burle Marx represents in the recomposition of living nature the elements he has gathered in his incursions into the unexplored hinterlands of Brazil, imparting to them a form of his own. The result is characteristic of a painter...'

But for all that he is none the less a horticulturist in the technical sense; he has not only his own experimental garden, as he had as a much younger man, but also his own large nursery, from which to draw the material he needs and where he propagates the new plants he has collected (e.g. the ten species of the genus *Helicoma* unknown to science until he found them and among which is *Helicoma burle-marxii*), and his newly discovered Aroids such as *Philodendron burle-marxii*. Probably no gardener before him has made such effective use of the giant leaves and strange shapes of tropical

inflorescences. But although he exploits them, although they suggest treatments to him, he does not depend on them; he could work, has worked, in the same spirit, using temperate-zone material to make gardens congrous with the modern townscape, modern building, latter-day feeling.

His work neglects no ancient tradition. Very interesting, and calling to mind the ancient Chinese and (in another context) the Japanese use of stones, is Burle Marx's use of beds of pebbles, standing stones dressed or rough, and other inanimate objects, artefacts, or *objets trouvés* (such as curiously shaped masses of granite) to balance or offset the shape of a plant, or dried roots of mangrove weirdly shaped. But he does not use these, any more than plants, for their own sake (although the ancient Chinese sometimes certainly did in their gardens), but as elements of a composition.

Another old element which he has reintroduced into garden design, but in entirely modern terms, is the decorated wall — not, of course, realistically painted or with realistic sculpted

367

366, 367 *Brasilia. State Ministry, Foreign Office.*

objects but decorated with brilliant tiled or mosaic murals. There are some fine examples of this in the garden he made for Sr Walter Moreira Salles at Gavea, and in the garden of Sr Olive Gomes at São José dos Campos, in the state of São Paulo. In the garden made for Sr Francisco Pignatari the wall has a relief design in unfaced concrete. Burle Marx uses such walls as wind-breaks, and also to delimit a view or to draw the attention in a particular direction. In the roof and court gardens, for example, at the Museum of Modern Art in Rio, the way in which walled and rectangular beds of plants massed for foliage colour are somehow given as much substance as stone artefacts is very remarkable. But the most careful thought is always given to making artefacts balance or harmonize with the plants associated with them. A good example is the blue tiled wall and the bed of *Iresine herbatii* in the Larragoiti Hospital garden; and foliage patterns are superlatively matched with murals and other artefacts in the garden of Sr Inocente Palacio in Caracas. Plant associations are quite as carefully thought out.

368-70 *Missouri Botanical Garden.*

But these formal, abstract gardens are only one part of Burle Marx's art. Like the pre-picturesque theorists and the great landscape garden artists of the post-picturesque reaction, he has a taste for wildness. Whether, indeed, Addison would have liked Brazilian nature is a question; but Rousseau would certainly have approved of Burle Marx's ponds with their masses of waterlilies, their ferociously 'natural' philodendrons, and of the way art is used to conceal art in their making.

In a number of his gardens, his own renewals of all the great styles of the past are combined, as in the grand garden made for Sra Odette Monteiro at Correias, in the State of Rio de Janeiro. There, the open landscaped valley has, as it were, been 'paradised' with flowers, masses of coloured foliage and rocks matched with giant-leaved plants, to make an abstract of a wilderness. Paths are as serpentine as ever they were in the gardens of China; lakes are in the picturesque tradition but with bold differences in the treatment of foreshores. In the great garden made for Sr Alberto Kronforth at Theresopolis, lines and contours in the landscape are empha-

sized and answered with masses of colour so vast that very large surfaces are no longer green or brown but the grey mauve of *Helichrysum petiolaris*, the red maroon of *Iresine herbstii*, the gold of *Chlorophytum sommusum variegatum*. Perhaps only in the tropics could just those effects be obtained, for the problem of deciduousness, of the winter-resisting herbaceous plants, hardly exists. The same bold effect was achieved in the Cavanelas garden about the bungalow residence built by Oscar Niemeyer.

The older European styles are not the only ones which Burle Marx has made his own, transformed and reinterpreted in new terms. There is an element of Japanese in several of his gardens, for example in the treatment of lakes and foreshore plantings in Sr Alfredo Baumann's garden at Itaipava (despite the fact that the plant material is so different) and in the treatment of the pool which receives the waterfall in Sr Palacio's garden (Caracas).

We have seen that in the history of gardening, as of the other arts and crafts, a certain pattern of events is, from

371

371 *Sydney Botanical Garden, with the Opera House in the background.*

372 *Interior view in climatron, St Louis, Missouri.*

time to time, repeated. A gardener with creative genius, a Seigen (chapter 5), a Pirro Ligorio, a Petrarch or an Alexander Pope, a Le Nôtre or a Henry Hoare, or for that matter a school of poet-gardeners, makes gardens which, being masterpieces of their kind, give rise to a style to be followed, at first in their country of origin, then outside its frontiers but still within the frontiers of its proper culture; and at last and occasionally, even beyond that frontier. The influence of such men and such works produces two kinds of imitators. First there are those who have skill and talent and can produce valid works of their own in the new manner because they understand the originator's intention and share his ideal; such creative imitators may surpass the first master or may, by taking his works as a point of departure, do original work in garden design themselves. The second and much larger class of imitators merely accept the new style as a vogue and degrade the originator's manner into mannerism.

Le Nôtre's manner and Repton's manner are both degraded into mannerism in the gardens made by most of their imitators, especially those outside France and England. 'Capability' Brown made one or two gardens in which he seems to have degraded his own style into mannerism. And, especially because of the boldness and strong character of Burle Marx's gardens, nothing is easier than for his imitators to fall into mannerism. Nevertheless, he also has his true disciples; and it is important for the present and future of garden art that there be as many of them as possible.

For a style in gardening to be accepted and widely followed, social and economic conditions must be such that the making of gardens in that style is materially possible. A garden artist who ignores social conditions will find no clients; if he finds one or two, still he can make nothing lasting, nothing which makes any strong impression on the art or continues

372

its history. In the Italy of the Renaissance there were many nobles and princes of the Church with the taste and education to desire, and the money to pay for, the great baroque gardens of their time; and presumably it is true to say that the artists in question would not have conceived such gardens at all had not the social and economic conditions been such as to create a demand for them. In pre-baroque Germany (and Holland), the Germany of prosperous free cities and a relatively wealthy burgess class, conditions favoured and produced small gardens, as they did, under Petrarch's guidance, in pre-baroque northern Italy. In seventeenth-century France social and economic conditions were such as to demand the Le Nôtre garden of extraordinary grandeur, expressing the arrogant assurance of the French Court, of the princely families and the most powerful nobles. In garden art, as indeed in all the arts, one element of genius is surely the *nous* which answers the call of the times. Only

the existence of quite a large class of rich nobility and gentry in eighteenth-century England made the works of Brown and Repton possible. And we have seen how the garden style reflected the social mores in Japan very closely.

All of which is some sort of guide to what we may expect in our garden art today, or at all events tomorrow.

British writers on gardening, with a touching faith in the propaganda about there being no more rich men left after the tax collector has done with them, have for some time repeated that there will be no more making of great gardens, and that we must now think only in terms of the small man's small garden. The facts are different and money has little to do with them. The latter-day rich in Britain and in Europe generally buy great gardens, they do not make them; but that is for want of inclination. The modern rich are not

323

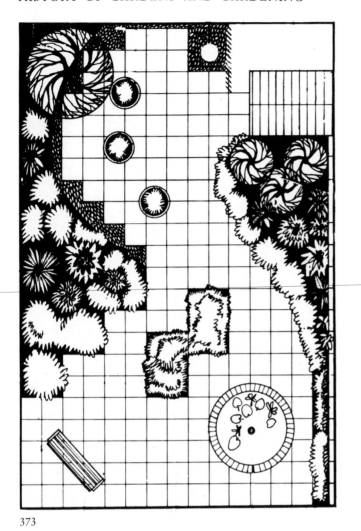

373

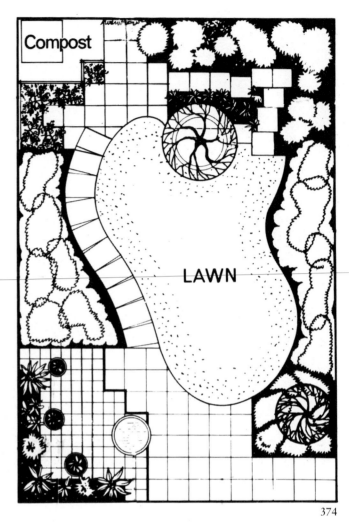

Compost

LAWN

374

leaders in the arts, they are followers, and dragging their feet at that. If they buy pictures they are old ones and bought, as a rule, by way of investment, any kind of property being preferable, nowadays, to money whose purchasing power declines hourly. But Europe is not the only continent in the world. Roberto Burle Marx has not gone short of clients, public and private, for large landscape gardens.

But that is by no means the whole story. Individual rich men in modern Europe represent nothing but themselves. Rich industrial corporations, on the other hand, are one manifestation of the popular will; municipalities are another. Public gardens are still made and maintained; and, increasingly, the grounds round large complexes of both industrial and residential buildings are being landscape-gardened. We

373, 374 *Winning designs for a small garden in the 1968 'Daily Express' garden design competition, Chelsea Flower Show.*

375 *Los Angeles, the arboretum.*

375

badly need a style which is congruous with modern building and social conditions. Burle Marx has created it for us.

But that having being said, it remains true that the class of small clients for the garden artist is more numerous than ever before. They must be considered in terms of certain social and economic realities which imply the limits within which the garden designer must work.

First there is a class of small-to-medium garden owners — large in Britain, rather small elsewhere — which can be discounted altogether. It consists of those who would not in any case accept professional advice, much less ask for it; who themselves do all the physical work which used to be done by the almost vanished jobbing gardener rather than

alter the nature of their garden to reduce labour. But a much larger and growing class of house-owner, while he likes to have a garden and even to do a little light gardening, also enjoys others of the ever more numerous leisure occupations and is not prepared to be owned by a garden. For these people the would-be garden designer has now to bear in mind a number of considerations which are relatively new. Obviously, to begin with, he must plan the gardens for such clients with all the modern gardening machines in mind; he must also remember that, taking into account the social habits of the middle classes in mid and late twentieth century, the garden to look at and the garden as a pretty collection of flowers will no longer do. What is clearly required and is increasingly coming into existence is the garden-as-outdoor-living-room, the garden-as-play-place. This

325

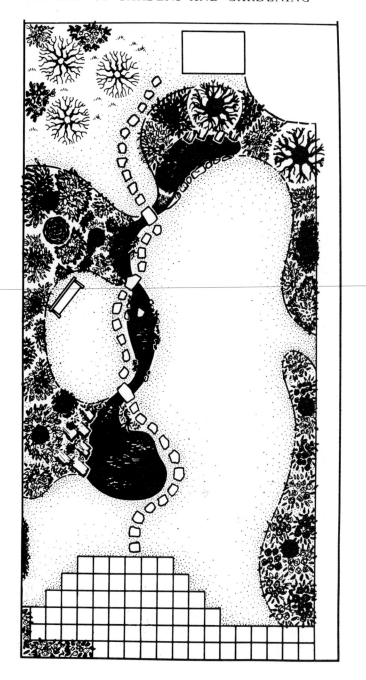

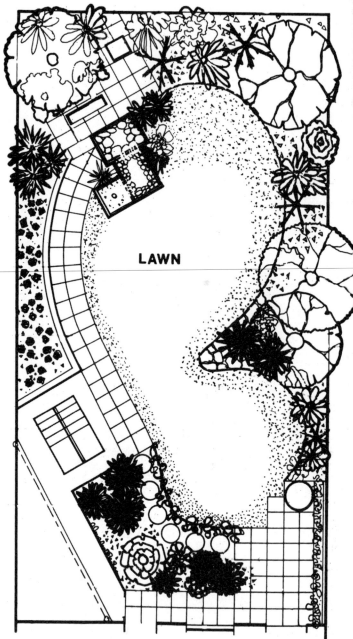

LAWN

means, among other things, making use of modern materials and construction methods to get part of the garden under cover, at least in the temperate zones of the earth; and it means using plants which are at once highly decorative, which suit with the surrounding artefacts, and which are undemanding of labour.

In short, we are back at a much earlier kind of garden, a garden with attributes which were interpreted in much the

376 *This design for a small garden won the 'Daily Express' garden design competition at the Chelsea Flower Show in 1966.*

377 *Chelsea Flower Show 1967. Winning design in the 'Daily Express' garden design competition.*

same way, although in different terms, in a different spirit and for different social reasons, by two ancient schools of garden artists, remote from each other geographically: Early and Middle Kamakura Japanese; and Humanist Italian. The attributes in question here have been discussed in both places — they are those which link house and garden into one living-unit in an area where house penetrates garden, or garden penetrates house. The garden in no longer a place for plants to live in, but for people to live in against a decor of plants.

Some of the best living garden artists have realized this very fully, and have done their best to give a new expression to this ancient arrangement. Perhaps the best of them now working, certainly the artist with the clearest sense of the garden-as-living-space, is Russel Page. Although he has worked chiefly for people in higher income brackets than the average, and for great corporations and institutions, his sound sense, his feeling for the genius of place and his realization of the importance of taking social conditions into account apply at every income level. He has the same kind of genius as Burle Marx for associating plants and artefacts, although he works, on the whole, with much more traditional and conventional elements of design and garden objects.

378 'Daily Mail' Ideal Home Exhibition: conventional small garden design.

379 Pool garden for suburban house.

380

381

380-81 *Lily pool and garden
room made by
the author to link
house and garden.*

382-4 *'Daily Mail' Ideal
Home Exhibition:
Modern suburban garden.
Burle Marx influence on
small garden design
in Britain.
Belgian garden exhibit.*

But garden artists cannot be of real use in improving the design and worth of small gardens unless they are given the chance to do so. What we are still doing in too many places, and particularly in Britain, is to design houses and ignore the garden, simply leaving the new house standing in an empty plot of land to be used or abused as the purchaser likes or can afford, whereas we should be designing house and garden as a unity. (It must be said, however, that some contractors of middle-income housing estates do design the gardens to harmonize with the complex of houses and blocks of flats.) Even in cold and wet climates the problem of the transitional area between house and garden is solved by putting it under transparent cover. Although this point, that house and garden should be a unity, has been made in practice by men such as Burle Marx and Russel Page (and earlier, and on a different scale, by Corbusier and Frank Lloyd Wright), their works have made small impression on the ordinary house-owner and on such institutions as influence him.

382

Nor has the work of modern garden artists yet made much impression on the taste and doings of the millions of small gardeners in the western world. The English are the people most interested in gardening, by a very large margin. The small gardens they currently design are usually pretty but are made of a few clichés collected from the past and neither functionally nor aesthetically expressive of our time. The same kind of stagnation afflicts other European countries. In America, more inclination is shown to use the work or at least the help and advice of professionals, and the best of the professionals are making gardens which begin to be congruous with the architecture they surround. Particularly good work has been done in making city gardens, for example, by Philip Truex. Though he works with conventional or traditional elements, his small town gardens are extensions of the living quarters of the house itself, and not simply some unrelated flower-beds and bushes.

383
384

Which all brings us back to the point that we need a guiding style, need to be shaken into our own times by a garden artist of genius. Burle Marx's lesson is there to be learnt.

But a question remains: to what extent does the garden style of Burle Marx depend on tropical plant material? Put in other words, can you make a Burle Marx garden with temperate zone plants?

This is a problem which arises in no other art. Paint is paint

385 *Covered pool-garden integral with house.*

and stone is stone in any time and place, but the material used by the garden artist is alive and must have its proper conditions in order to flourish. When the lead in garden art came from the north temperate zone, there was little difficulty in interpreting garden designs in the fashion of the times, in tropical materials, as anyone can see for himself in such English picturesque gardens as the botanical garden at Entebbe on Lake Victoria in Uganda, or the one in Singapore. But now that the lead is being taken in a tropical country, there is a difficulty.

But it is certainly not serious, perhaps not even real. The art of Burle Marx is in his way of using material, not in the choice of material, despite his special way of exploiting tropical plants, his passion for them and his botanical erudition. What he has shown us is how to bring plants and artefacts into a composition in our own twentieth-century terms; and how to get back, again in our own terms, to the garden-as-living-space, the garden-as-playground, without losing the garden-as-work-of-art.

386 *Terraced beds with serpentine outline: a New York roof-garden, by Philip Truex.*

387 *The principal problem of the city roof-garden is high winds; hedges are important as wind-breaks.*

388 Modernized 'gardenesque'; a New York city garden dating from the late 1950s.

389 *American gardeners make more use of Japanese styles than British gardeners. Japanese corner in a New York city garden, by Philip Truex.*

390 *All the European garden styles meet in America, even in the New York city gardens.*

391 *Terrace garden on a New York building.*

BIBLIOGRAPHY

ALLAN, MEA (1967): *The Hookers of Kew*, Michael Joseph, London.

AMHERST, A. (1888): *A History of Gardening in England*, London.

ANDRÉ, J. (1879): *L'art des jardins*, Paris.

ARAMBOURG, C. (ed. 1967): *L'Homme avant l'écriture*, Armand Colin, Paris.

ARBER, E. (1885): *The First three English Books on America*, Birmingham.

AUBREY, JOHN (ed. J. Britton, 1847): *The Natural History of Wiltshire*, Wiltshire Topographical Society.

BABUR, ZAHIR-UD-DIN MOHAMMED (trans. J. Leyden and W. Erskine, 1826): *Memoirs*, London.

BARDI, P. M. (1964): *The Tropical Gardens of Burle Marx*, Architectural Press, London.

BARRON, W. (1852): *The British Winter Garden: a practical treatise on Evergreens*, London.

BEAN, W. J. (1914): *Trees and Shrubs hardy in the British Isles*, Murray, London.

BERRALL, J. S. (1966): *The Garden*, Thames & Hudson, London.

BLOCH, M. (1966): *French Rural History*, Routledge, London.

BLOMFIELD, Sir R. (1892): *The Formal Garden in England*, London.

BONNEFONS, N. DE (trans. John Evelyn, 1658): *The French Gardener*, London.

BOYCEAU, J. (1638): *Traité du Jardinage*, Paris.

BUSHNELL, G. H. S. (1956): *Peru*, Thames & Hudson, London.

CANDOLLE, A. DE (trans. 1884): *Origin of Cultivated Plants*, London.

CATESBY, M. (1731-43): *The Natural History of Carolina, Florida and the Bahamas*, 2 vols., London.

CHAMBERS. Sir W. (1772): *A Dissertation on Oriental Gardening*, London.

CHARDIN, Sir JOHN (1711): *Voyages de Monsieur Chevalier Chardin en Perse, et autres lieux de l'Orient*, Amsterdam.

CHILD, V. GORDON (1958): *New Light on the Most Ancient East*, revised edition, Penguin, London.

CIBOT, Père P.-M. (1782): *Essai sur les jardins de plaisir des Chinois*, Paris.

CLAVIJO, RUY GONZALES DE (trans. G. Le Strange, 1928): *Embassy to Tamerlane 1403-6*, Routledge, London.

COATS, P. (1963): *Great Gardens*, Weidenfeld & Nicholson, London.

COLLIS, M. (1965): *Siamese White*, Faber.

COOK, M. (1676): *The Manner of Raising, Ordering and Improving Forest Trees*, London.

CUTLER, W. P. and J. P. (1888): *Life, Journals and Correspondence of Rev. Manaseh Cutler*, Cincinnati.

DARLINGTON, W. (1849): *Memorials of John Bartram and Humphrey Marshall*, Philadelphia.

DE GRAAFF, J. and HYAMS, E. (1967): *Lilies*, Nelson, London.

DE WIT, H. C. D. (1963): *Plants of the World: The Higher Plants*, 2 vols, Thames & Hudson, London.

DELILLE, Abbé (1782): *Les Jardins, ou l'art d'embéllir les paysages*, Paris.

DEZALLIER D'ARGENVILLE (1709): *La Théorie et la Pratique du Jardinage*, Paris.

DOWNING, A. J. (1841): *Treatise on the Theory and Practice of Landscape Gardening*, New York.

ELWOOD, P. H. (1924): *American Landscape Architecture*, New York.

EVELYN, JOHN (1658): see BONNEFONS.
(1664): *Sylva, or a Discourse of Forest Trees*, London.

334

(1693): *Aceteria, a Discourse of Sallets*, London.

(ed. E. S. de Beer, 1954-5): *Diary*, 6 vols, O.U.P.

FÉLIBIEN, ANDRÉ (1674): *Description sommaire du château de Versailles*, Paris.

FLANDIN, E., and COSTE, P. (1887): *Voyage en Perse*, Paris.

GILES, H. A. (1901): *A History of Chinese Literature*, London.

GILPIN, W. (1782): *Observations ... Relative chiefly to Picturesque Beauty*, London.

GOTHEIN, M.-L. (trans. Mrs Archer Hind, 1928): *A History of Garden Art*, Dent, London.

GROEN, J. VAN DER (1668): *Den Nederlandischen Howenier*, Amsterdam.

HADFIELD, M. (1960): *Gardening in Britain*, Hutchinson, London.

HAMMOND, J. (1656): *Leah and Rachel, or, the Two Faithfull Sisters, Virginia and Maryland...*, London.

HANMER, Sir T. (ed. I. Elstob, 1933): *Garden Book*, London.

HANWAY, J. (1753): *An Historical Account of British Trade over the Caspian Sea*, 4 vols, London.

HARADA, JIRO (1956): *Japanese Gardens*, Studio, London.

HARPER-GOODSPEED, T. (1950): *Plant Hunters in the Andes*, Hale, London.

HAWORTH-BOOTH, M. (1963): *The Moutan or Tree Paeony*, Constable, London.

HEDRICK, U. P. (1950): *A History of Horticulture in America to 1860*, O.U.P.

HENTZNER, P. (trans. Horace Walpole, 1797): *Travels in England during the Reign of Queen Elizabeth*, London.

HERBERT, Sir T. (1634): *A Relation of Some Yeares Travaile* [1627-30], *Into Afrique and the greater Asia...*, London.

HERESBACHIUS, C. (trans. B. Googe, 1577): *Foure Bookes of Husbandrie*, London.

HERODOTUS: *Histories*.

HESIOD: *Works and Days*.

HEYN, V. (1885): *The Wanderings of Plants and Animals*, Swann, Sonnenschein, London.

HIRSCHFELD, C. L. (1779): *Geschichte und Theorie der Gartenkunst*, Kiel.

HOME, HENRY, Lord Kames (1762): *Elements of Criticism*, 3 vols, Edinburgh.

HOMER: *Iliad* and *Odyssey*.

HOMMAIRE DE HELL, X. (1854-60): *Voyage en Turquie et en Perse*, Paris.

HORACE: *Odes*.

HYAMS, E. (1952): *Soil and Civilization*, Thames & Hudson, London.

(1953): *Vineyards in England*, Faber, London.

(1964): *The English Garden*, Thames & Hudson, London.

(1965A): *Dionysus*, Thames & Hudson, London.

(1965B): *The Speaking Garden*, Longmans, London.

(1967): *The Irish Garden*, Macdonald, London.

HYAMS, E., and JACKSON, A. A. (1961): *The Orchard and Fruit Garden*, Longmans, London.

HYAMS, E., and MAC QUITTY, W. (1964): *Great Botanical Gardens of the World*, Nelson, London.

HYAMS, E., and ORDISH, G. (1963): *The Last of the Incas*, Longmans, London.

IXTLILXOCHITL: *Historia Chichimeca*, appended to Prescott's *Conquest of Mexico*.

JAUBERT, P. A. (1821): *Voyage en Arménie et en Perse fait dans les années 1805 et 1806*, Paris.

JEFFERSON, THOMAS (ed. E. M. Betts, 1944): *Garden Book*, Philadelphia.

JEKYLL, G. (1908): *Colour in the Flower Garden*, London.

JOSSELYN, J. (1674): *An Account of two voyages to New England*, London.

KARSTEN, R. (1949): *The Civilization of the Inca Empire in Ancient Peru*, Helsinki.

KER-PORTER, Sir R. (1821-2): *Travels in Georgia, Persia, Armenia, Babylonia, etc., in the years 1817-20*, 2 vols, London.

KLEINER, S. (1713): *The Wonderful Home of the Incomparable Hero, etc. etc. ... Eugenius Franciscus, Duke of Savoy*, Vienna.

KRAUS, G. (c. 1894): *Augsbrugher Gärten*.

LA QUINTINIE (trans. J. Evelyn; abridged by G. London & H. Wise 1699): *The Compleat Gard'ner*, London.

LANEHAM, R. (1575): *A Letter: Whearin, part of the entertainment untoo the Queenz Majesty at Killingworth Castl in Warwik Sheer in this Soomerz Progress in 1575, iz signified*.

LAUFER, B. (1890): *Sino-Iranica*, Chicago.

LAYARD, A. H. (1850): *Niniveh*, London.

LEACH, D. G. (1962): *Rhododendrons of the World*, Allen & Unwin, London.

LEIGH, C. (1700): *Natural History of Lancashire, Cheshire and the Peak*, London.

LEMMON, K. (1968): *The Golden Age of Plant Hunters*, Dent, London.

LEPSIUS, K. R. (1849-59): *Denkmäler aus Ägypten und Äthiopien*, 12 vols, Berlin.

LIGHTON, C. (1960): *Cape Floral Kingdom*, Cape Town.

LOUDON, J. C. (1822): *An Encyclopaedia of Gardening*, London.

LOUDON, J. C., and LOUDON, J. (1832): *The Suburban Garden and Villa Companion*, London.

MCGUIRE, F. M. (1964): *Gardens of Italy*, Heinemann, London.

M'MAHON, B. (1806): *The American Gardener's Calendar*, Philadelphia.

MARKS, DOROTHY S.: 'How the American Vinery Trade Began', in *Bulletin of the Brooklyn Botanic Garden*, vol. 23, No. 3.

MASSON, GEORGINA (1961): *Italian Gardens*, Thames & Hudson, London.

MEANS, P. A. (1931): *Ancient Civilizations of the Andes*, Scribner, New York.

MENDEL, G. (1865): *Versüche über Pflanzen-Hybriden*.

MOLLET, C. (1652): *Le Théâtre des Plants et Jardinages*, Paris.

MONARDES, N. (trans. J. Frampton, 1596): *Joyfull Newes out of the newe founde Worlde*, London.

MYERS, A. C. (1912): *Narratives of Early Pennsylvania, West New Jersey and Delaware, 1630-1701*, New York.

NAVILLE, E. (1898-1908): *The Temple of Deir el Bahari*, 6 vols, Egypt Exploration Fund.

NICCOLINI, F. (1854): *Le Case ed i Monumenti di Pompeii*, Rome.

NOBUKICHI KOIDE, SABURŌ KATŌ and FUSAZŌ TAKEYAMA (1968): *The Masters Book of Bonzai*, Collingridge, London.

OLMSTED, F. L. (1852): *Walks and Talks of an American Farmer in England*.

PAGE, R. (1962): *The Education of a Gardener*, Collins, London.

PARKER, A. C. (1926): *History of the Seneca Indians*, Friedman, New York.

PARKINSON, J. (1629): *Paradisi in Sole, Paradisus terrestris*, London.
(1640): *Theatrum Botanicum*, London.

PEPYS, SAMUEL (ed. J. Warrington, 1953): *Diary*, 3 vols, Dent, (Everyman), London.

PESCHEL, J. (1597): *Belehrung über Wein-und Rosengänge, Labyrinthe, über Pflanzen der Bläume in Quintunx und Manches andere.*

PIERRE, Sir F. (1894): *Tell-el-Amarna*, London.

PLATT, Sir H. (1594): *The Garden of Eden*, London.

PLATTER, T. (trans. C. Williams, 1937): *Travels in England*, London.

PLINY THE ELDER: *Natural History*.

PLINY THE YOUNGER: *Letters*.

POLO, MARCO (Yule-Cordier edition, 1903): *Travels*, 2 vols, London.

POMA DE AYALA (1580): *Nueva Cronica y Buen Gobierno*.

PRESCOTT, W. H. (1886): *History of the Conquest of Mexico*, Allen & Unwin, London.
(Everyman edition, 1908): *History of the Conquest of Peru*, Dent, London.

PRICE, Sir U. (1794): *On the Picturesque compared with the Sublime and Beautiful*, London.

PÜCKLER, PRINCE (1834): *Andeutungen über der Landschaftgärtnerei.*

REA, J. (1676): *Ceres, Flora and Pomona*, London.

REPTON, H. (1795): *Sketches of Hints on Landscape Gardening*, London.
(1803): *Observations on the Theory and Practice of Landscape Gardening*, London.

ROBINSON, W. (1870): *Alpine Flowers for English Gardens*, London.
(1870): *The Wild Garden*, London.

ROHDE, ELEANOUR S. (1932): *The Story of the Garden*, Medici Society.

ROSE, J. (1666): *The English Vineyard Vindicated*, London.

SAGARD-THÉODAT, G.: *Histoire du Canada du Pays des Hurons*, Paris.

SAINT-SIMON, Duc de (first complete edition 1829): *Memoirs*, 21 vols, Paris.

SALISBURY, E. J. (1935): *The Living Garden*, Bell, London.

SANDS, MOLLIE (1950): *The Gardens of Hampton Court*, Evans, London.

SARMIENTO, P. (trans. Sir C. Markham, 1907): *History of the Incas*, Hakluyt Society.

SEDDING, J. D. (1891): *Garden Craft Old and New*, London.

SERRES, O. DE (1651): *Le Théâtre d'Agriculture*, Paris.

SEVERN, G. E. (1968): *Miniature Trees in the Japanese Style*, Faber, London.

SEVIGNÉ, Mme DE (ed. E. Gérard-Gailly, 1953-7): *Lettres*, 3 vols, Paris.

SIRÉN, O. (1949): *Gardens of China*, New York.

SITWELL, Sir G. (1909): *Essay on the Making of Gardens*, Murray, London.

SLADE, D. D. (1895): *The Evolution of Horticulture in New England*, Boston.

SLICHER VON BATH, B. H. (trans. Olive Ordish, 1963): *The Agrarian History of Western Europe A. D. 500-1850*, Arnold, London.

SOUSTELLE, J. (trans. P. O'Brien, 1964): *Daily Life of the Aztecs*, Penguin, London.

STRABO: *Geography*.

STROUD, DOROTHY (1950): *Capability Brown*, Country Life, London.
(1962): *Humphry Repton*, Country Life, London.

TAVERNIER, J. B. (trans. J. Philips, 1684): *The Six Voyages of Tavernier, through Turky [sic] into Persia and the East Indies*, 2 vols, London.

TAYLOR, G. (1951): *Some Nineteenth Century Gardeners*, Skeffington, London.

TEMPLE, Sir W. (1680): 'Upon the Gardens of Epicurus', *Miscellanea*, vol. I.

TEZOZOMOC (trans. from MS by H. Terneux-Compans, 1853): *Histoire de Mexique*, Paris.

THEOPHRASTUS: *History of Plants*.

TROLLOPE, Mrs F. (1832): *The Domestic Manners of the Americans*, London.

TS'AO HSÜEH-CH'IN (part trans. by H. B. Joly, 1892-3): *The Dream of the Red Chamber*, 2 vols.

VAN DER DONCK (1935): *A Description of the New Netherlands*, Old South Leaflets No. 69, Boston.

VARRO: *De Re Rustica*.

VAVILOV, N. I. (1951): *The Origin, Variation, Immunity and Breeding of Cultivated Plants*, Ronald, New York.

VEGA, GARCILASO DE LA (trans. Sir C. Markham, 1869-71): *The First Part of the Royal Commentaries of the Yncas*, 2 vols, Hakluyt Society.

VERGNAUD, N. (1835): *L'Art de créer les jardins*, Paris.

WALPOLE, HORACE (1771): 'The History of Modern Gardening', in *Anecdotes of Painting*, vol. iv.

WARD, F. KINGDON (1960): *Pilgrimage for Plants*, Harrap, London.

WHEATLEY, T. (1770): *Observations on Modern Gardens*, London.

WHISTLER, L. (1954): *The Imagination of Vanbrugh and his fellow Artists*, Batsford, London.

WILBER, D. N. (1962): *Persian Gardens and Garden Pavilions*, Tuttle, Tokyo.

WILKINSON, Sir J. G. (rev. S. Birch, 1878): *Manners and Customs of the Ancient Egyptians*, London.

WOOD, W. (1634): *New England Prospects*, London.

XENOPHON: *Oikonomikos*.

YOSHIDA, TETSURO (1957): *Gardens of Japan*, Architectural Press, London.

YOUNG, A. (1846): *Chronicle of the First Planters of the Colony of Massachusetts Bay*, Boston.

ZIRKLE, C. (1935): *The Beginnings of Plant Hybridization*, Philadelphia.

INDEX